CW00496016

1

Cover design by: Lizzy Gosney
Edited by: Luke Gosney

For Julian and Pasado (a.k.a. 'Dutch Frank')
- two of the finest fellow-travellers and all-round best human beings
a person could hope to meet on their earthly journey

4

Epicycle: Five very different stories of long distance cycling: battling ferocious winds in Patagonia; a gruelling 3000 mile mountain bike haul from Canada to Mexico; taking a recumbent tricycle from St. Malo to Budapest; exploring the extreme ends of Japan and a gentle meander from Lands End to John O'Groats.

Introduction

Adventure cycling is a curious pastime, generally undertaken by curious people. By 'curious' I mean 'inquisitive', though no doubt many would veer towards the alternative interpretation of 'odd'.

To set off on a bicycle laden with everything you need (for some people with everything you *have*) for weeks, months, even years suggests an uncommon perspective on life. We can't all be Ranulph Fiennes though. Some of us have adventure enough in just dealing with the day to day challenges of getting by. Some live them vicariously through films or books and some, like me, do their best to fit in whatever experiences they can while they fumble their way through life.

When I was young I recall spending long summer holidays endlessly meandering around the lanes of Kent on my battered, but much loved bicycle. Even then this was considered a bit strange. One day a concerned colleague of my father's called him up at work to say he had spotted me riding around some 20 miles from home and was that right? My Dad was a bit surprised (I must have been around 8 years old at the time) but reassured his colleague I'd passed my Cycling Proficiency test with flying colours and I was probably fine. Fifty years ago parents suffered a lot less angst about children exposing themselves to the dangers of the outside world and 'probably fine' was a perfectly acceptable statement.

After college I stopped cycling for a while, but when I moved to London and began commuting all the way across the capital from Finsbury Park in the north to Croydon in the south, I quickly decided that cycling to work was not only the quickest but possibly the sanest solution. At this period the majority of people still assumed that the only reason you would be riding a bike was because you were too poor to be able to afford a car, but I came to relish that 45 minute ride, twice a day. Whatever the weather (or traffic) threw at me I got a different view of the capital in different light almost every day and I enjoyed the quiet time alone with my own thoughts.

By the time I was 33, despite the fact that my career was ostensibly 'on track' (and even that phrase began to frighten me with visions of straight railway lines disappearing into the perspective, locked on a path to a predictable end) I began to get restless. I started reading more and more travel books, scouring bookshops in my lunch break for stories of the most remote destinations.

The crunch came on a wet winter's day in Uxbridge, a suburban offshoot of West London, working on a computer security audit for a large hospitality sector client. The work itself wasn't so bad. Previously I'd been a teacher in a school in Moss Side Manchester, so I was always grateful when my 'customers' weren't trying to stab me. I just felt an increasing sense of claustrophobia. I couldn't get a line of poetry out of my head, from Andrew Marvell's 'To His Coy Mistress':

"At my back I alwaies hear,
Time's winged chariot hurrying near."

At the time I was reading 'Uttermost Part of the Earth' - the story of early missionaries 'settling' Tierra Del Fuego. It was hard to imagine a more remote place. It also triggered in me a sort of historical angst, an overwhelming desire to see somewhere, some part of the world which had not yet been completely transformed and tamed by human ambition.

It took nearly a year and a half to get from reading about wild places to actually going. Finally, though, I handed in my notice and booked a one way flight to Buenos Aires. I had only a minimal plan and no real idea of what to expect but I spent five months cycling Patagonia, the length and breadth of Chile and Argentina before I finally ran out of money and energy and came home. I have never, ever regretted the decision to go.

Since then I've been on a number of epic bicycle adventures, each one very different and this book is my attempt to draw together the journals. notes and stories which I wrote about some of the early trips (if anyone is interested enough to actually read it I may add some of the later adventures for a second book).

I am sometimes asked wasn't it hard, to make that decision to go? The truth is, the going was always the easy part - the hardest was always coming back. Somehow I managed to fit all these journeys around a 'normal' life - work, marriage, home and even children. You don't have to consign yourself to some sort of nomadic, hippy existence for life to experience at least some adventure (and I have nothing against either nomads or hippies, but I enjoy having a home and a comfortable retirement too).

I am 62 now. A couple of years ago (pre lockdown) I rode from England to Spain with my son and as a follow-up decided to revisit the Rhine, this time from the coast to its source (I am sadly no fonder now of German drivers than back when I wrote the Four Rivers piece for this book). I have no intention of stopping my cycling adventures any time soon. As I write this I have a large (and hideously flatulent) Irish Wolfhound asleep with her head weighing down my feet. I am waiting for my two grandchildren to arrive to look after them for the day while their mother is at work. I also find myself wondering what it might be like to cycle from Hook of Holland to Nordkapp in the far north of Norway…

I hope you enjoy the stories that follow but most of all I hope you enjoy writing the story of your own life and whatever adventures that may hold for you.

Pat Foreman
Kent, August 2021

Who put the Pat in Patagonia?
Chile and Argentina 1993

21st January 1993

It's not often I'm conscious at 4:30 in the morning, or, come to that, at 3:00, 2:00 or 1:00 am either. Last night I woke up almost every hour. If I have to get up early I know I'll wake up at least three or four times in the night. It's like re-packing the bags – two seconds after I've taken everything out to check it's all there and packed it all away again I'm wondering if, in the process I didn't leave something out. I hope this isn't the onset of some senile neurosis – am I going to wind up wandering around the house with a pair of rubber gloves and a bottle of disinfectant cleaning the door handles

Anyway I managed to get up in time to make my way to the airport. En route I checked my passport and ticket sixteen times, thought I'd left my guidebooks at home (no) was worried I'd be 10 kilos over my baggage allowance (nobody cared), and wondered had I put any guns, explosives or things with batteries in my bag (apparently not). Then there was that nice man at the airport who came and wheeled away my bicycle. Well he looked nice enough, but suppose he was just a front man for the wrecking crew downstairs in the baggage mangling department?

As I wait in the departure lounge I slip into a day-mare… somewhere down in the lower levels of the airport there is a bare lightbulb swinging to and fro on a twisted wire. Underneath it, leaning back against the wall is a man in a dirty grey overall. He is fat, greasy and balding and scratching a wedge of hairy belly that surges between the top of his trousers and a dirty T shirt two sizes too small. He is yawning. In front of him a conveyor belt trundles hapless passengers luggage like prisoners paraded before a despot. In his right hand he twirls the tool of his trade, a four pound club hammer with short handle and octagonal faces…

Buenos Aires

Half of the pleasure in planning this trip came from the pure magic of some of the names of places I was aiming to visit - Buenos Aires, Patagonia, Tierra Del Fuego, Ushuaia, Mendoza, Torres Del Paine. To my mind at least, every time I read them they conjured up images straight from a Harrison Ford movie. Buenos Aires didn't disappoint (including having my own Harrison Ford moment rescuing a damsel - or maybe a dame - in distress).

The cardboard box with my bike and most of my bags inside appeared on the normal luggage carousel, looking relatively unscathed. Clearly the hammer-wielding baggage handler had been sleeping on the job.

I picked it up quickly and spent the next forty minutes re-assembling the bike, re-packing all my bags and trying to remember how I had ever managed to strap them all to my bike in the first place. By the time I'd finished the arrivals hall was empty. In fact, apart from a skeleton staff the entire airport appeared to be empty. As I wheeled my bike towards the one remaining open customs booth my footsteps echoed around the large hall and I started to feel uncomfortable. Rule number one in my personal travel guide is try to stay as inconspicuous as possible - especially around any sort of border crossing, transport hub, gangster hangout or any form of officialdom in general. My epic Patagonian adventure had been a long time coming and Argentinian Customs was the last remaining barrier before it could begin.

The small round lady manning the last booth in the line watched me every step of the way as I click-clacked my way across the hall. Not Good. Either she was suspicious or just plain bored, but she also had plenty of time to spend on me and (by the look of things) not much else to fill out the long hours of the graveyard shift till the next flight arrived early the following morning.

"Buenos Tardes," I gave her my winningest smile. It lost. Fortunately I was well prepared for this - if my face had been my fortune I would have been out on the streets years ago.

By far the hardest part of gaining entry to Argentina (and to be fair it would have been the same in most other countries) was down to the vagueness of my own plans. I had bought a one-way ticket in and had no idea how long I would be there or when (even how) I was going to leave. This type of serendipitous approach to planning rarely sits well with immigration officials, so under the circumstances I did what any well meaning, honest individual would do - I lied through my teeth. Yes, I was going to fly south to Ushuaia, then I was going to cycle north. In less than a month I would enter Chile (and therefore become someone else's problem). I neglected to mention that I would quickly be re-entering Argentina again, since, despite their frosty relations, the border between Chile and Argentina was much more porous than that at the international airport, and especially via the rarely travelled high mountain passes I intended to use. At this time the Falklands War was more than 10 years past, but remained a very sore topic for many if not most Argentinians (and would indeed prove problematic later in the trip). Nonetheless Señora Customs remained very cool and professional and I was just beginning to think I might be in when she sucked her teeth. Wherever you go in the world this is universally a bad portent. At a border crossing it's *really* bad.

"There is a problem."

"There is?"

"The bicycle"

"This bicycle?"

"Hmmmm."

She walked around it rubbing her chin(s).

I was dreading being stuck with some hideous import duty and hoping that it didn't look too valuable, though to be honest, you couldn't see much of it beneath the mountain of bags, bungees and various loosely-attached appendages that I'd intended to sort out as soon as I was outside the airport.

"You cycle, here?"

Avoiding the first, second, then third answers which sprung to my lips I settled for: "Yes, that's right."

"Hmmm."

Suddenly she smiled, as though a brilliant idea had just occurred to her, a masterstroke that would enable us both to cut through some apparent Gordian knot of import regulation.

"Is racing bicycle, Yes? Racing bicycle?"

Now I loved this bike, and forty years on I still do. When I bought it, it was a top of the range steel framed mountain bike. Then I set about modifying it for a long distance tour and in the process pretty much doubled its weight. Could it technically be described as a racing bike? In the sense that Elvis could once have been called slim, then yes. Did it look anything like a racing bike in its current incarnation? Like Elvis in his later bulging-catsuit years, sadly no.

Maybe she just didn't fancy the paperwork, maybe she had actually taken pity on me, but I was clearly being offered a get-out clause here so I grabbed it with both hands.

"Racing bike - yes. Racing. Yes."

"Very good. Racing bike?" Nothing if not thorough.

"Racing bike, yes, absolutely."

"Bueno. You can go."

Some border crossings go almost unnoticed. Some take days. Some turn out to be impossible, until you come back on a different day and sail through. I long since gave up trying to identify any logic or rules to any of them. The only thing that matters is getting through, and having achieved that you get away from the area as quickly as possible before anyone can change their minds. This would have been much easier to achieve if I'd spent a bit longer arranging stuff properly on the bike. As I skittered through the customs area and across the airport foyer I had to keep stopping to pick up a smorgasbord of small items of camping equipment that dropped off the bike every few feet.

Eventually I made it out through the door and into the cool evening air. I leant the bike up against a row of airport trolleys, dropped a pile of loose items next to it and allowed myself a small smile of triumph. South America. I was here. Now all I had to do was find my way into the city and find somewhere to spend the night.

Mission Improbable

To the googlemaps and Tripadvisor generation it may seem bizarre that I hadn't already booked myself accommodation and couldn't just plug the directions into my phone. In 1993 things worked slightly differently. The best I had was a very large scale map and the knowledge that if I couldn't find anywhere to stay one night out in the open was unlikely to kill me - at least I hoped it wasn't.

Having spent another half hour re-arranging all my kit on the bike (this was to be a theme for the next two weeks before I finally settled into some sort of organisation), I scratched my head, pedalled away from the terminal and started looking for road signs to the city centre.

At first things went swimmingly, traffic was very quiet, the road was well-lit and I seemed to be heading in the right direction. Then alarm bells started to go off. The road widened, the street lights disappeared and I found myself on what was quite clearly a six lane motorway. I cycled back to the previous junction, pulled out my map and re-checked all of the road signs for some form of alternative route. Unfortunately with the information available to me at least, none was on offer. It was late, I was tired and I just wanted to find somewhere to sleep. I found my bike lights, turned them on and set off down the hard shoulder. This was to be my early introduction to what became rule number 1 of Latin American Cycling: It's usually easier to ask forgiveness than to ask permission (the same rule, by the way, for some reason seems to work well in Japan as well). I knew the city wasn't far and was hoping that maybe I could just ride a short stretch of motorway then jump off at the first signed exit that looked like it might take me towards the centre.

After 40 minutes I hadn't seen any exits, but then again I hadn't seen much traffic either. The road surface was good, there was no wind and I was making good progress so I was beginning to think that maybe this wasn't such a bad idea after all. Until, that is, I spotted a row of lights across the road. Shit - a toll-station.

For a moment I thought about turning off my lights and seeing if I could just sneak past somehow. But then toll stations are rarely designed with large gaps to the side to let illegal or non-paying users slip by. Also, if (when) I got caught it would just make me look even more guilty (not to mention even more stupid - cycling on a motorway at night with *no lights*?). So I kept the lights on and pedalled boldly up to the first toll booth that had someone inside it.

Before I got within thirty metres I could see the guy reach for his radio. A few seconds later and three more uniformed guards issued from a small office to one side of the road and ran over to wait by the booth. Maybe my accommodation problems were solved after all - though a South American jail wasn't quite what I was looking for as a first night experience…

At this stage my Spanish was not great and unfortunately qualifications for an Argentinian Toll-Booth operator did not seem to include fluency in English either. This did not, however, stop discussions being somewhat 'spirited' shall we say. In fairness it wasn't too hard to work out what was being said anyway - something along the lines of "What the Hell are you doing?", "Are you completely mad?" ('loco' is pretty clear and is being used frequently here), "This is a motorway", and "Not permitted", were all pretty clear, helped by copious amounts of gesturing and waving.

I didn't really have much by way of a reasonable response ("It's a fair cop" was unlikely to help), so I settled for a hapless shrug, a goofy smile and pulled out my (useless) map to see if I could at least glean any idea of where I was, how far I had to go and how I might be able to get there.

At first there was much gesticulating that clearly indicated I should turn around and go back, but I dug my heels in at this.

a) I would just end up back at the airport with still no clear way into the city and

b) That would also require me to continue to cycle a significant distance along the motorway - surely something that we all wanted to avoid.

Somehow I managed to get the latter point across which seemed to strike a chord. Maybe they didn't want me to get picked up by the police so I could tell them I was sent this way by the guys at the toll booth…

Getting the map out turned out to have been the best move. Soon all four of them were poring over it, turning it round and trying to see if they could recognise anything.

Eventually they must have decided that since we were significantly closer to the city than to the airport, the lesser of two evils was to pretend they had never actually seen me and send me on my way to complete the last few kilometres on the hard shoulder to the first exit which, as far as I could tell, should lead me to the city centre.

I smiled and nodded gratefully, put my map away and shook hands with all four. Three of them wandered off back towards the small office, excitement over for the night, while the fourth, slightly crossly mimed 'pedal fast' with a warning glance.

I needed no further encouragement, jumped on the pedals and set off back into the night.

Forty minutes later I was cycling through downtown Buenos Aires. This part of the city could almost have been a Parisian suburb - not too surprising given that a lot of the architects responsible for BA's golden era of building were French.

Eventually I found a small hotel in a tall, thin, elegant but slightly run down apartment block, which was still showing a light and a slightly sleepy night clerk (with appropriately droopy mustachios) nodding at the desk.

After a brief negotiation I secured a room for three nights and even managed to persuade him that I could bring my bicycle into the room.

The only downside was that the room was on the third floor and the 'elevator' was a particularly Heath Robinson affair which looked as though it had been installed as an afterthought only a few years after the building had been erected. This consisted of a tiny wrought iron cage inside a rickety looking square frame which rose the height of the building inside the ornate curved stairwell. I unloaded all my bags and carried them up first then somehow managed to squeeze myself and the bike upright on its back wheel into the tiny cage and clanked and rocked our way up to the third floor.

I slept late the next day, still recovering from the long flight and jet lag, but woke to a lovely sunny summer's day and set off to explore the city.

First stop was La Boca, a working-class suburb near the old docks. What makes La Boca special is the 'Sesame Street - meets Acid House' style of decor: Every house, tin shack and window frame is painted a rainbow alliance of bright primary colours. It has a lively range of street artists and tango schools capitalising on its newfound role as a tourist attraction (an artistic barrio hits every tourist sweet-spot), but more importantly for me it also had a good range of steak houses. I'd heard a lot about Argentine steaks but never tried one and having missed out on supper the night before was ready to catch up with a decent lunch. Argentinians are unashamedly carnivorous, famed for the quality of their lamb and beef and (apologies for the pun) make no bones about the animate origins of their meat. The restaurant I picked had a life-sized model of a cow outside, was heavily decorated with cow hides, cow horns and heavy, leather-covered chairs. Slightly more disturbing was that even the men's urinals had been remodelled into facsimiles of giant cow backsides. I have no issues with eating meat or using leather, but peeing into a cow's rear end just feels wrong on too many levels.

Feeling decidedly peckish I ordered a medium sized T bone rather than my usual preference for a smaller portion and settled in to wait for my meal to arrive.

I was quickly presented with a knife and fork that would not have looked out of place in a gladiatorial combat and a dinner plate the size of a large-ish tea tray. These guys obviously meant business. Despite these clues I was still unprepared for the sheer scale of the challenge presented me when my 'lunch' arrived at the table - a paving-slab chunk of meat, around four centimetres thick and so large it leant over the edge of my enormous plate and drooped towards the table surface in at least three separate places. If it had still been alive it would have presented a valid contest as to who-should-be-eating-whom it was so big. I was not at all sure that it would have been physically possible to encompass that much extraneous material inside my relatively modest frame without risking splitting at the seams. Still, I *was* hungry, it smelled and looked fabulous and I was unwilling to look a complete idiot by sending it back and asking for something smaller, so I picked up my Gladius and Pitchfork and started to set to. It was at this point that a huge bowl of potatoes and corresponding bowl of salad appeared alongside. "You have got to be kidding," I thought, followed by "I wonder how much of this I could sneak back to my hotel room - there's enough here for the next two days easily…"

Portion control aside, though, the experience was practically transcendental. To my mind I can't recall a steak meal before or since that tasted anything like as wonderful as that first giant slab of Argentine beef. It was so good I managed to eat at least a third of it (a piece by the way approximately the same size and weight as my own head) before conceding defeat and laying down my weapons of meat destruction.

Within minutes a concerned waiter appeared. "Was it not good?"

I pointed towards my visibly distended belly, puffed out my cheeks and sighed.

"Too good, just too good…"

He kindly agreed to make up a doggy-bag the size of a small suitcase which I lugged back to my hotel for a well-earned siesta.

By early evening the weather had deteriorated and thunder was rumbling across the city. I could hardly contemplate eating any more, but a short walk, and possibly a long beer seemed like a good idea to try and lend my hard-pushed digestive system a hand tackling what was probably the hardest task I'd ever presented it.

I walked out into the hallway and immediately bumped into a very short, nearly spherical elderly Argentinian lady waiting for the elevator. I was just about to head off down the stairs thinking a) I needed the exercise and b) the little iron cage could start to get the wrong side of intimate if both of us were trying to squeeze in there, when the lift arrived. With one hand she threw the door open and with the other grabbed me by the elbow and practically tossed me in towards the back wall. She turned around, backed herself in then hurled the cage door closed again and stabbed the down button.

Perhaps she didn't want to end up face-to-face (well, let's be honest, face-to-chest) with a scruffy gringo in the elevator, perhaps she was just used to taking charge - either way, once I was in this position there was absolutely nowhere else to go till the lift reached the floor and she stepped out again, so I settled back, took in the neatness of the black lacey veil that covered the strict grey bun of hair on the back of her head and started to think about which of the local bars to head to and just how far I felt like walking.

The elevator started to descend and moved about half way between the second and third floors before the lights flickered and went out, the cage jounced to a stop and the señora screamed fit to stretch my eardrums. Power cut.

Marvellous. Not only was I not getting my beer, I was trapped in a very small cage with a hysterical septuagenarian widow. I kicked myself for not having got to the stairs quicker.

I reached out to try and calm the señora but quickly decided that touching her in these circumstances was possibly not a great idea. I tried to reassure her verbally instead.

"Calm, calm. Is Ok. Ok. Seguro, Si?"

I shook the sides of the cage to demonstrate that it had locked in place and was not going to fall all the way to the foyer.

She screamed again.

21

Maybe shaking the cage had not been such a good idea.

Gradually some of the other hotel guests appeared on the stairs to see what all the noise was about and check that the power was not just out in their rooms.

After a few minutes the hotel manager appeared and started speaking to the señora but with hardly any more success than I'd had in calming her down. After a while he gave up and turned to me.

"Power cut." He shrugged.

"You think? How long?"

He shrugged again.

Great.

Gradually most of the other guests disappeared. After a while the manager too left, but making signs to me that he would soon return. I hoped he was going in search of a generator or at least some means of manually opening up the lift cage to get us out.

While he was away I started to examine the inside of the cage, or at least as much of it as I could see above the Señora, who was now quietly (but at least invisibly) weeping to herself while she played over her rosary.

From long (and I must say, much-ridiculed) habit, I rarely go anywhere without my trusty Leatherman pocket tool strapped to my belt. This marvellous piece of micro-engineering has a tiny knife blade, screwdriver and very small set of folding pliers all folded into a bundle the size of a couple of matchboxes. In full McGuyver mode now I looked for any weak spots in my current micro-prison.

By the time the manager had returned I'd already undone four nuts and removed a large section of the interior cage of the elevator.

The poor man was horrified.

"Nonononono - stop, please. STOP!"

I shrugged. Evidently there was no generator and I had next to no faith in the Argentinian power grid miraculously restoring power anytime soon. The señora had started shivering in addition to quietly keening to herself and she clearly needed to get out almost as much as I now needed my beer. I set to work on the next panel of the external frame.

Eventually the manager resigned himself to the disassembly of his hotel and started to help by undoing some bolts from the other side. After twenty minutes we had another panel removed and a clear view across to the stairwell. The only problem being it was too clear. There was still a significant gap between the elevator and the bannisters with a long (and almost certainly fatal) drop two and a half floors down to the lobby below.

With someone to catch me I was pretty sure I could have jumped it ok but the señora did not strike me as a natural gymnast, not even in her glory years and there was zero chance she would do it in her current condition.

There was much discussion between the manager and the two guests who had remained to see out the end of this particular show. He disappeared with one of the guests and came back with two short planks of wood.

Fortunately the panels we had removed were more or less level with a flat section of bannister and with a bit of wiggling we managed to get the two planks across to form a (moderately) stable bridge to the staircase. Now all we had to do was persuade the señora to crawl across.

To her credit, once the manager had explained the situation to her and she caught sight of her doorway to freedom she seemed to forget all her fear and was mustard keen to try and make her way out of the gringo trap.

The only issue was, try as she might, she just could not climb high enough to get onto the planks in the first place. I watched her scrabble at the side of the cage like an overstuffed hamster for a minute or so before I finally bit the bullet, reached down, placed my linked hands under her copious rear end and pushing from my legs to try and avoid a slipped disc gave her an enormous boost up and onto the planks.

She shrieked again, but once she realised she was on the planks, with an almost catlike grace scampered across and into the arms of the waiting rescuers. I suspect that she was a little heavier than they were expecting as they lowered her none-too-gently to the floor of the stairs, but judging by the look of relief on her face she was far too happy to be bothered.

While the 'rescuers' gathered round to make sure she was Ok I was left to my own devices to scramble across our makeshift drawbridge as best I could and jump down the other side.

After making sure she was ok (she gave me the blackest of looks as though I was personally responsible for the power outage - maybe as a cunning plan to enable me to grope her rear end) I made off for the bar and one or maybe more well-earned beers, before the manager could catch me to ask me to help re-assemble the lift.

I'd already decided I'd walk the bike back down the stairs rather than try the elevator again anyway.

Ushuaia

Ushuaia sits on the shore of the Beagle Channel on the far south of the main Island of Tierra del Fuego. The Beagle Channel is narrow and the mountains behind it form the coccyx of the Andes range, and while not that high are very steep and very close to the shore.

As a result the landing there has to be one of the most exciting of any commercial flight in the Southern Hemisphere. The plane scrapes in low over the mountains then suddenly turns and swoops simultaneously in a steep dive before coming to rest on the short airstrip just outside the town. Sadly this was superseded in 1995 by a much more practical (but less entertaining) larger runway some 4km south of the town, built to accommodate the growing traffic of Antarctic cruise tourists.

My plane appeared to be roughly equally divided between those who thought this was a "Wheee" moment and those who were on the "Arrrggggh" side. I was transfixed by the view from the window. Snowy mountains, blue water dotted with icebergs, a frontier-like outpost of tiny buildings - this was the real deal, a gateway to proper wilderness.

In Buenos Aires I'd used my remaining time to get some slightly better maps (there were still huge blank areas but this was largely because, well, large parts of Patagonia are literally blank - nothing there apart from grass, sheep and/or wind) and found a better route back to the airport that managed to avoid the motorway.

I stopped briefly in Ushuaia town to pick up some supplies before heading straight off to Baia Lapataia - the very end of Ruta 3 and by general agreement the southernmost point of the continent.

Tierra del Fuego is divided in two between Argentinian and Chilean territory. To be fair the Chileans claim they have the southernmost point, but at the time they didn't have a road there and the Argentinians got to the encyclopaedia first so, nah.

Ruta 3 also forms part of the so-called Pan American highway that, in theory at least, stretches all the way up to the far north of Alaska. If you are a Northern-Hemispherist like me, quite literally the only way is up from here.

At the park itself I found a small wooden sign marking the end of the road: Buenos Aires 3,063km, Alaska 17,818km. Other than that it was deserted. I picked a small flat spot overlooking the shore, pitched my tent and set about rustling up some supper on my small petrol fuelled stove.

Today I find myself wondering if I'd bought petrol in Ushuaia or if I'd actually flown from Buenos Aires with fuel already in the bottle. I honestly can't remember but security was certainly a lot more lax those days, especially on internal flights so maybe I had been let on with my own personal bomb after all.

Over supper I sat and admired the view. Darwin sailed these waters with Captain Fitzroy aboard the tiny (90 foot long) eponymous Beagle between 1832 and 1833. The stretch I was looking at probably looked hardly any different 160 years ago. I contemplated the enormity of the world and the path that lay ahead of me. I had no real plans beyond 'head north, and see how far I get'. I liked the idea of getting all the way to Alaska, but to be honest I lacked both the confidence and the ambition to see myself making it quite that far. Equally, I didn't really care. I was so happy just to finally be here, in such an amazing, remote and beautiful spot. Half the world stretched out in front of me, just waiting for me to find it.

I spent three days in Lapataia, just chilling, re-sorting all my gear and wrapping my head around the journey to come. I slept badly the third night and woke several times - once to horrific screams which I eventually worked out was an owl picking up a midnight snack.

In the morning I realised I was really cold. I unzipped the door to my tent and put my hand down on half an inch of snow. Shit. It was still early January, and technically mid summer in the Southern Hemisphere, but the snows had come early to Tierra Del Fuego and I still had a mountain range to cross before the long flat plain in the middle of the island and the ferry across to mainland Chile. Time to go.

Before leaving Ushuaia though I had a short pilgrimage to make. The Estancia Harberton sits a short way along the shore of the channel and is the ancestral home of the Bridges family. Thomas Bridges was an Anglican missionary but also a keen linguist. He set up one of the first permanent missionaries to the Island and spent many years studying and documenting the language of the indigenous people while watching their slow progress towards extinction. Lucas Bridges grew up among the last remaining members of the local tribe and was the author of 'Uttermost Part of the Earth', the book which had kicked off my own personal mission that wet winter lunchtime in Uxbridge, quite literally the opposite side of the earth.

The estancia was simultaneously fascinating and mildly depressing. Since there wasn't a huge amount to see there I was happy to have closed the circle, and seen the outpost which had essentially inspired my trip.

In the centre of Ushuaia, not far from the shore there is a memorial to the sailors of the General Belgrano, sunk during the Malvinas (Falklands) conflict in the early 1980s. The war was still raw for most Argentinians I met. Some were still angry, though many more were philosophical and still friendly, though probably in a slightly more guarded way than they might have received a Brit in the days before the war broke out. Regardless of the rights and wrongs of the sinking (if there can be 'rights' for such a thing), I took a moment to consider the 323 lives foreshortened on that day, many of them conscripts much younger than I was already, all of them stripped of the chance to take the sort of journey I was now about to begin. With a quiet nod I turned away, swung my leg up and over the bulging mass of bags on the back of my bicycle and left them behind - grateful, not for the last time, to have been born in another time and place.

Fuegian Friends

The road out of Ushuaia begins climbing almost immediately you leave the end of the main street. Then it was a roughly graded dirt surface, though by now I should imagine it is silky smooth tarmac.

The road twisted and wriggled as though it was unsure itself if it was going the right way. Hairpin bends were a nightmare, trying to balance keeping the front wheel on the ground, getting grip to the rear and turning at painfully slow speed without toppling over. At first I got it wrong repeatedly and ended up in a painful pile in the road. After a while either the bends got less steep or my technique improved. I launched myself into each corner, trying to get enough momentum to carry me most of the way through without having to fight for drive till I was straight again. I still fell over a lot, but I tried to make the most of each crash by pausing to take in the magnificent views as I gradually worked my way higher up towards the Paso Garibaldi - the highest point on Ruta 3.

it was a long, slow grind and a painful introduction to the delights of climbing dirt roads in the mountains (something which I was to have more experience of than I care to recollect). By mid afternoon though I was nearing the top of the pass and eventually rewarded with the long, long view across Lago Fagnano and the broad expanse of the Fuegian plain stretching out to the north. Best of all, it looked magnificently flat!

I hurtled down the other side, obstinately refusing to touch my brakes as far as possible, wanting to translate every calorie of that long hard slog up into full scale kinetic energy on the way down - I had no interest in swapping any of it for heating up my brakes.

I stopped by the shore of the lake for a quick bite and a drink. Were they flamingoes over there? Did flamingoes even come this far south? The lake was large enough that there was a significant swell, with small waves rolling repeatedly onto the shore, so it felt more like the sea than a lake. Flamingoes. In the sea. In Patagonia. Maybe I was just hallucinating from dehydration. Either way it was a stunning view.

Pressing on I was by now fighting an increasing headwind. Well, to me it was a headwind. To the locals, as it turned out, this was a mild breeze. By early evening I was still fighting my way across the flat (now apparently endless) plain and nowhere near any form of town. There were barbed wire fences either side of the road, but precious little else to interrupt the view in any direction. I was just considering setting up camp in a ditch next to the road when a small track opened up to my left with a sign to a local estancia. The trouble was, in this landscape, the estancia could be a couple of kilometres up the track or another 80 kilometres away across the plain. I decided to give it a try anyway. If they were close enough I would be able to ask permission to camp on their land, and maybe blag some fresh water without having to filter it from a muddy puddle. If they were a long way off then I could probably camp by the track and be up and on my way in the morning before anyone noticed I was there.
Before it got dark though I crested a small rise and found a small cluster of wooden buildings hiding from the wind in the shelter of a small dip in the plain.

Conscious that I was trespassing on private land, and thinking of the monument to the Belgrano and whether there was anyone recorded there with relatives still living on the island, I approached the buildings a little cautiously. At first I couldn't see anyone, they seemed deserted. I shouted a loud 'Halloa' several times and eventually a small figure emerged from behind one of the larger blocks.

I say small - he was relatively short, but incredibly thickset, with magnificent Zapata-esque moustaches and bow legs that, as my mother was wont to say, "wouldn't stop a pig in a passage."

He also held in one hand the longest, sharpest-looking knife I had seen in my life. That in itself need not have been too disconcerting, were it not for the fact that it was also (along with half of his extremely hairy forearms) absolutely covered in blood...

He smiled, but disappointingly failed to show any of the gold- or silver topped teeth I had been so expecting to see.

"Hola."

Forget the teeth. This guy had a voice that was to Tom Waits as mountain boulders are to gravel - it almost made the air crackle when he spoke.

I pointed to the tent on the back of my bike (rather pointlessly I realised, since it was wrapped up tight in an anonymous waterproof sack) and in my best Spanish tried to mime the process of setting up camp, waving my arm in a broad arc to suggest I was happy to go wherever he might direct me.

He shook his head. Damn.

Then, waving the knife he gestured for me to follow him. I couldn't help but notice a large globule of blood fly off and land in the dirt, where it was rapidly soaked up and turned to the colour of distant murder.

Oh well. With legs like that he was bound to have a horse somewhere, and there was no way I would outrun a horse in this territory so I decided I might as well follow and see what fate held out for me.

He led me to another long low building, with a wooden veranda running the length of the front, pushed open the door and motioned me inside.

Surely if he was going to gut me like a fish he would do it outside where the sand would soak up all the mess? Why go inside where there would be so much more mopping to do?

Inside the building was a single long room, with tables and chairs set up at one end, old fashioned oil lamps set out on each table. The other end was lined with simple wooden bunks.

A-ha. The bunkhouse.

He walked over to one of the bunks and motioned towards the bottom bed. I could dump my bags here. He was offering me a bed for the night rather than having to set up tent outside. What a lovely, lovely man. If he weren't still holding that very very pointy knife I could have hugged him. As it was that would probably have been a fatal move, either accidentally, or, as Gauchos are famed for their machismo, possibly a visceral response to effeminate western ways. I settled for a broad smile and many 'Muchas Gracias'es.

I'd just finished unloading the bike and trying to shove most of my bags somewhere under the bed when he re-appeared at the door and motioned me again to follow him.

We went back outside then round to the other side of the building from which he'd emerged when I arrived. There we found the source of all the blood.

There was a huge open fire, maybe 8-10 feet across. Just outside the range of the flames, but leaning in towards them were three large iron crucifixes. Spread out on the crucifixes, cruelly pinned to them were three whole sheep carcasses, smoking gently in the heat. After a long day on the saddle the smell was nothing short of divine.

This was an Asado, a Patagonian barbecue, done estancia-style. My new friend was the cook, or at least on Cook's duty, preparing the evening meal, presumably for a small army of hungry Gauchos who were about to emerge from the range after a hard day's steer-wrestling (or whatever the equivalent is on a sheep farm).

He pointed to a long wooden bench under the eaves of the

building, and while I sat took his long, long knife (still slick with blood I may add) and carved a huge chunk of meat from one of the nearby carcases in front of the fire. He came back and held it out to me on the end of the knife. I picked it up, then immediately regretted it, since it was (D'oh!) searingly hot. In best comic tradition I tossed it from hand to hand, alternately blowing on my seared fingers and puffing 'hot, hot, hot' pointlessly, but apparently very amusingly at least as he chuckled his way back to a massive wooden table laden with onions and potatoes.

The potatoes he chopped roughly and tossed into a large cauldron sitting on top of an equally large standalone gas ring. The onions were chopped (using the same bloody knife, though I guess this was as good a way as any of cleaning the blade) then thrown into an equally massive frying pan atop a similar ring.

By this time my hunk of sheep had cooled enough to take a bite. While chewing I idly mused I would be safe enough if I went on a crime spree now since I sincerely doubted I had any fingerprints left.

My Gaucho friend Zapata returned, this time with a metal cup, full of water and a tin plate piled high with steaming potatoes and onions, together with a fork and a long and very sharp-looking knife. He pointed towards the crucified carcases - I nodded. Serve-yourself buffet was absolutely fine by me.

As I picked up my plate and headed towards the fire the gauchos started to drift in.

Given the amount of food I had expected dozens but in the end there were no more than five or six, plus Zapata of course. As each came in he handed them the same cup and plate he had given me, but without the knife - every one of them carried a long knife of their own, very similar to his and very much on display at the front of their belts. Knife and spurs I learned were the quintessential pieces of Gaucho kit, without which no self-respecting Patagonian cowboy would leave home.

I gingerly hacked a small chunk of lamb from the nearest victim, trying not to broil myself in the heat from the fire in the process, and wandered back to take my seat at the long wooden bench. A few of

33

the Gauchos nodded to me, but most ignored me, concentrating on their food and occasionally exchanging a few words with their neighbour, They all looked tired and I guessed we at least had one thing in common - we had all spent a long day in the saddle. If you think a hungry cyclist can eat a lot you should see how much a cowboy can put away.

Only once the last Gaucho had come in and been served did Zapata take a plate for himself and sat down at the far end of the bench.

After everyone had eaten their fill (which usually took three or four visits to the barbecue) they dropped their plates in a large bucket, sheathed their knives and re-took their places along the wooden bench. Some rolled and lit spindly cigarettes and the conversation perked up a little, but not much. It was noticeable to me there was absolutely NO alcohol nor was there, at any stage, any suggestion of someone picking up a guitar and singing by the campfire. The first was a bit of a disappointment to be honest but I was quite grateful for the latter. These were hard-working men, seriously tired after a long day out on the range. Allegedly they made up for it on their days off and (also allegedly) a popular pastime was knife-fighting - hence the secondary importance of the gaucho knife. Fortunately none of them showed any inclination to practice on this particular evening, and before long they started to drift off towards the bunkhouse.

My friend Zapata meanwhile had been busy cleaning and clearing away the plates and the food preparation area. There wasn't much left of the three sheep carcasses. He took a couple of pieces and stored them in some sort of galvanised meat locker, then threw the rest to the dogs who had been gathering patiently in expectation of this particular moment.

I went over and thanked him profusely for his hospitality, wishing again that I'd taken more time to learn Spanish before coming out here. He shrugged. As is often the case in many of the wilder parts of the planet, hospitality is a given, part of a mutual survival pact that knows at some point you may be dependent on your neighbour for help too, and there are rarely that many neighbours to choose from.

I made the universal hands-pillow-sleep mime then wandered back towards the bunkhouse, wishing I'd remembered to bring my headtorch with me since it was by now full dark. Inside, thankfully, one of the oil lamps was still burning, though most of the gauchos were already in their bunks. I spent a minute trying to remember which bag I'd put my sleeping bag in, and trying not to make too much noise while I rifled through the rest of my kit to find it, then spread it out on the wooden bunk, climbed in and groaned contentedly. Where I'd been expecting to have to pitch my tent by the side of the road and warm up a small bag of rice for supper I was indoors, warm and dry with a (very) full belly.

It's now more than forty years since that evening, but I still remember the sights, smells and taste of that meal.

I slept so soundly that by the time I woke up the bunkhouse was already empty. I repacked my bags and dragged them outside to put them back on the bike. There was no sign of Zapata either, so presumably even he had to work during the day as well.

I had one last look around before pedalling off back down the track to rejoin the 'main' road. There was a strong headwind blowing.

It took me five more days to reach Porvenir, the port for the crossing from Tierra Del Fuego to the mainland. There was a headwind every inch of the way. Around half way there I crossed the border from Argentina into Chile, the first of several times.

Waiting for the ferry to Punta Arenas I spotted two other cyclists. Ben and Frank were Dutch, and had followed a very similar route to me but somehow we had missed each other up to this point. It might seem strange to remark on this, in an area almost twice the size of Wales, but there really is only one real road through it, and very little traffic.

Ben was bearded, stocky and rode a well kitted out touring bike. Frank was blond, tall and gangly and was riding what looked like a converted racing bike, with very skinny wheels and tyres and various bags strapped on in a slightly haphazard manner. He had a goofy smile, a very measured manner of speech and a somehow infectious air of calm. I took to him immediately. I did wonder, though, how his bike was coping with the rough dirt roads.

We swapped notes and talked about where we were headed to once we reached the mainland. They both wanted to see Torres Del Paine, a huge national park famous for its mountains, glaciers and hiking trails. I had no specific plans and was by now thoroughly bored of battling strong headwinds on my own. I asked if they would mind if I tagged along, at least we could take it in turns to take the lead into the wind. Frank agreed immediately. Ben, I think was slightly more reluctant but went with the flow. When the ferry arrived we rolled our three bikes on together and lashed them into a corner near the bow, where, we realised too late, they would get thoroughly doused in salt spray.

During the crossing I stood in the bow and watched dolphins playing in the wake, dodging to and fro in front of the boat like some aquatic game of chicken. Eventually they got bored and went off, presumably to go and train some humans to throw fish for them.

Southern Chile

P unta Arenas was a pleasant enough town, with a typical central square and a memorial to Ferdinand Magellan. Unfortunately I can't recall paying much attention to any of it. The most striking thing about Punta Arenas was the food, and one food item in particular. This was to be my first taste of the Latin American equivalent of the Cornish Pasty, otherwise known as an Empanada. Actually, comparing them to a Cornish Pasty is a bit like saying the barmaid at your local pub looks like Jennifer Aniston. They come in all shapes and sizes and flavours but to a hungry cyclist they were manna from heaven. Cheap, easy to find, fit neatly in your hand or pack away in your bags and absolutely delicious. I ate them for breakfast, lunch and dinner while we were in the town. I would have filled my bags with them for the ride up to Puerto Natales but I thought the hammering they would be subjected to would likely turn them into some sort of dry soup at the bottom of my bag within the first few kilometres.

Despite Ben's initial hesitancy the two Dutch guys turned into excellent travelling companions. When you are cycling it's very hard to find someone who follows the same pace as you - we all feel comfortable at a different tempo, and even individually you will feel stronger on some days than others. For once, though, the strong headwinds may have helped in some small way. By taking turns at the head of our own tiny peloton we shared out at least some of the strain, and the rear two were happy to tuck in and follow whatever pace the leader felt able to sustain.

One particular day, though, defeated all three of us.

Patagonia is, of course famous for its winds, and we'd already experienced plenty of those crossing the island of Tierra Del Fuego. This particular day the wind started off stronger than any we'd experienced before, then proceeded to build in strength throughout the morning. From standing on the pedals in even the lowest gear we eventually had to concede defeat and all three of us got off to push. The wind, however, was not finished with us yet and continued to mount. At one point I stopped for breath, Ben and Frank a few paces ahead of me. Head bowed low against the dust, I leant into the wind, bracing myself against the fully-laden bike. The wind strength increased. Instinctively I grabbed both brakes and leant further forward. The wind got stronger again. I started to scrabble for grip. Slowly but surely, both wheels locked up, me leaning at something approaching 45 degrees, the fully loaded bike and I started sliding back down the road. It was a most unnerving feeling. Since then I've experienced a couple of medium-sized earthquakes. To find yourself utterly powerless in the face of an overwhelming force of nature is scary, humbling and deeply unsettling all at the same time. Slowly, almost gracefully, the bike and I gently slid back down the road, angling towards the verge, and eventually (and fortunately) toppled into a deep ditch. Not many seconds later I was joined, first by Frank, then Ben who had both suffered identical fates. The whole situation was so ridiculous we just laughed at each other with just a hint of hysteria at the same time.

With nothing else to do we settled down into our ditch, munched on some dried figs and the remains of a chocolate bar I had in my bar bag and waited for the wind to die down enough for us to be able to stand up again. It took most of the afternoon, but towards evening the wind finally began to be more humane and we eventually struggled up and out of the ditch with a view of just going far enough to find a slightly more comfortable camping pitch.

After five days on the road, filtering our own water from ditches, dining on rice, pasta, tinned tuna and gherkins (yes, sounds weird, but the dutch guys were carrying a supply and for the first few meals at least it tasted ok), when we arrived at Puerto Natales we fell on the first restaurant we found like a flight of avenging harpies. The restaurant owner can't have been happy about the sight we presented, hunched around a table in the corner, dirty, dusty and very dishevelled, but he could have had no complaints about the amount we ordered.

From Puerto Natales we continued north towards the Parque Nacional Torres Del Paine. The road was dirt all the way, mostly not too bad but with the odd section of kidney-mulching washboard. This stuff was truly horrendous to cycle on and I came to hate it with a passion. A lot like the miniature wave patterns you often find on a long sandy beach when the tide has gone out, but much harder, you could not design something which could so effectively make progress on a bicycle both hard and incredibly uncomfortable. Inevitably it took its toll on nerves, knees and equipment. With long distances to cover and still fighting strong headwinds we took to stopping every 4 or 5 kilometres just to check that nothing new had shaken off - nobody wanted to double back then cover the same terrain again just to pick up some vital piece of equipment that had shaken loose without us noticing. We became fixated on the road in front, scouring the next twenty metres for the route that looked like it might be slightly, just slightly easier. If it was easier it was hardly noticeable, and the mental toll of concentrating so hard was all part of the endurance experience. Fortunately there was relatively little other traffic to bother us. There was the occasional tourist bus, but mostly the locals drove ageing American pickup trucks - big square fronted Fords and Dodges from the sixties and seventies and rounder-looking models from the forties and fifties. They were inevitably battered, rusty and every single pane of glass in them was cracked from the showering of rocks and gravel they received whenever they passed another vehicle. They were, though, absolutely perfect for that environment and, not for the first time, I found myself daydreaming of one for my personal transport. Generally the road was at least fairly firm. What sand traps we did find were inevitably at the bottom of any small dip in the road, and the source of much hilarity as whoever was in front launched down an incline, determined to make the most of any gravity-assisted speed to climb the opposite side, then either snaked wildly from side to side or faceplanted completely when they hit an unnoticed pit of deep sand right at the bottom. Poor Frank with his skinny wheels and tyres had the worst of these but Ben and I were not immune either.

We arranged to leave our bikes at the ranger station by the entrance to the National Park, jury-rigged panniers to be able to carry them on our shoulders (a folding rucksack would have been much better and more comfortable, but you live and learn…) and set off for five days hiking around the park.

At first walking made a pleasant change from cycling every day, but our improvised rucksacks soon began to chafe shoulders and we realised how nice it was to have metal frames to hang all our luggage from. We also quickly realised that all those muscles we had built up in our legs were slightly different from the ones we need to be walking 80 miles and we discovered a whole new range of aches and pains. The scenery very nearly made up for it all, but there were times when naked dancing girls holding trays of hot hamburgers and cold beers would have failed to distract me from my personal discomfort. I decided never to give up the bike again (I did, of course), or at least to pick up a cheap rucksack before I went hiking again (which I didn't).

By the time we left the park tensions had started to emerge in our small group. Frank and I had become firm friends but Ben had started to feel frustrated at our slower pace and rather more laissez-faire attitude to planning. I really liked Frank's easy-going nature and I think he just found me less hard work than Ben. As a result Ben decided to head off on his own and Frank and I teamed up to continue our steady, if slightly shambolic drift northwards. It was all very amicable and Frank agreed to meet Ben in Santiago a week or so before their flight home.

For me it was the beginning of a life-long friendship. We exchanged greetings cards every year and photos of our families as they grew up. We even managed to meet up again in later life for a couple of gentle cycle tours of France and East Anglia. Frank changed his name to Pasado when he became a Buddhist and eventually I learned to call him that, even though he was always 'Dutch Frank' in my head. Sadly, despite his easy-going nature he nursed a darker side of which I was completely unaware until it was too late. I hadn't heard from him for a while, but had been too busy with my own life to pay much attention when I received an unexpected letter from his wife, Liesbet. Sadly poor Frank had taken his own life shortly before his 50th birthday. According to Liesbet, he'd carried the Black Dog of Depression for many years but had finally bowed out when it no longer made sense to him to fight it any more. I still find it hard to reconcile with that goofy, calm, gentle soul who made such an easy travelling companion. Like everyone involved in something like this I suspect, I also felt guilty, wondering whether there was anything I should have noticed, anything I could have said or done to alter the course of his life, though it seems unlikely. However he felt about himself, the world is a worse place without him.

In Chile, in 1993 though, all of that lay a long way off in the future as Dutch Frank and I set off to amble our way across the border and back into Argentina to see where the road would take us there.

Cry for me, Argentina

These days it's possible to continue north from Torres Del Paine and cross into Argentina that way. Back then, though, we had to go back south first, returning to Puerto Natales before crossing the Andes to pick up the notorious Ruta 40 to head north again on the Argentinian side. I say 'notorious' - in reality we met two, maybe three other cyclists who agreed that Ruta 40 was 'terrible', 'covered with huge rocks', or 'practically impassable'. Maybe they'd graded it the week before, but once we actually got there it didn't seem that much worse than any of the other 'roads' we were now used to in Patagonia.

Very much at our own pace we wound our way north to El Calafate, en route to see the Perito Moreno Glacier. In 1993 only a few specialists were even looking at global warming, and it certainly was not a widely accepted or even widely known phenomenon. Strangely, though, the Perito Moreno glacier appears to remain one of the few world-wide to be largely holding its own, seeming to gain, and shed ice at an equal rate.

In Patagonia, a land full of glaciers, Perito Moreno is well known largely because of tis unique location. . The glacier ends at a narrow, horseshoe-shaped spur off the giant Lago Argentino. What makes it especially interesting, though, is that there happens to be a narrow spit of land sticking out into the lake directly opposite. The result of this is that as the Glacier ebbs and flows, periodically it bridges the gap across to the spit of land, damming one half of the horseshoe lake behind it. Over time water builds up until the pressure finally breaks up the ice dam and rejoins the lakes again.

At the time we were there the glacier was in one of its 'ebbing' phases, but no less spectacular for that. The short promontory facing it provides an ideal viewing platform. I spent the best part of a day, just sitting on the grass, mesmerised, watching giant chunks of ice periodically calve off from the face of the glacier and plunge into the lake below. The glacier was near enough to be able to see these in great detail and just far enough away that the noise they made would reach you just a fraction of a second after the sight of them cracking off, or crashing into the water, which only made the experience somehow seem even more surreal. It really is an experience it would be a shame to miss, and, who knows? This particular experience could be a time-limited offer closing all too soon.

Further north, but still in the Los Glaciares region lie Cerro Fitzroy and Cerro Torre.

Mount Fitzroy is named after the Captain of Darwin's ship, Robert Fitzroy. Interestingly, though, it was not named by an intrepid Englishman. In fact it's quite probable that Fitzroy never even saw the mountain. It was actually named in his honour by an Argentinian explorer, Francisco Moreno in 1877, many years after the Beagle expedition had returned home. It's a stunning mountain (in fact has been my screensaver for years), though not quite as stunning as one of its near neighbours, Cerro Torre.

Cycling was not permitted in the national park here, so once again Frank and I left our bikes at the ranger station and shouldered our panniers to hike through the park. Yes, I had said I wouldn't do that again, and no, I hadn't bought a rucksack, but as I mentioned already neither Frank nor I were particularly rigid in our planning or in sticking to unnecessary resolutions. How lucky for both of us that turned out to be…

I'm sometimes asked, if there were one place I'd visited in all my travels I could take anyone back with me, just for a day to see, where would it be. Unequivocally my answer would always be Fitzroy. Torres Del Paine has always been more popular, but from my perspective that would always be just because Fitzroy is (or at least was) much harder to get to. Equally, from my perspective, its remoteness was an important part of its charm - it felt like the *real* Patagonia - really a long way from anywhere.

Having sorted bikes and bags we borrowed a (very) rough map of the park and asked the rangers where they thought the best hiking was. Without hesitation they said Cerro Torre, though they warned that it was quite remote, rugged terrain and we would need to be confident we were self-sufficient and capable of handling the hike. Naturally we puffed out our chests (to very little effect, it has to be said, on either of us) and tried to look like the intrepid explorers we wanted to be. They looked at us very carefully, then asked us to provide them with contact details of next of kin...

At the end of the first day's hike we stopped at the top of a small hill. There were a couple of low trees behind us providing some shelter from the wind, a small clearing in front and a magnificent view of Fitzroy itself as the sun set behind it. It was the perfect campsite. While Frank sorted the tent (we shared one while we were hiking to minimise the amount we had to carry) I set about lighting a fire. We were just about to settle down to cook some supper when we were both jolted to our feet by loud screams coming from the side of the hill. The screams were quickly followed by a very out-of-breath ranger running up the hill and into our camp. Without breaking step he ran straight into our campfire and started dancing in it. Frank and I exchanged glances while I started unfolding the tiny knife blade on the side of my leatherman folding pliers. The ranger looked around, found our pot with our supper in it, and promptly turned it upside down over the fire than jumped up and down on it. Madness was one thing, but messing with our dinner was another thing altogether. I was hungry and we only carried minimal supplies for our hike.

"No, no, no, no, no - NO FUEGO!" He shouted, by now seriously red in the face and matching around the ankles.

"Oh shit - light eventually dawned on me - no fires allowed inside the park. We were so used to just setting up camp in the middle of the wilderness (I thought of the massive bonfires the Gauchos lit for their asado), we hadn't even checked the park rules on our way in. It was a cardinal sin and I felt stupid and humiliated. The best thing I could do was stand there looking stupid and humiliated while the ranger finished shouting at us. Eventually, the fire well and truly out, he calmed down enough for me to apologise profusely and promise we would only use our small camping stove from now on, carefully propped up on a pile of rocks in a small area of cleared ground. He explained to us that it wasn't just the risk of wildfires - much of the ground in the park was a dense, peaty earth, made up of decomposing heather packed down over thousands of years. It was lovely and soft to walk on or sleep on, but unfortunately highly flammable. There had been numerous cases in the past of the actual ground being set on fire. Once lit these fires could burn underground for months or even years and were extraordinarily difficult to put out. Chastened, we apologised again and thanked him for his advice. If there's one thing I hate more than feeling stupid, it's being stupid.

The next day we broke camp early, eager to put the scene of our crime behind us. The hike towards Cerro Torre was lovely, but largely uneventful - until, that is, we reached the river. The river was also lovely but rather wide, very fast flowing and some thoughtless person seemed to have taken the only bridge with them the last time they crossed. Frank got the map out again. This was definitely the right path, and the bridge was right here. Except it wasn't. We dumped our bags in a pile and Frank set off upstream while I took the downstream side. We agreed to walk twenty minutes in either direction which should give us a range of an extra mile either side to try and spot the bridge. Forty minutes later we were back at the pile of bags wondering just how deep it actually got. Whoever had taken my bridge had done a thorough job - there was no sign of it anywhere.

It didn't look too deep, but it did look fast. I have crossed a few

45

rivers before and I know just how much pressure a relatively shallow stream can exert on you as you try to wade through it. I'm also a very poor swimmer, so swimming across even a short section was out of the question. Frank, being the tallest volunteered to go first.

He found a long branch first, to steady himself and probe in front to check the depth. Then he stripped down to his shorts (how on earth did he manage to stay that *white*?) and put everything else inside his panniers which he then threw over this shoulders. Prodding carefully with his stick he gently edged into the stream. At first it didn't look too bad at all, barely up to his long white skinny calves, though he *did* seem to be making a bit of a meal of it, grunting and puffing as though he was slogging through a six foot snowdrift. We'd deliberately picked the widest part, on the assumption that that hopefully meant the gentlest flow and (possibly) the shallowest too. It also meant there was still quite a long way to go. Frank ploughed manfully (if a bit whingeingly) on…

For quite a long way the water stayed below his knees. Then, within a couple of steps, it was up to his waist. At this point he was puffing like a steam locomotive (I could still hear him above the rushing noise of the water) and using the stick to brace himself downstream rather than checking the depth out front. Luckily it didn't seem to get any deeper, and although Frank was moving much slower at this point, after 8 or 9 rather hesitant steps he started to rise in the water again like a very pale (and frankly unattractive) Lady of the Lake. There was one more section near the far bank when the water briefly came up to his thighs again, but otherwise he was home and dry. Well, home anyway. When he climbed out on the far bank he threw his bags on the ground and bizarrely started running up and down the bank waving his arms in the air. I assumed it was just his version of a victory dance and started stripping down to my shorts ready to join him.

I shouted across "How was it?", but either the noise from the water was too much, the distance too far or Frank was too busy still doing his victory dance to hear. I packed my gear away, picked up my bags and my own long stick and got ready to step in. Unlike Frank I didn't

46

have any flip-flops and rather than get my shoes soaking and risk blisters on the remaining part of the hike I decided to go barefoot. By now anyone who knows anything at all about hiking, mountains or rivers will be wincing, but we were young, inexperienced and learning all the time.

I stepped down from the bank and put my foot into the edge of the stream.

Jesus, Mary and Joseph - that water was *cold*! Now that I was closer I could actually see lumps of ice tumbling in the current. OK Dumbo, it's called Las Glaciares Park for a reason - where do you think this water is coming from? Bugger. This is ice-melt from one of the glaciers snaking its way down from the Andes, probably the same one which twists pas the foot of Cerro Torre itself. No more than five or ten miles upstream this water is coming out of a solid block of ice. No wonder Frank was huffing and puffing. I was barely past my ankles and already catching my breath.

I shuffled on. At first my feet were in agony, burning from the cold and cut and scraped from the sharp stones on the river bottom. Very quickly, though, and rather more worryingly they started to simply go numb. This might have been a relief from the pain but it really didn't help when I was trying to feel my way across, avoid any deep holes and generally stay upright.

By the time I got to the deep section I could just about move my legs but couldn't feel anything below my knees. Still, i was committed now - might as well go forwards as go back.

I took one step, then another. Oddly, it wasn't quite as bad dipping my man-parts in iced water as I'd expected. Maybe my body had already started to acclimatise and I suspected that all the key elements had been sucked up well inside my body cavity, possibly never to return.

It wasn't till the third step that I realised Frank's waist, of course, was roughly on a level with my chest.

My feet scrabbled for grip, the stick flailed in the current, the water picked me up and - I was gone. In a tenth of a second I'd gone from intrepid explorer to a ragged lump of flotsam, heading for the sea at some considerable speed.

At this point I'd like to take a moment to express my very sincere thanks to a Mr Ortlieb of Germany. Some time ago Mr Ortlieb started making bicycle bags and panniers. He hated that his stuff kept getting wet, so he made them out of a sort of PVC canvas that they used for the softsides on lorries. They are very simple bags, with a rolltop closure that effectively seals them completely and keeps all of the water out. Fortunately for me, the unanticipated bonus of this is that it also seals all of the air *IN*.

My head went under briefly but I grabbed both bags in my panic and was just about able to keep breathing while I floated downstream on them like two bloated water wings.

The only problem I had now was how to *stop* floating and try and make my way to shallower water before I ended up in the South Atlantic.

I looked towards the far shore and saw Frank's skinny white frame flashing through the trees (not literally flashing) as he ran along the bank trying to keep pace with me. he was shouting something but I couldn't hear. Every now and then my feet must have bumped the bottom - it was hard to feel anything through my toes but I could sense the drag on my legs, and I kicked as hard as I could towards the shore.

I looked up again but Frank was gone - maybe he'd fallen, maybe the undergrowth was just too thick. I tried kicking again. if I didn't get out soon the cold would get me long before I drowned. I looked downstream instead, to see if there was any noticeable change in the stream.

There he was! My angel in white. Frank had run ahead and was now wading back out into the stream, waving a long stick in my direction. God bless him. Nothing on this planet could have persuaded *me* to go back into that water once I'd got out, but here he was, almost up to his waist a second time, coming to fish me out.

I kicked as hard as I could and just managed to manoeuvre myself within reach of the stick. As I grabbed it Frank dug in and I swung in a broad arc until my legs started scraping once more on the rocky bottom. Without letting go of the stick I scrambled as best I could in the direction of the bank while Frank heaved and pulled me in like a giant pale catfish.

Back on shore at last I sat on the bank, unable to stand, waiting for some circulation to restore to my (interestingly blue) legs. I was frozen, wet, cut and scraped and I couldn't have been happier. Frank had a huge grin on his face.

"Cold, huh?"

I nodded. "A bit."

At least I understood the victory dance now - he'd just been trying to warm up again.

"Let's not do that again. Next time, I'm gonna build a boat - ok? I don't care how long it takes."

Of course at some point we were going to have to go back the other way, but for now I was happy to cross that non-existent bridge when I didn't come to it.

"I can't believe you got back into that water to rescue me?"

He shrugged.

"You have the stove, the pans and half the food."

I smiled back.

"In that case you can count on me to carry them for the foreseeable future."

Thank God I hadn't picked a shorter, less food-obsessed travelling companion.

Once we'd dried off, thawed out and got dressed again I insisted on pausing to make a large pot of coffee and gave Frank most of what was left of my supply of dark chocolate. I kept a small piece for myself - after all, it wasn't as though he'd actually had to *swim* out to get me...

I took a perverse (and very petty) delight in just taking a tiny amount of that very, very cold water, boiling it up then drinking it. That'll show nature who's boss.

Once we were on our way again it didn't take long to reach our destination - the small lake at the foot of Cerro Torre. It was absolutely stunning - the wildest, most isolated and beautiful spot I have seen, before or since. The only thing which spoiled it was the small circle of tents and group of five or six other people milling about them right next to the shore of the lake. Goddamn it. We'd specifically chosen this route because it was supposed to be off the beaten track. Grudgingly we wandered over to say hello.

As it turned out they were a group of Austrian mountaineers. They'd been camped out here for the best part of a month, just waiting for the weather to clear at the top of the mountain to make their ascent. Cerro Torre is a needle-like monster of a peak, jutting up like someone has stuck a giant stone sword into the ground then broken off the hilt.

As I looked up I could see the sunlight bouncing off a great, mushroom-like cap of snow sitting on the peak.

"It looks ok now?" I said, unhelpfully.

The group leader who'd been chatting with us grimaced.

"Ja. Perfect now. 28 days, covered in cloud, high wind. Today we have no more time. We go home."

They weren't just milling aimlessly around their tents, they were actually packing up to leave. They'd travelled all that way, waited for the best part of a month and been unable to get further than the glacier at the base. After they left we had six glorious days of summer weather. Bummer.

Still, I've been on the receiving end of that kind of luck often enough to know there's no choice but to roll with it.

Speaking of luck, just as they were about to leave the leader came over to us again.

"Hey - would you like some food?"

Frank's eyes lit up

"Sorry?"

"Food. We bring a lot of food with us when we come. No good to carry it all back."

He took us to their stash. A large bag of potatoes, onions and numerous tins of fruit and vegetables.

"Wow. Ok, yes, that would be great. Thank you. Better than having to try to carry it back through that blasted river, anyway."

"What river?"

"Didn't you have to cross the river to get here? Man that was so cold."

"We came over die brucke…the, the…bridge, yes, bridge."

"There's a **bridge**?"

"Ja, of course. Sehr gefarlich - dangerous - crossing glacial stream."

After we'd pulled out our map and compared notes we worked out the bridge (a lovely new wooden one) was in fact only a few miles upstream from where we'd crossed. if we'd walked for half an hour rather than twenty minutes we'd probably have spotted it.

The route we'd taken was apparently the *old* path, used before they built the bridge and we'd missed the turn for the new one.

Oh well. We'd had an adventure. It hadn't quite killed either of us. And best of all we could relax now knowing that we didn't have to go back through it again to get home.

Over the next five days we did practically nothing. As I already mentioned the weather was stunning. We woke each morning and went to bed each night with picture-perfect views of the mountain in every possible lighting combination, and not a cloud in the sky.

We slept, cooked, ate, wrote in our journals and drank in the sheer wonder of just being there.

On one occasion I forced myself to have a quick bath in the stream (Frank was moving further and further upwind at mealtimes so I decided it was probably necessary). But I never went in further than my ankles, splashing myself all over, and was in and out in under a minute.

I also took a short hike round the edge of the lake up to the edge of the glacier, gave it a good hard kick out of spite, then walked back again.

We ate like kings (maybe medieval kings, but still it felt pretty good) thanks to our good friends the Austrians. Thanks to them, too, the hike back to the ranger station was much less exciting than the hike out. We found the bridge straight away and I stopped in   the centre for a ceremonial pee into the icy water. *That's for trying to kill me*...Funny how much you can appreciate a simple thing like a footbridge once you've had to deal with it *not* being there.

Checkpoints and Chilblains

From El Chalten we made our way north, aiming to cross back over into Chile at Balmaceda.

In the far south of Argentina we'd had to stop every twenty miles or so at military checkpoints thrown across the road. Mostly these were manned by shivering young boys, conscripts from the far north of the country who'd probably never imagined there could be a place where *summer* was this cold. None of them spoke a word of English, but regardless we were all required to fill in our details in a large ledger kept (I suspect) principally for the purpose of giving the conscripts something to do once they'd stopped us. The columns were always the same and we quickly worked out a routine, filling them in by rote.

Family Name, First Name, Nationality, Passport number, Occupation, Vehicle Registration number.

Since it was not permitted to leave blanks the registration number caused a bit of consternation to us cyclists. At first we scrabbled in the dirt to try to find a serial number on our bikes. After a while we realised it made no difference what you wrote, so long as you wrote something. There were a lot of ABC123's after that. The further north we got, the fewer checkpoints we found. What was interesting, though, was watching how the attitude of those passing through shifted as they became more blasé about the information required and the conscripts inability or lack of interest in reading or checking any of it. While completing our own entries we took a few minutes to scan back through those who had passed before us, just to see if we could find anything interesting. Unsurprisingly we found an awful lot of 'Mouse, Mickey', a 'Marx, Karl' and a 'Queen, Elizabeth'. People got much more creative when it came to occupation, though. My personal favourites were: 'Astronaut', 'Sumo Wrestler', 'Pope' and (either especially brave or especially foolhardy) 'Spy'.

Eventually the checkpoints faded out altogether and we left Argentina again to make our way back into Chile.

Of course when you put it like that it sounds very straightforward. Crossing the Andes by bicycle on unpaved roads is never going to be a barrel of laughs though. The best thing I could say is that, as long as you keep the pedals going round, you'll get where you're going eventually. Sometimes the going was better than others, sometimes (when the washboard combined with the sand and the rain) it was nothing short of Dantean in its hellishness. Mostly, though it was just a long hard slog.

Up to this point, although the weather had been mixed, our worst enemy had always been the Patagonian wind. Back in Chile we were subjected to five long days of relentless, torrential rain. Within the first hour, everything that I was wearing was wet through. After the first day, setting up and taking down camp in the pouring rain, just about everything I had was wet through. It stayed that way for the next four days. We went to bed wet, we woke up wet, we cycled wet and we cooked wet. In that time I can't recall seeing more than two or three other vehicles on the road or I would quite possibly have lain down in front of one and insisted they either run me over there and then or drive me to the nearest motel.

On the fifth day we stumbled upon a sign indicating a campsite, just 2km up a side track. Hoping at least for a shower block, or even a picnic shelter we decided to take a chance and check it out. Just about anything would be better than another wet night by the side of the road.

When we got to the site the gates were closed. Fortunately there was a guy the other side, working on his pickup truck in the rain. When we called him over he explained he was a part-time caretaker, but the campsite was currently closed until the new season started in a week's time. In a week's time if it continued like this we would either have shrivelled to a quarter of our original size or worst case dissolved away completely and washed down into the Pacific Ocean. As best I could I explained we had cycled all the way from Tierra Del Fuego, we were really tired and wet - could he not just let us set up camp in a small corner somewhere, maybe there was somewhere we could just stand out of the rain for an hour or so, remind ourselves what breathing just air was like.

The mention of Tierra Del Fuego seemed to capture his imagination and for whatever reason he took pity on us. He opened the gates and showed us through to a small flat patch of land just outside the main reception building.

he stood by and watched as we parked up our bikes and started to unload our sodden gear. I couldn't tell if he was a sadist or just plain curious. After a while he stepped forward.

"You know, if you want, you could have a cabin for twenty dollars."

A what? You have a cabin? With a roof and walls and everything?

I had a twenty dollar bill out of my wallet so fast it almost dried off some of the water soaking through it. Maybe it was a caretaker's sideline - who cared? At this stage I would probably have paid a hundred had he only known.

He took the soggy note, shook it slightly then carefully folded it into an outside pocket on his jacket and motioned for us to follow him. Rapidly piling all our stuff back onto the bikes we chased after him as quick as we could. Turned out this was not just a simple campsite, but more of a rich Chileans playground. City slickers from Santiago in the north came down here to go hunting, or hiking in the wilderness. Being rich folk, though, they liked their creature comforts when they got back in the evening. The cabin he showed us into was more like a giant Swiss Chalet. A huge log house with a massive open plan kitchen and living room, bathroom and three bedrooms leading off. Best of all there was an enormous open fireplace with a great stack of logs and kindling piled ready next to it. I pointed towards the logs and the fire. "Is ok…fire?"

"Si, si, ok" he nodded. Frank was smiling for the first time in four days and I realised I probably was too.

Within minutes it looked as though a clothes bomb had gone off as we tipped out the entire contents of all our bags and spread them out over every surface across the room. Next up was to get the log fire going and see just how many of those logs we could get through in one evening. Frank and I stretched out on the long leather sofas in our underwear like pale and very damp Romans. Once we'd warmed up a bit and singed a couple of items of clothing from soddenness to mere dampness, Frank set to in the kitchen, where he was delighted to find a full range of herbs, spices and sauces to spice up our rather bland rations. I went back outside to find our caretaker friend and persuaded him to sell me a rather nice bottle of Chilean wine for another five dollars to complete the perfect end to the day.

The following morning was muggy and overcast but at least it looked like our newly-dried out kit might stay that way for a bit longer. We thanked our host profusely then cycled off before he could see quite how much sand and dirt had made its way off our clothes and bags and onto the furniture and floor of his lovely log cabin.

Tales of Cake and Wine

From Puerto Chacabuco we took the ferry to Puerto Montt. I say 'ferry', it's actually more of a cargo ship that takes passengers too. The accommodation for the 24 hour sailing is fairly basic but it was worth every penny for the views of the fabulous Chilean fjords as we cruised in and out of the narrow waterways and around the islands of the Chilean archipelago. In some ways it was nicer that this was a proper working boat rather than a tarted-up cruise ship - it made the views feel like a travelling bonus rather than a luxury purchase.

Every traveller we met in the area raved about the island of Chiloe which lay to our west for most of the boat journey. Without exception though, they all talked about the incessant rain which seemed to bless the island. Having experienced quite enough damp sightseeing for a while we decided to skip this particular opportunity. In fact, by this stage, we were ready for a flat out run to drier, warmer climes.

The bikes were fairly crusty with salt by the time we arrived but we managed to hose them down in Puerto Montt before heading north for Osorno and Temuco.

Temuco is a relatively large city and has one of the highest proportions of indigenous population in Chile, mostly people of Mapuche Indian origins. Bizarrely it also has quite a high proportion of German descendants and not a few Basques. While this may have been associated with a certain amount of racial tension in the past, it has led to an interesting mix of cultures and, more importantly for us, some very excellent cake shops and superb tasting sausages.

Did I mention how much Frank liked cake? Frank really liked cake. In fact, the main issue with Patagonia, as far as Frank was concerned, was the large distances between coffee and cake shops. When you're cycling for 6 to 8 hours a day you burn a lot of calories, and inevitably your food intake goes up. For such a skinny guy, though, I've never seen anyone put away the sort of volume of sugary, creamy, icing covered calorie-bombs that Frank could demolish in a single sitting, and generally between meals. Meringues, cream puffs, lemon drizzle - you name it. You can imagine, then, his reaction when presented with a plate glass window-full of Black Forest gateaux, Bavarian cream cake, Topfentorte and the delicious, if scary, Bienenstitch or Bee-Sting cake. We stayed for a while to indulge Frank's gluttonous fantasies, but after two or three days even he started to waiver a little at the thought of yet more refined sucrose. I reckoned if you pricked his thumb at this point and drizzled some blood on the top of a vanilla ice cream you'd be hard pushed to tell the difference between that and strawberry syrup.

Bags full of emergency Bienenstitch then (not a phrase you will have read before, I guess), we left Temuco and pushed north in a full-bodied drive for sunshine, warmth and wine, aiming for a little town called Curico, right in the centre of the Chilean wine growers region and around 500 km away.

I have to say I loved Curico. In another life I could easily imagine myself living there. We found clean, comfortable and very cheap accommodation not far from the city centre. In the centre itself was a lovely Plaza de Armas with plenty of benches and huge shady palm trees where we were able to sit, relax, read or recover from the latest cakefest. Frank was happy to see an excellent collection of bakeries (though missing out on some of the Bavarian specialties Temuco could offer). Using Curico as a base we took our time to explore the countryside all around, and in particular to visit as many vineyards as possible. One particular, long, hot day, we'd been out for a while and were more than usually grubby, covered in a layer of sweat and road dust that would have made a passable outfit for one of those irritating living statue buskers. It was late afternoon when Frank spotted a sign leading off the road for Wine Tasting and Tours of the Vineyard. You have to be slightly wary in Chile, because these places could be anywhere between 2 and 30 km from the actual road, but we were both tired and thirsty so it seemed like it would be worthwhile checking at least. We'd only gone about 3km when we could clearly see a bunch of white farm building hiding in amongst a large stand of trees. The place seemed to be popular at least, there were quite a few cars scattered around the outside of the buildings. As we got closer I noticed that for some reason the cars all looked the same - all very large, all very black and all saloon cars, not a pickup truck among them. To go along with the cars was a matching collection of men - also all very large, all wearing black suits and dark sunglasses. As we rode up three of them swiftly stepped out from the group and quietly and efficiently surrounded us. On closer inspection they didn't look very Chilean and to go with the intimidating stares they were giving us they all carried suspicious-looking bumps under their suit jackets.

"Er, Hello. We're here for the tour? Wine-tasting?"

"Is close. You leave now."

"Really? Oh, that's a shame. There seem to be a lot of cars here. Is it some form of private function? Do you think we could just get some water before we go? We've really come quite a long way…"

"Is close."

Ok, well that much was clear anyway.

We were just in the process of trying to shuffle our bikes around when a small man in a sharply contrasting white suit and Panama hat came out of one of the buildings. Seeing us surrounded by goons he quickly walked over.

"Hello, can I help you?"

"Hi yes, sorry, we were hoping for a tour, or at least a small tasting - we didn't realise you were closed."

"You came here by bicycle?"

"Yes, well, actually we came all the way from Tierra Del Fuego by bicycle…"

59

It had worked before so was always worth a try.

"You came here, from Tierra Del Fuego, by *bicycle*? How far *is* that?"

"I dunno - what do you think Frank? Bit over 3,000km?"

Frank looked down at his odometer.

"No - I have 2,864 - remember we took the boat to Puerto Montt?"

"Please - wait here a moment. I will make some enquiries. One moment, please."

He walked back into the building. Frank, I and the men mountain waited.

A few minutes later there was a faint buzz as something was relayed into the earpieces worn by our three minders and without a word they walked off to rejoin their clones.

A little later and Geraldo Durrell re-appeared (for some reason he reminded me of the writer). "I'm sorry, we have the Russian Ambassador here today and security is a little... secure?"

"No problem. We understand. Thank you for your time."

"But...if you would care to let the Ambassador's group go first, you can perhaps follow behind them?" He looked at our dusty clothes and faces. "Perhaps keep a little distance?"

"That would be brilliant, thank you."

"I'm afraid we cannot invite you into the dining hall afterwards - they would not permit it, but if you wait here after I will bring you something to eat?"

"Marvellous - thank you so much."

"Not at all. 2, 800 kilometres by bicycle, now *that* is marvellous."

So it was that we tagged along behind the ambassadorial party, keeping well clear of the dark suits. We saw the huge brewing vats and the bottling plant and tasted a very nice Pinot Grigio.

At the end of the tour we went back to wait in the car park out front. After half an hour we started to assume we'd been forgotten and were thinking about heading off when a young girl in waitress outfit appeared carrying a large tray. There were two glasses of white wine, fresh fruit, bread, different cheeses, some cooked chicken and, a nice surprise, a small glass bowl of caviar.

After a few more days in Curico it was time for Frank to head off and meet Ben in Santiago, then home back to the Netherlands. I don't mind travelling alone, often in fact I prefer it. But Frank had been a brilliant cycling compadre. Easygoing, cheerful and entertaining - with the added bonus, of course, that he'd pretty much saved my life.

I would miss him. But I wasn't quite ready to go home yet, I wanted to see more of Argentina first. So as Frank headed north, I turned around to re-trace our steps back south. I'd heard of an interesting border crossing that involved a long ferry ride across one of the high Andean lakes and would take me into the Argentinian skiing region around Bariloche and San Martin de Los Andes.

Ferry Boaring

I passed back through Temuco again, but without Frank's magnetic addiction to cake shop windows felt no great desire to linger and shortly afterwards cut eastwards to start climbing up into the mountain country, heading for the wonderfully-named town of Panguipulli. For some reason I just couldn't separate this from the image of the two-headed llama in Doctor Doolittle called the Pushmi Pullyu. Sadly there were no two headed llamas to be seen, but it was a nice enough little town, sitting on the western shore of Lago Panguipulli and with great views of the Choshuenco volcano. I love volcanoes. I also love my grandchildren. Both of them are wonderful to visit, but perhaps slightly more challenging to live with. Fortunately Choshuenco (sometimes known as Mocho-Choshuenco) has been dormant for some time now, and when I was there at least was largely covered by a giant ice cap, though I understand this has shrunk considerably of late. Still the area around is highly geologically active and there are a number of Termas, or thermal hot-springs dotted around the area.

From Panguipulli the road loops around then follows alongside the lake before starting to climb in earnest up to the little, one-horse town of Puerto Fuy. From Puerto Fuy the only way forwards through the mountains is by ferry, which runs 14 miles end-to-end of the long, narrow Lago Pirihueco. These days there is apparently a shiny new Catamaran running regular services. Unfortunately when I was there I arrived a day late for the last ferry and the next one wasn't due to leave for another four days. I'd pretty much exhausted the sites of Puerto Fuy town within fifteen minutes of arriving, but since my options were wait, or turn around and descend a couple of thousand feet and cycle several hundred km south then back east again to the next road pass, I decided I could wait. There weren't a lot of accommodation options but I got a clean, reasonably cheap room in an otherwise empty hotel and set about sorting through all my gear. A couple of hours later I'd checked and tidied everything, serviced the bike and was looking at my watch thinking surely it should be nearly Monday by now?

I spent a lot of time updating my travel notes. I went for a paddle in the lake. I drank quite a lot of tinned beer.

Friday evening things livened up a bit when the hotel suddenly filled up. There was a large party of hunters who'd come down from Concepcion on the coast hoping to bag a wild boar. They were friendly enough, and one of them even asked me if I wanted to come out with them the next day. I took a look at the large number of guns they were carrying, the even larger number of beer cans they'd emptied and decided if they *did* find a boar it was going to be a bit of a one-sided massacre and if they *didn't* find one there was every chance they'd end up shooting one of their own party. I politely declined - it wasn't as though I could claim to be busy...

The next day they came back empty-handed and settled for launching another all-out attack on the hotel beer supply instead. I wondered if hunting in Chile was a bit like cricket at home - i.e. not much to do with hunting really, but more about an excuse to sit drinking with your mates. I also began to wonder if I should get a quick order in for half a dozen cans to store in my room in case they ran the bar dry.

The next day they were up and out again before I could be bothered to explore the hotel breakfast buffet (bread roll, packet jam and instant coffee). I mooched around the lake shore again for much of the day and wondered whether I should have taken them up on their offer - at least I would have had a bit of exercise. Later that afternoon I wandered back to the hotel to find they'd returned early. They were all gathered around a large muddy pickup truck and from the excitement I gathered they must have actually shot something - though from this angle I couldn't tell if it was a Boar or an unfortunate member of their party. When I got closer I looked into the back and saw one of the largest wild animals I'd ever come across. When they'd said they were hunting wild boar I'd pictured something the size of a medium dog, maybe a small domestic pig at most. This thing was a giant, easily the size of a small cow it completely filled the flat bed of the truck. When they came to slide it out it took six men to lift it. It was black as night, covered in thick wiry hair and had tusks that would have done a sabre-toothed tiger proud. Perhaps they weren't overdoing it with the number of guns after all - I'd have wanted a bazooka to tackle this thing.

There was much celebrating at dinner that evening, though pretty much just the same volume of beer drunk as the previous night. In the morning they, and the boar, had already gone by the time I saddled up and rolled down to the quay ready, at last to board my ferry. It was a beautiful trip, but I was mostly just glad to be moving again.

At the other end of the lake there was a bus waiting to take any foot passengers on to San Martin. For a while I was tempted, it would be a good way to make up at least some of the time I'd spent waiting in Puerto Fuy - no, that's a lie. I wouldn't really make up much time, but I was feeling lazy. As it happened the decision was made for me. I made the fatal mistake of asking the bus driver if I could put my bike in the luggage compartment. What I should have done, of course, was put it in first, then tell him I'd done it. Path of least resistance. Get out of your seat and force me to take the bike out? Too much work. But don't even look at me and just say 'no' - easy-peasey.

Hence I found myself alone again, pedalling up to the very appropriately named Hua-Hum pass. "Ho, hum" I kept thinking to myself.

Hua Hum is one of the lowest of the Andean passes but unfortunately it's not a straight drop from there straight into San Martin. The road continues to rise and fall and as the rain started again I questioned the bus driver's parents marital status numerous times.

Only 55 km from the ferry terminal but it turned into one of the longest and toughest days I can remember. Following my mantra, though, of 'just keep the pedals turning' eventually I rolled into the pretty ski resort of San Martin de Los Andes.

Gun Control

I gave myself a day off in San Martin to enjoy the relative sophistication of good food and actual shops and restaurants after the slightly claustrophobic isolation of Puerto Fuy. Apart from being back in Argentina, this was a popular tourist resort, summer and winter and noticeably wealthier than anywhere I'd passed through on the Chilean side of the mountains.

From San Martin I started to make my way north again, shadowing the route I'd followed up through Chile, but this time on the eastern side of the Andes. News arrived that one of my friends was getting married and wanted me to be best man, which was great, but for the first time put a duration limit on my travels. I would run out of money before too long anyway, but, with fond memories of the warm weather and other delights of Curico in mind I decided to fast-forward a little and jumped a bus up to the wine-producing region of Mendoza.

After a few days cycling around I settled on the town of Tupungato as a convenient base from which to explore the region. While staying there I found a particularly good restaurant and ate there three days running. It wasn't busy and I got chatting with the waiter. Eventually he asked me if I was staying for the weekend and if I'd like to take a trip up into the mountains with him and his friends. I thought about it for a while and decided he was probably genuine so said yes.

I met him and two others outside the restaurant early Saturday morning. It was cool, but bright and looked like it was going to turn into a really nice day. We bundled into a very battered looking car and headed out of town towards the nearby peaks. You're never really far from the mountains in Chile. Chileans are very fond of saying you can go skiing in the morning and lie out on the beach in the afternoon. Tupungato is practically in the foothills of the Andes, though, so it didn't take long to find ourselves in among the peaks.

As we climbed the road got narrower and rougher and I realised I had no idea where we were going or what we were going to do when we got there. Each time we reached a junction it looked like we took the smallest, roughest road of the two. The higher we got, the slower our pace and the more I got bounced around the back seat. We'd been going for about an hour and a half, and hadn't seen another vehicle (or person or even animal) for the last hour of that, and I was starting to get nervous. I was struggling to imagine what could possibly be of any interest at the end of such a remote, and clearly little-used trail when the car suddenly veered off the road and scrabbled to a halt in a small lay-by followed by a large cloud of dust.

Without a word said the other three opened their doors, got out and walked round to the back of the car and popped the boot lid. When they re-appeared all three were holding handguns and I got ready to say goodbye. My waiter friend smiled and gestured for me to get out of the car.

As it turned out, their idea of fun was to go out at the weekend to a remote spot and shoot …rocks. They even handed me one of the guns with gestures clearly indicating 'go on, have a go…' I was still feeling jittery so did my best to use up as much ammunition as quickly as possible without worrying too much whether I actually hit anything (well, obviously I hit *something*, but nothing I could have said I was *aiming* at). Needless to say they were fairly unimpressed with my gun skills.

Eventually they got tired, or bored and, ears still ringing, we all climbed back into the car and headed back to town. They dropped me off outside the restaurant, slapping my back as though we were the greatest amigos of all time. I never saw them again.

I've seen any number of beautiful mountains, sunsets, rivers and ruins - but I don't remember any of them as well as I remember that day.

In Mendoza I followed up a lead provided by another cyclist I'd met coming south as I went north. Jose was a local Mendozan, living in a tiny house in the suburbs with his wife and young daughter. A keen cyclist and (rare now in Argentina) an anglophile, he held an open house policy for any cyclist travellers passing through. I simply turned up on his doorstep and he welcomed me in with open arms. He insisted I take his daughter's room (she would move in with them for the duration). While his wife was preparing supper he sat me down and picked my brains for details of my journey so far. For a native Argentinian he seemed to know relatively little about the far south of his own country, or perhaps he was enjoying the vicarious thrill of an adventurous ride that was slowly slipping out of his reach while he settled into family life. Or perhaps he was just being polite. Anyway, it seemed a small price to pay for a soft bed and a warm supper. A couple of times I tried to offer him money for the room but he would have none of it. He was fascinated by my LED bike lights which apparently hadn't made their way to the stores in this part of Argentina yet.

The following day I explored Mendoza while Jose was at work. In the evening he told me his boss was also a keen cyclist and wanted to meet me. If it was ok we could take our bikes and meet up at one of the parks in town after supper. It would have been churlish to refuse, and cycling without any bags or luggage always made a pleasant change so I said I would be glad to.

When we got to the park Jose's boss was already there. I said hello and he spent the next ten minutes telling me what an accomplished racing cyclist he was, how many races he'd won, how strong he was. I say telling me, in fact he told Jose who was expected to perform simultaneous translation. Jose did his best but I told him not to worry too much - I pretty much got the gist of it within the first fifteen seconds and wasn't overly interested in hearing the rest anyway. I took a more or less instant dislike to the man. He was a Boor, a Braggart and a Bully and I could see Jose was slightly intimidated by him. After a while he broke off his monologue and pointed to a small hill rising in the centre of the park. I could just make out what looked like a path winding round it a couple of times before finishing at the top.

"Let's race to the top of the hill. I will beat you."

I looked at him. His shirt was straining to hold in a nascent, but promising beer belly. Tucked into the pocket at the top was a packet of cigarettes - unfiltered I should imagine, the only sort a man like that would smoke. Now I'm no Charles Atlas myself, I have arms like sticky the stick man and no upper body strength to speak of. But 6 months more or less continual cycling up and down mountains lugging 30 odd kilos of gear is going to leave a bit of a mark on anyone. Perversely I quite liked climbing anyway - having no upper body mass just meant there was less weight for my legs to have to push up. And right now I felt like I was floating without having all those bags strapped to my bike. I shrugged. I'm not really into racing but if that's what he wanted I might as well see what the view was like from the top of the hill.

"Ok".

He set off straight away pedalling for the hill. I waited for Jose to follow then tucked in behind. When he got to the bottom of the hill, instead of waiting for us all to line up he just jumped on the pedals and carried straight on up the path.

'Ok,' I thought, 'no surprise there.'

To begin with I just followed Jose, but the gap gradually widened between him and his boss. By the time we were halfway up I couldn't be bothered to hold back any more so overtook Jose and fairly quickly caught up with Bossman. By this stage he was still going, but puffing quite hard so I just hung on, a couple of metres from his back wheel.

That's where I should have stayed. It would have been the grown-up thing to do. It would have been the polite thing to do. But he'd really pissed me off - not least by flagrantly trying to cheat a head start.

I waited till he was about thirty metres from the top then quickly and quietly went past him. I even stayed seated in the saddle.

When we got to the top he was really quite red in the face - not just from exertion, though, he was angry - really angry. We waited for Jose to join us. When he got there Bossman barked a few words at him then turned away and rolled off down the hill. Jose didn't bother to translate and I didn't ask.

"Look, I'm really sorry about that - I should have let him win. I hope I haven't made a problem for you."

Jose shrugged.

"When he was younger, he really was a good racer - very fast, quite famous in Mendoza. But, that was years ago. I think he does not like how things have changed."

"Probably not. Shall we go home?"

"Si."

Jose was quite subdued on the way back to his house. I began to worry that I really had made a problem for him. It would not surprise me if Bossman was vindictive. I decided probably I should move on the next day.

It was getting close to time for me to head back to Buenos Aires for my flight home, but I wasn't quite done with the Andes yet. Jose had told me about an old, little-used pass into Chile. It was, he said, a very pretty climb up a narrow dirt track. At the top I would have to hike up the last section, but there was a Gendarmerie at the end of the road where I could leave my bike, and an ancient Refugio at the top where I could spend the night. I had no desire to cross back into Chile at this stage but I thought this might be a nice farewell to South America.

In the morning Jose had already gone to work by the time I was up. I wondered what sort of reception he faced while I was loading up my bags. Before I left I put out my two LED bike lights on the table for him - a thank you and an apology.

The Bold Gendarmes

I headed back south and west from Mendoza and eventually found the road Jose had shown me on his map.

At first it was very pretty, winding gently into the foothills as it followed a bright blue stream back up towards its source. There was a grassy bank and tall trees providing shade from the increasingly fierce sun, and I stopped and sat down for an idyllic late breakfast/ early lunch.

Party time over I packed up my things, topped up my water bottle with filtered water from the stream, and set out for the more serious part of the climb.

Fairly soon the road switched from a gentle incline to a series of more severe switchbacks, each one with a horribly tight and steep hairpin bend at the end.

That in itself would have been quite manageable, even almost enjoyable, were it not for the fact that the road surface rapidly deteriorated and became rockier and rockier.

It got harder and harder to keep any sort of momentum going, especially going into the hairpins, and I found myself having to stop and push more and more frequently. Probably if I'd taken the time to turn around and look back down the trail, the view would have been spectacular. Instead I got more and more fixated on making it to the top before dark. I laughed grimly. I thought I'd be saying a fond farewell to the mountains. Turned out the mountains had another message for me altogether.

It was late afternoon before I finally spotted the Gendarmerie high up above me. By this time I was pretty much pushing the bike all the way. it was too steep, too rocky and the surface too slippery to get started properly if I did get back on the bike, and I'd only get a few metres before some huge rock would bounce me to a standstill anyway.

I guessed the guys stationed at the Gendarmerie didn't get many visitors. There were three of them in total and they all turned out to watch me shuffle my way up the final ascent. About 100 metres from the station I looked up to see two of them scrabbling down to meet me. One took the handlebars of the bike, while the other pushed from behind and they motioned me to walk ahead. Well I hadn't been expecting that kind of service from the local law enforcement, I must admit. But I was very grateful and stumbled up to the top relieved to finally be rid of my Sisyphean burden.

The Gendarmes couldn't have been more welcoming. They plied me with tea, and insisted on giving me food as well. My bike was parked carefully in the corner.

While I ate the older one of the three sat and questioned me avidly on my journey - how far I'd come, what had I seen, did I like Argentina? (I did, I really did).

After a while the questions turned to my home life. Where did I live and what did I do? Married? Children? Girlfriend?

Finally I finished my meal and feeling hugely refreshed I started to get ready to move again.

Where was I going? I wouldn't be able to cross the border now, the Chilean side would be closed.

I explained - that was Ok. I didn't want to cross. I just wanted to hike up to the top, spend the night in the Refugio, then come back down. Could I leave my bike here overnight?

They looked puzzled. Not cross? Just go all the way up...then come back down again?

I shrugged. When you looked at the road I had just climbed it didn't seem the most sensible thing to do, but I was here now.

The older one stood and patted me on the shoulder.

"It's getting late. I will guide you up the mountain"

"That's ok, I'm sure I'll be fine it's a pass, after all."

He shook his head.

"The path can be difficult. If you fell…"

"Well, OK - if you insist, thank you."

While I sorted my overnight essentials into my makeshift pannier-rucksack he went off into the interior of the station and came back a few minutes later in shorts and a very jazzy-looking red beret pulled jauntily over one eye. There was a faint itch at the back of my head, but I pushed it aside while I finished sorting out my gear.

There was no sign of the other two Gendarmes so I assumed they had gone off to polish their guns or something.

My new friend handed me a spare hiking pole and waved for me to follow him up a narrow path at the back of the building. The 'track' itself continued to switchback up the mountain but we followed a much steeper trail that cut across it going straight uphill.

We'd been going for about an hour when he stopped to sit on a rock next to the trail and motioned for me to join him. I sat down and looked back across the view - it really was magnificent. He passed me his water bottle. I shook my head, thanking him, but pulling out my own. He shook his head in return, pointing up towards the peak.

"No agua - only nieve…snow." Good point. Whatever I had would have to last me the rest of the night and the following morning. I took his bottle and drank thirstily, thanking him. He reached into his bag and shared out a couple of fresh figs - my favourite.

It was then that he tapped me lightly on my thigh.

"Strong legs, yes?"

Oh shit.

Now don't get me wrong. I think I'm pretty liberal-minded. I'm certainly no homophobe. But an unwanted advance is no fun for anybody, and even less so when there are just the two of you at the top of one of the remotest mountain passes in the Andean chain.

I *liked* my friend the Gendarme. He wasn't at all threatening, he'd been nothing but kind and he was helping me out. But I didn't like him *that* way. Plus of course, I didn't really know him. Plus, and not to be forgotten, he also had ready access to firearms should he so desire.

I gently stood up and picked up my stuff. I pointed to the sky.

"It's getting late - you should probably be heading back. I'll be fine from here, really."

He argued briefly - he should take me to the hut.

"No honestly - I can see the path, look."

It was true, there was really only one way up now.

He shrugged, looking only slightly put out, shouldered his rucksack, shook my hand, then set off back down the path.

I watched him go for a while, then turned and started to climb again.

I reached the Refugio around 45 minutes later. I've stayed in a few mountain huts before, but this one really was an emergency shelter only. A small stone hut, no bigger than a garden shed (or possibly a large outhouse), it had slates for a roof, with several large holes visible even from where I was standing some way back down the path. It had a wooden door which consisted of a mixture of air and some rotting wooden planks dangling loosely from a single hinge. The whole thing lay in the centre of a small clearing which was covered in a 5cm layer of snow.

Inside it was even less prepossessing. There was a single rusty iron bedstead, with enough broken springs it could probably double as a fakir's bed of nails, and ...well, nothing actually - that was it. Light and fresh air was provided courtesy of the numerous apertures in the door, walls and roof, and presumably running water via the same facilities when weather permitted.

I went back outside and made a small snowman while it started to get dark. There were plenty of rocks for his eyes, and I didn't think the door would miss a couple of splinters taken off for stubby little arms. He only needed a scarf and a hat, but by now it was beginning to get quite cold really quickly. I needed every item of clothing for myself so snowy would have to do without.

I couldn't say it was the worst night's sleep I ever had, because technically I never actually got to sleep. The combination of the bitter cold, the painful bed (I tried putting my sleeping bag on the floor but that was no more comfortable and even colder) and, above all the endless series of small scratching noises put paid to any possibility of nodding off, no matter how briefly. The scratching noises were almost certainly just rats, mice or some other micro-mammal, poking around to see if the human had brought any food to this desolate spot. But they just *could* have been the sound of a randy gendarme sneaking up the path, gun in hand.

The night lasted forever, but, as all nights eventually do, it started to fade away. As soon as there was enough light to see the path, I was up and packed and bounding back down towards the gendarmerie. I wasn't quite sure what would happen when I got there, but as it got lighter I was more and more comfortable with putting the worst of my imaginings down to paranoia plus a bit of oxygen deprivation.

I was almost disappointed by the time I reached the station to find no sign of my guide from the previous day. One of the other Gendarmes greeted me and wheeled my bike out for me to re-pack my gear. I may have looked a little hurried while I was doing this, but I gave him a cheery wave and a loud "MUCHAS GRACIAS!" as I set off back down the bumpy little track.

Of course the track hadn't improved magically overnight, but my mood had, and in addition, this time Mr Gravity had switched sides and was giving me a huge boost. I bounced and ricocheted my way between rocks, grinning like a loon. What had taken me all day nearly to climb I rocketed down in not much over an hour. I shot out back onto the highway in a cloud of dust, put my head down and started pedalling for Buenos Aires and home.

As so often happens with plans we make when we're travelling (or just plans in general), it hadn't quite worked out as the sendoff from South America that I'd anticipated, but it was a sendoff nonetheless.

Four Rivers and a Tricycle
Across Europe from St. Malo to Budapest on a 3-wheeled recumbent

I n May 1998 I set out to cross Europe from West to East by bicycle.

To make it interesting, I thought I'd follow the valleys of some of the great European rivers: the Loire, the Moselle, the Rhine and the Danube. To make it more interesting, I thought I'd do it on a 'Windcheetah' or 'Speedy' 3 wheeled recumbent.

As it turned out, the plan worked on both counts.

(A note on style: in the story below I regularly refer to 'we' rather than 'I' - although this was very much a solo trip Gonzalez, so named after the 'Speedy' recumbent, was such a strong character that I felt he deserved inclusion in the story on more or less equal terms.)

Part 1 - Courtesy, Cows and Catastrophe
From St. Malo to the Loire

Windcheetahs were built to order, at the rate of about 5 per week. I picked up number 383 from Bob Dixon at the Seat of the Pants Company, where they were built, on Saturday morning, the 16th of May 1998, manoeuvred it into the back of my car, and headed south for the English Channel.

Gonzalez, as he was instantly christened, is built for speed, long and low like a sports car. Just how low I began to realise while I was sat in the queue to board the cross-channel ferry at Portsmouth, examining in intimate detail the wheel nuts of a huge Landrover to my left and the tyre tread of a large motorbike in front of me. If you can imagine suddenly becoming the size of a small child again, spending most of your day at least 4 feet lower than you would normally be lends an interesting perspective to any experience.

We rolled off the ferry in St Malo around 6 am and it was already warm. I plastered my Dickensian-white body with factor 50 sunblock and resigned myself to the fact that my nose would compete admirably with Rudolf the Reindeer's by the end of the day.

It took us about an hour to find our way out of the town, since all the road signs tried to lead us onto some form of four lane motorway. Unsurprisingly, there are very few signs which indicate "Lovely little D road going nowhere in particular except South-ish". I suppose it would take up a lot of space, but still, it would have been nice.

I was pleasantly surprised by the courtesy of almost all of the French drivers, who always slowed behind me and gave me plenty of room when overtaking. Eventually I put this down to three factors:

1) They slowed down in order to see what the hell it was in front of them

2) The French are enthusiastic about cycling - it's not just a poor man's transport or something in the way (by contrast see the section on Germany later)

3) I suspect their first assumption was that it was some form of handicapped vehicle, and the French have always had a strong respect for invalids and the 'Mutiles de Guerre' (War wounded).

Whatever the reason, for someone with the same perspective on the road as the average small furry mammal, it was very re-assuring to be accorded so much consideration. The one exception, though a minor one, as we trundled through the streets of St Malo, was a large car with GB plates which shaved my elbow as it went past. The driver's window went down and a large head came out followed by a number of chins: "That's the lazy way!", he shouted. I assume he was referring to Gonzalez laid-back seating position. I smiled back hypocritically, but thought this was just a tad ironic coming from Michelin man in his gas-guzzler.

On our first day we stopped early at a municipal camping site at a small town about 65km to the south. I felt guilty about covering such a small distance, but didn't want to repeat the mistake of my South American trip when my knee blew up on the second day and I had to spend a week rebuilding it. As it turned out we would have a remarkably similar experience this time but for very different reasons. The campsite was small but neat and clean. I talked to a retired couple from Guernsey about their earlier cycling holidays. The man was saddened that his granddaughter, who was 20, as he put it "doesn't have the time to smell a rose or watch the ants".

"Maybe she'll learn," I said. "Maybe," he replied.

Before this trip I'd done little more than a few quick test runs on a Windcheetah. So far, though Gonzalez was certainly living up to expectations. He was reasonably quick (given the amount of baggage we were carrying), except going uphill where I think a 'normal' bike would definitely have been quicker.

He was, more importantly, very comfortable; not just in the seating department, but in the back and shoulders, which is where I tend to suffer most on long distance tours. Throughout our trip, if I felt tired it was from simple physical exertion. Even after a long day I had no difficulty getting back into the "saddle" again.

Above all though, he scored heavily in the PR department. Almost everyone who saw us looked twice, and more than half either laughed, hooted, smiled or waved as we went past.

I've never enjoyed food more than when I'm cycling, and after breakfasting on a fabulous little 'Rouge Gorge' Charentais melon, I remembered another of the many reasons for liking France - there are always good eats available somewhere.

During the morning I was joined for about 20km by two young boys on mountain bikes, brothers maybe, with matching helmets and cycling jerseys.

I didn't slow down particularly, but the elder was determined to keep up with me and overtook me on a couple of climbs. I justified this to myself on the basis that he wasn't carrying over 30lb of gear, but have to admit, sometimes it feels like I'm cranking a giant wheelbarrow up the slopes. Still, the climbs are when I get to look around me more, and being so low, that generally means taking in the roadside verges in some detail. At one point the poppies and other wild flowers were livened up by a string of fabulous yellow irises.

Lunch was taken under a shady tree by the edge of a small lake, and I rather enjoyed dipping bits of bread into my, by now semi-liquid, piece of Roquefort.

In the afternoon an old woman cycling the other way flagged me down with her walking stick in order to let her small herd of cows pass by.

"I doubt you'll pass beneath them," she laughed. I hadn't actually intended to try, but it was a nice idea. One strange fact is that, even more than people, the cows in the field were absolutely fascinated by

Gonzalez. Almost every cow I passed stopped, stared and tracked me so long as I was in sight. It was a very strange feeling watching an entire herd swivel in unison through 180 degrees, ruminating gracefully. Being on your own all day can do very funny things to your social skills, but I got very fond of my bovine fans during the trip, and soon got into the habit of greeting them very loudly wherever I went with "Bonjour Mesdames les vaches, Bonjour!".

By the end of the afternoon I was very hot and quite tired, and that was where I screwed up. I spotted what looked like a small campsite beside the river and pulled in to check it out. It turned out to be a sailing club, the campsite was on the other side of the river, I'd have to go into Chateau-Gontier, over the bridge and double back.

A Windcheetah, as much fun as it is, is not the most manoeuvrable of vehicles. It's not easy to pick up and has a very broad turning circle. Consequently it's often easier to back your way out of a tight spot, just as you would in a car. Cars, however do not have joysticks which can drop forward when you're inattentive, nor do they have contra-rotating pedals when you go backwards. Like so many things in life which can completely ruin your day, it was such a small thing - a tiny 'ping' - but I knew straight away that it was a small noise with a big family of trouble behind it.

The pedals had caught the joystick on their way round, pushed it down just a little too far and snapped the plastic universal joint at the bottom. Result - absolutely no way to control the steering. From now on I could go as far and as fast as I wanted, but it was Gonzalez who would decide what direction we were going in.

Part 2 - Michelangelo, Madness and a Menage a Trois
The Loire Valley

I phoned Seat of the Pants back in Altrincham and explained my little 'problem'. Bob Dixon, who runs S.O.P., couldn't have been more helpful, but even he couldn't do much on a Friday before a Bank Holiday weekend, so I waited in Chateau-Gontier for four days while a replacement steering joint was airfreighted out from the UK. I whiled away the time reading and re-constructing the broken joint with a combination of wire, plastic cable ties and epoxy resin. By the end I had a construction that Michelangelo would have been proud of. Unfortunately, steering joints, like parachutes, tend to score higher on functionality than artistic merit. What I needed was something that Isambard Kingdom Brunel would have admired, and I wasn't so sure that either of us would have trusted it to hold at 40 mph downhill. I kept my repair job in reserve and took the bus into Angers for a day.

Angers is one of the first major towns you come to on the Loire tourist trail. It has its fair share of cafes, fountains and a castle with the top sawn off. In Angers I came across the same problem that was to dog me across France - if you want to eat, you have to do it between 12 and 2, if you want to buy anything you have to do it outside of those hours. In the US, shops are open nearly all the time. In the UK, they're open more or less when most people want to shop. In France, they're open when the staff don't have anything better to do (like eating).

The following day my new steering joint arrived. Only problem was the old one refused to go away. No matter how hard I tried, I couldn't get the grub screws out which held in onto the joystick. Strangely enough, no amount of foul language loosened them either. I tried every word I knew and even invented some new ones but nothing doing. I had no choice but to stick with my repair job until I could find a proper workshop. I pushed Isambard to the back of my mind, put my faith in Michaelangelo and set off for the Loire.

At Gennes I found a near-empty campsite, slightly run down, but with a great view over the river. The French couple to my right prepared a "barbecue" by pouring petrol over a pile of twigs and green branches collected from the river bank. I decided I was far enough away to be safe from their attempt at launching a beefburger into the stratosphere, but could only wonder at the mingle of flavours that must have gone into their rather charred supper.

The following day was my first experience of driving Gonzalez in the rain, and the first time of several that I wished Bob had been able to fit my front mudguards before I'd left. At slow speeds I got wet elbows. Any faster and I looked (and felt) like a particularly ill-favoured mermaid sat in the middle of the Trevi fountains. Gonzalez lifted two beautiful arcs of water from the front wheels which blew back gracefully into my face and torso while the slightly higher spume from the rear wheel dropped artistically onto the centre of my head. At Saumur we stopped at a cafe and I consumed their entire stock of croissants as well as any number of thick black coffees while several tons of water obediently followed Mr Newton's laws outside. Eventually we had to move, and set off like a performing arts display of water culture, following the road along the banks of the Loire. I'm sure I could get an Arts Council grant for this sort of thing in the UK.

After a while the rains relented and we were able to enjoy some fabulous cycling along a tiny road atop a high levee right next to the river. At Usse we stopped for thirty seconds to admire the chateau which is supposed to have inspired the story of Sleeping Beauty, made the obilgatory offering to Fuji, the god of all pictures, and carried on. Frankly, I was enjoying myself more on the road.

Later on, of course, it started raining again and I got my first, and last, puncture of the trip. Fixing a puncture on a windcheetah requires a few feats of the imagination, since you can't simply turn it upside down to remove the wheel as there is neither a seat nor handlebars to rest it on. After numerous experiments building a roadside jack with the panniers we were eventually successful (in a wobbly sort of way) and were back on our way again in under a half an hour.

Camping while we were in France added another dimension to the trip. At Henrichemont the campsite appeared filled, for some reason, with people whom I could only describe as either mad or just plain bizarre. Half of them spent the entire evening shouting at each other for no apparent reason, the other half simply drove around and around the campsite in their car, occasionally honking the horn for good measure. One man seemed to be trying to train his dog to choke itself by pulling on the end of its own leash which was looped over the branch of a nearby tree. What's more the dog appeared more than willing to oblige. It was all too surreal for me and I went to bed early with a bottle of cheap wine.

I was woken up in the middle of the night by furious swearing (in French), followed by an hour or more of hammering, sawing and banging. When I got up in the morning I expected to see at least a two storey timber building put up next to my tent, but nothing appeared to have changed. I know that being in a tent at night tends to heighten the imagination as to what is going on outside, but this was all too weird and I was glad to be on my way at first light.

At Montbazon I'd barely got the tent up when I was besieged by the charming and rather curious trio of Monique, Monique and Jaques. Somewhere in their mid fifties they would have done well as the stars (and certainly the title) of a black and white French art house film. They were very friendly, very polite, full of questions about Gonzalez and, as best I could tell, all lived together in a tiny caravan which would have fitted inside the average garden shed. While they wanted to know all about our trip, I was more interested in finding out about their domestic arrangements. Unfortunately they were more successful in their enquiries than I was. Before I went to sleep, I wondered whether one (or both) of the Moniques had changed her name to save confusion......

In the morning we passed the first of many cycling tour groups. I got some very envious looks from some obviously saddle-sore stragglers at the tail end of the party. They eyed Gonzalez' armchair-like upholstery in the way a thirsty drinker looks at a bottle of ice-cold beer.

Over the next few days I tried a new regime of stopping every hour to drink, stretch and occasionally eat something. I'd been getting badly dehydrated and I think letting my blood sugar level drop too low (I lost over two kilos in the first two weeks). This seemed to work much better and I rarely felt particularly tired from then on.

As if by way of compensation, however, the wind picked up and turned head on, my knees started creaking badly and hayfever rendered me half blind for most of the day. I'd been told I might expect knee problems when I first switched to a recumbent, but to be honest I think mine were more related to the leading role my knees have played in a couple of low speed motorcycle crashes in the past. It should have been purgatory. I took some antihistamine, kept to a low gear and a high cadence to keep the pressure off my ageing joints and Gonzalez lived up to his proper name as a 'Windcheetah'. Drag from the headwind was markedly less than on a conventional bike, and half the time we were below the level of surrounding crops and hedgerows which cut the wind down even further. Despite the ill omens, I ended up rather enjoying myself.

As we worked our way across France I started to get into the rhythm of long distance cycling again. Every day seemed to have so many ups and downs (geographical, physical and emotional) it was difficult to keep track of them all. In general, though, we were swinging along pretty nicely through some of the pleasantest roads in Europe.

Part 3 - A sidenote concerning self-sufficiency, support and serendipity
How much baggage can you carry?

I always thought consistency was a much over-rated virtue. Any of us with any sense of honesty or decency knows that we are all a bag of contradictions held together within a loose framework of how other people expect us to behave. Still, most of the time, what we do is only a partial representation of what we think or feel. You might think, for example, that setting off to cross Europe requires someone with a big chunk of self confidence or at least a strong belief in their own good luck to get to their destination.

I, however, approach travel with all the self-confidence of a paranoid rabbit running out of Prozac and with a keen sense that my luck is about to run out just round the next corner.

Why go then? What holds the journey together if you feel like that? Why do people strike matches to check if there's a gas leak? Yes, stupidity is of course one reason, but also because we like sometimes to prove ourselves wrong by tackling worries head on - and the fact of the matter is that we almost always get by (though maybe the gas test is not the best example).

What I find interesting is HOW we get by. It's called lots of things, the nicest name I know for it though is Serendipity. I like the word Serendipity because it's own definition is self-contradictory:-

Chambers calls it "the faculty of making fortunate or beneficial discoveries by accident". This is a bit like saying "the ability to generate good luck".

If you set out on anything trusting purely to luck to get you by, you deserve everything bad that happens to you. If you think you can plan and prepare for every eventuality you're in for an equally nasty surprise, nobody is entirely self-sufficient.

But, if you're prepared to think a bit about what you're doing beforehand, if you can apply a little intellect to problems as they arise, if you're prepared to grab an opportunity as it floats by, and above all if you can trust yourself enough to think that whatever happens (short of dying at least) you'll find a way to get around it - what will surprise you is how rare it is that things don't work out.

End of lecture. The practical aspect of all this was that:

a) I carried enough tools with me to re-build the Queen Mary from a Meccano kit (ask someone over 40 if you don't know what Meccano is)

b) I still didn't have what I needed to fix the only two things that broke

c) I wasted an inordinate amount of time and energy worrying that they might break

d) When they did break, I got by anyway.

It's axiomatic of course that you always start a trip like this with too much stuff, the habits of 'civilised' living are not so easily discarded and it takes a while to remember how little you really need. In general I pride myself on my ability to travel light, but if you're aiming to cover 2,000 miles on a bicycle unsupported, there is a certain amount of baggage which comes almost as a pre-requisite. Tent, sleeping bag and stove take up the space under the seat and 2/3 of one pannier. A fleece and Gore-Tex jacket against less than ideal weather are enough to fill that side. Spare inner tubes and enough tools to take the bike apart and put it back together again (steering excepted) may not be strictly necessary but make me more confident about getting to my final destination. A pump of course comes in handy. If you add to that at least one change of clothes, water and food, you have two reasonably full panniers and a small bag to go on top.

I sent two boxes of stuff home, but was reluctant to part with either my tent or my tools, if only for their symbolic contribution to my feeling of independence (in fact, after France I needed neither). However, Gonzalez has no way of carrying anything on the front and the net result of all of this was that the rear rack was loaded to capacity.

I had to re-jig the load 2 or 3 times a day, and after 200-300 miles the rack started to sag and had to be 'persuaded' back into shape periodically. It wouldn't really be fair to ascribe this to any particular weakness in the rack itself. In fact, thinking about it, every rack I've ever had has broken at some point. They're simply not built for the sort of pounding they get on a really long distance tour.

The net result of all this was that, although I was covering some good ground and I was actually enjoying my tour, still I started to fret. As ever, I worried more about what might happen, than what had happened, and my two biggest concerns were that either my Michelangelo steering fix would let go in a big way on a fast, sweeping right hander (on a left hander the worst I could hit would be a ditch, on a right hander at the wrong moment and I'd be eating radiator), or that the rack would finally break, leaving me no way to carry all my kit.

As it turned out, I was right about one, wrong about the other and worried too much about both.

Part 4 - A Belgian, a Dutchman, a Turk and a Mancunian
From the Loire to the Moselle

At Clamecy I rather foolishly followed the road signs to a campsite. These took me 3km out of town (back in the direction I'd come), up a pig of a hill with an incredibly steep and nasty drop on the other side and deposited me next to the canal, not 200 meters along the towpath from where I'd started.

Having got the tent up, I settled down to console myself with what turned out to be my best ever tuna and rice fry-up and a beautiful bottle of white wine I'd picked up passing through Pouilly that afternoon.

A nice Belgian gentleman took great pleasure in calling me away from my cooking, right over to his enormous caravan, in order to point out to me that it was going to rain any second. How kind. I walked back to my tent as it started to spit. Some people can make it very difficult to like them.

The next day, I thought I should try to give the knee a rest as far as possible, and thanks to a blinding piece of map reading (though I say so myself), I managed to plot a route which wound its way between the hills, following the canal du Nivernais, with only one serious climb. En route I met the only other recumbent encountered on my trip, a Dutch made M5. It's Dutch pilot, Wim, was following one of the pilgrim's routes to Santiago da Compostela, though he became a bit hazy when we got onto the subject of the Pyrenees. Given my own concerns about baggage, it was a relief to note that Wim appeared to have a small cottage strapped to the back of his bicycle, under the cover of about an acre and a half of plastic sheeting. I began to understand his reluctance to talk about mountains.

In Bar sur Aube I once again found myself head-to-head with the French conceptions of when dinner should and shouldn't be served. Having cycled all day, my body wanted fuel and wanted it now and my stomach was not going to be pacified with any considerations of gallic etiquette. In fact, after 30 minutes of pounding the streets in search of something open there was a severe danger of civil war breaking out between knees, stomach and head, all of whom had competing claims for my attention and very different requirements. If I'd found an ironmongers open I'd have settled for boiled candles with string dips.

As it happened, the issue was settled by the unexpected appearance of a Turkish kebab house. The owner appeared inordinately pleased to see me, which I could only put down to the fact that he got very few customers who:

a) wanted to come in and sit down

and

b) were actually capable of standing on their own.

I got this from the fact that there was one table, two chairs and a lot of rails, shelves and counters for people to lean on. In fact, I had an excellent meal which was only marred by the fact that I was unable to understand most of what he was telling me about world cup football. On the other hand, I'd hardly count myself as a football fanatic, and he either didn't notice or didn't care whether I was following. Having communicated very successfully on a gastronomic level we parted considerably happier, if not necessarily wiser. I'm sure there is a lesson here - I'm just damned if I know what it is.

As the days progressed and the mileage mounted, both the steering and my feelings about it got twitchier. From the outside the

Michelangelo bodge looked OK, except for the tell-tale migration of some air bubbles between my glue sculpture and the main body of the plastic joint. But on fast descents it wasn't easy to tell whether it was the steering getting vaguer or my ability to picture imminent and painful death becoming more precise. For days I kept my eyes open for a helpful-looking garage or bicycle shop, but a sixth sense told me somehow that those establishments which were commercially best equipped to help me were probably personally least interested in trying.

At Thonnance-les-Moulins I decided to stop early and take some time to investigate a bit closer. I was sat outside my tent staring at the offending item, trying very hard to develop X-RAY vision and wishing I'd been bitten by a radioactive spider or something when I was younger, when I was brought back to the real world by a booming Lancashire accent about 2 inches from my left ear; "By 'eck, I din expecasee wunathem arteeyah".

My Guardian Angel had arrived and I didn't even know it. Of course Guardian Angels aren't normally depicted as Ian of Stockport, but then I wasn't expecting Bruce Willis in a vest either.

Ian was the only person I met who knew what a Windcheetah was. More importantly, I'd barely finished explaining (a little wearily, to my subsequent shame) what the problem was, than he dropped himself onto the wet grass next to me and immediately set about working out how to fix it. Within a minute it started to rain. In half an hour we had the old steering joint off, the new one in its place and Gonzalez re-assembled and ready to roll. Ian brought a few useful tools with him, but most of all he had a bag full of energy and a simple confidence that we should be able to fix things. Serendipity in action.

My gratitude must have seemed out of all proportion to the simple offer of help he'd given me, but the key difference was that now I KNEW I was going to get to Budapest. The following day I felt like I was flying and by 4pm I was camped on the banks of the Moselle.

Part 5 - Mastication, a mole, the Moselle and more disasters
The Moselle Valley

Not long after I'd begun to enjoy my pristine steering mechanism again, I stopped at a rundown little roadhouse for breakfast. Chez Janine looked about as busy and popular as Bates Motel, but I was hungry and had no plans to try the shower, so I parked Gonzalez outside by a table and went in to see what they could offer to eat.

Janine, if it was she, wasn't exactly delighted by my arrival, but after a few minutes came outside with a small mountain of hot bread, some cheese, butter and homemade jam. She perked up a little when she saw Gonzalez however, and as soon as she'd put the tray down wandered over to inspect him. Just as I'd taken a huge mouthful of bread (and was therefore incapable of saying anything other than FNNNMMMMFFFFPPPHH) she leaned forward, tossed my cycling helmet to one side, grabbed the joystick and began furiously wiggling it from side to side with a strength and forcefulness which belied her advanced years.

Even as I watched, it occurred to me that she had probably never been the tenderest of lovers, and I winced again at the thought. The years of advanced jam-making appeared to have given her the triceps of an East German shot putter. By the time I'd chewed and swallowed my breakfast though, she'd either worked out how the mechanism operated or had lost interest and Gonzalez appeared to have survived his destruction testing unscathed.

Further along the road I passed yet another tiny roadkill. This time it was a poor dead mole, with shockingly pink little feet. He looked so out of his element, so exposed out there on the tarmac, that I got a sudden urge to pick him up and put him back on the grass. Since there were no hand washing facilities available, however, and it was getting close to lunchtime, I compromised and flicked him into the verge with the toe of my boot. I decided there's no such thing as dignity in death whoever you are.

I left the river just before Metz, crossed into Germany and followed the Saar valley north to re-join the Moselle again at Trier.

All along the Saar and the German part of the Moselle run excellent purpose built cycle paths. Unfortunately for us these were designed more for heavy German roadsters than for a thoroughbred racer like the Windcheetah, and Gonzalez and I took a fair pasting from poorly cobbled sections, raised concrete joints and tarmac-splitting tree roots. It was bound to take its toll sooner or later,........ and sooner rather than later it did.

The rack, under a combined attack of too much weight and a great deal of shaking, had been sagging faster and faster. One evening, having unloaded all my bags, I bent down to straighten it again and the over-fatigued metal snapped clean in two. Yuri Geller might have been pleased, I however, was stuffed. No rack meant no bags, no bags meant no trip. I did the only thing I could think of. I left the bike exactly where it stood and went into the village for a bottle of wine and a sulk.

If I followed my intended route, along the Moselle and then down the Rhine, I was still about three days ride from friends in Mainz. I couldn't go far without any kit though, I didn't want to give up and there was zero chance of getting the rack fixed in the village where I was staying. I had another look at the map. It did look possible, that if I cut across the hills which lay between the two rivers (an area known as the Hunsruck) I could probably make Mainz in a day.

I could make arrangements to leave my bags at the Guesthouse where I was staying, stay with Kurt and Carola in Mainz while my rack was fixed and come back and pick up the luggage later.

The other advantage, I thought, was that crossing the Hunsruck without any baggage would be a doddle.

This was probably to be the biggest mistake of the entire trip.

Part 6 - Kwai-Chang Caine and Mr Spock meet Attila the Hun
A study in Teutonic Road Rage

T he following morning I'd hoped to make an early start. Instead, I sat working my way through an enormous breakfast watching thunder and lightning hammer along the river valley like a carpet layer working along the edge of a corridor. Eventually both worked their way north and the clouds decided to give me a break.

The long slow climb up into the Hunsruck passed without problem. Once at the top, though, I moved onto busier A roads. I was so used to people waving to me in France, that at first I was pleased to see similar signs of interest. It wasn't long though before the intention behind the gestures was clarified as something much less friendly, as waving was re-inforced with honking, then shouting. I can't ever remember having been on the receiving end of such concentrated aggression and naked intolerance before, and I hope never to be so again.

This was a form of road rage which I was not used to. Knowing what a law-abiding people I was dealing with I checked and double checked that the road that I was on wasn't prohibited to cyclists, but as time passed it became clear that a key part of the problem was Gonzalez. It appeared to be a combination of the fact that he dared to be different and, as in France, the first assumption was that I must be handicapped. The fact that I then had the temerity to come out onto the open road seemed sufficient to send some drivers into near apoplexy.

Unfortunately this was to be a recurrent experience throughout my time in Germany, and despite that country's many attractions for cyclists, was sufficient to make me very glad indeed when I finally crossed the border into Austria. Gonzalez and I were united in our determination to fight our way through, apart from anything else we had no other choice, but for the first time I was genuinely worried about being involved in an accident.

By the time I got to Mainz bike and body were still intact but mentally I was a gibbering, fuming wreck. It took a bottle and a half of top quality Riesling to calm me down, a week's break to get back my will for cycling, and I shall never, ever forget the mean, aggressive and belligerent behaviour exhibited by German drivers. I would have given a lot to see any one of them sat on the sharp end of their own three-pointed stars.

General bad behaviour warrants a general condemnation. Fortunately, whenever things get to the brink of intolerability, an individual will pop up to redeem your faith in people. Mine came in the shape of Herr Schefius.

Herr Schefius, appropriately enough, is the chief mechanic in a Mercedes Garage. When not at work he eats, drinks and for all I know sleeps in the basement garage of his home, tinkering with old cars and anything mechanical. One of his many hobbies is to pull old bicycles out of skips and re-build them. Herr Schefius spent many happy hours welding, re-inforcing and generally re-engineering my rack until he was finally happy with it and prepared to release it to me and send me on my way to Budapest.

As a boy I can vividly remember watching David Carradine on TV as Kwai Chang Caine, the Zen master/Kung-Fu expert, and even at the time I thought there was something vaguely inhuman about the quiet calm with which he faced aggressive and abusive behaviour - he even looked like Mr Spock, and I'm sure would have made a very good Vulcan. What's more, despite their much-vaunted pacifism, both of these characters always ended up either beating the crap out of the baddies or dropping them unconscious to the floor with a quick pinch to the neck.

I'm afraid that when I'm surrounded by people who are being very aggressive and shouting abuse at me, it's only too likely that I'm eventually going to start feeling aggressive too and will start shouting something appropriate back. Since this is not going to do anything for either my long-term or short term health prospects, I decided to modify my plans a little and went back to my maps to try to find a route which would carry me down to the Danube with as little contact with German Automobile culture as possible. Fortunately (though presumably it's no coincidence) Germany has a wide network of long-distance cycle paths and farm roads to keep incorrigible and reckless cyclists like me separated from the rest of the traffic.

The other, and more grudging concession I made to prevailing car culture, was the decision to find and fit a tall flag to the back of Gonzalez to raise his visibility. Though undoubtedly sensible, it still felt like raising a flag of surrender, and both Gonzalez and I baulked at the idea for some time before dropping pride in favour of prudence.

After a week of over indulgence in food and fine wines Gonzalez was re-fettled and I was braced to continue our journey south through the Rhine valley and the Black Forest to the Danube.

Part 7 - The Good, the Glad and the Highly Eccentric
It takes all sorts...

Southof Mainz the Rhine valley broadened out into relatively flat, rich agricultural country. After an hour's cycling one morning I pulled off the side of the road to check the map. A farmer who'd been working in his field close by pulled up in his tractor and turned the engine off. Subconsciously (and unfairly) I prepared myself for some aggressive questioning or a lecture on trespassing. Instead he turned out to be one of the few people in Germany who were genuinely interested in Gonzalez and wanted to know more about him and our trip. After a while he wandered back to his tractor and I was just about to pull back on the road when he ran up again and tipped a double handful of gorgeous red cherries into my lap - "for under way...". What a nice man.

It seemed this was to be my lucky morning. At the next town I spotted a larger than usual bicycle shop on one side of the high street. The shop itself looked closed, but as I pulled into the courtyard next to it, I came across the owner who was in the process of opening up, chatting with a friend. We struck up a three way conversation and it quickly became clear that he was a real cycling enthusiast. At first he thought I was French (since I'd told him that I started my journey in St Malo), but when I explained that I was actually from England he just smiled and tapped me gently on the shoulder; "There are only good men, and bad men - it really doesn't matter where you come from."

It may not seem the most profound of homespun philosophies, but it came from the heart of the man, and I was touched. I explained what I was looking for and why, and after a while he dug around in his workshop and emerged with one fluorescent orange flag on the end of a six foot glass fibre pole. We both agreed that the pole was just a bit OTT for poor old Gonzalez (whose dignity was already dented by having to carry a flag in the first place), but fortunately it came in three sections, so we settled for two thirds and four feet in height. He absolutely refused any form of payment, beyond taking Gonzalez for a quick spin around his yard. I took his name and promised him a postcard from Budapest.

At that point a lady arrived with a flat front tyre and I decided I should get on. As I was leaving, Karl-Heinz was continuing the process of slowly opening up his shop from the back forwards, while politely chatting with the lady with the puncture. I got the feeling that opening up in the mornings would always take him some time.

From there on the day passed reasonably quickly, following a maze of small cycleways, sometimes well marked, sometimes not but mostly paved and mostly out of the way of the demolition derby. In the afternoon I came across a number of places which supposedly offered rooms, but either there was no-one at home or Tuesday was their rest day, so it wasn't until late evening that I found a place to stay.

Mine host for the evening was just that - a perfect host. For an hour and a half I watched him take care of his customers and guests with consummate skill, moving round the restaurant like a powerful invisible force, sitting down at their table to write out the bill, always exchanging more than a word but less than a conversation. He had loud braces, a warm smile and (I discovered) a Honda GoldWing motorcycle which was the love of his life.

The following day things got a little tougher . It all started well with a beautiful, well surfaced cycle path along the pretty little Nagold valley. After about 25 km though, things deteriorated quickly as the 'cycle path' gradually transformed itself into a rubble-strewn mountain track that compared rather poorly with some of the trails I used to follow through Snowdonia on a fully suspended mountainbike. If Mike Burrows weren't still alive, he would have been turning in his grave at what I was doing to his marvellous bicycle. This was not what Gonzalez was designed for. Apart from being physically exacting and tough on frame and wheels alike, it was very difficult to actually get up the slopes. You can't really get off and push a Windcheetah, and it's hard to get enough grip on the rear wheel as you can't shift your weight back any further when you're stuck in a narrow little bucket seat.

Still, we got to the top somehow, and just as I was whingeing to myself about how tough it was I bumped into a group of twenty or so middle aged ladies doing their own bicycle tour. Despite the fact that most of them had walked up they were happy as Larry, just to be out and about together and having a good time. We enjoyed lunch together but I didn't hang around too long, as I felt that part of their fun probably came from the fact that they were just getting away from the men for a bit, and I don't suppose it was that often that they got the chance.

Having lost a lot of time, energy and (most precious of all) patience in my little mountain biking expedition, I decided to try the roads again. This was only partially successful as I still managed to get lost three times trying to find may way through the next town. By the time I reached Sulz on the river Neckar I was ready to drop and was glad to find a cheap clean guesthouse by the river.

As I cycled through the town the next morning, I was pulled up short by the most amazing Heath Robinson house I'd ever seen. In prime position in the centre of town, on the corner of the main bridge, it was absolutely covered with homemade balconies, wind powered generators and (the piece de resistance) a gazebo made from the cutoff windscreen and roof of a VW Beetle mounted on 4 tall wooden poles. This masterpiece was topped with two or three life size wooden storks. In Germany especially this sort of thing is Simply Not Done, and this man had to have a serious disregard for peer pressure and the comments and suggestions of his neighbours to get away with it.

While I was taking a photo, the owner must have spotted me and Gonzalez and threw open one of the upstairs windows and shouted out for me to wait while he came down. True to my best expectations he was every inch his own man in a highly conformist society. On the short side, with a pronounced limp he was probably in his late fifties with magnificent silver curled up moustachios and what looked very much like pizza stains of a highly dubious vintage down the front of his shirt.

As an 'inventor' he was particularly taken with Gonzalez, though his main idea, being partially disabled was to fit a motor to the back. I told him that I knew of a Windcheetah which had had a jet engine fitted, but that might prove a little too lively around the narrow cobbled streets of Sulz. I have to say I particularly admired the man because I have a strong suspicion his architectural genius would have met with some fairly powerful resistance from the good burghers of the town, but he went on building anyway.

My only regret was that when he asked to take Gonzalez for a spin, I politely said no. While this might have been prudent (Gonzalez's steering had already been subjected to the obligatory forceful wiggle) it was less than generous to one of the few people who had shown some appreciation of his eccentric design. Lesson number one:- it feels better to be generous than to be smart.

Having scuttled away far too quickly, I wasted a good half hour looking for a cycle path which was marked on every map in town, including my own, but which this morning had clearly slipped into another dimension for a bit. I should have listened to my eccentric friend who had told me quite clearly that there was no path. Lesson number two of this encounter: - always trust the truly eccentric more than the social consensus - they are probably more in tune with the vagaries of inter-dimensional shifts.

We carried on along the Neckar valley for a while before biting the bullet and striking out and up into the high Schwarzwald. Despite two long hard climbs we thoroughly enjoyed ourselves. Once out of the valleys the highlands here are very beautiful - flat(-ish) open countryside - and there seemed to be a difference in the light, and even the people, which I couldn't quite pin down.

Every 100 metres or so, scattered across the land there was a farmer in the same dinky green tractor that looked like it had been built in the Trabant factory in the early fifties. The one exception was a large, proud lady in pinafore and headscarf at the helm of a magnificent fire-engine red vintage machine, its polished bonnet ploughing through the field of corn like the prow of a land-locked boat.

A rather philosophical note from my diary sums up some of the feel-good factor of that day:

" I don't know whether we've gone that much quicker or that much farther, not that it matters, but I feel better for having in a small way claimed back the roads for those who, like Gonzalez and me, have the time to take pleasure in what they pass through, rather than simply where they lead.

In the early evening we rolled over a small rise and looked out from the top of a high limestone cliff across the valley of the Danube. It was beautiful and it was the last river of our trip.

We went at the descent like a rat at a drainpipe.

Part 8 - Da, da, da, da, da -dum, dum -dum, dum
The German Danube

Nowhere does the Danube look anything like blue, but like most of us it's certainly at its prettiest when it's still very young. For the first few kilometres we followed a well-laid gravel path along the bottom of imposing white cliffs and meandered to and fro across delicate wooden bridges that, fortunately, were just wide enough to cater for Gonzalez's double-wheeled front end.

As the valley widens out, the 'path' follows the river much more loosely, and picks its way through a network of small country roads and farm tracks. It is signposted fairly well, but you have to concentrate, and without the excellent Austrian guidebooks which I picked up in a German bookshop, I would have been lost much more often.

"Was Friseure konnen, konnen nur Friseure" - my German is still not good enough to decide whether this meant: "What hairdressers can do, only hairdressers can do" or "What a haircut can do, only a haircut can do".

Either way it struck me as particularly weak, but after a half an hour wandering around Hochstadt an der Donau, this ludicrous slogan in a shop window was about the only thing which stuck in my mind.

From Sigmaringen to Ingolstadt, the Danube valley presents

pleasant cycling through open country, but there is not much to stop you sliding gently into a somnambulist stupor (Gonzalez's comfy seat and inability to topple over are particularly well suited to the gentle art of sleep cycling).

There were some high points though. Ulm and Neuburg are both very pleasant towns (for places you would probably not want to live in).

Other memorable moments:

1. Crossing the Danube to look up and see some high tension electricity cables decorated, not with the usual fluorescent plastic footballs, but instead with steel cutouts in the shape of swallows diving and gliding above the river.

2. A sea of real swallows surging and swooping over the road and part of a nearby field - not a good place to be a fly, I thought at the time.

Cycling along the top of the river embankment I was joined for a while by an old boy on a heavy steel 'racer'.

" - Look at me! I cycle this part of the river back and forth every day. Eighty kilometres every day! Summer or winter, rain or shine. And how old do you think I am? Go on, guess - 68! What do you think of that then?"

Aside from the fact that I was clearly not going to get the chance to tell him what I thought of it, I supposed I thought it was admirable, but couldn't he find another route occasionally? It all seemed a bit like those behavioural stress symptoms you see in animals who've been kept in too small cages for too long, pacing backwards and forwards day in, day out.

Still, most Germans that we met paid absolutely no attention to Gonzalez whatsoever, the only people who wanted to know about him were a Dutch couple we met outside Ingolstadt. I think if he could have left Germany under his own steam he would have gone off in a Snit. Where he would have got a Snit from I don't know, but I decided to look for one for both of us before we crossed the border into Austria.

Each day seemed to dedicate itself to a different species of wildlife. One, for example, was most definitely Vole Day. Dozens of the little devils scurried across my path all day long, like little black furry clockwork beetles. The only other wildlife pedestrian we encountered that day was a tiny brown and black stoat who stopped briefly to shoot me a quick "wotchewlookinat?" look, then ducked back into the undergrowth - presumably in search of his friends the voles.

By now, too, I could almost watch the corn growing in the countryside. It got inches higher every day, and Gonzalez and I sailed through long avenues of maize, well above our heads like going up the grand drive to a Brobdingnagian manor house.

In one of the larger towns en route I stopped for an ice cream lunch. We pulled up outside a small cafe, right in the centre of town, with tables and chairs on a platform built out into the street. In best Continental fashion I parked Gonzalez and dutifully pulled up a chair, sat down and waited.....

Since both hunger, thirst and Old Father Time were against me spending the rest of my natural on a pavement in a small town in Germany, I eventually got up and ventured inside the cafe. It was pleasantly cool and dark inside, so much so in fact that the young lady whom I took to be the waitress appeared to have nodded off behind the counter. While I was trying to think what sort of noises a customer makes, in order to wake her gently, she woke of her own accord and, seeing me, jumped back as though I was a stranger she'd just caught in her bedroom (which I suppose, in a way, I was). I asked politely for my ice cream and wandered back outside.

After another few minutes wait I came back in again to pick up my ice cream from where it had been left, very lonely, on the counter. Having finished it, I wandered back in again, and this time had to forage as far as the kitchen before finding my little help mate in order to pay. Unfortunately she was very aggrieved when I failed to add a tip to the bill in payment for her non-service. I wondered whether she was under the impression that the possession of youthful good looks, long blonde hair and a shapely figure warranted a 10% addition to the bill on their own - if so she was not accounting for grumpy old farts like me who were more interested in getting their ice cream down their neck and being on their way.

Once I got into a good pedalling rhythm I spent much of the day enjoying the simple pleasure of just propelling myself through the countryside. The Danube was becoming wide and flabby by now, and although we didn't see that much of it we didn't miss it that much either. One afternoon, around 2 pm it started to rain, not heavily but persistently, though at least it was still warm. I tried, half-heartedly, for a room in Passau, but with no (or as it turned out, good) luck. Fortunately the route through the town itself was reasonably direct, and within an hour or so I was on my way on the other side of the city. Then the river was on my right, a good tarmac path beneath me and the sun came out. For an hour or so I cranked my way downstream to Obernzell, where I found a clean and pleasant pension with a view over the river and had one of the best meals I can recall, watching the sun go down from the restaurant verandah.

After a glass and a half of local white wine I was quite heady with the hedonism of it all and all was once again well with the world - not least (I'm afraid) because this was to be my last day in Germany.

Part 9 - The hills are alive...
The Austrian Danube

P assing into Austria the valley becomes very steep again. It must have taken millions of years for the Danube to wear its way down so far, and in another moment of wild philosophising, it occurred to me that for the river, the trees which lined either side of the valley must seem like mould sprouted on yesterday's bread, while it goes about its business patiently digging deeper and deeper.

After heavy rain overnight, everything was wet under-wheel (and since Gonzalez is a messy roller I was pretty wet too). This was to be national Snail-and-Slug day, and they were suddenly all out on patrol.

Fortunately for them, our gastropod-molluscy friends have developed a cunning evolutionary defence against being crushed by roving cyclists :

- it's not camouflage, it's not poison, it's not cunningly imitating a sharp little tin-tack. No. It's the "I-will-make-a-disgusting-mess-when-I-die" tactic.

I have to say that I have some respect for this particular line of defence, for two reasons:

1. It works on me at least, and I swerved all over the path to avoid the little buggers.

2. Exactly the same principle is probably the only thing that kept me from being embedded in the front of any number of large vehicles

while cycling through Germany.

Of course, it's not foolproof. There are those who might take a childlike (to say "childish" sounds too critical) delight in the crispy crunch of a tiny invertebrate exploding beneath their wheels. Such is life.

The first part of the Austrian Danube is really lovely, with a dedicated cycle path tracing every twist and turn of the river along the edge of the steep valley.

In many places, however, the cycle path is the only route along the valley, so I was more than a tad put out to come whizzing round a corner only to find the whole width of the path blocked with criss-crossed "police-crime scene" -type sticky tape. I had no idea why it should be so, but there was no mistaking the general message which was quite clearly against the concept of any further cycle-type progress along this particular route.

I'd just turned round and was contemplating my options (not good and not many), when a couple of Dutch ladies came whizzing round the same corner. I flagged them down and explained the dilemma. They had read the sign which I'd missed explaining the path was currently being re-surfaced and would be opened again later that afternoon.

"Let's give it a go then," they said, more to each other than to me. Shamed by my own lack of intrepidity I immediately volunteered to join them they helped me man(woman-)handle Gonzalez around the tape barrier.

Oh wonderful Dutch ladies, you made my day! Not only did you save me a good 20 mile detour up and down the valley sides. Not only did you remind me of the need to "give it a go". But, bless you, you sang your hearts out as you pedalled the next 30km or so along the newly-tarmacadamed path and made a bright summer's day out of a grey sow's ear. I am forever in your debt.

Eventually, of course, we came across the road gang who were in the process of re-surfacing the path. They were most definitely less than impressed with us. By rather feebly pretending to be with the two ladies, though, who were laughing and smiling and waving their way through, oblivious or careless of the dirty looks, I got past without too much acrimony.

In Aschach I treated Gonzalez to a 2,000 km birthday present - a new bell, and got myself a pair of gloves. I think we were both rather fond of our new acquisitions, and we pinged our bell repeatedly over the next 30km or so. Sometimes we pinged it discretely, sometimes we pinged it happily and sometimes we pinged it defiantly. It was most definitely a worthwhile addition to the team.

The Wachau is one of Austria's main wine-producing regions, and together with the first 30 km or so of the river's length is one of the Danube's prettiest sections. The path here winds its way through some very attractive villages and is quite suited to the gentle pace we set ourselves.

At one point we were going so slowly that we were overhauled by a group of sexo-, septo- and octo-genarian Americans who stopped to have a chat. Their guide, a pleasant enough, but rather orderly gentleman from Koblenz, was like a puzzled Alsatian trying to round up a bunch of highly eccentric sheep. They were having none of it and (the octogenarian in particular) were clearly more interested in Gonzalez's pedigree than the stone age remains of their itinerary. We chatted quite happily for a quarter of an hour, with the guide nervously circling and nipping at the occasional heel (to no effect whatsoever) before they decided as a group to move on. Poor man. The victim of a culture clash if ever I saw one.

A little later in the same day I came across a group of cyclists heading the other way. They each wore a plastic Viking helmet and had a fluorescent green plastic bulb attached to their handlebars which they squeeked incongruously as they passed. I have absolutely no idea why.

To me, this is one of the greatest pleasures of travelling. You cross the threads of so many other people's lives, catch them, like a photograph found in the attic of the house you move into, at one particular instant during a long and complex story, and try to extrapolate from that who they are, how they came to be there and where they are going to.

Gonzalez and I pinged our bell madly, but we couldn't compete with plastic Viking helmets and fluorescent green squeakers - I considered looking out for some in Vienna.

Before we'd parted, the octogenarian American (and I apologise to him profusely if I've overstated his age, but for the purposes of this story it doesn't matter) told me he'd actually thought about buying a Windcheetah, but 4,000 dollars was a little expensive - "still, maybe sometime in the future, eh?"

And why not. Why not indeed. With a plastic Viking helmet and a fluorescent green squeaker, my man.

I felt rather obliged to go into Vienna, but frankly once there I was rather bored. Museums and Galleries do little for me, and one western European shopping zone is much like another. If you looked up, you saw a lot of baroque buildings. If you looked to your left or your right, you saw a lot of plate glass and late 20th Century retail architecture. Benetton, McDonalds and Co have established a stranglehold on the streets of the world's major cities that I suspect will not be relinquished while cities themselves still stand.

Only the cafes really offered much in the way of new street life, but even for a hardened pedal-pusher they looked suicidally calorific.

A small boy screaming (with that penchant for repetition that only small children can really sustain) "Ich bin hungrig, Ich bin hungrig, Ich bin hungrig....".

A Yorkshire terrier yapping hysterically. Its owner, whose years failed to be concealed behind enormous, almost opaque sunglasses, but whose vanity was openly displayed by the attempt, at first ignored it completely, then swung it viciously, all four feet in the air and still yapping, through 360 degrees on the end of the lead. And afterwards I felt guilty because that was exactly what I'd wanted to do with it.

These, I'm afraid, are my principal abiding memories of Vienna, the city of music and culture. I don't really feel that it's a pity. Like chemical catalysts, I think we are all able to extract different things from different raw materials. Vienna, I'm sure, is packed full of experiences for those with the interests and capacity to draw on them.

I was more interested in heading on into Slovakia.

Part 10 - Eastern Bloc - Buster
Slovakia and Hungary

Cycling along the Danube as I left Vienna, probably the most remarkable thing was the number of naked people wandering around. On a sunny day, it would appear to be almost de rigeur to wander along the banks of the Danube stark naked - or in one chaps' case, to get up and take your equipment out for an airing on the cycle path. Fair put me off my breakfast.

As we got nearer the border Austria began to look more eastern European, more run down and distinctly poorer.

On my final day in Austria I pulled into a little gasthaus on Orth a.d. Donau, just 20 minutes before the skies opened and there was a massive hailstorm. I drank two large tumblers of water, then went to use the loo, where there was a large sign saying "Kein TrinkWasser" (Not drinking water) - just a little too late. Why the sign was over the loo rather than the basin I can't say. Maybe guests have been caught before lapping from the toilet bowl like dogs. Whatever, I felt reasonably confident I'd survive.

As we got nearer to Slovakia there was a gradual change in the atmosphere, distinctly different from the other frontier crossings we had made. At the border it was much as expected, though. Lots of people in oversized peaked caps, sporting little bits of red and gold and with carefully studied non-expressions, who deliberately take too much time to look at the passports handed them until you are SO grateful to have them put a little rubber stamp in your red/black or green book and let you on your way. Who they think they are fooling I have no idea, but the idea of anyone catching a petty cigarette smuggler in this way, let alone a ring of international terrorists I find frankly ludicrous. As a sort of rite of passage I suppose this little piece of theatre has some entertainment value, but I can't say I'm sorry to have seen most of them disappear in western Europe.

The outskirts of Bratislava were much as I'd anticipated - that is, frankly, a mess. If we think the term "concrete wasteland" has become a tired cliche over here, the expression still has a great deal of life left in it if we recycle it for eastern Europe. It will take some time to clear up the physical and cultural damage wreaked by fifty years of the Communist State.

For me at least, as one of those who are only visiting, the depression of urban Slovakia was made up for in a large part by the pleasant countryside and the genuine friendliness of the people I met.

There are, of course exceptions to every rule. At one point I managed to get myself fairly comprehensively lost. Having decided not to follow the rough dirt path along the river in order to give both Gonzalez and myself a break from more mountain biking, I took what I thought was a road to the next village. Since I wasn't sure, though, I thought I'd stop and ask two sweet little old ladies by the side of the road.

I don't know whether there are such things as parallel universes or multiple dimensions where all things are possible. I hope not, since as far as I'm concerned there are more than enough different versions of what's going on in this dimension to keep sanity stretched taught as a drum-skin. Here, allowing for my ignorance of the Slovakian language, are at least two alternative versions of what followed from my simple question (I'm sure there are many more)....

Version A (my first version)
Me: "Hello, sweet little old ladies! Tell me, if you please, is this

112

the way to Zlata Novy?"

S.L.O.L's: "Why certainly young man. Just follow this road round to the right, then left at the next crossroads. Have a nice journey!"

Version B (which came to me some 30 minutes later)
Me: - as version A.

S.L.O.L's: (To each other) "Ha, look at this foreign fool on his backwards bloody wheelbarrow - says he wants some pickled herring and sawdust. Best get rid of him quickly Wanda, before he starts foaming at the mouth or something. (To me) 'YES, YES - THERE IS A SAWMILL AND FISH PICKLING FACTORY THAT WAY. YES, YES. JUST FOLLOW THIS ROAD, LEFT OR RIGHT, DOESN'T REALLY MATTER'. Thank God, Wanda, he's going. How the Hell did they win the Cold War anyway?"

So it was that Gonzalez and I set off down a road, which became a lane, which became a track, which became a rut, which became.....well, a field actually. Determined not to give the old bat the pleasure of seeing us turn back, we pressed on. Every time I saw a line of trees I was praying for just one thing - tarmac. As we bounced across ditches and ploughed over fields I longed for the black stuff like a man in a desert longs for an oasis.

Eventually we found a farm, the farm led to a track and the track led to a road - whoopee! The question of which direction to take was by now more or less irrelevant, at least we were finished playing 4 x 4's. Within a few minutes we were back on the road to the Hungarian border at the twin towns of Komarno and Komarom with our final off-road expedition and a big fat tailwind both firmly behind us.

At the crossing there was again much scepticism on the Slovak side, but this time a lot of hilarity too once we got over to the Hungarian side. We were back at last in the land of the laughing, smiling and waving.

The Guide Book said that the Slovak side of Komarno/Komarom was much more interesting and much less touristy than the Hungarian side. I rapidly decided the Guide Book could go screw itself. I liked

113

Hungary. It might have been seedy and run down in places, like Slovakia, but it felt so much more optimistic.

The countryside between Komarom and Tata was superb; vineyards, orchards and wheat fields in gently rolling hills. This cycling idyll was marred only slightly by the quaint old toothless shepherd who smiled and waved at me, then quite happily left his pack of semi-rabid pooches to chase me some half mile down the road, slavering at my rear wheel.

As it turned out, this incident was the final proof I need to found Foreman's Inverse Law of Cycle Friendliness. This states that the degree of warmth towards bicycles and cyclists exhibited by any human population is in inverse proportion to the degree of viciousness exhibited by the canine population or equally to the number of miles of bicycle paths available.

I have yet to cycle through a country which contradicts this rule.

In Tata I managed to find a room in a private guesthouse. It was damp, smelly and none too clean, but it had a fabulous view, and the landlady (a sort of Hungarian version of Elvira, Queen of the Dark) and her son were warm and very friendly. Once again Gonzalez was subjected to much stick wiggling.

After dinner (Pizza with mandarin oranges, peanuts, artichoke ham and shrimps - strangely enough it tasted great), I wandered up the hill to the "observation point" above the town. I was admiring the Salmon pink full moon on my way up when I gradually became aware of a gentle murmuring noise. When I got to the top, just around the other side of a domed monument, there were twenty or thirty people sat cross legged in a crescent, incanting gently to the same pink moon. I have no idea whether they were Buddhists, Satanists or waiting for the return of their leader from the planet Tharg. Any way it seemed rude to intrude on their ceremony so I retreated quietly and settled for the emergency backup viewpoint some 50 meters down the hill.

The following morning we left Tata under a heavy grey sky spitting with rain. The road climbed high into the hills above the Danube and would have been very pretty had the weather been better.

Passing through one small village an elderly lady spotted us out of the corner of her eye, whirled on her heels like a ballet dancer and laughed like a drain once she got a full view of us. "Halloo, halloo, halloo...." was all she said. I have no idea what she meant.

After a short stretch of busy road alongside the river, we climbed back up into the peace and quiet of the hills again and both the weather and our spirits lifted simultaneously. It really was glorious country. By now I wanted to prolong our cycling through Hungary as much as possible, so we stopped early in Esztergom to give ourselves an extra day for the short hop from there to Budapest.

Some of the other transdanubian cyclists I met were complaining bitterly about the volume of traffic and lack of dedicated cycleways in Hungary. On the other hand I found the road manners to be impeccable after my experience of Germany, and Gonzalez appreciated being out on the open road with all that tarmac again, so we left them to commiserate amongst themselves.

Hungary has some fantastic architecture left over from its days of European Empire, and Esztergom is well endowed with some magnificent 18th and 19th century buildings, albeit a little the worse for wear, which look down rather haughtily from a small hill, across the river to the abysmal concrete legoland in Slovakia on the other side.

I liked Esztergom a lot, even after having to abandon my dinner when the DJ arrived early at my restaurant carrying the most destructive dose of aftershave ever known to mankind. He was presumably only able to walk and speak through it himself because it had already dissolved most of his olfactory organs and half of his synapses. "Essence of toilet block", it smelt like someone had dissolved half a dozen of those blue cubes you find in public pissoirs in half a litre of petrol with a dash of raw sewage for added zest. Since I couldn't have tasted anything had I been able to eat any more, I left money on the table for my meal and tried to make it out of the door without breathing any more than necessary.

Between Esztergom and Budapest was another mixture of busy main roads and idyllic country lanes. We had a little fun negotiating Gonzalez onto the tiny ferry across to Szentendre island, but there were plenty of helping hands to get him on board. Unfortunately, there were slightly fewer hands available at disembarkation time as many had gone back to their seats to discover large splodges of black oil all over their fingers - oops.

On the outskirts of the city itself, the traffic became considerably heavier and the roads considerably worse for wear. By this point though, we were practically old hands at the art of coarse cycling. Through a combination of footpaths, railway tracks, pavements and genuine (if somewhat bumpy) cycle paths, we managed to work our way right through to the centre of Budapest without using any of the main roads.

After more than 2,900 kilometers we had reached our destination.

Long Division
By mountain bike along the US continental divide from Canada to Mexico

Preface

The Great Divide Ride runs from the Canadian border in Montana to the Mexican border in New Mexico and follows the North American continental divide all the way along the roof of the Rocky Mountains. It is something over 2800 miles long, 90% off-road, takes around 75 days and involves climbing a total of around 125,000 feet (that's from sea level to the top of Everest 4 times, give or take a small mountain or two).

The route followed a mixture of dirt roads, forestry trails and the odd piece of single track. It was originally mapped out by a voluntary organisation called 'Adventure Cycling', who also helped organise loosely-structured groups of cyclists to take on the route together.

This was the nearest I ever got to riding in an organised group but for once the geography of the trip (off-road through some of the remotest and wildest parts of the states) meant that some form of companionship was probably wise. Luckily for me the group I went with was full of fiercely independent characters who, while happy to help each other out at any time were equally content to go their own way during the day.

Although not meant to be technically challenging (this was a tour, not a race) riding off-road is considerably harder than long distance cycling on tarmac. We were also entirely self-contained, there was no support vehicle or sag wagon to carry our bags or pick us up if we got tired. Everything had to be carried on the bikes, including food for up to five days and often water too.

Montana, where we began, was stunningly beautiful, but the trail was very remote and covered some of the most difficult terrain of the whole route. The mountains here rose steeply above narrow valleys and we often had to get off and push up rock-strewn forest tracks.

Most of the 'towns' en route consisted of a gas station, a small store and if we were very lucky, a bar, but frequently we would go for two or three days with only sight of a farmhouse or barn in the distance. At night we camped off the trail beside a stream or lake or in primitive forest service campsites with pit toilets and either a spring or an old fashioned pump for water supply.

In Colorado we barely dropped below 8,000 feet for nearly a month. At night the stars were bright enough to see by, even without the moon..

In New Mexico the group was hit by a bout of Giardia, a nasty little water-born parasite which announces its presence with violent diarrhoea, vomiting and nausea. These are not good cycling companions, and although not struck myself, I volunteered to shepherd part of the group via an alternative road route to find a clinic and get some medicine. We were regularly treated to the most spectacular natural firework displays on the planet as the evening thunderstorm did its stuff. Often it was so warm that the rain seemed to evaporate before it even reached the ground, but great shards of lightning blasted anything bold enough to poke its head too high above the desert.

After breakfast on our last day we set out from the Hachita Café and just pumped for the border. As we got closer we were all counting down the miles. At first 22, then 9, then 5, then suddenly someone turned on the turbo boost and we were hammering through the last three miles like our lives depended on it.

Then, ...we were there, at the end of the road and suddenly the summer was over.

We passed through forest fires and drought, mud, rock and snow. We saw bear, moose, elk and even wolves. Was it long? Yes. Was it tough? Undoubtedly. But superlatives are really wasted on a ride like this. Put simply, it was a blast, and any one of us would leap at the chance of doing it all over again.

From a Map to a Plan

Imagination and memory, two sides of the same coin, and they both serve us extraordinarily well. Nobody likes to believe they are taken in by estate-agent speak or advertising copy, but if there wasn't something in all of us which wanted to believe then probably neither of those jobs would exist. Would any of us ever fall in love without a little selective blindness, a little imaginative enhancement? They are our mental shock-abosrbers, without which our poor minds would either get shaken to pieces by the rocks and potholes of the real world, or would simply refuse to get out of bed in the morning. Every now and again, of course, reality bites; the minor crack in that dream house turns out to be major subsidence; that charming free spirit turns into an obsessive inability to commit to anything. As we get older, normally we tend to keep imagination on a tighter rein and pay out some of the slack to memory. In my case the risk that goes with an over-extended imaginative capacity just seems to spice it up a bit. Thus it is that I found myself wandering in and out of a series of what memory would describe as 'lively' relationships and what anybody else would probably call disastrous, yet I never seemed to lose the appetite for them. So it is too, that I can get so much pleasure out of planning a long journey well before I get stuck in the everyday mud of actually undertaking it, and the pleasure never seems to pale no matter how far the last one missed its mark.

If I had to pick a point at which my imaginary journey began, it would have to be with the maps. I love maps. I could spend hours in Stanfords in Covent Garden spinning globes, opening long flat drawers and poring over roads and contour lines. In fact I often do. They can tell you. In this case, though, the maps in question came to me via the Internet.

"Bikecentennial" began life in the United States in the early seventies, organising a mass bicycle ride across America to celebrate the bicentennial of the Declaration of Independence. The event was such a success that they carried on organising mass rides and cycle touring in the US. After a while they changed their name to "Adventure Cycling" to reflect their ongoing mission, "to promote the use of the bicycle as a means to exploration and adventure". They do this through two key activities: charting suggested routes for long distance tours across the US and organising and facilitating groups of cyclists to undertake these tours. The maps I ordered from them, a series of six, covered the "Great Divide Mountain Bike Route", or Great Divide Ride for short. According to the description, the GDR "paralleling the U.S. Continental Divide for 2,470 miles from Canada to the Mexico border, is the longest off-pavement cycling route in the world" and is "designed specifically for dirt-seeking bicycle tourists". I wasn't sure about the idea of being a "dirt-seeking tourist"; it sounded somewhere between a Sun journalist in Ibiza and a pervert on a dodgy holiday in Thailand. As I read through some of the descriptive text on the first map, though, I could feel my imaginative synapses firing off left, right and centre, shooting like rockets in all directions to explode in dramatic images of myself conquering mountains and fighting bears.

I quote:

" There are many wild, remote stretches along the trail not elaborated upon in detail here. Hot and dry weather, high elevations, wild animals, inclement weather (including lightning storms), and other potential hazards are plentiful ".

At this point my imaginative brain (which we'll call 'I-B' for now) was standing at the front of the room cheering wildly while my real world brain ('RWB'), relegated to the back of the room muttering words like "cold", "wet", "unpleasant" and "dangerous" was being cheerfully ignored.

It went on:

" There is plenty of surface water along this portion of the route, but it typically can be safely ingested only after running it through a good water filter. Also pack along bug repellent and sunscreen. Carry bicycle tools, tire pumps, spare tubes and first-aid gear. Be prepared for any eventuality."

While I-B was jumping up and down like a drunken teenager going "dangerous water! Yes! – Any eventuality – I can do that!", RWB was looking on in disbelief: "Hello? Diarrhoea and vomiting mean anything to you? Any eventuality? How about a boil on the backside or losing your front teeth on a rock?"

If there was one thing, though, which tipped me over the edge, which had me fantasising for weeks and sent RealWorldBrain off in a huff, his head in his metaphorical hands, it was one short phrase towards the end:

"Carry bear repellent…and understand how to use it safely".

It would be fair to say at this stage that I had absolutely no idea what bear repellent was, but it was clearly powerful, dangerous stuff and needed skill and courage to use it properly. The reason imagination is so risky is that it will quite cheerfully volunteer you for something which your saner self would have you taking one step backwards in line. In my mind's eye, at least, I was quite clearly the man for the job. I already had my Davey Crockett 'coonskin cap on, my buckskin shirt with the tassels down the arms, moccasins and a seven foot flintlock musket over my shoulder. Now you might ask how you might go about carrying a seven foot rifle on a bicycle, but my imaginative brain would only pooh-pooh such trivia. I was away on a glorious mixture of childhood fantasy and adult adventure.

That was how it started anyway, and at that stage I could indulge all the pleasures of an armchair traveller in the way that a lapsed dieter could sit and gorge themselves on a box of their favourite chocolates. So long as I wasn't really intending to go, I didn't have to worry too much about the possibility of future reality upsetting current fantasy.

Every now and then I would get the maps out again to show them to a friend or just to trigger off another fantasy about epic achievements or incredible scenery. Then something changed. Little by little I began to take my daydreams a little further, I pushed my imagination a little harder to see if I could picture what it would really be like. I wondered what sort of bike I would use, what equipment would I carry, how would I prepare myself for the physical demands made on me. I was beginning to think of it as an option rather than a fantasy. There was a subtle, and at first imperceptible shift from daydreaming to planning. Now this, this was the really dangerous sort of imagination. This was the sort of imagination that thinks it can take on reality on its own terms and still beat it. Instead of just idly fantasising about this I was starting to convince myself that I could (theoretically) actually do it (if I wanted to, that is...I just don't want to...at the moment). I started cycling to work every day (do me no harm anyway, good to get a bit fitter). I started spending more time in camping shops and bought some new cycling clothes and weather gear (I can always use those). I renewed my subscription to Adventure Cycling (they send you an interesting magazine every couple of months, and it's like supporting a good cause in a way, isn't it?). I sent an email to the Tours Department just to, you know, find out how much it cost to do the Great Divide, and how many people did they have for the next trip? When was the deadline for signing up then?

When it did finally happen the whole thing came in an avalanche: sign up for the trip, pay a deposit, hand in resignation at work, buy a new bike, get an air ticket, pack the bags and arrange for a house-sitter. I must have done the lot in less than a week, but by then I'd already done it in my head at least twenty times. By this point I thought I had a pretty good idea what to expect and how I would deal with it. There was one thing that did keep me awake at night though, from that point on, almost until I got back home. Not the risk of having made a bad decision to leave my job, nor the chance of being eaten alive by bears or mosquitoes. I was simply afraid of failure, the idea that I had finally bitten off more than I could chew and either physically or mentally, I found out I just wasn't up to finishing it. From the moment my daydream became a plan, it was the one fear I couldn't shake. As it turned out, it was also the one with the most justification.

Security, Salt and Salvation – Getting Across The Pond

Carrying a bicycle on a plane is both surprisingly easy and potentially very frustrating. It's easy in the sense that there are far fewer technical restrictions or barriers to doing it than you might think. It's frustrating because it's just uncommon enough to throw the average airline functionary into what my mother would call "a bit of a tizz". By her definition, a "tizz" would be a situation where your perception of problem is larger than your intellectual or emotional capacity to deal with it. Technically I suppose this could arise from either a very big problem or a very small capacity. It's difficult to think of a bicycle as a really big problem, so I leave you to draw your own conclusions. Being forewarned and forearmed I arrived at Gatwick good and early with the bike already half disassembled and packed up nice and snug inside a custom bike bag. I'd stipulated when I bought my ticket that I'd be carrying a bike and I was pleasantly surprised to find that this information had even managed to find its way into the computer system when I was checking in. Things, I thought, were going swimmingly, ...until the frown. The frown meant consternation. Consternation at this point was not 'A Good Thing'. Consternation called for consultation (though not with me of course). Consultation called for Security. Security decided this was one buck which needed passing forthwith, absolution was granted all round and the nice lady behind the counter gave me a nice smile and told me they would now like to X-Ray my bicycle.

At this point I should probably point out that I hate flying. It's not because I'm afraid of crashing, it's not because of the recycled air and viruses or the risk of deep vein thrombosis. It's for the same reason as I hate going to the Doctor or talking to Policemen. In all of these circumstances there are a fixed set of Rules to The Game, and number one of these is that at no time can you ask the question "Why?". As a passenger it is considered very bad form to challenge anything you are asked to do by an "airline official" and is all too likely to set you off on the slippery slope from docile sheep to potential security threat in the blink of an eye. I decided I had plenty of time, it was going to be entertaining to find out how they would get it into the X-Ray machine, and I was very unlikely to get an explanation if I asked for it, so let's go X-Ray the bike. Perhaps they think it is a STEALTH BIKE, invisible to radar which I am smuggling out of the country disguised as a..., well, as a bike, actually. Maybe they are concerned it may have cancer of the cranks. Whatever, no-one was prepared to suggest simply opening up the bag and looking at it. They had a very expensive X-Ray machine and they were going to use it.

Unfortunately the machine happened to be located on the other side of the airport so we had to go for a little trolley push marathon to get there. I was escorted there and back by another branch of "Security" in the form of a 3 feet 9 inches tall Puerto Rican lady.

"Why do they want to X-Ray it?" she asked me, with a look that suggested she was trying to decide whether to be Security defending the airport from the likes of me or Security defending me from the likes of mad bicycle bombers. I took a shine to her straight away.

"I don't know," I replied.

We carried on while she tried to work out what an Iranian terror cyclist would look like and whether I fitted the bill or not.

At the X-ray machine I passed the bag over to the attendant who loaded it onto the conveyor.

"Why do they want to X-ray it?", he asked.

"I don't know," I replied.

A few minutes later, "It's a bicycle", he confirmed to anyone who was listening or cared. In this category there were only two potential candidates, me and "Security" and neither of us were too surprised by this information.

We trolleyed back to check-in where we were sent on to load it into the luggage cage. There, another security person asked me "Why did they want to X-Ray it?".

Of all the answers which rose to my lips, I settled for the one which was most likely to get me and the bike on board the plane today.

"I don't know," I replied.

If you ever fly to the States and have to fly through an airline hub to change planes, I can recommend Dallas/Fort Worth as a destination. For a start, everyone around you at check-in in London and most of your fellow passengers on the plane will be talking with such a strong American accent (and, it has to be said, so loudly too) you will feel like you're already half way there. For Texans, it would appear, buying a plane ticket is like getting an invitation to a party. In the waiting area outside the gate life stories, even whole family histories are swapped like Pokemon cards (though without the same trading value of course) with double marks gained for every point of intersection discovered between yourself and a complete stranger: ".....really? You know my daughter went to school there....", ".....oh? My first husband was in the navy too, where were you posted?" and so on.

When we arrived at Dallas Immigration was polite, efficient and swift. I couldn't shake the feeling that I was missing something, but then there was still Customs to be navigated. Queues at the Customs point were a little longer, though they appeared to be moving quite well. I couldn't help noticing that the queue which built up behind me, though, was considerably shorter than the two other lines. Clearly some people had seen the enormous black bag on my trolley and concluded that I might take some time to process.

At the front of the queue a largish American lady was testing out the tensile strength of thread holding the buttons onto her uniform blouse. To say she was puffing out her chest does no justice to the immense strain she appeared to be exerting on the fabric.

"You have a bicycle with you sir?"

Well, she didn't need an X-Ray machine. "I do."

"Have you cleaned the wheels?"

Thorough or what? Now tyre cleaning had not been high on my list of priorities when packing for this trip, but I would have had to be very silly indeed not to know what the correct answer was to this question, and I had a connection to catch.

"I have." (Fingers crossed).

"Thank you, Sir. You may go."

From Dallas I was flying on to Salt Lake City to stop with friends for a few days before driving up through Utah, Idaho and Montana to the meeting point near the Canadian border. Being an internal flight the service provision on board was a little more basic than the previous one. Food was provided in the form of a "Bistro Bag" which you picked up yourself from a cooler in the tunnel when boarding. In my case it would more accurately have been called a "Bacillus Bag" since I ended up spending the whole of the next day in bed with food poisoning.

Salt Lake City might seem like a bizarre place to start a journey across The States, but it is very close to the Rockies, and I'd been offered a warm welcome, free accommodation and a lift to Montana which struck me as a great opportunity to hit the ground running.

Salt Lake is probably best known as the home of the Mormons. Unfortunately my knowledge of comparative religion is about as profound as the average teenager's understanding of monetarist economics. However, I did manage to pick up a few meagre fact-lets about the City and its founders' religion while I was there, so here goes. Sometime in the 18th century Brigham Young and his followers in the Mormon church decided to head west in a bunch of covered wagons to find a place where they could build their own community and practice their own religion without interference or persecution.

What form this persecution took I'm not exactly sure, though I have an idea that Mr Young's business successes and his habit of taking on more than the usual quota of wives in a synchronous rather than sequential approach probably did little to endear him to the sort of shiftless, unmarried young men who are most likely to be at the forefront of any low-grade social protest cum lynch mob. The complaint "they come over here and take all our women" probably just made a change from the usual "they come over here and take all our jobs". Personally I've always been baffled by religious persecution anyway, it all seems far too vague for me. Now persecuting people who ignore you when you hold a door open for them, that I can understand. Whatever the reason, I can only assume it was a very powerful one, because having cycled through the Rockies I know that anyone who managed to drag horses and a covered wagon over them without the benefit of a road must have had some very significant motivation.

Having crossed one of the Rocky Mountain ranges though, they were rewarded with the sight of their promised land and dropped down into the valley below. Unfortunately for them the 'promised land' of the Salt Lake valley consisted of scrub desert and a gigantic lake so full of salt it was practically toxic. In summer the temperatures hover quite happily in the low hundreds Fahrenheit (low forties Centigrade) and drop well below freezing in winter. It did, though, have two advantages: there was nobody else there and the only way out was up and over another mountain range to the West. Probably everyone was just too knackered to carry on.

Other little snippets of Salt Lake history I discovered included the fact that all of the main roads were built wide enough to be able to turn a wagon and eight oxen in one manoeuvre (three point turns had not been invented yet). This was an amazing piece of foresight on the founders' parts since a wagon and eight oxen appeared to me to equate quite closely to the size of the average American 'family car' of the 21st century. The down-side comes if you are foolish enough to try and use your own legs and feet as a way of getting around the city. This will rapidly turn into one long nightmarish game of "Frogger" with the very significant difference that you only get one life and it's yours. Crossing the road is a bit like playing chicken on the main runway at Heathrow. You can barely see the other side when you set out and by the time you reach the halfway point you feel like a snail in the middle of the Champs Èlysées on Bastille day.

Salt Lake also hosts the world's largest genealogical database. People come here from all over the world to try to trace their family tree. The records are housed in a huge building right in the centre of town and the whole things is funded and promoted by the Mormon church. This was the bit that really puzzled me. I barely managed to trace my own ancestry back to my grandparents before I started to get bored. "Good Kentish Stock" they may have been, as my mother insists, but I seriously doubt whether any of them knew the business end of a pencil from the end which you stick in your ear. Why a relatively obscure church on the other side of the planet should want to know more about them than I did was beyond me. So I asked someone. Now before I find myself on the worldwide Mormon blacklist or people start painting white X's on my door, I should point out that I have no idea as to the accuracy or the veracity of the explanation I was given. All I can say is that it was a Mormon who told me this and I found it entertaining so I relate it more or less as heard.

Apparently one of the tenets of the Mormon church is that there is a kind of SAT test to get into Heaven. As well as being on continuous assessment while we are down here, we have the opportunity to accumulate various brownie points to assist our ultimate passage through the Pearly Gates (or not). One very good way of doing this is to convert people to the one true faith, in this case the Mormon Church. No surprises there then. However, the Church in this instance goes a little further than most in extending its concern for the welfare of souls to include all those poor devils who were born (and died) before this particular route to salvation had been made available to mankind. As far as more conventional Christian or Islamic faiths are concerned, of course, this would be a road to nowhere since there are precious few records remaining of any census taken prior to the first century AD. However, if your Church only started in the 19th century there is a potentially enormous mailing database of lost souls available to your marketing department. Once their names and identities are known they can be baptised in absentia and welcomed into the real kingdom at last. Young Mormons can earn themselves large numbers of brownie points by tracing these individuals and then undergoing baptism in their names - "proxy-dunking" as my guide rather irreverently described it. Assuming this works, it did occur to me that had I died and spent a couple of very happy centuries in an Islamic garden heaven, full of sunshine and cool tinkling streams and lovely handmaidens feeding me grapes, I might be less than pleased to find myself suddenly yanked out of there in a puff of smoke and dumped unceremoniously among a bunch of rather straight laced harpists banging out a cover version of 'Crazy Horses' somewhere up in the clouds. Maybe there is a Court of Appeal for cases like this. Would the correct term for such a confused and contradictory state be "proxymormon"? I can never quite get my head round the minutiae of this sort of thing and suspect this is at the heart of my own difficulties with religion. Anyway it seems like a very public spirited sort of thing to do and comes in very handy if you want to find out where your Aunt Betsy really came from.

Meetings with Moose – Acclimatising in The Rockies

I stayed in Salt Lake City for about a week, recovering from the unpleasant after effects of the 'Bacillus Bag' lunch, getting my body clock re-aligned and acclimatising to the altitude and temperature change from back home.

Jeff and Stacey, the friends I stayed with were the most generous and solicitous hosts anyone could have asked for. Jeff is in his mid-thirties, has the sort of whisper-fine platinum blonde hair and beard that you look straight through, and looks out on the world through improbably large eyes, magnified two or three times by the big, round almost pebble-like lenses of his spectacles. Combined with an uncommon degree of kindness and courtesy, this has the unfortunate effect of hiding a considerable intellect and a pin sharp wit from most casual observers. Stacey is athletic, blonde, pretty and very witty and, as I frequently remind myself, very happily married to Jeff. Were it not for the fact that they so thoroughly deserved each other, I could quite easily have been jealous.

The Friday after I arrived Jeff took a day off work to drive me around the city in search of a new tent. I could spend hours in U.S. outdoor shops, I find them fascinating. Whereas their UK counterparts are mostly about woolly pom-pom hats and thermos flasks, the American versions are simply enormous and carry a vast range of gear designed to enable you to survive just about anywhere short of the surface of the moon. In the West especially, even a moderately sized supermarket such as Wal-Mart will carry a quite terrifying array of knives and armaments as well as fishing equipment, traps, canoes, tents, flares (the fiery sort as well as the outmoded jeans) and a vast array of other 'survival' equipment. You begin to understand that 'outdoors' for these people means something different from crossing the threshold from a warm living room to go and wander around a rather well tended country park. Their outdoors has teeth and claws, deserts and blizzards and they have no intention of taking it on without being well tooled up in advance. I was beginning to get the idea this might be a little different from a quick jaunt in the Lake District. For the time being I decided to pass on the semi-automatic assault rifle and the 14 inch skinning knife, though I did linger briefly over the mini crossbow. I pictured myself leaping to the rescue of a fair maiden cornered by a wild, rabid Grizzly. As it reared up to its full twelve feet I thrust myself in front of the fair wench and with a William Tell-like thwang loosed the deadly bolt straight at his heart. At this point at least, I had the wit to realise that this might as well be fitted with a rubber suction cup on the end for all the effect it was likely to have on a real bear. Apart from that, any fair maiden I was likely to encounter out there would more than likely be pretty well tooled up herself and might not thank me for getting in the way. I remembered a story from the Lewis and Clark expedition. Lewis and Clark were sent by Thomas Jefferson to explore and map out the West in the days when nobody really knew what was there. They were the first people of European origin to see the Rockies, and one of the things they came to hate on their trip was Grizzly Bears. The main reason for this was that they seemed to have nothing in their armoury capable of providing effective defence (or offence come to that) against them. In one encounter they came across a medium sized bear while out on a hunting trip, fired everything they had at him, then had to run like hell for the boats when he took umbrage at this, turned around and ran straight at them as though he'd suffered nothing more than a nasty bee sting. When they returned two days later they finally found the bear dead and discovered no less than seventeen bullets in the body, five through the lungs and two through the heart. At this point they decided it would be diplomatic to leave well alone and tried to avoid any contact with bear in future. This particular story was to provide something of a long running theme to my own trip through the Rockies. I put the crossbow down and unashamedly abandoned the fair damsel to look after herself. I know for a fact there are safer ways of impressing women and nobody is going to find a mauled half eaten dead guy very attractive, no matter how brave.

I did look at the (then) new high tech Global Positioning Systems (GPS) which seemed, at first, like they might be a very useful navigational tool to carry out into the wilderness. On reflection, though, I remembered that none of the maps I carried had any recognisable grid references marked on them. The concept of knowing exactly where you are to within a few metres but having absolutely no concept of where anything else is in relation to that appealed to a kind of existentialist philosophical irony in me, but in practical terms was about as useful as the proverbial chocolate teapot. In the end I settled for a new lightweight tent and a waterproof stuff sac on the basis that at least I would know what to do with them.

On the way back from the store we stopped off to pick up Stacey from her work and were making our way home through the rush hour traffic when she suddenly turned to Jeff and shouted excitedly: "Oh Jeff, look! It's the Salt Lake i-car!"

I leaned forward from the back seat, anxious not to miss any of the sights of this fine city. "What's an i-car?", I asked.

"There – look!"

Just ahead of us and to the left was a small, fairly battered and fairly old Japanese car. Even if I were interested, it would not have been easy to tell the exact make or model. The car was completely covered in sculpted papier-mâché eyes - the Eye-Car. They were of various sizes and all looking in different directions, but they were very definitely eyes.

"Jeff, pull alongside so Pat can get a better look".

Jeff duly obliged and, committing several minor traffic offences in the interests of tourism and entertainment, managed to catch up and get alongside this roving monstrosity.

As we pulled closer I could see that the roof of the car was also covered with what looked like sea shells, interspaced with what I was now guessing were life-sized glass eyeballs. Other than the fact that he was driving around in a car covered with big papier-mâché eyes and glass eyeballs, the young man inside the car displayed no outward signs of insanity.

"Hey, that doesn't look like the regular guy"

Aha! This then, is the irregular eye-car driver.

"Maybe he just borrowed it"

"Yeah, maybe he's on a date"

This latter thought is almost too enthralling to contemplate. You finally manage to persuade the girl of your dreams to come out with you, the one you always thought was way above you, who would only ever look down on you if she noticed you at all. "Pizza and a movie? OK, whyn't you pick me up at eight."

Yes! Jubilation, exhilaration, anticipation... But. You need a car. It's Friday night, and so does everyone else. You're desperate. Dad's going to a meeting of the local Pooh Bahs' craft circle. Mom's going out bowling with the boys. Brother's away and sister won't co-operate. There is ONE option though....the Eye-Car. Well, at least you'll find out if she's really interested in you as a person... or maybe not.

Maybe there's a vogue for this sort of thing in Salt Lake City. I seem to remember one of Jeff's previous girlfriends had a penchant for gluing small plastic action figures to the bonnet of her car to make little tableaux-vivants. As performance art goes, it's hardly earth-shattering. But then, when I recall some of the more infamous recipients of Arts Council grants back home, I think it's fair t say it's a lot more fun than three men walking around with a plank tied to their heads, and nobody out here in Utah seems to think they should get government funding for doing it. After a while the Eye-Car turned off and disappeared behind a posse of large four wheel drive pickup trucks. Still, I made a mental note to check the local news just in case there was a story about a deranged adolescent running amok in the Pizza Hut when his date refused to get into the car.

The following Saturday I got my first taste of Rocky Mountain Biking, when Jeff took me up into the Wasatch mountain range, overlooking the city itself. It was the first time I had been on the bike for over a week, and in particular I wanted to see how much the altitude might slow me down (Salt Lake is at about 4000 feet above sea level). In the event, the answer was to be "not enough", but we'll come to that in a bit.

We set out fairly early and after around five or six miles climbing fairly steeply through the edges of the suburbs, picked up the bottom end of the Mueller Park Trail. After California, Utah has to be one of the most popular venues for mountain biking in the US so there are huge numbers of trails to choose from. We choose an intermediate one on the basis that I thought it would be stupid to risk injuring myself just before I'm due to start a 3000 mile bike ride and Jeff just thought it would be stupid to risk injuring himself anytime.

The Mueller Park trail turned out to be a beauty. To begin with, it followed a narrow, twisty path, winding its way through the woods up into the mountain. To be fair, the scenery didn't get the full attention it deserved for the first 3 or 4 miles, though, as the path was very narrow and quite technical, with lots of rock and tree roots to negotiate. To make it more interesting there were some very sheer drops coming right up to the edge of the path and the trail was already quite busy with hikers, dogs and other mountain bikers coming back down and zooming around blind corners at quite a lick. By the time we were around two thirds of the way up, the crowds had thinned considerably and we were treated to some really pleasant riding through the woods. Although still narrow and with the occasional 'tree root surprise' thrown in to keep us on our toes, the trail became relatively smooth hard-packed dirt and switchbacked up and around the mountain through tall stands of evergreen and hardwood forest. At one point I stopped for a pee (I hadn't yet mastered the art of doing this while staying on the bike – more of which later) and was buzzed by a tiny green and black hummingbird. Now I know I don't look much like a flower (not even in the softest light), but the same thing happened more than once on this trip. From what I can remember of TV nature programmes humming birds and bees are drawn to the source of nectar by patterns of ultra-violet light on the plants and petals which we can't normally see. I can only assume that this particular chap was drawn off course by the unexpected presence of around 3 square metres of fluorescent cycling gear in the middle of the forest. Poor bugger probably thought he'd hit the jackpot, if only he could find his way in to where the nectar was…At this point I decided it might be judicious to be moving along now. We carried on climbing for another couple of hours, but when we reached the top we were rewarded with some spectacular views out over the city and the Great Salt Lake itself.

By this time Jeff was suffering from fairly severe cramps in his legs and my backside was pretty tender so we sat down on the grass for a while and contemplated nature. At least we looked as though we were contemplating nature. I strongly suspect Jeff was thinking about a recent job offer he'd had and the prospect of moving himself and Stacey out to San Francisco to start a new life, with all the questions, risks, fears and excitement that such a prospect offers.

I was thinking long and hard (again) about the journey I had in front of me. Foremost in my mind, as ever, was the fear that I wouldn't be up to completing it. I've done a few ultra-long distance cycle tours before, but I knew from the start that this was always going to be the most difficult and the most challenging. I'd trained fairly hard and thought I'd prepared quite well, but I was looking at nearly 3000 miles over 90 days, through some of the wildest mountain country the US has to offer. That seemed like a lot of opportunities for a lot of things to go wrong. As it turned out, of course, a lot of them did, but then if you never step into the unknown, it makes it really hard to ever learn anything new.

After a while we got up, picked up the debris from our little snack-fest (a snack to a cyclist is like Krill to a Blue Whale – it's amazing just how much you can hoover up in one go) and looked around to try to decide which was the route down the other side of the mountain. After a brief discussion about the direction of the sun, compass bearings, ridges and other topographical features we got on our bikes and followed the first mountain biker to go past us. I've always maintained there is no such thing as 'safety in numbers'. There is, however, security in numbers. If you imagine yourself as a young wildebeest (and if Buddha was right you might even find yourself in this situation) my guess is that you are no less likely to get eaten by the lions in a herd of other wildebeest than you would be quietly wandering the plains on your own, but you probably feel like the odds are better. Likewise, if there are five other people going in the same direction as you it doesn't necessarily make it any more likely that it's the right direction – you'll just feel happier if you know you're not the only one lost.

The descent turned out to be a little more technical and a lot more hairy than the climb up the other side, beginning quite steeply and with a lot of loose shale and rocks. At this stage I should probably point out that I'm not really a natural mountain bike rider. I'm not good at technical climbs, and too afraid of crashing to really let rip downhill. On this occasion though, after a three hour climb up a long and twisty trail I decided I was ready to present gravity with my payback chitty and enjoy a fast and twisty descent. Instead of tensing up and trying to fight the bike I decided that I probably wasn't in control half the time anyway and it didn't make that much difference where I tried to steer – I was better off just holding on and letting the bike do its own thing. Unfortunately, just as I was beginning to gather some serious speed, dropping back down into the woods and around 50 or 60 feet ahead of Jeff, I swooped round a tight corner, high on the upside of the track to discover someone had erected a large furry building smack across the trail. Fingers grabbed brake levers, wheels locked, gravel flew, jaw gaped…and the furry building blinked.

The bike and I snaked our way another 30 feet down the trail and clawed to a stop about 40 feet from the largest living creature I've ever met in the wild, a huge bull Moose. My head appeared to be on a level with his shoulders, then came his neck and a broad head with a wide, downturned mouth. The whole thing was topped with a six foot wide hat stand.

Before starting the trip I'd read and been told a lot about the wildlife I might meet, but most of it had focused on potential encounters with bears – where I might expect them, differences between a Grizzly and a Black Bear, what to do if I came across them. The only advice I'd come across about Moose was, by comparison very skimpy indeed.

"Moose? Well, you're very unlikely to see a moose. The trouble with moose is that they're mean and they're very thorough. If they decide they don't like you, they'll stomp you. Then they keep on stomping you until you're raspberry jelly on the trail. Don't mess with moose."

This one didn't look mean. He looked more like a family moose. I only hoped he wasn't wearing his best fur today as the large cloud of dust I had thrown up was drifting gently towards him, and I didn't want him to interpret this as being 'messed with'.

He blinked again, snorted (probably the dust), then turned and with improbable agility leaped up the mountainside and back into the trees.

I was still taking in what I'd just seen, and thinking how glad I was not to have had the raspberry jelly experience at this stage of things when there was a horrible choked-off scream behind me, followed by a long scrabbling noise like a small avalanche and some more choked-off swearing and gurgling noises. "Ah," I thought, with rabbit-in-the-headlights like calm and composure, "that'll be young Jeffrey arriving then…" I may be being very unfair to Jeff of course, since he's not the sort of man to swear a lot, and in fairness I couldn't really make out much of the gurgling noises he was making as he desperately tried to convert large amounts of kinetic energy into heat before it converted itself into broken bones and redistributed flesh. On the basis that some of that flesh was quite likely to be mine, I was very glad indeed when he managed to squeeze by me, closely followed by a large cloud of dust and a small shower of pebbles. Jeff being Jeff, he was so pleased just to have stopped, he'd already forgotten why he'd had to slam on the anchors so quickly in the first place. I apologized anyway and pointed up the slope to where we could just see the back end of my furry friend disappearing up into the mountain, accompanied by the sounds of small trees being broken in two, in the way that you or I might push long grass out of our way.

"Oh yeah," said Jeff, "Moose," confirming my highly unqualified zoological classification at least, "- don't often see those around here. Looks like a young one."

"Jesus, if that was a young one, what do the grown up ones look like?"

We watched, then listened till we could hear him no more, this time keeping one ear open for anyone else coming down the trail, just in case. I apologized once again to Jeff for stopping so suddenly.

"Oh, hey, no problem. You know, you want to be careful with Moose, they can be real mean."

I promised him If I ever came across one again I would treat it with all the lickspittle respect and courtesy I could muster and try not to get its coat too dusty.

A little further down the trail we were treated to another delightful (if somewhat safer) nature-moment when we found ourselves flying through a flock of giant, bright yellow butterflies, rising and scattering in front of my front wheel in one continuous wave.

When we finally got back to the house we treated ourselves to a giant bucket of Einstein Brothers Bagels with a variety of different cream cheeses and a cold beer straight from the fridge. It has to be said that days don't really come any better than this.

Northern Exposure – Heading up into Montana

A few days after our narrowly missed demonstration of Moose-Stomping, Jeff, Stacey and I set off for the long drive up into Montana. The plan was that we would spend a couple of days hiking in Glacier National Park, then they would drop me off at the rendezvous point where I would meet the rest of the group taking on the Great Divide Ride this year, and they would head back home.

From the back of the car I had plenty of time to contemplate some of the differences which separate our two countries, and one which particularly caught my eye was the American approach to signage.

A large sign by the road read:

"WARNING! UP TO $299 FINE FOR TRACKING MUD & DEBRIS ON ROAD"

The spirit of commercialism is so strong in America it turns up sometimes in some unexpected ways and unusual places. With the possible exception of some of the former communist bloc countries just about everyone is used to psychological price limits where something is priced at 19.99 whatevers because it seems a lot less than 20 whatevers. Only in America, it would appear, is this applied even to road traffic fines:-

"Only $299, that seems like a bargain, let's go track some mud!"

In fact, road signs in general are far more verbal than in the UK. Presumably the influence of multilingual Europe has restricted what we try to say to a series of universal symbols. Here there are no such constraints on the road signer's muse, though sometimes they are forced to abbreviate in order to save space. It took me a while to work out what a "PED XING" was, other than a Chinese dissident - PEDestrian crossING. One of my favourites was:

"NO DUMPING - PIT RESTORATION" - we are restoring this 20th century pit to its former glory so please don't put any old 21st century rubbish in it?

One of the more obscure, but more sympathetic was a yellow diamond which said simply 'ROUGH BREAK'.

Even straightforward tourist information signs are very literal, whether this is because of fear of litigation or just a general lack of irony I don't know. On a visit to the Garr Buffalo Ranch, a large wooden billboard exhorts all visitors to:

'Be sure to stop and relax from time to time'

'Ask lots of questions'

'Use insect repellent' and my personal favourite,

'Beware of dangers; rusty barbed wire and nails, badger holes, old farm equipment'.

Provided you can navigate this minefield you should have quite a good time.

Although the drive to Glacier National Park is nearly 900 miles, for the most part it requires slightly less driver input than the trip down to the shops at home. The roads are big, wide, long and straight, and since Jeff isn't too fettered by concern over speed limits we made excellent time. One thing which started to worry me though was the sheer size of Montana, and this is where trying to describe it is about as adequate as trying to photograph it. It's big. It's VERY big. And there are not that many people living there. Such towns as were marked on the map took about 90 seconds to drive through even if you stuck to the 20 limit.

Yet another ghost joined the happy throng sitting on my shoulder whispering doubts into my ear. If it took this long to get anywhere with Jeff nudging three digits in a great big four litre four-wheel drive jeep, how long was it going to take with my spindly shanks laboriously cranking the pedals round on a one-wheel drive bicycle?

Just to add to my gloom the weather started deteriorating rapidly. By six o'clock we were driving through pouring rain. By ten, it was so heavy that we decided to stop and pull into a motel in Kallisper. Jeff and Stacey started debating the merits of different motel chains – should we go straight into the "Ball 8" or should we check out the "E-Z Sleep" first? Apart from the fact that as far as I could see there was no discernible difference between any of them, I was too preoccupied with my own thoughts to care very much. I sat in the back drawing up a mental league table of serious but not life-threatening medical conditions, ranked in terms of a) how easy they would be to fake and b) how good a justification they would be for turning back now and catching the next plane home. It was cold, it was dark and there was so much water around it didn't seem to matter whether it was coming down, going up or just mooching around. It wasn't even as if I was in the middle of nowhere; if anything it felt as though I was right on the very edge of nowhere, and in all likelihood, about to drop off it into who knew what any day now. In a couple of days my friends were going to get back into their nice warm dry car, drive all the way back to their nice warm home and abandon me here with nothing but a bicycle and a very small tent. I hadn't even done anything wrong – well, not in the legal sense of wrong anyway, though there might be a couple of ex-girlfriends who could put up a strong moral case against me.

I went to bed with a sinking feeling. I would have preferred the Motel receptionist, but with my current run of luck didn't fancy chancing my arm, so not for the first time I hunkered up with nothing but self doubt and apprehension to keep me company.

Kallisper didn't do itself much justice by night, but by day it was a little bigger than the one and a half minute wonders we had encountered en route and, with the rain stopped, it looked quite pleasant. One thing, which was still quite hard to get to grips with though, was the way that (with the exception of the very centre of town) all the buildings were so spaced out along the road. From a Londoner's point of view it seemed like a very profligate and untidy way to lay out a town - but then space is hardly at a premium here.

One other thing which was impossible to get to grips with was the American Shower Tap design. Call me simple but there are only two things I require of a shower tap: to regulate the volume of the water and to regulate the temperature. This is generally, and easily, achieved in the UK by having one hot and one cold tap. Americans, it appears, feel this is too complicated and insist on having one tap to do everything. What you must then master is the correct combination of pulling, pushing, twisting or tilting required to achieve the result you wanted. This generally feels more like a technique required to crack a safe than one for taking a shower. Perhaps if I'd had a stethoscope handy I might have been able to work it out. As it was, I was reduced to alternately flashing one part of my body through a scalding dribble or jumping in and out of an icy torrent.

Later that morning we drove into Glacier National Park and pulled up at the Visitor Centre. On the way up I'd noticed how the mountains had gradually changed from being just big, to being big and very, very steep. I don't know whether the others noticed the same change, but then my interest was far from academic. I was still trying to picture myself going up and down these damn things on a bicycle and couldn't take my eyes off them. As the same time odd thoughts were going round my mind like "I wonder if Holland has a Continental Divide?".

In the advance material I'd received from Adventure Cycling we were advised to obtain some 'Bear Spray' before setting out on the ride. Inside the store at the Visitor Centre they carried a small range of these behind a locked glass cabinet. They ranged from pocket size to something like a small fire extinguisher. I asked the little grey-haired old lady behind the till for some help. After opening up the cabinet she pointed to the two smaller canisters.

"These here are what we normally sell to the tourists, though they're pretty durn near useless." From her expression it wasn't easy to decide whether she meant the spray or the tourists were useless. "These here are what the rangers carry."

Despite her unusual sales technique I started to like her. There was something about the way she pronounced "what", as though there were an extra 'H' at the beginning, or the 'h' and the 'w' were inverted, "hwat" that made her sound like the lovable but grumpy grandma from the Waltons. Of course she may have been a bitter old child-molester for all I knew, but I was enjoying our conversation and I had a sneaking suspicion she was too.

"And do they work OK?" I asked, pointing at the big ones.

"Ain't none of 'em bin et this year," she replied, again not quite clarifying whether she meant the sprays or the rangers.

"So what would you recommend?" I asked, wondering how far she'd take this.

All the way, as it turned out.

"I'd recommend you don't get out of the damn car." At this point she closed the glass door on the cabinet, slowly but firmly, turned the key and walked back to the checkout. I did wonder whether she'd been reading up on any of the sales gurus' techniques for handling difficult customers and had maybe just misinterpreted the phrase "Close that Sale" as meaning close it down. Maybe she just thought it was down to me to grab the stuff if I really wanted it. Whatever, it was clear that as far as she was concerned we'd brought the conversation to a conclusion, so I decided to postpone buying anything until I was sure it was really necessary.

The park appeared to have a strange microclimate all of its own, split in two by the mountain range, which runs through it, and during the first week or two of the trip we found this quite often when crossing the divide backwards and forwards. Since it had started raining hard again this side, we decided to head over the top to the other side to see if the weather was any better there. By the time we got to the top of Logan Pass we were at 6,500 ft and in clear blue sky. There is a short hike from here across the snow (of which there was still quite a lot) to a hidden lake so we decided to jump out of the car and make the most of the break in the weather. Once there we were treated to an outstanding view across a small valley with a frozen lake tucked into the bottom of it. The mountains around were very black and incredibly steep sided. The one opposite was hump shaped with a large gash running down the centre from top to bottom. It looked disturbingly like a builder's mate bending over to pick up a hod full of bricks, so we re-christened it Buttcrack Mountain. By the time we made it back to the car, the clouds were rolling in quickly and pretty soon it was hailing hard enough to cover the car park with a complete layer of small icy ball-bearings to a depth of half an inch or so.

I made another mental entry in my now expanding Book of Bad Omens and Portents.

Next morning was D-day when I was due to meet up with the rest of the group who were planning to tackle the Great Divide Ride this year. I always start a long trip by getting my hair cut really short. At first it was just a question of practicality – a low maintenance haircut is simply less hassle when you don't know where the next shower's coming from – but by now it has become almost a rite of passage. Since it was likely to be a 300 mile drive to the nearest barber's Stacey very kindly offered to give me the once-over using Jeff's cordless beard trimmer. It took a few passes, but in the end achieved the desired effect – fluff level number 5. We managed two more short hikes that morning before we had to head off to Whitefish for my rendezvous.

On the way out of the park there were a number of cars pulled over by the side of the road. We stopped to see what everyone was looking at, and in plain view, just the other side of a small river was a very large Black Bear. He was lazily poking around the edge of the river in a very relaxed way, but all the same I was very glad to be on the opposite bank and within easy reach of a car. He didn't seem too bothered that we were there, but then he didn't seem as though he would be too bothered either to knock our heads off if got between him and something interesting, like food.

At the Visitor Centre we stopped for just long enough for me to pick up one of the fire extinguisher sized Bear Sprays – it suddenly seemed like a bargain.

146

Whitefish is a very pretty little town in the far north of Montana, close up against the mountains and around 60 miles from the Canadian border. When we got there we parked the car and went looking for a restaurant where we could grab some food before trying to find the rendezvous house.

We had just sat down to pizza when six cyclists rolled up, parked their bikes outside and started ordering large quantities of food. I knew that the only other European in our group was French, so when one of them tried to order a Four Seasons pizza and a glass of wine in a very outrageous accent the coincidence became too much to doubt. I walked over to their table and introduced myself to my first six Great Dividers.

On the road at last

That evening, fourteen of us gathered at the SunCrest Lodge, Whitefish, Montana for our introduction to the Great Divide Ride. There were two leaders, Evan and Larry. Their main role was to handle group finances and provide guidance, moral and technical support throughout the trip. Richard, Mark, Paul, Dean, Donn, Brian, Mike, Chris, Jack, Pierre, Sue and I made up the rest of the group. Our eldest member, Pierre from Lyons was 69, Evan was the youngest at 24. Overall the average age was probably around 50. One of the ghosts who'd been haunting me quietly keeled over and dropped off my shoulder – one concern I'd had was that I would find myself surrounded by 26 year old Triathletes, the sort who add house bricks to their panniers before a big climb just to make it more challenging. This lot at least looked relatively normal and it was re-assuring to find I was on the younger side of the median line, at any rate. Had I known at the time just how fit some of these old boys were I might not have taken so much comfort from it. For the time being, though, I still had more than enough ghosts to be going on with. After I'd found a bed and dumped my gear on it I wandered back downstairs. There seemed to be people everywhere, fiddling with bicycles, packing and unpacking gear, preparing food, loading film into cameras. In one way it was quite re-assuring. It looked exactly how a team preparing for a grand expedition were supposed to look (though there were no huskies in our case) - lots of highly purposeful hustle and bustle. It could have been a ship leaving port, a troop train off to the front or a camel train about to set off into the desert. On closer inspection, though, the problem was that while everyone seemed to be very busy doing something, no-one seemed to be getting very far. New brake blocks were being put in and then taken out again because they were back-to-front. Fuel was being poured into camping stoves at a rate slightly slower than it was gushing over the side to soak feet and shoes. I tried to help by demonstrating how to cover both your feet and your hands with fuel at the same time. If anybody'd been foolish enough to strike a match at that point we'd have all made Michael Flatley and Riverdance look like a bunch of clodhopping yokels...I'm sorry, look *more* like a bunch of clodhopping yokels. Most of all though, people were strapping huge, vast, mountainous piles of luggage onto bike trailers that sagged, wobbled and tipped over under the strain. I thought of my own, porky, overinflated panniers upstairs, then I thought of hauling that lot over a hundred and twenty-five thousand feet of elevation gain, up some of those steep black mountains, on dirt trails, and I thought we would all be going back to school for some swift and painful lessons in the not-too-distant-future.

Sue, the only woman in our group, had both a heavily laden trailer and a full set of panniers, and was the first in line for re-education. Evan took one look at her rig and tore into it like a terrier at a rabbit warren. At first, I felt sympathetic as her kit was tipped out all over the floor of the main room. As the mountain of clothes, gadgets, tools and more clothes began to mount though, I realised no matter how fit she was, she might as well have had a full-sized sea anchor tied to the back of her bike for all the chance she had of hauling that lot over the first mountain pass we came to. As the pile of stuff to go got bigger, and the pile of stuff to take got smaller, one by one people started drifting off to have another rummage through their own little packs of 'necessities'. This was to become something of a theme for the trip, and barely a week went by when somebody wouldn't send a little parcel of goodies home as we got better at knowing what we really needed and more calculating about how much stuff we were prepared to carry over the next mountain.

Eventually we all gathered in the main room of the house and spread ourselves in a circle around a large pile of group gear. This consisted mostly of cooking equipment, stoves, fuel, tools, water filters and some food. While this was being divided out among us everyone took turns to introduce themselves and talk a little (or in some cases rather a lot) about who they were and how they'd come to be here.

Mark was raising money for Children's and Aids charities, Donn wanted to celebrate his 50th birthday in style, Mike would be 65 soon and wanted to do a great ride before it was too late and Pierre was fulfilling a lifelong dream to see 'the deep America'. In many ways I couldn't have hoped for a nicer or more interesting bunch of travelling companions, and for the first time in a couple of weeks I started to develop a good feeling about this ride.

We were paired up into shopping and cooking teams, each of which would take it in turns to buy food for the group and prepare supper, breakfast and lunch for the following day. At the time, I have to admit, I was more than a bit sceptical about the likelihood of this working out in practice, but so long as we didn't starve I figured we could put up with whatever we got for a couple of months. I am sure the same thoughts were going through most people's minds. We were going to be pretty close to these people for the next three months, assuming all went well, and we had a long way to go with some difficult challenges on the way. We were all wondering what it was going to be like, who would make it and who might not, what would we be like by the end of it?

Then the talk turned once again to bears. For anyone camping or hiking in the US, bears are always a great topic of conversation. There are at least two good reasons for this. One is that if you go camping in say, France, you are very unlikely to get eaten by anything (except maybe very slowly by sandflies), whereas in the US you are also very unlikely to get eaten by anything, but none the less, there are things out there which are quite capable of eating you should they decide they are fed up with berries and salmon.

Regardless of the statistical risk, the mere fact that they exist is enough to spice up your outing and turn it, with a little imagination, into an adventure.

Secondly, while everyone talks (and writes) a lot about bear behaviour and what to do and what not to do, the amount of conflicting advice suggests quite strongly that none (or a statistically significant proportion) of them know what the hell they're talking about. Like the English weather, there are enough different opinions and a small enough chance of anyone (including the experts) actually knowing what is going to happen, to keep the conversations going on endlessly.

Thus if you are out trekking in the woods the advice is:

- Carry a bell, this will warn the bears of your approach and give them time to clear off.
- Don't carry a bell. Bears rely on smell much more than hearing. If they can hear the bell they won't associate it with humans anyway, and they may just come and have a look-see out of curiosity.

If you are attacked by a bear, you should:

- Climb the nearest tree if you can and try to get out of the way
- Don't climb a tree, as bears climb better than we do and like this game lots
- Shout and scream at the bear and make yourself as big as possible
- Keep very quiet and make yourself into as small a ball as you can
- Blast him with your pepper spray
- Don't blast him with your pepper spray unless he is less than 3 feet away, you are absolutely sure he's not feinting, the wind is blowing away from you and you can be sure to give him a full five seconds in the face – otherwise you'll risk blinding yourself and probably just piss him off
- If you have a gun, shoot him

-       Unless it's a pocket howitzer, don't bother, and if you survive you'll probably end up in jail anyway.

In a nutshell, granny from the Waltons had a point. The best way to deal with bears is not to have anything to do with them. Don't look at them, don't speak to them and above all don't invite them into your parents' home for a party while Mom and Dad are away. Anything that can quite literally knock your head off with a backward flip of one paw or open up a car to get at a piece of chocolate without using either the doors or the windows has not had to develop a lot of social inhibitions.

Of course there remains the possibility that they might turn up anyway as an uninvited guest. Supposedly bears can smell a bacon sandwich from as far as 50 miles away. The principal precaution we have to take therefore is against any kind of smell. Now with 14 people cycling and camping in the back woods for three months with only occasional motel or launderette stops, you might think this is going to be a bit of a tall order. We are told, though, that people smells are not so much the problem (though if you're cycling along behind the others and the last one in the pack you might disagree) as non-people smells. Top of the list of these, of course, is food or cooking. Not only did we have to do all cooking at least 100 yards away from the main camp, we should avoid keeping food of any kind, even chocolate or biscuits about our person or in our tents at night (there were a few winces at this – as I mentioned before cyclists do like to snack). All the food we did have had to be bagged up and hung in a tree at night. If we'd been cooking something smelly we were even advised to change our clothes afterwards and bag the smelly ones with the food (nice!). The anti-smell precautions even extended to smelly toiletries such as toothpaste, deodorant, soap or antiseptic cream, any of which could be deemed as 'interesting' smells by our friend Yogi. Everything had to go in the bags at night and dangle in the trees well away from camp.

As it turned out we were able to relax these precautions quite a bit when we got further south, but in the first few weeks we were actually camping in the area where the rangers released problem

Grizzlies (i.e. ones who'd already caused people 'problems', been captured and taken away to a remote spot to be let loose again), so for the first few weeks at least we were relatively diligent in following these precautions. Our competence in them was another matter altogether…

That night I turned in to my shared room with Mike and Dean looking for a good night's kip ready to make a good start the following day. It didn't happen. Within about 15 minutes I was wide awake again listening to the windows rattle in sympathy with Dean's stentorian snoring. By the sound of things they were the only thing which were in sympathy with it. I could swear I heard Mike muttering something in the corner that sounded remarkably like '..sumbitch…' We hadn't put foot to pedal yet and the group dynamics were off to a flying start – I was looking forward to it. I moved my mattress out to the landing, closed the door quietly and made a mental note to pitch my tent at the opposite end of camp from Dean whenever possible.

The following morning it would be fair to say that we breakfasted like Kings, but it would only be fair if you had in mind very greedy kings with a penchant for lycra. There were eggs, bacon, pancakes, syrup, fresh fruit, muesli and toast. The only thing missing was Marmite and I think I was the only one who noticed, to be honest. If there are two things the Americans do really well, they are breakfast and gluttony. When you combine the two of these you're looking at quite a spread. Fortunately, since this was going to be our first cycling day, an activity which would normally come under the 'being greedy bastards' category, could be neatly re-categorised under the 'stoking up with essential fuel' section. This only works, of course, if you are actually going to do more to burn it off than push the remote button on the garage door opener – a fact which I am afraid to say seemed to have escaped rather a large number of my fellow-travellers' compatriots we met along the way.

Living and sharing with people for three months continuously you are bound to pick out some of those foibles or eccentricities which make every one of us unique (and we only hope, not too offensive), but in the case of Paul, the contract accountant from New York I was starting early. While everyone else was getting stuck into all sorts of high-fat, high-sugar, high-cholesterol goodies, Paul's right hand was firmly wedged inside a box of dry cereal which he was gradually munching his way through. After a time this combination became so common a sight that it was almost as though the cereal box were a prosthesis attached to his right arm. It seemed like the only times I ever saw him without it were when he was cycling or bathing.

By the time we'd finished clearing away the debris, the two shuttle buses had arrived to take us up to our start point at the Canadian Border. I wouldn't say it was easy to get 14 bikes and 12 trailers into the back of a minibus, but fortunately there were at least 10 experts on hand to assist so, on the whole, we were quite lucky to get away inside an hour.

Inside the bus, it didn't take long for the talk to turn back to our favourite subject again – Bears. Around half the group had actually bought the fire-extinguisher sized pepper sprays, the rest had decided not to bother. Chris, a retired Fire Chief from Long Beach, California was among those who had decided to do without.

" A bear may be able to run 35 miles an hour, but I can move pretty quick too when I'm scared, and I doubt he'll get up to that sort of speed when he's slippin' all over the place in my sh*t…"

An interesting theory and certainly a worthwhile addition to the Great Bear Behaviour Debate.

The Port of Roosville has precious little claim to being a port (being around 600 miles from the nearest ocean) and probably less claim to being a '-ville' since it consists of an immigration shed and a duty free booze shop. Still, it sits on the US/Canadian border and it's the nearest crossing to the Continental Divide so it seemed like a logical place to start our ride.

Everybody apart from Pierre and I cycled across the border first so as to start their journey in Canada itself. I have a pathological distrust of border crossings and prefer to avoid them unless I have to, and I suspect Pierre didn't feel like cranking up his rusty English too early in the trip. My cynicism was fairly justified when, having watched 12 cyclists go past them 30 yards, do a U turn and come back, the US immigration officials stopped every one of them to find out who they were and where they'd been. These are the sort of people who would follow the instructions on a packet of corn flakes before making their own breakfast.

After a 20 minute pantomime with everyone swapping cameras to try and get a team photo at the start we finally got on our bikes and were under way just before lunchtime.

The first few miles were relatively flat and followed a long straight paved road directly south, past the local airport and parallel to a range of snowy peaks just off to our left. It gave us plenty of time to contemplate what we had just started.

It was a long road ahead of us. For many of us, and for me in particular, it would turn out to be one of the most mentally and physically challenging journeys of our lives.

Whatever the future held, we had one thing in common – we had at least made a start.

Mountain Men

Despite the fact that the road was paved and relatively flat, it didn't take long before we were strung out along it to the point where we were mostly out of sight of each other. To begin with I stayed with Mike, my cooking and shopping partner and our resident Okie. Mike came from somewhere called Yukon, Oklahoma, which I was about to say I recognised, until I realised I was thinking of the Yukon, Alaska which is about as close to Oklahoma as London is to Addis Ababa.

Mike didn't cycle particularly quickly, but that didn't bother me too much as a) I wasn't in a hurry and b) since we'd volunteered to be first on cook duty everyone had to stop and wait for us when they got to the first supermarket anyway so we could buy and then distribute the food for that night. When we got there it wasn't too difficult to find the supermarket in question. Apart from being the biggest building for 20 miles it was probably the only one in the state with more bicycles than cars lined up outside. I say 'cars', though in practice the vehicle of choice in these parts was almost always a pickup truck – a fact for which I had cause to be very grateful much later on.

I consider myself a pretty good cook and even quite enjoy food shopping most of the time. My first group shop, though, turned out to be much more of a headache than I'd allowed for. In the first place working out measures for 14 people is one thing, working out measures for 14 very hungry cyclists is another thing altogether. I hoped I'd be safe by adding 50% onto everything I got. Then, whatever culinary delight you have planned, you have to be able to cook it relatively quickly over a maximum of 3 little camping stoves (so you wasted your time learning how to perfect that cheese soufflé I'm afraid). Then you have to take into account that whatever you buy, you are going to have to carry it over at least one mountain if not several before you get to eat it and, if it comes in a container that won't burn, the chances are you'll have to carry that over a few mountains before you can dump it too. Tinned food might be popular at mealtimes but was not going to make you popular when you were handing it out for porterage. Since we were going to be hammering our bodies more or less continually for the next three months we needed to make sure we were getting the right balance of enough carbohydrates to fuel a small power station during the day and buckets of protein to rebuild our worn and tired muscles at night. To make things even more interesting we had four vegetarians in the group, so we were faced with the choice of either making two separate meals every night or sticking to a vegetarian menu most of the time. As far as I was concerned, anybody who discovered a wheat or dairy allergy was going to get a Mars Bar and a carton of orange juice every night, and good luck to them.

From the expression on Mike's face when we went in, I rather gathered that this was the first time he'd seen the inside of a supermarket in a number of years, so I grabbed the trolley and headed off for the dried produce shelves while he looked for the bread. Beans and rice, dried pasta, bagels, peanut butter, bread, cheese, jam, cereals and Pop Tarts; these were to be our staples for the next quarter of a year. In actual fact, with all the exercise we had, it turned out to be a relatively healthy diet most of the time – with the exception of the Pop Tarts. They were undoubtedly a good source of energy, but this was mostly, as far as I could see, because they consisted of sugar-coated sweet pastry with sugar-infused fruit substitute and flavourings with added sugar and sweeteners. The 'chocolate' ones were even worse.

It was only a few miles from the supermarket to our first campsite and since Mike and I had done the shopping, we were able to distribute the food among the rest of the group and set off at the head of the pack while everyone else was still trying to fit what they had into their luggage.

The countryside reminded me of Norway in many ways; one or two small farms lying in the flat beds of the valleys with tall mountains climbing like a black curtain in the background. We even startled a few white-tailed deer grazing in one of the meadows. They watched us for a while, then spun off into the woods, flashing their tails behind them.

At Grave Creek I pitched my tent at the edge of a noisy, bubbling river and started to pump water from it to fill our two large cooking pots. One by one the others arrived and started filling up the small space until it looked more like a refugee city than a wild and remote campsite. Actually it wasn't quite as wild or remote as we might have liked, since we seemed to be sharing it with one of the extras from the film 'Deliverance' who was parked in his pickup next to the river.

A few of the guys went over to make polite conversation but found that this didn't exactly cover too much ground as far as our fellow guest was concerned. Blessed with only one remaining incisor, he appeared to favour a liquid diet and was working his way through a six pack perched on the seat next to him. According to the others he explained that he was just thinking about 'whether or not to go and see the doctor tomorrow'. We all hoped it was not because he'd run out of medication. It did occur to me that Bear Spray might actually be multi-functional under the right circumstances and I carefully tucked mine into the pocket next to my tent door.

After supper the rest of the group got started on their first attempt at bear-bagging (putting all the food and smelly stuff out of reach up in a tree) while Mike and I cleared up the dishes and put everything else away. One of the first lessons we all learned from this (though it was Dean who paid the price of our education), was that if you put absolutely everything into one bag it will a) be extraordinarily difficult to haul it high enough up into the trees in the first place and b) when it comes down, it will do so with a considerable amount of force.

Having got one end of the rope over a high branch our intrepid engineers attached the other end to the bag full of food, toothpaste and toiletries, then organised a team of pullers, using a thick branch as a crossbar to pull on the other end and haul the bag up off the ground. The weak spot in this design turned out to be the branch which snapped in two before the bag was half way up, deposited half the pullers flat on their arses and made a valiant attempt at decapitating Dean as the bag, rope and branch plummeted to the ground. Fortunately it only caught him a glanicng blow, but he ended up with a nasty shiner all the same.

I decided to leave the engineers to it and went back to my tent where I painted imaginary scenes of carnage to match the muffled, shouts, screams, swearing and assorted sound effects coming from the other end of the woods for the next forty minutes.

Having slept far better in my tent than in the house in Whitefish, I got up around 5:30 the next morning and started to pack my stuff away so as to get a swift start after breakfast. Mike and I were still on cooks' duty, so we had to lay out the breakfast and lunch things and put some water on to boil. Fortunately, someone else had already got the infamous bear bags down by this stage, so all we had to do was unpack them.

Mark was one of the first to be ready to go, so we set off together while the rest were still eating breakfast. A Lutheran Pastor, he now heads up one of the largest voluntary social services organisations in the US, based in Washington. Fit and with seemingly boundless determination and patience, he was to make an excellent cycling partner, and eventually a good friend and I spent much of my cycling time in his company.

We turned away from the valleys and the tarmacadamed roads and for the first time headed up into the mountains following dirt tracks and trails. It didn't take us long to find our first test. After a long steady climb up to the Whitefish Divide, just past the crest, we discovered the bridge had been washed out by recent storms, so we had to unload the gear, take off our shoes and socks, roll up our trousers and brave the near freezing water to carry our stuff across the river and up the bank the other side. In all, it took four trips across and back, but for some reason it was the second crossing which turned out to be the most painful. I think by the third we had lost most of the sensation in our feet.

A few miles after the crossing the rain began and before long it became clear that it had set in for the day. I switched to Gore-Tex gloves which did indeed prove to be waterproof, though not in the way I had hoped. Instead of keeping the water out, they rapidly filled up with cold rain which had run down my sleeve and into the cuffs, keeping my fingers nicely immersed in a constant bath at a temperature just above freezing.

The trees on either side of the road showed lots of marks which looked very much like they had been clawed by bears, and we even found some scat on the trail but no sign of live bears at this stage.

Then, as we were coming down a badly rutted section, Mark got his front wheel caught in one rut and the wheel from his trailer in another and jacknifed in a big way just in front of me. He wasn't hurt, but the back end of his bike was bent badly enough to stop him being able to change gear. I thought for a moment I was going to hear some new Lutheran swear words, but if he was thinking them, at least he never got as far as voicing them. We straightened his bike out as best we could with nothing but a pair of pliers between us and he struggled on for the next 20 miles to Polebridge with only a couple of gears.

Polebridge is a true western town, with an ancient mercantile store and a genuine saloon. The store also happened to sell some of the best bread and pastries I have ever tasted. Other than the store, the saloon and the hostel, though, it's a pretty small town and very isolated.

A little girl at the store adopted me while I was trying to write postcards outside.

"Do you have any friends?"

"Yes I do, though most of them are a long way away."

"Do you have anyone to play with?"

"Well, yes. In a way I'm playing with all those men over there."

"You're lucky. I don't have anyone to play with."

I suppose scenery isn't much consolation when you're four.

The hostel we stayed at had no electricity and only outside pit toilets, so we were just as well off pitching our tents outside on the lawn. John, the owner, was a kind of miniature Grizzly Adams, kind and very hospitable but not exactly garrulous. You don't move to a town like Polebridge for the social life. Still, it appeared that even this was a bit too hectic for him. A few days later and further down the trail we bumped into a friend of his, on his way up to the hostel to take over for a few weeks "while John gets away from it all, on a Mountain Man retreat". Where the hell you could retreat to from a town like Polebridge took some imagining. Besides, if they all came from places like this it wouldn't take too many Mountain Men at any one retreat to create a population greater than that of whatever 'town' they had left behind. Marlene Dietrich may have famously said "I vant to be alone!", but these guys were clearly in a different league altogether.

John's house was decorated very much in his own unique style. On the walls of the outhouse were, among other things, his degree certificate from a mid-western university, mounted perilously and presumably ironically close to the toilet paper, and a preserved sample of Puma shit stuck on a board with notes for easy identification. At least the notes said it was Puma shit. Personally, and I may say fortunately as far as I'm concerned, I am in no position to be able to verify or deny this. At least I couldn't see any traces of lycra in it.

That evening was the turn of the fabulous duo, Donn and Richard, to delight us with their cooking. Donn was our resident Hippy/ Liberal/Gourmet/Photographer from New Orleans. He was also probably the member of the group who was most concerned about his ability to keep up on the trail. It wasn't that he wasn't fit enough – nobody was even going to make the first two days of a ride like this if they weren't already a very strong cyclist. No, Donn's issues were twofold. One was to do with being off-road. Donn was a road rider through and through. He found the physical and mental concentration required for mountain biking on dirt roads all day long took away from his pleasure at just taking in the scenery. The other issue was one of pace. Donn liked to go slow. In theory, that shouldn't have been a major problem. Everyone rides at their own pace, and he still covered the same ground as the rest of us. I suppose the key thing is that it's not much fun if you permanently feel as though you're being pushed to go faster than you'd like. It's fair to say that no-one openly pressurised him at all, in fact the very opposite. Everyone was very supportive and encouraging. Still just turning up at camp to find everyone else has already set up their tents, had a wash, cleaned their bikes and either eaten or are waiting for you to cook can't have been much fun. The advantage of Polebridge at least was that most of us had already gorged ourselves on bread and pastries from the general store which prevented us from doing a very passable impersonation of Pavlov's dogs as our scheduled suppertime came and went. A second advantage was that John had offered us the use of his kitchen. Given that the principal part of Donn's chosen recipe for the evening turned out to be roasted vegetables, this would have been a particularly spectacular achievement using only three camping stoves. Instead of which, while someone set up his tent for him, Donn and Richard proceeded to fill both ovens, use every hob, cover every inch of work surface with pots, pans and chopped vegetables and generally do a very good impersonation of how I imagine the kitchen at The Savoy would look on Christmas Eve. Still, however long a day he may have had, all Don's cooking skills and his pride as one of the group's self-nominated gourmets came to the fore and he pulled off something of a triumph as we feasted that night on roasted red peppers, mozzarella and cauliflower rice, onions and courgettes and fresh fruit salad. As time wore on feasts on this scale were to become much less common as we all became less ambitious, more concerned with how much we had to carry and realised that actually, people would eat just about anything provided it was hot and there was lots of it. Certainly it was the first and last time anyone carried two whole cauliflowers on their bikes.

It rained again during the night, and I lay in my tent with a very full belly, but seriously beginning to wonder how much fun this was going to be if we had to plough our way through mud the whole of the length of the Rockies. Apart from anything else my joints were already beginning to ache from the cold and damp and I knew from bitter previous experience that after another day's rain every single thing I possessed would be wet through and would stay that way until we hit a town with a guesthouse and a Laundromat, or the sun came out.

By the time Mark and I had packed our gear and were ready to go the following day it was a cool, grey morning but clear and dry. From Polebridge there was a long, steady climb up to Red Meadow Lake. I remember it as being long and steady because by the time I was only halfway up it, I suddenly remembered I had left my cooking stove back at the campsite. Everyone was supposed to carry a share of the group equipment, and we had each been assigned specific items as our own responsibility. One of mine was one of the three stoves that we used and I realised too late that because Donn had used the kitchen to cook in the night before we hadn't used any of the stoves. As a result, I'd forgotten to pick mine up after the meal and it was still sitting on the camp table where I'd unloaded it when I arrived the previous afternoon. I agonised for a while over whether or not to go all the way back down into camp to pick it up, but in the end decided I'd either risk having to buy a new one, or I'd buy several beers for whatever kind soul picked the damn thing up and carried it for me that day. The climb steepened considerably for the last three miles and turned into one of those cruel optical illusions where each twist and turn of the road looks as though it will end at the crest. When we finally reached the top we were rewarded for our efforts by a beautiful view across a deep ice-blue lake trapped by steeply-banked mountains on all sides. By now the sun had finally come out, but after working up a temperature on the way up, the air was distinctly chilly at 6,000 feet and after we'd eaten a few biscuits, piled on some more clothing and taken a few photographs we were keen to be on our way again. Not for the first time I wished I were a little more like some of our more laid-back colleagues on the ride and could find it in me to take more time and linger more over views like this one on our route. For whatever reason it's in my nature that if I'm set a target, I have to try and achieve it as quickly as possible. Thus, if I had a destination for the day I found it difficult to relax until I'd reached it. Places like Red Meadow Lake were clearly so special that I would force myself to take the time to stop and stare, and I think I got better at this as time went by, but no matter how hard I tried I could never quite shake the urge to be moving on, to be knocking off another mile on the way to my goal.

The descent was rapid and very rocky which on this occasion seemed to work in my favour having panniers rather than a trailer – if only because I was confident I could probably stop quicker than the other guys if I had to. Not for the first time either, I was amazed at how well, and how hard the front suspension worked on my bike, keeping the front wheel pretty well in touch with the ground and hence, on more than once occasion, keeping my soul in touch with my body as a consequence. Eventually we moved onto a smooth-packed dirt road, and finally tarmac and around 2pm rolled (almost triumphantly) into Whitefish, the little town where we had all gathered only three days ago.

It seemed like a long time to cover a distance which had only taken something like a couple of hours in a minibus, but then we had taken a fairly circuitous route (even the Adventure Cycling maps called this section "madly meandering"), we'd gone some way out of our way to visit the charming 'town' of Polebridge and once off the tarmac we had seen probably two or three cars (or more accurately pickup trucks) at most.

Whitefish was our first designated 'layover' day. Although this was probably a little early (normally we would only get a rest stop once every seven to ten days), Evan, our Adventure-Cycling group leader had decided, probably wisely, to break us in gently and everyone was looking forward to the opportunity of stocking up on fresh pastries, good coffee and cold beer. While we were waiting for the others to arrive I wandered into the local bookshop to see if I could look up a startling blue bird I'd seen on the trail. After a while I

164

managed to find it and discovered that it delighted in the name of a "Lazuli Bunting" which struck me as a glorious name for a beautiful bird. As pleased as I was, though, I couldn't really compete with Jack and Chris. When they got back into town, they told us the story of how they'd encountered a large Black Bear in the middle of the road. Having come to a very rapid halt they'd watched while he sniffed the air, stared at them for a while, then wandered slowly off in the opposite direction. Evidently wheels, lycra and fluourescent colours don't make it into the Bear's Big Book of Easily Recognised Meals.

When Dean finally arrived at the Hostel he smilingly passed over my errant cooking stove without a word of complaint. In return I passed back as much beer as the others had left in the fridge from the twelve-pack I'd originally bought and apologised for having ever complained about his snoring.

One thing which everyone had in common after only three days of real mountain biking, was a sudden and overpowering urge to shed large amounts of luggage. Those items which only 72 hours earlier had felt secure of their place in the 'necessities' category found themselves dumped unceremoniously in the 'unwanted luxuries' bag being packed and wrapped and ready to ship off home.

I lost at least half of my toolkit (which must have weighed four or five pounds) as well as several bulkier items of clothing, deciding I would rather put several layers of dirty thin clothing on top of each other than carry clean bulky warm stuff, just in case. In the morning the hostel was full of piles of discarded clothing, tools, cameras, medicaments, toiletries (deodorant was high on the chopping list – apart from attracting the bears, you were on a losing battle if you thought a spray or a roll-on was going to keep you fresh over five days of cycling in the wilderness, and if we were going to smell we might as well all smell together), and portable hi-fi units. In the afternoon, these were transformed into a seemingly endless stream of anonymous brown paper packages making their way to the Post Office and from there winging off to the four corners of the world. Nor was this to be the last such purge. The Post Office was high on everybody's list for a visit whenever we lurched within reach of civilisation, and the list of necessities got smaller every month. The only exception to this was Paul, who, if anything actually accumulated more stuff as he went along and added it to his mobile motel-on-two wheels. In fact, he positively took pride in the amount of gear he was hauling. By my (highly unscientific) calculations, by the time he'd finished this amounted to something in excess of lifting eleven and a quarter million pounds of equipment through one vertical foot (excluding himself and his bicycle) or for the metrically-minded, 1.6 million kilos through one vertical metre. When you look at it this way, you can begin to see why that extra 35mm film, or the spare torch start to look like excess baggage.

Having got rid of a quarter of my gear, the next thing I did was to go out and buy some more, in this case 3 extra plastic water bags. In the long term, I realised I would need these to carry the additional water required when we were travelling through drier and hotter areas further south. In the short term, they suited my immediate need which was to increase dramatically my wine carrying capacity while in the northern woods. It was one thing to jettison a whole load of clothing and tools, but another thing altogether to be stuck out in the woods for days on end with no hope of a decent drink at the end of the day. Between us, Sue, Evan and I had rapidly formed the nucleus of a Great Divide Wine Appreciation Society and spent part of the day decanting a couple of bottles of California's finest into my three new Platypus bags with a view to bringing a little civilisation to the wilderness. At this stage I didn't realise quite how much I was going to need it.

Funny Bones

Whoever it was who described the English and Americans as "two nations separated by one language" had a fair point. It's not only simple differences in meaning or usage which separate us, but more complex issues like interpretation, literalness and the total lack of the "Carry On..." film format in the US. Not that I'm a huge fan of Sid James or Kenneth Williams, you understand, but there's a sort of shared cultural heritage here that's difficult to ignore for even the snobbiest of cultural snobs. This particular social observation came to me rather forcibly when I nearly choked while we were passing a couple of road signs which clearly meant nothing to my transatlantic cycling colleagues (they didn't mean much to Pierre either, but this is definitely NOT the place to get into a discussion about the French sense of humour).

The first proudly proclaimed itself to be the entrance to the "Creston Sod Farm", which immediately prompted two significant questions in my mind.

1.   I never knew they actually grew them in the ground and
2.   if that was the case then why the hell didn't somebody stop them.

I feel that I have come across far too many sods in my career already: ignorant, rotten, rude and stupid to name but the four most common varieties. To have finally tracked down the source seemed like as good a reason for a tactical missile strike as any that I've ever come across.

Shortly afterwards, and in total keeping with my "Carry On.." frame of mind, we ran straight past none other than the "Gobbler's Nob" Ranch.

"Blow me," I thought, "That's a funny name.

Just to prove that all good things come in threes, later the same afternoon entertainment was provided from an unexpected quarter when we stopped for a quick snack break just outside the entrance to another ranch. Two dogs hurtled around the corner barking furiously. Most cyclists, though, have developed a way of dealing with encounters with dogs, and more often than not the easiest route is simply to face them down. Consequently, when none of us moved they skidded to a halt and considered us more curiously. The larger one, a black lab, suddenly realised we had food, did a quick volte-face and immediately became inordinately friendly. He sat in front of Brian's front wheel and practiced sitting up on his haunches in his best begging pose. Brian was especially impressed with this fluent piece of opportunism and decided the least he could do was to reward such a bravura performance. Unfortunately the only food Brian had to offer was a handful of dry cereal and a muesli bar. The black lab sat back on his haunches and chewed this for a while in a pensive pose. Evidently he was not impressed however, and in yet another lightning-like switch of attitude he wandered slowly round to the back of Brian's bike and while Brian was packing away promptly emptied his bladder all over his trailer, presumably on the basis that if you can't do sarcasm, you can at least do irony. Dog humour at its best.

As on most journeys, the people you tend to meet almost always range from the good, the bad and the indifferent. On the whole, though, I had found Montanans to be a generally welcoming bunch, and usually interested in hearing our story.

Just as I was beginning to get used to small-town friendliness, though, we stopped at a dirty little roadside café in Columbia Falls for a mid morning treat of coffee and cakes, and I was delighted to discover a standard of customer service compatible with the worst transport café in the UK . The fact that it was 11am and the sign on the door still said 'Closed' even though the place was half full of locals might have been an indication of what to expect. If there had been a piano player he would have stopped and turned round as we walked through the door – certainly everyone else did. Of course it's difficult to make collective assumptions about the relative IQ of a group of people you've never me before, so I won't. One observation which did occur to me was that at least the floor of the café appeared to be level, since one old man in a hunting cap was drooling out of both sides of his mouth at the same time. They looked like just the sort of people who like to use the phrase "…these here parts" as some kind of tribal territorial claim as in "We don't like/take to/get/want x in these here parts", or "You're not from…" etc., etc. The last time I'd felt this welcome was when I'd taken a girlfriend to a dominos match in a rural pub in Lancashire. She'd compounded the crimes of being a Woman, and a Southerner and wearing a Short Skirt (though I think there might have been a faction who were divided on the desirability of the latter) with beating most of the old boys at their own game. To be fair, though, I'm not sure the lot in the café could have played dominoes without taking their shoes and socks off to assist with the arithmetical challenges.

After they'd determined that we weren't from you-know-where (the shorts, bicycles and accents may have been a bit of a giveaway) they turned back to whatever it was they were concentrating on before. Unfortunately this included the waitress. At least I assume she was the waitress. She may actually have been paid to sit behind the counter and look at the newspaper, of course. After a few feeble and very British attempts to attract her attention on my part, I was just about ready to give up and move on. Mark, however, is made of sterner stuff, and going up to the counter, very gently turned down her newspaper and asked her very quietly for three coffees and a glass of water in a voice of which Quentin Tarantino would have been proud. It wasn't exactly menacing, just very clearly expectant of being complied with. I was impressed and a little jealous at the same time. It did occur to me, though, that this sort of thing might be easier to

169

carry off in a country where you're never quite sure who might be carrying a gun – the very country which fostered that nice Mr Tarantino in the first place of course.

After a while, a longer while than was strictly necessary, but not long enough to start complaining, our coffees arrived, delivered without hostility but without much grace either. Having inspected mine very carefully for any trace of phlegm (I couldn't find any), I drank it quickly (it was so horrible I couldn't have tasted it if there were any), left my money on the table and went out into the fresh air, happier than ever to be back on my bike again. Thinking back over this incident now, I may have been a little unfair here, and maybe my recollection of the café in Columbia Falls has been exaggerated over time – then again, maybe not, and I'm not even sure the floor was that level.

Anyway you look at it, cycling across the US is not something that's likely to figure in most people's experience, and we drew many and varied reactions from the people we met on the road.

Jim, a local homeowner, flagged us down by the side of the road and was clearly delighted to see us. He gave us comprehensive directions (we were having a little route discussion at the time), said we were welcome to use the picnic table in his garden or even stop overnight, if we wanted. He retired from the military and moved out here from New York sometime ago so it would be fair to say his horizons were a little broader than some. Only five miles down the road though, we stopped to chat to another resident out working in his garden. Although friendly enough on the surface, when he found out how far we were going, his first response was "Boy, you must be really rich!" and suddenly he had lost the plot altogether. None of us was that rich, and you certainly don't have to be rich to cycle across America, you just have to want to do it enough. His comment had just that hint of bitterness of a disappointed man and made me sorry that he could miss the point of our journey so entirely.

At Big Fork, we stopped for the first time at a commercial campground right on the edge of Flathead Lake. The town was both prosperous and pretty and the campsite very pleasant with one major exception. Right next to us was a huge RV (Recreational Vehicle or mobile home) of the sort that Americans seem inordinately fond of retiring to, through some kind of atavistic urge to return to the days of covered wagons, I suppose. The prime difference being that not many covered wagons had space for a TV, dishwasher and tumble drier, and consequently had no need for a large, and very noisy generator to be parked outside running flat out all day in order to power these essential domestic appliances. I made a mental note to kill them, set fire to their RV and smash the generator before I went to bed, but they turned it off before it got dark.

At Big Fork it was Paul and Sue's turn to do the cooking. Perfectly rational and pleasant human beings in themselves, they are, unfortunately, probably the worst matched couple in the group. To begin with, Sue was an early riser and one of the fastest riders among us. Paul was not. Although he made every effort to arrive earlier when he knew he had to go shopping or to cook he simply ran on a different clock speed to Sue. If the pace at which he did things didn't infuriate her, the deliberateness with which he did them would. It seemed strange to see two patient, kind and generous souls ready to stab each other in the eye over the simple process of preparing a meal. Actually, if there was any eye-stabbing to do Sue was the more likely candidate. I think Paul would have settled for documenting his grievances and taking her to some kind of outdoor cooking tribunal. To both their credit, they managed to complete the entire trip without inflicting any significant damage on each other and nobody starved on their shift, but then I suppose there are married couples who go through fifty years of the same sort of tension day in and day out, so maybe it's not that surprising. In the end we all got our dinner, nobody got hurt and the only loss was probably a few millimetres ground off Sue's upper and lower molars. The real damage was yet to come, and it was to be me doing both the inflicting and the receiving of it.

Once again Mark and I made an early start, but we were so busy admiring the herds of llama on either side of the road (apparently imported from South America and farmed here for their wool and for

171

use as pack animals in the mountains) and the wild deer periodically springing across the road in front of us, that we missed our first turning and overshot by around three or four miles before we realised and had to turn back. The rest of the morning was spent climbing and falling through the forest, interspersed with plenty of deep muddy puddles running right across the track. Having lost the advantage of our early start we eventually caught up with Richard who had stopped by the side of the road with a flat tyre. Most impressive of all though was Pierre, our eldest and only French member. Although another early riser, Pierre was very independent, and generally liked to ride on his own. For some reason he reminded me of Pepe le Pew in the Looney Toons cartoons. He never seemed to be going that quickly, but somehow or other, at some point he would end up in front of most of us. Over the next weeks and months just about everybody developed a deep seated and abiding respect for his astonishing strength and stamina as well as his self-effacing politeness and generosity. For one thing, the only time he ever stopped was to take photos or to help someone else who was stuck. Having owned a camera shop in France, he'd retired some time ago and passed the business on to his sons, but clearly his little Leica camera was a source of great pride and joy to him. We got our first inkling of just how strong he was physically though, when we discovered that somewhere on one of the more rocky sections he'd actually lost the rear wheel to his trailer but carried on dragging the full weight along the ground for three or four miles before he noticed that something was wrong. Fortunately Evan found the wheel, saw the little furrow ploughed into the track and worked out what had happened, and he managed to catch up with Pierre before the trailer frame was ground away completely and he started distributing his luggage all over the trail.

Cedar Creek would have been better named after its predecessor on the road, Bug Creek. A muddy bog next to the river, even at midday it was infested with nasty, buzzing and hungry mosquitoes. The fact that we can make Dodos extinct without even trying but are apparently completely unable to even make a tiny dent in the population of these vicious little buggers strikes me as particularly unfair. I have no idea of course what it would have been like to have been bitten by a Dodo, but at least you would have seen the little sod coming, and given that they couldn't fly they would have had to use a ladder to get at anything above your ankles anyway. After a (very) quick wash in the near freezing river I put on as many clothes as I could and covered my face and hands with neat DEET. This is supposed to be the most powerful insect repellant available. Aside from little issues like mosquitoes clearly not being able to read the instructions (or maybe they just had bad colds and couldn't smell anything), this feels about as pleasant as covering yourself in an oily, smelly version of liquid plutonium and judging by all the warnings is probably only marginally better for your health.

Eventually I gave up and ran back to my tent for an afternoon snooze. I came out for just long enough to fill up my supper bowl and dived back under cover again to eat it and settle in for an early night.

I may have got an early night, what I didn't get was much sleep. I always knew this ride was going to be physically challenging, but my biggest worry about my physical capacity to complete it had always centred on my knees. Most long cycle rides that I'd done before had at some point generated a certain amount of discomfort in my knee joints, but I'd always previously managed to ride through that. This time, though, I wasn't sure. Riding off-road is always far tougher on your legs and on the joints in particular. Not only are they the drivetrain responsible for propelling you up and down various mountains, but they have to double up as a suspension system as well, absorbing all the shocks, bumps and twists that the trail throws at you. Having front forks or a suspension seat post certainly helps iron out a lot of the bumps, but you can never really get a smooth rhythm going in the same way you can on the road. One moment your foot will suddenly slip forward as the back wheel skids in some mud, the next it will stop suddenly and jar your whole body as you bang into a rock or a tree stump. Around midday my right knee had started creaking ominously and all my previous worries and concerns started crowding into my tent and buzzing round my head, worse than the crowd of mosquitoes I'd dived in there to escape.

Whenever I'd had problems before, I'd always been able to stop or ease off for a bit to allow my body to acclimatise to the stresses and strains. One of the difficulties of being in a group, apart from the already fairly punishing pace we had set ourselves, was the fact that it would be extremely difficult, if not impossible, to back off for a while without losing track of the rest of the team. Our schedule was designed to get everybody to the Mexican border by the end of August and with only one day off for every 7-10 days cycling and an average mileage of around 45 miles per day there was very little leeway for slowing down or taking time off. Even if I'd wanted to carry on on my own I had no cooking implements, no water filter and very few tools with me. With stretches of up to five days between towns of any kind it would have been pretty lonely, isolated and risky, even for someone used to covering long distances alone. I thought the chances of doing any permanent damage to myself were fairly slim, my biggest worry was that having started the ultimate mountain bike ride, I might not be able to finish it.

Just the other side of the river, a mile or so down the trail, a paved road lead all the way to Holland Lake, our next scheduled camp. One option would be to take to the tarmac for a day and rejoin the group in the evening. Unlike some of the others, though, I was really enjoying being out in the wilds, away from any traffic and I actually liked wrestling my bike and luggage through the mud, over the rocks and up the track to the top of the next hill. I finally dozed off, but none the wiser as to what my best course of action would be.

In the morning I decided to stick to the trail. It saved me having to go through a whole load of explaining with the rest of the group, and since everybody was finding it difficult in one way or another, I didn't want to look like a whinger; I'd always managed to ride through any difficulties before and I thought that at least this way I would be with other people if I did have any problems.

Big mistake.

This section proved to be one of the more difficult ones to navigate from the map and although we didn't actually get lost, we

174

backtracked twice because we thought we'd gone wrong when we hadn't and added another 8-10 miles to our total. Most of the time we were surrounded by trees, with the occasional view of the mountains through a clearing to one side. By 10:30 I didn't give a damn about the views, we were grinding our way up a narrow, very bumpy piece of single-track and my right knee was quite clearly shot to pieces. Most of the rest of the day was just about pain control. There was no option but to carry on until we got to the campground at Holland Lake. Having dismissed the choice of taking the road route in the morning the only way left open was to carry on along the trail and hope that at some point the surface would improve. After a while it widened out a little and we were overtaken by an elderly couple in a pickup truck. They pulled up in front of us and insisted on inviting us into their cabin half a mile up the road for cookies and coffee. I seized on the opportunity to rest my leg, however briefly and we sat in the warm and chatted for half an hour. The gentleman told us about the salt lick he'd put at the bottom of their garden to attract the deer - 'not to shoot them, though', he almost apologised, just because he liked to watch them. He showed us his latest acquisition, a stuffed fish mounted on a board which wiggled and sang "Take Me To The River" while his wife plied us with hot coffee and homemade cookies. They talked briefly and rather sadly of their only son who had died at the age of 53 from a brain stem haemorrhage, but otherwise they seemed healthy and very happy in their little mountain retreat, and for a while they took my mind off my own discomfort. As I hobbled down the steps on the way out the man noticed me limping and insisted on rushing back in to dig out some liniment for me. It smelled of horse piss and camphor, but I didn't see what I had to lose so rubbed a large gob of it into my leg and thanked him for his kindness. For the last five miles or so the others couldn't understand why I was pushing ahead so hard but the simple fact is that more than anything else I just wanted the day to be over. By this stage I no longer cared whether I was doing any damage or not, I just wanted the pain to stop. At least one thing was clear, and that was that I wouldn't be doing any cycling off-road the next day.

At Holland Lake, after pitching my tent, I hobbled down to the bar inside a giant log cabin on the lakeshore. Paul entertained us on the piano with a strange selection of Barry Manilow's finest and Rachmaninov's fastest while the rain set in for the evening outside and I sat down to the serious job of anaesthetising myself as quickly as possible, with a few bottles of Moose Drool beer. At first, my mood was as black as the clouds outside, but after a while, the beer and the music started to cut in and the day began to mellow out a little.

The main problem before me was trying to decide what was the best thing to do. The only thing that was clear for sure now was that I wasn't going to be able to complete the whole route off-road as intended. That was difficult enough to accept, much more worrying was whether I was going to be able to continue at all, and if I did, how I was going to keep up with the others' punishing schedule. Maybe it was the effect of the Moose Drool, but once I got off the bike and stopped pedalling it didn't feel anywhere near as bad, and despite the pain during the day, I still found it difficult to believe that I'd actually done any serious damage internally.

It wasn't until morning, when I made a quick trial circuit of the campsite, that I found out just what an effective anaesthetic Moose Drool really was. My knee felt like it had just disintegrated beneath the kneecap, and just for fun someone had replaced all the pieces with a bag of rusty screws. I assume the word "excruciating" comes from crucifixion, so I wouldn't say it was as bad as that (though I have no plans to find out), maybe just the equivalent of having only one foot nailed to a wooden plank. Whatever, it hurt like hell every time I bent the damn thing. I had little choice but to try to make it to our next stop, Seeley Lake, by road. Fortunately for me, though less so for them, I would not be alone in taking this particular diversion. Overnight, long tall Mike, my cooking partner and our resident Oakie had made an incredibly tough decision. Having spoken to his wife he decided not to continue with the trip. I cannot express how much I admired him for the way in which he made this choice. I know how bitterly disappointed I was to have missed even a day, we had all of invested so much of ourselves in undertaking this journey in the first place. How strong did you then have to be to turn around and say "I made a mistake, this is not for me"? Poor Mike just kept asking "When am I going to start having fun, boys?" He simply was not enjoying himself and decided that now was time to call a halt. If I reach the age of 65, and am still able to make bold mistakes like that and deal with them as well as he did, then I will be proud of myself. Whatever else happened to me on the trip, I was glad to have met Mike McKee and I am grateful to call him a friend.

Donn, too had not been having much fun on the off-road sections, and with a more difficult piece of single track ahead of us decided to join Mike and I on the road that day. At that point he was still undecided about the whole trip though, and thought perhaps he might carry on by road all the way. I set off ahead of the other two in the hope I wouldn't cause myself too much embarrassment by wincing all the time in front of them. The track down to the road was mostly downhill so I rode most of the way with my right leg stuck out straight in front of me and pedalling every now and then with just my left foot. By the time I reached the road at the bottom, I was sweating all the same and decided to rest for a few minutes and see if the others caught up. In fact, the first person I saw was Pierre which rather surprised me, he looked like the last one to be having any problems. The only problem Pierre had was with navigation, having turned right instead of left when he came out of the campsite. This was to be something of a theme for Pierre's trip and overall he must have covered at least a hundred miles more than anybody else. Still, it was typical of the man that when he found out where he'd gone wrong he simply waved cheerily at me and set about the long laborious business of climbing all the way back up the hill again.

A few minutes later Donn and Mike arrived and we set off together. Fortunately the road to Seeley Lake was relatively flat, beautifully smooth (by comparison to what we were used to) and not much more than 20 miles in total. Unfortunately it took me almost three hours to cover, I was sweating buckets all the way and by the time we arrived my right knee was doing a very passable impersonation of a very large spherical puffy red thing and a very poor version of any recognisable piece of human anatomy. After I'd got my tent set up, I sat down with my leg under a small mountain of ice Mike had found for me and contemplated the future. After about five minutes of this I decided a) my leg was very cold and b) I didn't want to contemplate the future, what I really wanted was a beer. Mike and I had an additional issue to deal with in that we were still on the rota to do the shopping and cooking that day. Since neither of us felt much like being mother at this point, we solved both problems rather neatly by walking (him) and hopping (me) over to the nearest bar, drinking two large beers ourselves and ordering two six packs and six large pizzas to take away for the group supper that evening. We could stock up on cereal, biscuits and bagels at the gas station in the morning and then our duty would be done, Mike's for good and mine at least for the next six days.

The woman behind the bar was very friendly, shapely and very charming, with long dark hair and a flashing smile. She also turned out to own just about everything in town including the bar, the launderette and the campsite. In fact the gas station was the only other business in town as far as I could see and I suspected she had her eyes on that too. Despite his, shall we say advancing years, Mike clearly couldn't resist chatting her up, but slipped into it with a smoothness and a dexterity which left me struck with admiration. This was a hitherto hidden side to his nature, but he clearly had the country boy charm down to a tee. Within 15 minutes he'd negotiated us a reduced rate at the campsite, got us both invited into her home so I could pick up my email using her phone line and was patting her none-too-gently on the backside and calling her "darlin'" like they were long-lost friends. Mike was definitely no "New Man", but, boy, was he good at being an old one.

For the next few days we stayed in Seeley Lake and, like ball bearings stuck in a pinball, bounced pathetically backwards and forwards around a small triangle bound by the gas station (coffee), the bar (beer and food) and the campsite (sleep and laundry) while I tried to work out what to do. Mike was clear that he was going home, but refused to leave until I got sorted out. Donn decided to turn the journey into a road trip and tried very hard to persuade me to join him. Probably my own feelings are best summed up by my journal entries for the next few days:

Monday 26 June. Still in Seeley Lake.

It was so hard to say goodbye to the rest of the team this morning. In the end I was so choked I had to turn away and asked Mike to cross over the road with me on the pretext that I wanted some breakfast. Every ounce of me wants to be back on the trail with them, I am surprised at the strength of my own motivation. My legs, heart and lungs are as strong as they ever were, and I love this type of riding, the hills, the rocks, the technical descents, everything. Just one small piece of my anatomy is rebelling and stopping me doing what I want to do. I find it so frustrating if I could scoop my own knee out with a spoon and replace it with a rusty door hinge I'd do it now.

Donn is still here with me and is tremendously supportive and Mike, Mike continues to be one of those people who can continually restore your faith in human nature.

Although feeling slightly better, the knee is still pretty cranky this morning and I have to fight my own impatience and frustration, to stay here and give it a chance to heal. I went to the local medical centre where a very nice lady relieved me of $57 and told me to keep off it for a while. My faith in the medical profession is undiminished. However, after consultation with an 'expert' in Missoula, when I phone back in the afternoon they suggest I come in for shot of cortisone. This involves sticking a large bore needle through the side of my knee and injecting the stuff directly into the joint, but frankly at this stage they could get out the Black & Decker and an 8mm wood drill and have a go at it and I wouldn't care. If it gets me back on the road again I'll be happy.

I have to wait a couple of hours while they deal with a gentleman who has somehow managed to shoot an arrow through his own hand, and I pass the time trying to work out what contortions you would have to perform to be able to do that. By the time I'm called in I'm still unsuccessful, but if anybody out there has any ideas I'd be fascinated to know.

The procedure takes only a few minutes and thanks to a local anaesthetic feels just like someone is poking a long needle under your kneecap only without the pain (or without much of it anyway).

Poor Mike has played nursemaid to me all day long and by the time we leave he looks shattered. I hope to be able to persuade him to let me get him dinner tonight at least.

Donn looks set to head off for Helena by road tomorrow, and I try to encourage him to do that, since he needs to find out whether he will be happier doing a road tour, and whether he would want to do it solo.

I will be staying here at least another day, and Mike still refuses to leave without me.

Tuesday 27 June 6:30am.

Sleepless night, from frustration more than anything else. The bad news is that this morning my knee feels worse than ever. This might just be the result of someone poking around inside it with a 3-inch needle, or then again it might be something else. Right now I feel so angry and frustrated I could just smash the damn thing with a hammer and be done with it. I can't see myself cycling to Helena this week, so we will have to try and find an alternative way out of Seeley Lake or I will have to persuade Mike to go on ahead.

Too angry to think clearly so will have to go over the road for a coffee to calm down.

11:59 am. After much thought and a few phone calls I have a plan at least for the next few days. Mike has decided to leave the tour and I respect that decision and understand how difficult it was for him to make. Donn is still not sure. But I am loving every minute of this ride, including the climbs, the rocks and the rain. I can even live with the mosquitoes if I have to. I will do everything I can to re-join the team.

Brian from Adventure Cycling is taking over from Larry as one of the leaders this week, and having spoken with him he has kindly offered to pick us both up on his way over from Missoula tomorrow and drop us in Helena a day early. With a layover day planned for Friday that gives me five days to rest and try to heal my knee. I plan to set off with the boys on Saturday morning. I will go as slowly as I am able, rest often, raise my seat another inch and Mike has (once again) kindly offered to lend me his Bob trailer to see if that makes things any better. If my knee dissolves once again, I will have to accept that and go home to see if I can get the damn thing fixed once and for all.

Later that day I was sitting in the Launderette (the warmest place to pass the time) reading my book, when I felt the chair I was sitting on wobble briefly. I thought no more of it until the following day when I heard that Montana had experienced a minor earthquake at exactly that time, with the epicentre a little west from where I was, and realised that my wobbly chair was just one of the extending ripples from the main shock.

Mike finally managed to book a flight home from Helena, but it cost him a small fortune in cash plus several minor body parts. For the price he paid I could fly round the world twice and it began to look like getting into Montana was going to be very much easier than getting out of it.

In the event it was Larry, rather than Brian who came to collect us and drove us into Helena in his pickup truck. As nice a place as Seeley Lake was, I don't think either of us were too sorry to get a view of it through a rearview mirror.

It took us just under three hours to cover the distance it would take the others nearly four days to cycle, though we did have the advantages of a rather flatter and more direct route and a V8 engine to help us along. One of the nice things about cycling long distance is that when you do get back into a car it always strikes you as miraculous how fast you can go and how easy it is. How many times when you're setting out on a journey do you worry about how many hills there are en-route, how steep they may be, what the road surface will be like and which direction the wind is blowing? But every morning these were our first concerns. These were the things that could make the difference between a relatively easy day and a very tough one. From the back seat of the pickup I thought again about what I was doing. Stepping into the truck meant that physically I'd already failed the challenge I'd set myself. Whatever happened I could never say that I'd cycled all the way. That was disappointing, but in itself wasn't really the issue, I didn't start this in order to get a certificate. What was really frustrating me was that no matter how much I had wanted this, no matter how hard I'd pushed myself, there was absolutely nothing more I could do. Probably I was acting like a spoiled child, and there are no doubt millions of people on this planet who aren't able to do even everyday things, let alone all the things they would like to do, because their bodies won't let them, but this was a first for me, and I hated the sense of helplessness it gave me. At this point it occurred to me that what had been taken away in terms of the physical challenge had just been added to the mental challenge of the trip. In all honesty I was even less sure that I was up to the task at this point, but at least it gave me a new target to focus on. I could still try to get to Mexico, one way or another.

Larry dropped us at a cheap motel, not far from the centre of Helena. Once again Mike turned his charm on the receptionist and got us a better room than the one we'd originally been allocated. I watched him the way I would watch a gymnast performing on the parallel bars or the rings, conscious of the fact that if there was such a thing as a parallel universe then he was inhabiting it here and now and I was firmly on the other side of the barrier.

While Mike was glued to the phone trying to organise shipment for his bike back home I tried out the triple American combination of bed, t.v. and remote control. After 45 seconds I could feel my brain beginning to melt and slide out of my nose so I turned the t.v. off and went out in search of some food. Unless you're absolutely determined to drag yourself out into the wilderness, food is never very far away in the States. Whatever sort of retail outlet you might be, it never hurts to carry a few lines of snacks, just in case your customers suddenly feel faint from lack of eating. I couldn't be bothered to look for a supermarket, so I walked into the first place I saw with lights on, a Chemist's as it happened, and bought two packets of biscuits, some chocolate and a four pack of beer. Not exactly a balanced diet but it would keep us going till morning.

After a good night's sleep, followed by a simply enormous breakfast, Mike and I headed into town to try to locate the nearest bike shop. Mike needed to get hold of a box to package up his bike, and then needed to see if he could persuade them to let him leave it there for UPS to pick up in a day or so's time. Provided he could find a female shop assistant when we got there I had no doubt he'd have any trouble. I wanted to get a new bag for Mike's trailer and a box to package up my panniers so I could send them back to Salt Lake for storage. We eventually found the shop but it didn't open till ten, so in his inimitable fashion Mike grabbed a woman who happened to be passing and asked where we could get a cup of coffee. There was a brief flicker as that inter-dimensional shift thing happened again, she smiled at him and said:

"Just follow me, honey…"

One thing that Mike and I did have in common was that neither of us was going to hesitate for even a heartbeat when that sort of offer came along.

Beck, as it turned out, was just charming. She chatted happily to us as she lead us through the sidestreets and brought us to a small coffee shop about 5 minutes walk from the bike shop.

She had one son in the Forces, stationed in Frankfurt, who she was going to visit soon, and another who would be going on an exchange student visit to Aberystwyth. I told her that Frankfurt was nice anyway and decided it was probably better not even to discuss Aberystwyth.

After a leisurely coffee, Mike and I wandered back to the bike shop where he not only succeeded in getting a box and leaving his bike there, he even managed to persuade the young girl at the counter to use the bike shop's UPS account to get him a discount. All I got was the directions to the skip on the other side of the parking lot where I might be able to find a smaller box to pack my panniers in. Such is life. I might not have minded so much if I hadn't been the one to spend £80 on a new bag for Mike's trailer while he bought diddly squat. She even called a taxi for him to get to the airport. While we were waiting I took all of my stuff out of the panniers and threw it into the new trailer bag and boxed up everything I needed to send back to Salt Lake. When the cab arrived I shook Mike's hand and wished him a safe journey home. I knew he could have been there two or three days ago if it weren't for me, but I certainly appreciated his company and his moral support. It did occur to me to ask for a few lessons on smooth talking while I was at it, but I knew I'd never carry it off anyway.

Since I was the only person on the trip to try both, it's probably worth mentioning the difference between trailers and panniers at this stage. In the past, the only way to carry a reasonable amount of gear on a bike was to use pannier bags strapped to a front or rear luggage rack. Rucksacks are virtually useless on a long trip as you can only get so much in a reasonable sized one, they hurt your shoulders like hell after a couple of hours bouncing over rocks, and your back gets horribly sweaty (or more horribly sweaty...or horribly sweatier... nasty anyway). Panniers transfer all the weight to the bike, but obviously affect the handling a lot. Off-road, it's generally a good idea to get as much weight as you can in the front ones or the bike tends to wheelie when you're going uphill (good for teenagers, bad for those who prefer not to fall off). Over the last few years though, more and more people have started to switch to using a trailer for touring. One of the best known is the BoB Yak, the one I borrowed from Mike, and the same as 12 other people were using on this ride. This consists of a tubular steel frame, shaped a bit like an arched window frame laid on the ground, with a single small wheel at the back and a fork at the front which mounts onto a special axle for the rear wheel of your bike. Advantages are that you can carry more, the bike tends to handle better, and the weight is shared between bike and trailer. Disadvantages are that you have one more thing to carry if you're flying or getting on a bus, and that you *can* carry more – and as a result, you almost certainly will. If you're going down a very steep hill and try to use your brakes, you will also find that the trailer has a nasty tendency to try to overtake you on the way down. Since it can't overtake you without turning you through 180 degrees this has rather unpleasant consequences for your downhill style, even if you do still get to the bottom of the hill. Most people use a single big waterproof bag (like the one I'd just bought) to go inside the trailer, then strapped smaller bags with things they were likely to need during the day on top. The trailers are very tough and handle remarkably well over rough ground, though it's probably just as well you can't see what's going on behind you – when you follow someone else down a rocky slope it's rather scary to see just how high the trailers bounce and how wide they swing from one side to the other. I decided to switch in the hope that moving the weight off the bike would put less pressure on my knees as the bike was thrown around and I had nothing to lose by trying.

Once Mike had gone, I hitched up the trailer, picked the bike and trailer up off the floor where they'd fallen straight after I'd hitched them together (there's a technique to doing this on your own, which I hadn't yet mastered) and set off for the campground where I was aiming to meet the others. Up to this point we'd met with nothing but courtesy from the few car and truck drivers we'd encountered on the road. A lesser-known fact about Helena, however, is that it appears to house Montana's total quota of arseholes, all in one place. Aside from the usual round of cutting up and horn blowing, their drivers have an inordinate fondness for verbal abuse when it comes to cyclists. A favourite one which, as a London cyclist I was pleased to see had crossed the Atlantic more or less intact, was to overtake, blow the horn, swing in to the point of forcing said cyclist off the road and shout something like "Hey, if you paid taxes, you could ride on the tarmac!" You could always reply to this of course, but then what's the point? I have grown more intelligent beings in window boxes and I would rather talk to them any day. Helena is not an unattractive town, but if you ever visit Montana I'd put it low of your list of priorities to visit – unless you like your vegetables behind the wheel of a pickup truck, that is.

The campground manager was not much better, something like a cross between Adolf Hitler and Basil Fawlty. He seemed pleasant enough while I was checking in, but then while I was filling out a registration form, an elderly gentleman turned up with an RV and had the temerity to question, very politely, why the charge was more than he'd been told on the phone.

"That's the cost, you can take it or leave it…"

"But, on the phone…"

"WHO did you talk to on the phone?"

"I don't know, but…"

"OH! I see. So you want me to give you a discount on the basis of some MYTHICAL person you just invented?"

"No, but…"

"Are YOU calling ME a LIAR?"

"No…"

"Good, because I can tell you I've beaten the SH*T out of better people than you, boy."

This, I could believe since he was twice the size and half the age of the gentleman he was addressing.

"Well…whaddya want? Are you staying, or do you want to go now?"

"No, we'll stay.."

"AND DON'T SHOUT AT ME! I deserve some respect too you know, or do you think just because I work behind a counter, you can abuse me as much as you like?"

At this point we both looked around just to see whether there was anyone else in the room, an astral projection or something. I was tempted to ask him about medication – as in whether he'd forgotten his or whether he'd like to try some of mine – but as this was more likely to end up with me pulling a ballpoint pen out of my eye, I sloped off quietly to go and pitch my tent.

The next day was a recuperation day for the team, and a try-it-and-see day for me. Since the campsite was a good five miles outside the town it took me a painfully slow 45 minutes to get into or out of town. I met Donn and some of the others at the coffee shop. Donn was definitely committed to doing a road trip from now on. He'd already dropped his bike off in the bike shop for a service and to get the tyres changed and tried very hard to persuade me to join him. I told him I was going to take the road for the next two days as far as Butte, but that I really wanted to re-join the main route if at all possible, but I said I'd walk with him to go pick up his bike if he wanted.

As we entered the shop I thought I caught sight of some funny looks exchanged between the shop staff, and one scurried off into the workshop at the back. Donn wandered around, smiling and talking to everybody. After a while a very weary looking mechanic came out of the workshop and walked up to us.

"Well, your bike's nearly ready, just have to…"

"Ah, good. Now while you're here, can I just explain to you…"

"What exactly is it you want doing to your bike?"

"Well, if you can imagine…"

"NO. NO MORE STORIES! Just tell me what you want me to do!"

Did I mention that Donn could talk a lot? He liked to talk, and he was good at it. It was just that he had a way of working round to what he was trying to tell you by using analogies or by telling you a story. Obviously the guy in the workshop had already had all the stories he could take and was looking for some straightforward instructions to get back to work on and get rid of the bike as quickly as possible. None of us actually met Donn on the road again after he set off on his own. But several of the group came across people who told them they had met a lone biker nearby. We always knew it was Donn when they began with "Boy, he could talk, though."

I thought I'd stick with the road for a while, to see if I could rebuild the strength in my joints without bouncing all over the place on a rock-strewn trail. Unfortunately the only road south out of Helena was the Interstate Highway. Cycling the Interstate was an interesting experience, but not necessarily one I would recommend. I remain to be convinced that it was actually legal (I couldn't imagine anybody getting too far down the M4 on a bicycle) but lots of people seemed to do it, and many more assured me it was OK, at least in Montana. The surface was good and there was a reasonably wide hard shoulder, but I kept a very close eye in my mirror for any sign of one of the big eighteen-wheeler trucks that tended to blow by like a minor tornado. At first the road rose and fell fairly gently among open, golden brown hills. Aside from a residual nervousness I felt this wasn't too bad a reintroduction, and the only truck which did nearly get me was the one which did a U-turn across all four lanes and nearly killed three car drivers as well, so that was OK. After a while, though, the hills started to steepen, and the road rose to a steady incline for the next 15 miles, topping out at a little over 6000 feet. Fully-laden it wasn't exactly a breeze, but it was the best I could do. To my right, was a steep drop down to a white river I could just about hear rushing between rocks and pine trees at the bottom. On the other side of the valley, I could occasionally make out the trail the others would be following and felt a mixture of envy tinged with the knowledge that it would be a much harder climb than the one I had to deal with.

I was still struggling to come to terms with the size and the emptiness of mid-western America. Had everything else not been so empty, I might have missed Basin, my destination for the day, altogether. Basin was not what you might call a teeming metropolis. If there was such a thing as a one-horse town, then Basin probably would have been pleased with a timeshare on a donkey.

The first thing I discovered in Basin was a Ghost Bar. It had all the signs of a bar (literally), it even had a row of pickups parked outside, but when I tried the door it was locked and when I managed to find a window that was vaguely transparent and looked inside, it was obvious it hadn't seen either people or beer for some years now.

The town's main 'attraction' (at least that was what they called it) was the "Merry Widow Health Mine". The idea of a health mine was an intriguing combination I hadn't come across before, and not an association that immediately sprang to mind (as opposed to "health farm" or "death mine" for example), so I thought I'd have a look.

There was a minor gold rush in Montana in the 1850s, and the mine originally produced a limited amount of both gold and silver. It had long since become uncommercial until a local 'entrepreneur' (I'm sure there's a case for moving this word next to the word 'crook' in the dictionary, just for clarity) reopened it recently as a health resort. Like many mines, it contained relatively high levels of Radon gas. Radon is called Radon because it's radioactive. In Yorkshire and Lancashire they spend large amounts of money re-housing people who are unfortunate to live above old mine workings, and have Radon gas leaking into their homes. In Basin people paid $3 an hour for the privilege of sitting in a cold, damp, dark mine breathing the stuff. The local campground was full of geriatrics in huge RVs hobbling around on sticks or burning up trails in 4x4 electric wheelchairs. I didn't know whether these were the people who had come there for the cure, or whether that was what you looked like after sitting in a radioactive mine for several days. Whatever, with my own perambulatory problems they made me feel right at home. I was not, however, tempted to take the cure myself.

Two residents of the campsite with no mobility problems whatsoever, were a pair of over-tame chipmunks who visited me in the early evening while I was trying to update my journal. I suppose the other residents thought they were teaching them to do cute little tricks for food tidbits, but this particular Chip 'n' Dale passed from cute to bloody nuisance in the space of about three seconds. Having mugged me unsuccessfully while I was sitting on the ground, trying to type up my notes, the thieving little toe-rags started to tear into my tent and all my luggage to see what they could help themselves to. It's one thing to share food with the wildlife when you've got an 18 foot RV with fridge/freezer and larder packed to the gunnels with snacks and meals for two. It's another altogether when you've just about got enough for one day, and you had to haul that up a 3000 foot climb under your own steam with a gammy knee. This was nature red in tooth and claw and I was quite prepared to fight for my supper if not exactly for my survival. I tried very hard to bounce a few rocks off their cute furry little heads without any of the neighbours noticing, then I stopped worrying about whether the neighbours noticed or not,

189

and went at them with everything I had. Still they kept coming back. In the end, I decided the easiest way was to eat everything I had which was edible there and then, and let the little buggers rummage through my dirty underpants to their hearts delight (served them right).

As it started to get dark, I noticed some very ominous and very black thunderclouds moving in from the southern end of the valley. I moved everything I could inside the tent, banged all the pegs as far into the ground as they would go and just got into my sleeping bag in time, as the thunderheads started to roll and boom all around the edges of the valley.

Normally I like dramatic weather. I have only been frightened of thunderstorms twice in my life, and this was one of those occasions. It felt like there was someone very big and very angry up in the sky and that they were intent on smashing things up until they had fully vented their spleen. What made the storm worse was that it appeared to get trapped in the bowl between the mountains and rattled around and around, moving away, then coming right back again. I had some very ungenerous thoughts that the lightning would find one of the large metallic six or seven tonne RVs much more attractive than my flimsy little nylon and aluminium tent, not to mention the fact that several of the occupants looked to have more metal parts in them than my bicycle had in total. The wind slapped and scrabbled at the sides of my tent like a hungry dog at the kitchen door. Lightning smashed and blasted the side of the valley, until I began to wonder whether there would be anything left when I came out. The strikes were so close there was barely any noticeable pause between the crash of the strike and the boom of the thunder. Rain and hailstones pounded on the tent and the ground all around. It seemed like nature at this point was very much in favour of very flat things and very much against anything which had the temerity to raise its head up above the ground. Deep inside my sleeping bag, I did my very best to oblige.

When I finally wiggled my face out through the tent zip in the morning, I firmly expected to see something like the battle of the Somme with nothing but mud and a few blasted tree trunks (or a smoking zimmer frame) in the distance, but the world appeared to be remarkably intact. Although it had stopped raining when I got up, it started again once I had all the gear packed and was ready to set off. As I pedalled like mad for the cover of the Interstate flyover, the rain turned to hailstones the size of large peas, gave me a full (and painful) face and body massage, and stopped abruptly as soon as I reached the bridge. The really bad news was that I'd forgotten it was Sunday, and whatever facilities Basin might have been able to offer in the culinary area (and there were never going to be many) were very firmly shut down, closed and sealed for the Lord's Day. Thanks to Chip 'n' Dale (and I cursed their cute little heads one more time for luck) I had no reserve supplies left, so unless I fancied a breakfast of soap and toothpaste I was going to be cycling to Butte on an empty stomach. This was a little more serious than you might think, since a cyclist needs fuel just as much as a car does. Without food, and the right food at that, you very quickly hit something known as the 'bonk'. Everything starts to feel twice as hard as it should, you slow right down and begin to feel very weak, often without even knowing why. To make things more interesting this was to be my first crossing of the Continental Divide.

The road snaked upwards through a deep sided gorge, to emerge on a long empty plateau which rose gently the final 500 feet to the Divide itself. I saw my first raccoon, squatting down by the side of the road and looking very put out, as though I had caught him in the middle of his morning motion (which I might well have done, of course). The trail crossed and recrossed the road I was using and at one time I came off the tarmac to give it a try and see how I got on. I managed about 500 yards up the slope to join an old disused railway bed, hanging on the very edge of the gorge before I turned round and went back. Cycling on the trail was so much harder, I was hungry and my main priority had to be to get to Butte first, then worry about what route I should take from there. I saw some cowboys, real Marlborough men, and a couple of Marlborough women too, unloading their horses from a sixty foot trailer by the side of the road. I stopped to rest on a pile of gravel in the middle of a bare flat plain, and spent a while listening to the wind and staring at the blue and brown hills on the horizon. I'd travelled alone and been in some wild and desolate places before, but I'd never had to cycle along motorways to get there, and it made a bleak combination. When I reached the Divide I was very disappointed. I had been hoping for a dramatic, wild and rocky high mountain pass. What I got was a bloated beer belly of a hill, with a four lane highway running through the middle of it. I stopped to take a photo, more out of a sense of obligation than anything else and sat on a rock to think again. I asked myself Mike's Big Question – "When am I going to start having fun?". The only answer I could come up with was "Not while you're sitting on a rock next to the Interstate, mate." I climbed back on the bike, and with the thought of being able to eat soon to motivate me, I pushed off down the other side of the hill. From the crest of the divide the road sloped down almost all the way into Butte. I pedalled as hard as I could at the top, then tucked myself down into a racing crouch to see how fast I would get up to. With a long, but steady gradient, I topped out at a very modest 43mph, with the trailer swinging unsteadily from side to side behind me, but I managed to keep my feet off the pedals until just after I had rolled into the suburbs of the town itself nearly five miles later.

Just before the exit to the Interstate I was surprised to see another cyclist with the very distinctive yellow reflective triangle which Adventure Cycling handed out to all their tour participants. I didn't recognise him, but stopped to talk. It turned out to be Tim, our new group leader for the next few weeks, and a very welcome sight he was too, since I had absolutely no idea where the campsite was supposed to be. Tim very kindly offered to guide me there and I very rudely turned him down on the basis that if I didn't get something to eat soon my stomach would have started to digest my brain (if it hadn't already). Tim was very understanding and guided me at just the right speed (ie as fast as I could go) to a nearby Denny's restaurant, where he politely watched me tear my way through a plateful of pancakes, syrup, fruit salad and a yoghurt in around 45 seconds. By the time I'd finished, I had enough blood sugar back to remember my manners and asked him if he wanted anything. I think I may have put him off the idea though, and he declined.

At a population of around 33000, Butte was far and away the biggest town on our itinerary and very appropriately named, as far as I was concerned. The town was big, noisy and ugly, and had a campsite to match. It was heaving and I think the noisiest I place had ever had the misfortune to stay. Things weren't helped by virtue of it being the Sunday before the 4th of July. Everybody seemed to have decided to light all their fireworks early, probably in case there should be a sudden rush in two days time and they might have to wait in a queue to let them off or something. Given the security and safety warnings surrounding Guy Fawkes' Night in the UK, it was unsettling to see small children from the ages of four and upwards being actively encouraged to throw lighted fireworks and crackers at each other, or under passing cars. At least I didn't see any of Chip 'n' Dale's relatives hanging around or I might have bought a few bangers to throw myself. Since the others had stopped well before Basin the previous night, I knew they were going to have a long day of it, and probably wouldn't be getting in till quite late. On the basis that they would be tired and hungry and would probably need all the help they could get to get any sleep that night, I emptied everything off the bike, cycled round to the nearest supermarket and filled Mike's trailer to overflowing with beer and snack food. In fact it was so full I had to stand on the pedals to get the damn thing moving at all. Once I was rolling it felt fairly stable, but I might as well have been towing the Space Shuttle for all the effect my brakes were likely to have, and besides, I didn't want to give myself a hernia trying to start up all over again, so I didn't bother trying to stop till I got back to the campground. It's surprising how liberating it can feel, shooting two or three stop lights with a 40 or 50 pound shopping trolley rumbling along behind you. Who would want to be a train driver, when you could be a runaway train driver?

While I was waiting for the others to arrive, I took a good long look at the maps for the next few days. Up to this point I had been relatively lucky, we were still in a populated area and for the last few

193

days the main route had shadowed the State and Interstate highways between towns. From this point on though, the trail began to strike out into real wilderness. The next town with a population over 3000 was probably Steamboat Springs, nearly 700 miles away. There were very few roads of any sort and as far as I could see, no realistic alternative route. I was struggling to keep up on the road, and there was a very real risk that I would just become a liability for the rest of the group if I broke down in the middle of nowhere and they had to find a way to get me out.

When Evan and Brian arrived we sat down to talk about my options. Both were incredibly supportive and did everything they could to encourage me to keep going. Brian suggested that maybe a bit more rest would help, and offered to give me a lift up to Elkhorn Hot Springs where I could take another couple of days off, bathe my leg in the thermal spa, and wait for the others to catch up with me there. I hated the idea of giving up, unless I had no choice and with the chance to spend a few days at a health spa thrown in (I did check that there was no Radioactivity involved first) I didn't see what I could lose. I gratefully accepted his offer and joined the others in attacking the trailer full of booze. Despite the beer the fireworks kept us all awake until 3 o'clock in the morning, when they were replaced by the sound of someone in a big V8 pickup with a hole in the exhaust cruising aimlessly round and round the campground for an hour or two. I say aimlessly, they might have had a very specific purpose in mind, but unless it was to keep as many campers awake as possible they appeared signally to fail to achieve it, whatever it was.

In the morning I had my first and last opportunity to watch the process of breaking up camp from beginning to end. First up, as ever, were Mark and the twins, Jack and Chris, closely followed by Pierre and Sue. They lit the camping stoves, put on the water, made coffee and laid out the breakfast things while most of the others were still groaning in their sleeping bags. I hovered guiltily round the edges of the group while they packed their gear away and made their own lunches for the trail. It felt very strange being part, but not part of them, and I was uncomfortable and envious as I waved them off on their way. After they'd gone there was quite a long pause. I sat and drank coffee while I waited for the second shift to emerge. First Paul, then Richard, Bryan, Evan and Other Brian crawled into the sunlight and made their way up to the breakfast table like blind puppies snuggling up to a teat (-sorry guys but you really did look like that, you know). After a while the place took on the air of a refugee camp for bag ladies, as people started wandering backwards and forwards in various states of dress, some eating, others just holding bits of food while they thought about it. Tents, bags, bikes and clothing were strewn over most of the site, sleeping bags and cycling shorts slung up in trees to air, open jars of peanut butter and half-eaten bagels rolled off the top of the picnic table. There were people squatting, standing, walking and lying down, picking over bits of luggage, folding up tents. Gradually (in some cases very gradually) the tide of chaos started to turn, then ebb back as all the different elements were pulled back together again, folded up and packed down and re-assembled into little compact units of man (or woman), bike and trailer. By around 11:30 it had started to rain again and just about everything and everyone had gone apart from me, Brian, Dean and Tim. Dean had been trying to dry his tent properly, but given up once the rain started. Tim was waiting for Dean as he had to ride 'sweep' that day, following behind the last person to leave and carrying all the tools in case of any breakdowns on the trail. Brian and I were waiting for his girlfriend to arrive in the car to take us up to Elkhorn Hot Springs.

Eventually Dean and Tim headed off, the rain started to come down even more heavily and I started to feel even more miserable. I should have been grateful to have the option to be inside a nice warm car and have myself and all my goods delivered to my next location, but I couldn't help but feel twinges of guilt and sympathy at what I knew my fellow team members would be undergoing on the trail. It would be hard for them to have fun today. The clouds were so low they probably wouldn't even be able to see much of the scenery, assuming they had the inclination to look up from their rain-gear. As for myself, I still didn't really know what I was doing here. Half

195

crippled and still trying to make out I had a chance to complete one of the toughest cycle rides in the world, dragging myself along behind the rest of the group like the littlest boy in the schoolboy gang, the one at the back who's always shouting, "Wait for me! Wait for me!", pedalling up and down the Interstate and hitching rides in the back of pickup trucks or cars – what on earth was the point, after all? I didn't know what the answer was, the only point I could think of was not giving up. I opened one of the leftover beers and sat down with Brian to watch the rain.

The only place with any shelter was on the veranda of one of the tiny log cabins which the campground rented out to those who couldn't be bothered with tents (or could be bothered with weather forecasts – depending on your point of view). We picked an empty one and set up a couple of chairs. Except after a few minutes the noises coming from inside the cabin suggested that it wasn't empty. In fact they indicated that it was being put to very good use indeed. Actively. Brian probably wasn't too worried, since his girlfriend was due to arrive any time, but assuming I managed to carry on, and unless I was unfortunate enough to come across a very amorous and very short-sighted bear, it was going to be sometime before I was likely to be indulging in any of that kind of extra-curricular activity and frankly I could do without being reminded of it at this stage. We moved to another cabin at a discreet distance. It rained harder. We drank more beer.

Some people might have got upset. Some people who had just driven two hundred miles expecting to pick up their boyfriend and go home. Those people might have been less than pleased to find him sitting in a pile of bikes, bags and beer cans, giggling over dirty jokes with a very disreputable looking character with a limp. They might have been even less impressed to find out they were going to have to squeeze their new friend, and his bike and all his bags into their little rental car and drive another 70 miles further south.

Anna, though, was not one of those people. She took one look at us, laughed like a drain and said "Great! We can spend a day in the hot springs and YOU [stabbing Brian in the chest with a manicured finger] can buy me dinner. Let's go!"

Either the Chrysler Neon she was driving had elastic sides, or the beer had greatly improved our packing skills, but we managed to get all of the stuff inside somehow and set off around midday.

I watched the road through the steamy back window, and thought again of the others struggling through the mud with their heads down, and I still knew I would rather be with them.

Elkhorn Hot Springs once had the misfortune of being visited by Barbara Bush when she was First Lady. At least it was a misfortune as far as most of the locals were concerned. Elkhorn was remote and very quiet and at the end of a very poor and very long dirt road and most of the people in the area liked it that way. Once Barbara'd discovered it she wanted to share it with all her friends, so she told the State Highway Department to widen the road and pave it (so they wouldn't get their Lincolns dirty) and told her husband to tell somebody else to pay for it. It's no wonder Montanans don't like Washingtonians (DC, that is). An unintentional compromise was achieved when either somebody's money, Mrs Bush's interest or Mr Bush's term ran out before the new road got more than halfway. The advantage of a rented Chrysler Neon of course is that nobody gives a shit how dirty it gets. Anna threw the little car into the mud, ruts and gravel with an absence of mechanical sympathy which seemed to be nicely complemented by an absence of any sense of mortality. She was "InvincibleWoman", and for a while there, I almost believed her, until we met a large and very hairy-arsed pickup truck doing the same thing coming the other way, when she became "EscapeByTheSkinOfMyTeethWoman". The funny thing is, as far as she was concerned they were one and the same thing. We sprayed some gravel, kicked up some mud and indulged in a minor forest clearance programme, then were on our way again with every bit as much gusto as before. I felt like my Gusto account, by comparison, was seriously overdrawn.

Elkhorn Hot Springs consisted of a large wooden lodge, with a bar, restaurant and around a dozen basic rooms on the first floor, half a dozen log cabins scattered around the woods nearby and two outdoor pools with changing rooms and a sauna. The Spa was 'natural' in the sense that it was fed with hot water which bubbled up naturally directly out of the ground nearby, otherwise it looked like any other outdoor pool. Inside the Lodge, the far wall looked like it had been rammed by a stampeding herd of Moose, Elk, Deer and Goats, the front row of which had just managed to get their heads and necks through the wall before getting stuck with a permanently surprised expression on their faces (though this may have had more to do with where the second row ended up). Climbing up onto the mantlepiece above the big log fire was a stuffed mountain lion (funny how cats always find the warmest places). In one corner was a big silver backed wolf and in the other was an 8 foot high Grizzly (which prompted some rather unpleasant comparisons with my 8 inch high can of bear repellent – try convincing Bears that size doesn't matter). In fact, there wasn't one of these animals that wasn't bigger than me, not to mention having a lot more sharp and pointy bits attached to their bodies than I did. Outdoors in the wild, they must have been magnificent creatures. Indoors, as drinking companions, their principal redeeming feature was that they were all well and truly dead. I certainly wouldn't have played cards with any of them.

I booked myself into one of the small rooms upstairs, while Brian and Anna took a cabin. The greatest luxury of being in a room rather than in my tent was not so much a question of comfort as of space. I normally slept pretty well while I was camping, but it was a real relief to be able to just tip the contents of my luggage straight out onto the floor and just spread it around a bit – so I did. I dug around in the pile for a while until I found a spare pair of shorts, then wandered off to check out the springs.

The first thing I did when I got there was to fall over. The pools were surrounded by wooden duckboards, either to stop people slipping over or to make it easier for the ducks, but in order to allow for wheelchair access someone had also built a wooden ramp coming down from the main path to the poolside. With the combination of rain, steam and spray from the pools this had become, wet, slimy and very, very slippery. In one sense I was lucky - if I'd tried to come down it in a wheelchair I'd have ended up in Idaho (though the wheelchair would probably still be wedged between the slats of the duckboards at the bottom – nice design work, fellas). It was too cold to sit around for long worrying about splinters or broken bones, so I picked myself up off my arse and staggered round to the steps into the first pool. Being midweek, and possibly influenced a little by the lashing rain, there were only three other people there, and they were all in the second, and larger of the two pools. I assumed the smaller one was the kiddies version and would therefore do me just fine. Had I been in less of a hurry I might have noticed just how much steam was coming off it, or possibly the fact that the water was actually flowing over the edge of this one into the bigger one. I might even have noticed the large pipe which fed water straight into the smaller one. Frankly I didn't care much, I wanted out of the cold and rain and away from slippery wooden things. The first thing that hit me was that the other three weren't staring at me because I'd fallen over, they were staring because it was the first time they'd seen anybody change colour so quickly, from Blue Stilton to Steak Tartare in a very short space of time indeed. It was remarkably hot. Very hot, in fact. In fact, I thought I might just climb back up the steps and sit on the edge for a minute or so while my feet got used to it, then gradually re-introduce the rest of me. It did, though, take away almost all the pain in my knee, and I secretly cursed all those people who'd been telling me for days to pack it in ice at every opportunity. I held my knee directly under the inlet pipe until I thought it was pretty well cooked, then got out to dry myself off and go in search of food.

Elkhorn must be one of the most laid back places on the planet. The staff at the lodge are almost exclusively students working through their summer vacation, but whether it was their influence, the hot springs or just the remoteness of the location, everything went at its own pace there. Eating (or drinking) at the Lodge was always a lottery as they continually ran out of one item or another. If there was a 'special' on the menu, you soon learned to get your order in fast, as they were unlikely to have more than a half dozen portions available. Nobody there though was the least bit embarrassed about this; there wasn't any ice cream because no-one had been to the store today "-why don't you have a beer instead?" Conversely, when the rest of the group showed up late the following day, some of them well past the closing time for the restaurant, someone in the kitchen volunteered to make a large pan of spaghetti Bolognese that we could heat up and serve ourselves when we were ready. Somehow it just served to make it feel all the more 'homey'.

Whatever it was, the atmosphere of the place had a very powerful effect. Possibly there was something in the water from the spa. Possibly it was just the relaxed and friendly people. Possibly one of the students got their drugs supply mixed up with the coffee. I don't know what motivated me, but I did something I'd never done before and I very sincerely hope never to repeat again. I went horseback riding. Sherlock Holmes famously descibes horses as "stupid in the middle and dangerous at either end". I have always been extremely suspicious of any form of transport that has neither brakes nor an off switch, but I suppose this was my first and last opportunity to be a cowboy for a day.

The horse rides were organised by Jenny, a very pretty local girl with long blonde hair in a pony tail, bright eyes, a flashing smile and biceps of steel. She looked as though she could pick me up and twirl me around her head like a majorette's baton if she felt like it – in fact she almost looked as though she could do it while I was still sat on the horse. She was very patient though, in a country-girl-meets-city-dudes-all-the-time sort of way, except when she got bored of me trying to hoist myself into the enormous wood and leather saddle and gave me a leg up worthy of one of the space shuttle's booster rockets. We set off in line up a narrow, rocky trail climbing steeply through the woods, heading for the top of the mountain. My horse, Dando, was probably one of the most docile creatures in the universe, but had an entirely understandable predilection to stop and eat flowers and grass at every opportunity rather than drag some bony-arsed cyclist up a mountain and back. Every time he stopped and bent his head down for a little snack I did what Jenny had told me to do which was yank upwards on the reins and dig in with my heels. I suspect he liked this about as much as you would if somebody pulled your head back and poked you in the ribs every time you put a spoon in your breakfast bowl. His neck came up, his ears flicked a couple of times and he broke into a trot to catch up with the horse in front while I clung to the pommel of the saddle with both hands, and tried to will my testicles up into my body before they were slammed flatter than a marshmallow on an anvil. After a while, I stopped worrying about trying to keep up with the others all the time (Dando probably knew the way as well as Jenny) and Dando and I reached a compromise – I let him clear out the local flora every now and again, in return he wouldn't tip me off into the nearest gully. When we finally got there, the view from the top of the mountain was panoramic, with sharp triangular peaks rising in every direction around us. I paid for my pleasure in the descent, though, when it emerged more and more clearly how badly built I am for horse riding. I seem to have very narrow hips, such that even touring style bicycle saddles feel too wide for me. Dando was built exactly like a large hairy barrel, and with each jolt on the descent, I felt like I was being pushed further and further into the splits by Olga Korbut's gymnastics instructor. No wonder cowboys are bow legged. I couldn't stand in the stirrups because of my knee, it felt as though someone was trying to wrench my legs out of my hip sockets like pulling the wing off a roast chicken, and I doubted I would ever see my testicles again. One good thing though; it was absolute bliss when we stopped. I gave Dando an affectionate pat on the neck, though I think he was too busy defoliating a small patch of pretty blue wildflowers to notice, and said goodbye forever to any thoughts I may have had of a career as a cowboy, a jockey or in the Horseguards (it wasn't too much of a wrench, trust me).

Brian and Anna had already gone home to Missoula by this point, and most of the others were enjoying the delights of a layover day lounging in the hot springs and eating and drinking even more than usual. By the time I got back from my John Wayne experience, I was very happy to join them.

The visiting population at the springs had swollen considerably during the day and was an odd mixture of people. There were what I assumed to be locals who climbed out of beaten up old pickup trucks in dirty jeans, cowboy boots and Stetsons. There were the ubiquitous RVs, though generally smaller than usual as I think the rough road may have filtered out some of the more titanically proportioned vehicles. These usually belonged to older couples, people either retired or semi-retired (though they all looked in much better nick than anyone I'd seen at the Merry Widow health mine). Finally, there was a motley collection of VW Beetles, small vans, hire cars and ex-delivery trucks from which emerged an even more motley collection of people, whose only common feature was a slightly dazed look about them. This was the overspill from the influx of something like 10,000 or more hippies, new age travellers and hangers-on to the annual Rainbow Gathering just outside the nearby town of Jackson. I tried to find out what the purpose of the gathering was, but even the people who had been there didn't seem too sure. Their main motivation seemed to be a rather touching faith that if you got enough people together in one place with like minds then something good was bound to happen. None of them looked as though they had spent too much time studying modern history, so I thought mentioning places like Nuremburg wouldn't go too far as a counter-argument.

Despite my foray into torture-by-horseback, the hot springs felt as though they had done me some good so I was moderately optimistic about rejoining the guys for the short ride to Bannack the next day. At no more than 28 miles and (by comparison with our normal ride profile) relatively flat it looked like it would be a gentle re-introduction to the trail. Despite that I deliberately decided to wait until the early risers had gone, so I wouldn't feel the need to push myself so much to keep pace and could take my time travelling on my own, or with some of the more relaxed riders in the group. By 10:30, though, I was champing at the bit. Paul still had his prosthetic cereal box attached to his left hand and Dean had only just got to the stage of laying his tent out over a nearby fence rail to dry in the sun. Going at this pace was like trying to breathe through my ears, I just couldn't do it. I jumped on my bike and set off down the hill.

Leaving camp is always the best part of the day. It felt so good to be back on the road again, to be working my way towards the day's objective and, even though I was on my own at this point, to be back as part of that group endeavour again. The quiet of the forest contrasted with the mush of gravel under fat tyres and the leg muscles felt good winding those pedals endlessly round. Once more, I found the door to that big empty room inside my head and while my body pushed onwards, I stepped in and wandered around to see what I would find. I never really found anything tangible in there, it was just a nice, quiet place to be for a while.

I broke off from my mental perambulations for the first stop of the day at Ma Barnes' Country Market. General Store, Launderette, coffee shop and International Gossip and Bullshit Exchange, it served most of the needs of the local community for a radius of about twenty miles around. When I got there the coffee and gossip were in full flow and there seemed to be a rising market in Bull. In the corner, four old boys in wool-lined tartan hunting caps and dungarees were debating the merits of the different presidential candidates with a forthrightness and candidness that we Brits rarely achieve while still sober. It was difficult to tell if they actually favoured any of them much over the others, but while I was picking up some more chocolate and sipping my coffee, I learned at least two new words which I gathered were not meant to be flattering and I filed away in my database of derogatory expressions and insults for potential recycling. Unfortunately I have no idea of the derivation and therefore couldn't begin to guess at the spelling or I'd put them down here for your own reference.

From Ma Barnes' the road followed a flat, wide valley through open grassland and a few fields to the next town, Polaris. Polaris is a town in the sense that Britain is a World Power – someone once called it that and nobody bothered to check up on it since. There was one house and a small wooden shed. The shed was the local post office. You could tell this because it had a very large wooden flagpole outside it with a stars and stripes fluttering from the top. I doubt they ever took the flag down because there probably wasn't enough room for it inside the shed. There was a very friendly lady inside it who sold me two postcards and some stamps and told me she'd been very busy today with 'lots of folks coming by on bicycles'. I did a quick mental calculation and figured there couldn't have been more than five people in front of me at most. Out here that was enough to make a crowd.

Polaris was more significant for me because it marked the point where we officially completed the first section of the Great Divide Ride. Outside the post office I folded up the first map (Roosville, Montana to Polaris, Montana: Section 1 – 528 miles) and wondered how much I would get to see of the remaining five sections. At this point my knee was mildly uncomfortable, but the road had been either flat or downhill so far and generally pretty easy going. I was far from confident.

I was still pondering my future when Evan pulled up and offered to cycle along with me for the next few miles. My thoughts had put me in a rather darker mood than before so I appreciated his offer of some company for a while, not least because I knew from my own experience it would be really hard for him to go slowly enough to keep alongside me for long.

It was clear that coinciding with the change of maps we were moving into new country at this point. The trees were mostly left behind and the landscape gradually opened up into wide rolling plains, interspaced with ranges of tall, bare hills, more desert than alpine. In fact the scenery throughout the route probably varies more with altitude than with latitude, and the contrasts are much greater and occur much faster climbing and falling than they do moving from North to South.

We stopped for a while to stare at an American Bald Eagle, perched on the top of a large wooden structure in the distance. As far as we could tell, the wooden frame, a bit like a set of rugby goalposts but with the crossbar much nearer the top, was used by local farmers to construct huge haystacks, but for the eagle it must have been a godsend in such a wide, flat treeless landscape. It gave him the chance to rest his wings while he scanned the buffet table before him for lunch. I tried not to look like a gopher.

I had thought that the next few days would probably be crunch time for me in terms of my ability to keep cycling, but it turned out to be just the next few miles and the crunch came rather more literally than anticipated. Evan and I had just left our feathered friend to his window shopping, and were pedalling up a very gentle incline when I felt something give within the joint and was rewarded with a very sharp pain from underneath the knee cap every time I bent my right leg. This was getting ridiculous. It was the sort of slope that would barely have had an asthmatic eighty year old breathing hard. My head, heart, lungs and limbs wanted to sail up and off into the horizon, but I was like a car with a big V8 engine and a broken propshaft – I was just struggling to connect the power to the road. Have you ever tried to cycle without bending your legs? It's a challenge, I can tell you. I tried standing up, I tried pedalling with one leg and then I gave up and tried drugs. I swallowed a small handful of Ibuprofen on the basis that if I couldn't feel the pain that was almost as good as it not being there, if not quite. Bannack was still a good ten to fifteen miles off, and the only way I was going to get there was by repeatedly bending my leg, so my body better get used to it. All complaints in writing and to be tossed in the pending file until further notice.

Conscious that there was nothing he could do, and not wanting to ruin his day as well, I sent Evan on ahead to enjoy the rest of his ride and cranked my way slowly, very slowly across the plain.

One reassuring thing about cycling, unlike most other human endeavours, is that there is essentially only one route to your goal. No matter how far it is, no matter how hard it may seem, so long as you keep the pedals turning you will eventually get there, as surely as night follows day. It became something of a Mantra for me over that last ten miles or so, "just keep turning the pedals – it doesn't matter how slowly, so long as they keep going round". I was still about five miles outside Bannack when Tim finally caught up with me and shadowed me for the rest of the way. Even then he had to wait for me at the top of even the slightest incline. The words "painfully slow" have never felt so appropriate.

Bannack is a ghost town turned into a State Park. It sprang into existence more or less from nothing, from Montana's first gold strike on 28th July 1862, became the territorial capital for a year then followed a long (and presumably tedious) slope to decline, struggling to keep itself going after the gold ran out, until it finally gave up and the last person left sometime during the late forties/early fifties.

The campsite was one of the prettiest we'd seen. There were a few tall shade trees, and a flat piece of grass alongside a small twisting creek with tall, rounded hills curved round and sheltering it from behind, and a stark cliff face in front, a way off on the other side of the creek. I coasted in, dropped my bike, took off my shoes and socks and went and paddled in the creek, splashing water onto my now hot and swollen knee.

After a while I climbed out and put up my tent. Then, in order to avoid having to talk to any of the others about the day's ride, I thought I'd take a short walk (or in my case, hobble) along the road to what remained of Bannack itself, now preserved as a State Monument. At the time it struck me as something of a depressing monument; a big, bleached emblem of failure, but then the thought struck me that Americans in general tend not to think of buildings in the same way that we Brits do. We have too much history and are too wrapped up in it anyway, so we have a tendency to think of buildings as very permanent structures, erected for future generations as much as our own. Things are much more temporary in the US, and a building is often only as good as the purpose it serves; they are thrown up and torn down with what seems to us something like reckless abandon. In some ways, the preservation of a place like Bannack went against this trend, and I thought there was a healthy lack of sentimentality about the place. It came, it served its purpose, it went – what's the problem?

I kicked around the wooden sidewalks for a while, and peered through dusty windows and gaps in the bleached white boards into the empty rooms, but my heart wasn't really in it.

I started back towards the camp for supper and to tell the others of my decision. It made no sense to carry on - my Great Divide Ride was over.

Below is my journal entry for that evening:

Having nursed my knee for almost a week now, bathed it regularly in the hot springs and cycled one-legged for about 95 miles, I had only covered 11 miles of relatively easy dirt road this morning before an excruciating pain shot through my leg. Given the terrain we have ahead of us I risk creating a problem not only for myself, but for the rest of the group too, if I keep trying to continue with this ride. I have no doubt I could ride further and might be able to keep up for a few more days, but it is simply not feasible to ride this sort of terrain, fully loaded on one leg only and still keep pace with the group.

It is therefore with an enormous sense of frustration, failure and regret that I have decided to leave the group. Tomorrow I will head for the nearest town, Dillon, and decide what to do from there. I still have around 30 miles to cover and a 6000 ft pass to climb to get there, but it's all on road and I have all day (or longer if necessary).

A few weeks ago, my prime frustration would have been that I had worked so hard to prepare for this trip and looked forward to it for so long. Today that is counterbalanced by the sense that I will miss the people I have met and been travelling with and will miss the shared experiences they will have on the trail.

Jack, Mark, Chris, Pierre, Sue, Paul, Brian, Richard and Dean - I wish you all the very best on your epic journey and bon voyage all the way to Mexico.

Thanks are also due to Evan, Larry, Tim and Brian of Adventure Cycling who did their level best to help keep me on the trail for as long as possible.

In the morning I would begin a new journey – the long road home.

Trust me, I'm a Doctor

It was a bitter cold night, and for one reason or another I didn't get much sleep. At one point I wriggled my head out through the tent flap and lay flat on my back staring up at the sky. I looked over toward a low set of hills, the route the others would be taking in the morning, and thought how much I would be looking forward to tackling it were it not for the failure of one little piece of bone and cartilage. Everybody had been really sympathetic; a few had tried really hard to see if there wasn't a way to keep me going somehow. Jack, bless him had even offered to haul all my gear for a while, and had really meant it. Chris, ever the more down-to-earth one of the pair we had all come to know as "the twins", stalked off to the far side of the campsite where he somehow managed to blag a can of beer from a family with their RV parked over there, walked back and tossed it straight over to me with a "Here, maybe this'll help some". Just before sunset we'd all climbed to the top of one of the small hills behind the camp and taken a series of group photos. It really was an idyllic spot.

Tim had very kindly offered to accompany me as far as Dillon, so after breakfast we packed up our gear and got ready to head off back up to the road while the others carried on into the hills towards Wyoming. We were just about to leave when Pierre walked up to me and asked in a very hesitant way if I could do him a favour. I wasn't sure what I'd be able to do for him at this stage but said I would be delighted to try, whatever it was. Pierre had a rather neat, and very expensive Norwegian tent, designed for all sorts of weather conditions. At some point during the night though, the main zip on the entrance had finally given way and now Pierre had no means of closing it securely against such nuisances as cold, rain or mosquitoes. I readily offered to lend him my tent for the remainder of the trip – it seemed unlikely that I would need it for a while now – but suggested that rather than throw his old one away, he might like to offer it to Tim who had been praising its design for days now, and might be able to post it home from Dillon and get the zip fixed at a later date. A deal was struck and with a little sadness, but glad to have been of some use I handed my tent over and set off with Tim up the hill. At least it was one less thing to have to carry.

At first I wondered whether I'd done the right thing in giving up. There was a long slow climb up to Badger pass at 6,700 feet and for the first part I managed OK. Tim spotted a coyote off to the left of the road and we watched him for a while as he shadowed us, loping along in parallel at a relaxed 10-12mph.

"Looking for sheep," said Tim, "or maybe a calf or a sick cow." I'd forgotten he was a farmboy, and therefore likely to have rather a different view of coyotes from my romanticised city perspective. But I was wrong.

"Beautiful, isn't he?" he said.

"Yes," I agreed, "I think he is."

By the time we reached the top of the pass, there was a steady dull ache throbbing through my right leg and I knew I'd made the only choice I could have made at this point. Fortunately, after a quick bite to eat and a wee, there was a long steady descent from the other side of the pass all the way down to the highway leading to Dillon. Tim had been to Dillon once before, and thought he could remember a small motel which would be reasonably clean and cheap where we could base ourselves for the night while I tried to sort out my ongoing travel arrangements. When we got there, though, we discovered that the Rainbow Gathering at nearby Jackson had just broken up and Montana was awash with new age travellers working their way home. Still, after looking around town for a bit we managed to get a room, dumped all our stuff inside and headed downtown to see what we could find. After cycling around for a while it became clear that there was rather a large scale culture clash taking place here and we saw a couple of incidents involving some fairly aggressive posturing between the travellers and locals. One old man made the mistake of blowing his car horn at a large group of people who were taking their time to cross the road in front of him and was presented with a phalanx of single-finger salutes and some very Anglo-Saxon language for his temerity. In fact, as we looked around it seemed like it was the hippies who were being more territorially assertive than the locals, perhaps because they sensed an unusual (for them) security in numbers. They knew, of course, that many aspects of their culture, beliefs and way of life were diametrically opposed to those of most small-town Montanans, but in the event, it appeared to me that they were the ones who were making more of an issue of it. Despite the fact that we were technically travellers ourselves, it was an ugly atmosphere that neither Tim nor I were very comfortable with, and we tried our best (rather unsuccessfully) to distance ourselves from the rest of the invaders in the hope of looking more or less what we were – disinterested bystanders. I had one major advantage over Tim in this, in having an English accent (albeit a very downmarket one), and I used it shamelessly to defuse some of the suspicion and wariness we encountered while we were in town. I knew I wouldn't be able to afford to fly out of Montana, not without trading in some of my few remaining body parts and organs which were still fully functional and hence had at least some residual value. Instead I was banking on either hitching a ride south in the back of someone's pickup truck or finding a Greyhound station and taking the bus. It became clear fairly quickly that hitching was not going to be an option at this point. All of the rainbow tribe's vehicles were crammed to the gunnels and nobody else was in the mood to take chances. My first piece of luck, though, was to discover that Dillon was on a more or less direct bus route to Salt Lake City. Tickets were sold at the gas station in the middle of town, and if they weren't completely full I would only have to change bus once and could be back in Salt Lake by around 6 the following evening. I pedalled to the gas station as fast as my left leg would take me. When I got there I couldn't find any sign of a ticket office, but the guy behind the counter told me the manager would be able to help me out with any information I needed and could also sell me a ticket. While this was technically true, it took much longer than I'd anticipated and it was much more difficult to decipher the information I was given since the manager appeared to be suffering from an obscure variant of Tourette's Syndrome. Tourette's is a very unfortunate condition, for those of you who haven't come across it before, described as:

"A disorder characterised by a variety of facial tics, muscular jerks, and involuntary behaviour, sometimes involving compulsive imitation of others and use of offensive language."

In this case the problem seemed to be triggered by an ill-advised attempt on the manager's behalf at multi-tasking by trying to serve me at the same time as supervise the removal of an old coke machine from the rear of the shop. To be fair, he was doing his best, but the two gentlemen removing the machine were not the most gifted of individuals, the bus timetable looked formidably complicated from my side of the counter and the two tasks were more or less mutually incompatible from the start. He rarely managed to get through more than three words to me before looking up in a panic towards another tearing or crashing sound from the Laurel and Hardy removals team and unleashing a torrent of invective regarding the slow but steady destruction of his gas station and most of its merchandise;

"Okay, now when did you – HEY! For chrissakes will you watch that over there? – Okay, yeah, tomorrow morn – no, no, no, NO NO! STOP! Will ya look whatcha doing? NO! Back it up. Yes, thank you – lemme see to Salt Lake C...JESUS! What the hell was that? Hey asshole, I told ya, go ROUND that...City, yeah there's one at 11:40, change at...SHIT! What the HELL are you doin?..." and so it went on.

Eventually I managed to buy my ticket and left as quickly as I could to try and find a cardboard box in which I could pack the bike.

The local bike store were unable to help, having thrown all their old boxes our recently, but pointed me in the direction of a department store where I asked someone, who asked somebody else, who sent me down into the basement where I found the cleaning lady who was in charge of recycling the cardboard.

At first she was unwilling to help, as she'd just packed all the boxes up ready for collection, but I smiled sweetly at her (at least internally I did – other people have told me the outside effect of what I think is smiling would curdle fresh milk, but it was the best I could do) and kept talking and eventually the British accent worked some of its magic and she invited me back into the warehouse to see if there was anything suitable. After a while we found a bike carton flattened and bundled up with a load of other cardboard and she very sweetly sliced open the plastic banding holding it all together and handed the box to me while she reached for her tape gun to bundle the rest up again. By this time she was even prepared to offer me some tape to re-assemble it. I thanked her profusely and scurried back to the motel room with my booty,

The next day Tim was due to start south again to meet up with the others and we shared breakfast at a small diner on the edge of town and talked for a while about his trip and what it meant to him. He worked 8, 9 or 10 hour days on a production line packing stuff into cardboard boxes for Amway, and had to plead, persuade and cajole his bosses to get just long enough off work to spend two weeks cycling with us on the Great Divide trail. Still he was happy to take time out to help me, and generally seemed happy with most of what life threw at him. The lady at the shed-sized post office in Polaris had given him a little booklet of religious tracts, a bible analysis for each day of the year and after we'd ordered our food he ran out to his bike to fetch it so that he could catch up on the last two days he'd missed. He read them with an openness and a genuine interest, which I found completely disarming. As with the others, I was very sorry to see him go as we headed our separate ways and wished him a good day's cycling, before turning round and heading back into town. I had to wheel the bike and trailer around to the gas station with my empty bike box resting on top of the handlebars and seat, but got there in plenty of time to disassemble everything and pack it away. No matter how many different variations I tried though I could not work out how they got a bicycle and two wheels into one of these cartons in the first place without the sides bulging like a Sumo with wind.

While I was waiting several more people drifted up to join the loosely assembled crowd of bags, boxes and passengers just outside the door, and I tuned into a conversation between some of my forthcoming travelling companions:

"Yeah man, I'm like ridin' the bus...yeah well I reckon it's where the least Heat is, y'know? 'Cause like where there's heat, there's............well...Resistance, man and where there's Resistance there's like............Friction.........Yeah."

I stifled the temptation to ask what comes after friction in order to complete my education in Physics.

Not one of the group who were travelling with me wore a watch. I assumed this was because they didn't like to feel trammelled by the demands of western timekeeping. However, since the buses DO like to be so trammelled, they all asked me independently, at fifteen-minute intervals or less, what time it was.

The bus was much more comfortable than I'd anticipated, but the journey was marred slightly by one incident. A man in his fifties or early sixties was becoming increasingly drunk at the rear of the bus and increasingly abusive in an argument with one of the hippies. It was galling to me because I didn't hold with either side and they were both filling the atmosphere on the bus with their stupidity, vitriol and aggression. The older man was clearly drunk and aggressive; the hippy on the other hand was sober but didn't have the sense to know when to let an argument lie and taunted the other childishly. Eventually the bus driver intervened and the drunk left, without argument at the next stop. I wondered what he'd do, stuck at a five building town in the middle of Utah, but he seemed less concerned about it than I was.

The woman next to me was from Los Angeles. When she heard I was from London, she unconsciously changed her style of speech entirely and started saying things like "You must forgive our unorthodox attire, we've been camping for three days". I may be wrong, and people from LA may use words like attire all the time, but it sounded very strange to me. She kept rummaging in her bag and sighing and seemed unable to find what she was looking for. When I asked her if I could help, she explained that she must have left her bottle of water behind at the gas station. Since I had plenty I offered her one of my bike bottles to drink from. She accepted gladly, then said something about she would "get me some more at the next stop". I thought this was overly polite over a little water but thought nothing of it. When we did finally stop I got off and refilled both bottles from a tap in the washroom. As we were getting back onto the bus she offered me a small plastic bottle of mineral water. "Oh no, I said, that's OK – I filled mine up from the tap." She paled visibly.

"You drink tap water?", she asked, with the subtext that not content with my own folly I had deliberately or otherwise poisoned her into the bargain. It was at least another two hours before she thawed enough to resume conversation but she was clearly expecting to erupt into projectile vomiting or violent diarrhoea at any moment and it would be all my fault when she did.

The bus got into Salt Lake a little early at 7:45. In my hurry to get out of the bus station I bolted the handlebars back on the bike with the cables all mis-routed, but decided I could live with that for the next ten miles and pedalled like fury for Jeff and Stacy's place in North Salt Lake. Unsurprisingly my knee gave no indication of problems at all, but then it was only a short climb and on tarmac. Jeff and Stacy were both away for the weekend, but when I let myself in with the spare key it was almost like coming home. Like a kid in a toyshop I went mad on the luxuries of a home-based existence. I stripped and threw everything into the washing machine, ate two bowls of cornflakes with fresh, cold milk from the fridge and emptied everything out on the floor where I could pick things up, as I wanted them without having to search through endless bags. Ah, the delights of civilisation.

The problem with being back in Salt Lake so quickly was that I now had to decide what I was going to do next. Every bicycle trip I've ever made seems to ram more highs and lows (physical, mental and in this case altitudinal) into a few weeks than I usually get in a few years at home. It would be nice to suggest that spending a week and a half in Salt Lake doing nothing was all part of a carefully worked out plan to rest, repair my worn out joints and get back on the road. The truth is a little less tidy. For nearly a week I fell into a complete mental paralysis. I had no idea what was wrong with my knee, I almost certainly couldn't afford to see a specialist in the US and I didn't know whether my travel insurance would cover me for it if I did (though on the basis that rule number one for any insurance company is 'never pay out' I think it's safe to assume not). I felt frustrated, humiliated and isolated. My mind kept rotating through all the different options, like trying on hats none of which would fit: go home, see a doctor, do a road ride, get back on the trail...I sat and read and drank and ate...and got nowhere. Having spent the last week or so agonising over leaving the group or carrying on I found myself in a similar mental trap over my next move. The only options I could think of at this point were as follows:

> a.   pack my bags, buy a plane ticket and go home with my tail between my legs;
>
> b.   try to find a doctor, or preferably a specialist in Salt Lake to see if I could get my knee fixed;
>
> c.   rest for a while, keep my original plane ticket and return date and fill in the time with a road trip.

I think I only kept the first option open in order to give my personal demons of depression something to occupy themselves with. It was probably the most sensible thing to do, it was certainly what most people I'd spoken to expected me to do, and there was a cat's chance in hell that I was actually going to do it.

Seeing a doctor also seemed a very sensible thing to do. Somehow the fact that my mother has used the word "sensible" to indicate the contrary to just about every decision I've made over the last 40 years meant that (subconsciously at least) it sounded the death knell for just about any course of action it got attached to. Worse than the mark of the Black Spot, any option whose principal recommendation was that

215

it was the "sensible thing to do" usually had the survival chances of a three-legged fawn in the Serengeti. If you added to this my innate mistrust of the medical profession (which had not been in any way diminished by the needle-under-the-kneecap experiment at Seeley Lake) it wasn't looking too promising.

Any way I looked at it, rest seemed like the best prescription at this stage, so I set about resting with a vengeance.

Once again Jeff and Stacey were a godsend. Despite the fact that they were in the midst of major upheaval themselves and trying to plan a move to San Francisco within the next few weeks, they did everything they could to support me morally and practically while I tried to reshape the course of my summer.

I filled their fridge with bagels, cream cheese and beer and exercised their Blockbusters video rental card ruthlessly. In less than 48 hours I achieved complete metamorphosis from epic traveller to complete couch potato. Inside another 48 hours I was heartily sick of it. In this respect I think I was much helped by American daytime TV., which has the same nectar-like attraction as a bag of really sticky sweets and after any continued period of exposure a similar effect on the constitution – i.e. a kind of bloated nausea. I was also getting no nearer any kind of decision as to my next move.

In an effort to break out of the rut I was in, I put aside an entire day to draw up a remedial plan of action. Going home was only an option if everything else failed. This left only two headings for action; sort out my knee and decide where I was going to go with it when it was fixed. In addressing either of these questions I had one great ally – the Internet. At this time (and for my younger readers) this was still a relatively new phenomenon and reliant on something called 'dial-up' using an actual telephone line. Since local calls were all free in the US, however, I was able to spend hours researching online, digging out crucial information that would have taken weeks or months to find out any other way.

There was no shortage of potential road trips cycling in the US, but one which I had considered in the past was the Pacific Coast Highway. Since Jeff and Stacey were in the throes of moving to San

Francisco anyway, this had all the hallmarks of a predestined choice. I pulled off several accounts of other people's journeys, concentrating on the stretch of road from Seattle in the north to San Francisco in the south. I ordered a set of maps and two guidebooks and sat down to work out how long it might take me. I looked up plane and train timetables and fares to various places in Washington state and California. Subtly and piece by piece an alternative journey started to take shape inside my head.

On the subject of knees the Internet was even more forthcoming. There was simply masses of information on every illness, injury or deformity known to man and even more on just basic anatomical and medical reference material and background. I studied diagrams of the anatomy of the human knee joint, I read volumes on its physical characteristics and mechanical operation. I dug deeper into the various types and causes of malfunction, injury and pain associated with this one unsung hero of the human skeletal team. Half a dozen people had created full size websites listing every detail of their own case histories, of injuries, treatments and surgery with no shortage of full colour images to illustrate their woes. It was bizarre, but oddly re-assuring and actually very helpful.

In my hunt to track down the source of my problem, and hence to come up with some sort of prognosis for recovery I began to narrow down the possibilities and develop a much better understanding for what appeared to be going on inside my own body.

As it appeared to me, there were two basic sources of problems with human knees – ligaments and cartilage. Ligaments are the most common source of pain. Unlike a ball-and-socket joint, such as the hip, which has a structural integrity all of its own, the only thing holding your knees together are the tough, elastic ligaments which run either side of the joint and across the back connecting the top half of your leg to the bottom. If these are subjected to an unusual amount of strain or if the muscles are unbalanced, pulling more on one side than the other they will start to rebel and alert you to signs of their maltreatment by sending waves of pain up to your brain indicating it would be a good idea to stop whatever you're doing now and sit down for a bit. The usual remedy seems to be rest, stretching and physiotherapy, though if there is a major misalignment some corrective surgery may be called for. I was fairly sure, though, that this wasn't the source of my current difficulties.

For one thing, it failed to account for the rather unpleasant grinding and clicking noises, which accompanied the processes of standing up or sitting down. For another I couldn't see how it would have caused the amount of swelling I'd discovered that first day at Seeley Lake. From everything I'd read it looked as though my problem was related to the layer of cartilage lining the inside of the patella or kneecap. This seems to serve the dual function of lubricating and cushioning the joint as the patella slides backwards and forwards over the end of your thighbone. Although there are no nerve endings in the cartilage itself, if it gets worn or becomes roughened it will cause swelling in the surrounding tissue, which will in turn switch on the pain signals. Any roughness in the surface can also account for various clicking and popping noises when you bend the joint. To cut a long story short, it looked a lot like I'd just worn the damn thing out.

I turned my attention to remedial measures. On this subject, however, the information was less forthcoming and less clear when I did find it.

Surgery was one option, which I rapidly dismissed. Entering the knee from the side it's possible to shave off the inside layer of the cartilage, smoothing out any rough parts and hopefully making the whole thing run nice and cleanly again. This was ruled out on a number of counts:

a. It would take far too long to arrange and then to recover from;

b. It would probably cost more than putting a man into orbit;

c. I didn't like that word 'hopefully' which occurred in more than one description;

d. If I was wearing out cartilage it didn't make any sense to me to cut any more out;

e.　　I'd already had all the experience I wanted of people poking sharp metal objects around underneath my kneecap.

Having given up surgery my remaining options could be divided into three categories: the simple, the cycling-related and the unscientific, anecdotal or fingers-crossed variety.

The simple solution was rest. So far, so good on that one then.

As far as cycling was concerned there were a few things I could do which would at least alleviate the problem. I raised my saddle almost as high as it would go to keep my legs straight as possible and reduce the amount they would need to bend. Shorter cranks on the pedals would also have helped, but I was unable to get these while I was in Salt Lake. I'd already given up cleated pedals, which tend to lock your feet into one position and even removed my toe clips so that my feet could slide around the top of the pedals as much as they liked. This made for much less efficient pedalling (which was bad) but meant that I could change position and angle of my feet constantly throughout the day and meant that I was much less likely to be contributing to the problem by having my feet fixed at an angle which put an unnatural pressure on one side of the knee or the other.

Everything else was in the 'unlikely to do much harm/might possibly help' category. I bought three different types of knee bandage and tried them out in rotation. There was one plain white elastic support bandage, a slightly fetishist neoprene one and a top-of-the range item with adjustable Velcro fastenings and a ring of 'healing magnets' surrounding the kneecap itself. If truth be told I was more than a little embarrassed about buying the latter since it came perilously close to the concepts of crystal healing, praying for relief or putting the hairs from a dead cat under my bed – that sort of thing. Rather more effective was the practice of dosing myself up with ibuprofen every day to keep the swelling down and alleviate the pain. I supplemented these with handfuls of glucosamine and chondroitin – basically vitamin tablets that are supposed to promote the growth of new cartilage and help with joint problems in general. And that was the full extent of my treatment and recovery programme. Short of spending several thousand dollars and who knew how many weeks trying to get to see a competent specialist though, I doubted whether there was much else to be done or that any GP could have told me any more.

Jeff and Stacey were very keen on me coming out to the west coast to join them out there for a while, but something kept holding me back from committing myself to a road ride. I went over my plans again. If I could sort out my cycling and drug-taking regime to the point where I could keep the pain under control, there might just be time to take a trip out to Colorado and try a bit of the Great Divide Ride again. I really dislike giving up on anything I've started, and one way or another I'd been planning this trip for some years now. I wanted to see the Rockies, I wanted to rejoin my friends and cycling companions and above all I wanted still to get to Mexico to prove to myself I had the mental, if not the physical capacity to carry off the challenge.

I checked my maps and itinerary again. If I moved quickly I could get a bus to Steamboat Springs, Colorado and be there a good three or four days before the rest of the group were due to arrive. I could try out my legs, at my own pace, on different sections of the trail to the north and south. If it all went horribly wrong I could disappear before they even arrived. If the offroad stuff was just too hard I might stay and have a proper farewell party with them and I'd still have time to come back and cycle most of the pacific coast road. If things went well and the drugs did the trick I could think about joining them, at least part of the way through Colorado, which was supposed to be one of the most beautiful sections of the ride and one that I was most reluctant to miss. Still unable to make up my mind, I did what I always do to resolve the situation - I went and bought a ticket. At worst I would just have to handle a little more humiliation and frustration before I came home. Humiliation I could deal with. I have had some experience in this area. Humiliation is just Nature's way of educating the stubborn.

Just before I left Salt Lake I made one more trip to the Post Office. Whatever happened I had decided I should send Mike's trailer back to him. If I was to continue with any cycling from now on I would have to be absolutely fanatical about reducing the amount of weight I was carrying. As efficient as the trailer was it weighed nearly twelve pounds on its own and that was somewhere between a third and a half of what I was prepared to carry in total. I even abandoned my two front panniers and decided I could carry everything that I really needed in a handlebar bag, two rear panniers or strapped onto the rear rack. Anything else would have to go.

The guy behind the counter at the post office had me giggling like a schoolgirl. I could have stood for hours listening to his little patter with the customers. He was one of those individuals whose wit and energy sometimes just overflows the boundaries of the routine and fills it up with fun.

1st customer: I'd like to cash this money order

Postman: Certainly...what's this number here?

Cut: Number?.........I dunno, that was printed on it.

Postie: PRINTED - really? Oh well...........Oh dear.

Cust: What?

Postie: Well, you see here where it's been signed? Invalidates it I'm afraid. It's ruined. Totally worthless. Might as well toss it in the bin...

Cust: WHAT!

Postie: Nah, just kiddin...you want that in tens or Twenties?

2nd Customer: Mind if I borrow your stapler (reaching across)?

Postie (watching him)

Cust: Hey it's broken!

Postie: Yeah, I know. Customers broke 'em all. What can you do? Say, do you have a pen I could borrow? Customers took all those too. Are you hot by the way? I'm hot. Boy, it's hot in here. Air conditioning's broken. ANYONE ELSE HOT IN HERE?

...And so it went on.

Steamboat Reunion

"Good morning ladies and gentlemen. My name's Richard and I'll be your driver today. Before we leave I'd just like to run over a few rules with you. Please note that there will be no smoking, drinking, drugs or profanity allowed on this bus at any time. At the rear of the bus is a restroom provided for your convenience. Note I say convenience rather than comfort, as you will discover if you try to use it. Gentlemen, please note that this is a unisex facility so out of consideration for the ladies I would ask you to remember the courtesies regarding the positioning of the toilet seat. If you are unsure of these please feel free to consult with me at any time. Whenever you are moving in the aisle please be sure to hold onto the grab rail above you or one of the seat backs. Please remember this bus will be travelling at speeds of up to 65 mph and, in the event of an emergency will stop very quickly. If you are not holding onto something you will continue to travel at 65 mph until you reach the front of the bus at which point two things will happen. One, you will know what a bug feels like when it hits the windshield and Two, you will scare the hell out of me. Thank you for your co-operation."

I was beginning to like Greyhound buses. They were a source of all sorts of unanticipated amusement, and the bus driver from Salt Lake to Steamboat Springs was not the least of these. As we passed through Dinosaur valley in northeastern Utah he very kindly slowed to point out the life-sized concrete Brontosaurus off to our left and the giant "Ty-ranner-saurus Rex" up ahead painted a rather fetching shade of pink.

We pulled into Steamboat Springs in the late afternoon, and the bus dropped me at a Pizza restaurant on the far side of town. Rather than cycle straight out to the campground I thought I would take the easy option and get to know the town a little first. The first Motel I stopped at had a gymnasium, sauna, Jacuzzi, two bars and cable TV and cost $110 a night. The second one had a coke machine and cost $40 a night. Even though I don't drink coke it was a fairly easy decision.

Steamboat was a very pleasant town, even if evidently something of a tourist trap. At least the mountains and the greenery made a pleasant change from the seemingly endless desert we had crossed to get here. I think I would not enjoy cycling across the states much if I were going coast-to-coast. There is an awful lot of nothing in the middle, and at least the Rockies offer a more varied diet of scenery.

I found an excellent coffee shop at the back of the local bookstore and sat sipping a large espresso and reading a copy of 'Steamboat Today'. I gave up on the news pages fairly quickly in case I should accidentally atrophy my brain and scanned idly through the classifieds instead. I was especially pleased to find an ad for "The Merchant of Sandwich", local caterers who offered "Burgers, Brats and Dogs – Grilled to order". This is the sort of place that should exist in every town. The only issue I had was how to get the Brats and Dogs into the shop in the first place, until it occurred to me that this was maybe the cunning genius of making it a burger joint too.

The campground was next to the river, a few miles west of town. It was clean and comfortable but very busy and I decided to head out onto the trail as soon as possible. I was, though, increasingly nervous about trying to cycle again. Although there was no pain at this stage my left knee had now started to pop audibly. The trouble with Paranoia is that you don't know you weren't being paranoid until it's too late.

Heading out of Steamboat Springs the road climbed fairly steeply up through a calendar picture of a valley with a small stream beside the road, big red Dutch barns everywhere and lots of horses outside in the paddocks. The first hamlet I passed through was the intriguingly named Mad Creek. My experience of American culture thus far being that it tended very much towards the literal I thought better of stopping to fill up my water bottle here and pressed on up the valley.

Next stop was Clark, which proudly advertised itself as having an elevation of 7,700 feet and population unknown. Now this was just plain lazy, as there can't have been more than 50 people living within a ten mile radius so it wouldn't have taken that much effort to count them. The Clark Store had put up several billboards along the road warning you of its imminent arrival and the various retail delights, which it had on offer. These included: Food, Coffee, Hats, Boots and Home-Bred Worms. I wondered whether these were simply worms who had been trained not to pooh on your carpet or whether there was some other virtue in them I was missing. What exact benefit the homebred variety might have over their cousins from the Big Worm Factory was a mystery to me, but then I never had the patience to be a fisherman (nor the inclination to keep them as pets either). I stopped for a roll and coffee but decided to skip the Vermicelli.

From Clark the road turned to dirt and started climbing much more steeply, switching up and down like a roller coaster until I finally crested the summit and wound my way down to Steamboat Lake (some 30 miles north of Steamboat Springs). Here, unfortunately, I had to pick up the tab for my first miscalculation. This is evidently a very popular part of the country at weekends. It was now the weekend, and there was a sign outside the campsite indicating that it was full. Since my tent took up all of 12 square feet and this place looked to be around 40 acres, I remained reasonably optimistic that good sense and pity might prevail and someone would direct me to a far corner of the site where I could kick back and relax and above all not push my luck by cycling any further on my first day back. Unfortunately optimism is notoriously unreliable at keeping you warm at night, and the woman at the entrance booth to the campsite would have none of it. This was beginning to piss me off. It wasn't as though I could jump back into my monster truck and drive another 60 miles to the next town. It was late, I was tired, my knee had started creaking and there was shitloads of space there. But none for me. There was another campsite around six miles up the road, but she didn't know if they had any space and no, I couldn't use her phone. I wished her an early death and re-incarnation as a guard on the Tokyo subway where she might learn something about squeezing people in. The six miles was of course nearer nine and included going up the road, doubling back on myself and climbing (and then descending) a small mountain in between. Still the site looked OK and there appeared to be space. Since it was a forestry service site there should normally have been a camp host who lives in a trailer on site. There was non-one in the trailer, but some boys who were sitting outside pointed me to a large notice board near the entrance. I carefully followed the instructions on the board which told me how to pay for my site if there was no-one around, put a $10 bill in one of the envelopes provided, wrote my name and site number on it and posted it into the little box to one side.

I had just got my tent set up and unpacked everything and was starting to feel more comfortable with life when a large truck pulled up and a young couple stepped out, looking at me as though I were a stain on their carpet. They were accompanied by a roundish man in a pale green uniform, probably in his mid fifties who turned out to be the camp host.

"You have to move."

Now this sort of approach could be considered provocation by people with the patience of Mother Theresa, in whose ranks I would never contemplate myself, but I felt that at this stage it was better to remain relatively calm and polite when I asked why.

"This spot is reserved", pointing to a small stained note the size of a matchbox tacked to one of the tree trunks.

Okay, I missed the little note when I pulled in, I was probably tired. Where should I move to exactly?

Nowhere. The camp is full.

I was now a little less calm. I paid for a site, I put my $10 in the envelope and posted it like a good citizen.

225

"You shouldn't have done that."

I was just on the verge of pointing out that in this case the six foot sign by the entrance is missing the words "DO NOT" in several key strategic places, as in "DO NOT fill out one of the envelopes provided", "DO NOT put $10 in it" etc., and what could have become a very entertaining philosophical and semantic debate was diverted by the arrival of a tall woman in cut-off jeans and a T-shirt carrying a large Martini in her left hand. She was Brenda and was camped on the site next to mine. She had overheard our conversation and had come over to see what the fuss was about. She had also noticed, alone of the other people involved that I was on a bicycle and had only a very small tent. "Our site's got plenty of space – why don't you just move your tent a little this way and you can share with us?"

This was so sensible it baffled everybody for a moment, including me. Before the camp host could respond I'd already pulled up my tent pegs and moved my bike over.

Brenda and Roman, her partner, were welcoming and friendly and took away the sour taste of the previous encounter like a cool glass of water after a long hot day. In fact they had something even better than a cool glass of water, which was a long, stiff, dry Martini. They insisted on sharing their supper with me and were already making plans to get me breakfast before I got under way the following day.

Once his problem had gone away, even Cecil (pronounced "See-Sill") the camp host tried to be ingratiating, but I got my own back by turning down flat his invitation to attend the forestry service 'interpretation' on 'blowdown' (whatever that was). This may well have been fascinating stuff, and I might have been cutting my nose off to spite my face, but then again "sod him", I thought, and "sod him again".

One thing I did notice before I went to bed. There were an awful lot of claw marks on the trees in this area. I hoped the young couple who'd moved onto my site had lots of nice smelly food inside their tent. And yes, I know it wasn't really my site, and they were probably (possibly?) very nice people too. As far as I was concerned, though, Roman and Brenda were wearing the white hats which meant that the other two got to wear the black hats. It kept life simpler that way.

I debated quite a long time where to head to next. Although I could have continued north and made the next town, Savery, fairly easily, it was a long climb back up from there and I might not be so lucky again with a campsite on my way back. I could have camped wild in the woods, but I hadn't seen many suitable places up to that point and frankly I didn't want to push my luck. In the end I decided to head up to Columbine which was the crest of the climb for this particular section, then turn around and head back to Steamboat Springs via an alternative route. Once back in Steamboat I could head out for a series of one or two day rides or check out some interesting looking single track up around the ski slopes without the pleasure of hauling an extra 30 or 40 pounds of luggage at the same time. This would give me another chance of testing whether all of my body parts were up to the job ahead of them before re-joining the group the following Friday.

It didn't take me too long to reach Columbine, and I nearly passed straight through it since it appeared to consist of two wooden huts and a fenced in corral. Hopes of a decent cup of coffee evaporated pretty quickly and I turned around to follow the highway back down to Steamboat. The descent was fairly unexceptional apart from the fact that I smashed my previous downhill record with a 52 mph run down the side of the mountain.

Back at the KOA (Kampgrounds of America [sic]), things were a little quieter than when I'd left, but there was always some form of entertainment going on. In this case there was a father and son double act struggling to put up a tent which looked as though it should be big enough to house the population of Belize. I may have been wrong, but I wasn't convinced that they'd ever done this before. Once clue was that the father was banging in the tent pegs with a claw hammer, and, treating them as though they were nails holding his house together (understandable analogy I suppose) he didn't stop banging them until the tops were completely flush with the ground. A little later he crawled underneath the flysheet, then stood up inside it, his arms waving like some sort of mad green ghost. I couldn't see the son, but the father was clearly panicking:

"Don't do that. DON'T DO THAT...YOU'RE STILL DOING IT!"

Whatever it was can't have been fatal as the tent went up anyway. Once up it was a very strange cruciform shape, and despite the fact that it covered an enormous ground area didn't appear to have space to fit more than one normal human being lengthwise in any direction. This didn't look as though it would be too much of a problem though since both father and son were almost exactly cuboid in shape. I recalled an old science fiction film where the heroes were trying to reconstruct the physiology of a lost race of aliens from just the size and shape of the doorways in their abandoned city. They could probably have done a fairly good job from just this tent.

The problem with these large campsites is that they turn into a complete madhouse at weekends and during the holidays as people take the opportunity to inflict their children on somebody else for a change and the kids take the opportunity to shed any remaining behavioural constraints they may have been under at home. As a result there is generally not much sleep to be had and generally the best thing you can do is to get out as quickly as you can in the morning and head for the nearest point of civilisation for coffee and relative quiet.

Back in the bookstore-cum-café I selected a couple of large pastries and ordered a stiff double espresso. The young girl behind the counter had bright red dreadlocks and a pleasant gap-toothed smile.

"Say – are you from England?"

"Yes, that's right, London."

" Oh London, in the midlands, near Melton Mowbray!"

"Ye-es, more or less."

About the only thing I can remember about Melton Mowbray is the never-forgotten taste of quite disgusting pork pies which used to be made there and shipped all over the country to be foisted on an unsuspecting, and largely uncaring public through chains of greasy spoon cafes, newsagents and petrol stations everywhere. Maybe this poor girl was unfortunate enough to eat one once and it turned her head. Maybe she saw them on the shelves in every newsagents in London. Maybe too much caffeine will fry your brains. Whatever, I took my coffee and Danish and sat down to the Steamboat classifieds.

In one of the local bike shops I bought a map showing most of the single track mountain bike trails in the hills around the ski slopes and decided to try the Spring Creek Trail which started just on the outskirts of town. It was a lovely piece of forest track that wound its way fairly steeply up a narrow canyon, criss-crossing the stream at the bottom 14 or 15 times. It was moderately tough, and I was frequently struggling for grip with semi-slick tyres among the loose dust and rocks, but I was really enjoying myself. There were only a few other bikes on the trail, and all of them coming the other way. One woman, either incredibly rude or incredibly out of control came straight at me at around 30 mph on a very narrow hill section. I took the gentlemanly option of putting myself in the bushes out of her way, but blessed her in a very un-gentlemanly way once she was past. It was only once I reached the top and started looking for the road back into town that I read the note on my map which said:

"Many riders prefer to do this trail in reverse, climbing up the buffalo pass road, then descending on the glorious single track through the canyon".

Well many riders might, but I rather enjoyed doing it my way. Coming down I ended up racing the local fire tender, overtaking rather precariously when they braked for corners, then being overtaken again as they built up speed on the straights. It maybe wasn't the most sensible thing to do, the roads were covered in loose sand and gravel and I had to dab with my feet a few times to keep upright, but I was having a great day out on my bike, and I wasn't sure how many more of those I was going to get.

On the outskirts of town I picked up yet another example for my collection of classic American signs:

"Howard Orvis – Family Dentist / Oral Rehabilitation".

'Family dentist' I could understand, since in the US the word 'family' is universally associated with good and trustworthy, a bit like the word 'natural' – nobody much is going to object to that. I was not at all convinced, though, at the idea of having my mouth 'rehabilitated'. Was there a suggestion there that I had criminally irresponsible teeth? Is plaque really that antisocial? How about "Loose gums cost lives," as a slogan?

I stopped at one of the outdoor gear shops to see if I could get a small gas powered camping stove, just to make myself coffee in the mornings. I had thought that I could live without until either I rejoined the main group or I headed back, but the trauma of finding absolutely nothing at Columbine and going two straight days without caffeine was still burned in my memory. The guy who owned the store was very friendly but unable to help. He told me he used to be a ski instructor and guide but was getting a bit old for that now so he'd decided to open his own store instead. His shop was a little way off the main street, though, and he was finding it hard going. He had a 1950s single cylinder BSA motorbike that he rode to work in the summer and he just loved talking to customers. I tried several times to buy something from him, but unfortunately he never seemed to have in stock any of the stuff that I needed. Every time I went in though, he recognised me, gave me a big toothy grin and told me once again how much he loved that BSA.

Next day I took another excursion, following the trail south this time. The road followed the Yampa River (I love that name!) out of Steamboat and was relatively flat for the first ten miles. Just as I was passing a small ranch a fox ran across the road in front of me. He was young, but quite big, and his coat was a strange blonde colour. He was either very accustomed to people or very cheeky as he stood and stared directly at me for some time through wicked-looking small black eyes.

At the next turning I discovered a minor obstacle. There was a huge barrier across the road with a sign "ROAD CLOSED – UNDER HEAVY CONSTRUCTION". I didn't have to think too hard about this one, since there are very few places you can't get through with a mountain bike and in any case there was only going to be one way to find out if this was one of them. The next four miles were pretty badly churned up and there were quite a few bulldozers and heavy construction traffic around, but they didn't seem to mind me as I threaded my way through them. The bike was certainly much easier to manoeuvre through the rough stuff like this with my much lightened load but it still took me a fair while to bump, drag, hoist and push my way through the mud and ruts. My efforts, though, were repaid in spades once I'd got past the construction zone, and the next ten miles were a sheer delight. A narrow trail at first wound its way up a deep canyon alongside the river shaded by stands of pine and aspen. At the top of the canyon the trail cut across the top of a narrow, but very high concrete dam then followed a red cinder path swooping, twisting and climbing along the shoreline of the Stagecoach Reservoir. A large deer stood just off the trail, maybe 15 feet into the woods, and we played a quick game of 'now you see me – now you don't', as we both bobbed our heads around the trees to get a better look at each other. I felt more alive than I had done in years and I knew again why I had tried so hard to come back to this. Out in the wild it quickly becomes clear to anyone with any sense what a poor sort of animal we are. A large brain and opposable thumbs may be pretty useful when it comes to opening car doors (though, come to think of it even there Bears manage very nicely without, and once they open a door it stays open believe me), but when it comes to getting by in the wilderness we're pretty slow, weak and frail. I'd certainly learnt something about human frailty. Still, for five minutes there, winging my way along that path, blasting down one slope with just enough momentum to scrabble up the next, flying round corners throwing dust and gravel up in my wake I knew what it was like to be sleek and fast, flying through the woods, feeling the power in my own legs throwing me forwards, up and sideways, and it felt like real freedom to me.

Gravity, though, always gets its own back. After leaving the reservoir I turned onto a forest road which climbed steadily and dustily up into the mountains. Dropping down into low gear I settled into a long steady rhythm and slowly ground my way uphill. Perversely, I quite enjoy climbing on a bicycle, but it is a very different sort of satisfaction from that pleasure gained from sheer speed. Every turn of the pedals is one step closer to overcoming a physical obstacle, a barrier to my further progress. All I have to do is slip down a gear or two, keep pushing, pushing and pushing and I know that I can grind even a mountain down to size. Still, grind is very much the appropriate word, and this type of contrast is exactly what a day spent cycling in the mountains is all about. After a while the road levelled out onto a broad plateau and spent a while skirting the edge of a large alpine meadow. The climb was starting to take its toll and I thought about stopping there for the night. I slipped off the road and followed what looked like a promising path down to a small clearing next to a stream. The remains of a campfire told me that someone else had thought this was a good spot to stop before me. Looking around though, I wasn't so sure. Bears quite like to follow streams when they're on the move as the going is a lot easier than fighting their way through the woods. They have also discovered that lazy humans tend to leave food scraps lying around campsites so they tend to associate these places with snack shops. I checked my watch. It was still relatively early, and only another 8 or 9 miles to the campsite at Lynx Pass, my original destination. For the moment there was just a dull throb coming from my right knee – the acute pains had yet to return and I decided I had spent enough time on my own, it would be nice to have some company around for the evening. I turned back to the road and carried on. At nearly 9,000 feet Lynx Pass represented a fair climb for the day, but the road was reasonably good, I stopped regularly and just under two hours later I crested the pass and rolled down the other side and straight into the forestry service campsite. I talked briefly with the camp host, a friendly grey-bearded man with a checked shirt stretched to its limit, the fabric making little parentheses between buttons as it tried manfully to cover up a blue undershirt on a swollen paunch. He apologised for the noise coming from his generator, and said he would turn it off soon, "the wife wants to run the dishwasher". I thought briefly about towing a dishwasher and a generator up a 9,000 ft pass behind a bicycle and realised what insanities can be made to seem quite normal

232

through the luxury of an internal combustion engine. I drew some ice cold water from a rusty hand-pump up on the hill, contorting myself to try to hold a plastic water carrier under the outlet while keeping the large iron handle going fast enough to maintain the water flow, took out my new little gas stove and boiled up some rice and threw in the contents of a small tin of tuna. Another entry from my journal just about sums up my feelings at the time:

As I set my tent up I can see clouds building and now thunder is crashing and rolling almost continuously around the pass. Good timing, I think. There is a giant yellow beetle buzzing around making a noise like an electrical short and one of the tiny green humming birds, hardly bigger than the beetle, with an iridescent red throat is bored with dive bombing me and hovers just inside the old rusted barbecue. The only nuisances besides the mosquitoes are the chipmunks that run around chuntering in high-pitched squeaks trying to steal food. What an ace day.

In the night coyotes sang me to sleep.

As I left the campsite the Chipmunks were clearly getting very pissed off with me, chirruping their displeasure like a record played too fast as I scared them from the side of the road back into the grass. From my point of view this was a Good Thing. The little buggers had moved way out of the cute zone and well into the Bloody Pest category.

From Lynx Pass I dropped down to the highway, then followed a long curving route back to Steamboat Springs via Yampa. Although a bit longer than the way out it was all on tarmac and mostly downhill so represented a fairly easy day. In the morning I picked up yet another example for my sign collection:

"FINGER ROCK REARING UNIT"

I rather liked the idea of someone looking after young rocks, nurturing them until, as little boulders they're ready to roll out into the world. Maybe the ones here were special long pointy ones, designed to be made into signposts (I couldn't think what else you could use finger rocks for) to point people on their way. Cycling a long way on a flat road will do this sort of thing to you.

You might think that a cyclist would have no interest in petrol retailers, but until you have spent time in a country as big and as empty as this it's difficult to understand the real significance of the gas stations out there. More than the post office or even the bar (though they occasionally double up as these) the gas station represents the social hub for a community from miles around. It's the one place everybody, even the most anti-social hermit, has to go to at least once in a while and the food stores or coffee shops attached to them are always great places to take the social temperature.

At Yampa I pulled into the truck stop for coffee and a sandwich and turned the dial on my mental radio to tune in and out of the conversations around me.

Two couples on holiday together from New York were laughing and joking with each other and making some less than flattering observations on culture in the West (west of the US that is) just loudly enough to create a little isolation zone around their table.

In the corner the official BS table was giving it loud, a large and rather overweight deputy from the sheriff's department in the chair. People came and went like players in a cheap poker game, but the coffee and the BullShit kept flowing.

At another table a young woman with more lines on her face than she looked like she deserved tried to keep her small daughter quiet while she counted out the money for their lunch. Then she snapped and slapped the child hard on her leg and I saw the process of passing those lines on had already begun. If you didn't feel like going out to see America, you could always set yourself up in the corner at a place like this and the people side of it at least would pretty much come and see you. I paid my bill and moved on.

On the way back through Steamboat I saw a group of kids floating down the river in inner tubes. After all the sweat and dust of cycling up mountains it looked like a very attractive way to travel indeed. I stopped off at my favourite outdoor shop just in time to see my friend there working up a pretty major sweat of his own trying to kick start his old BSA into life. He gave me another toothy grin:

"Sometimes she just don't like to be coerced, y'know?"

There are those who don't believe you can have a relationship with a machine, but I suspect that they are either lacking in imagination or just using the wrong machines. I gave him a push down the road and eventually the bike fired a couple of times, hesitated, fired again, then picked up on the throttle. He waved to me as he accelerated down the road, then slowed sharply, did a u-turn, drove back up the road to the shop, pulled up and after a few seconds blipping the throttle turned the engine off. As I collected my bike I must have had a slightly puzzled look on my face because he smiled and said:

"Just wanted to make sure she was OK."

When I checked into the KOA I found out that Evan had made a reservation for the Adventure Cycling crew for the following night, two days earlier than scheduled so I decided to cycle out and meet them on the road the next morning.

The obvious place to meet them was the Clark store. The place was like a little Oasis with coffee, cakes and cold drinks. There was no way on this planet they were going to pass this place by so I knew I was safe waiting for them there.

When I got there I parked my bike outside with its distinctive yellow reflective triangle hanging form the saddle, got myself a coffee and cake and settled down in a chair on the veranda to wait for the first passers-by to be reeled in like fish on a line. Like most fishermen though I didn't quite get what I expected. I didn't recognise anybody from the first cyclists who arrived – a husband and wife, followed a little later by a group of five older men. It seemed the Great Divide Ride was starting to get quite busy at this point. The husband and wife team were cycling the whole route and had passed my group further back up the trail. The older men were doing the ride one section at a time, coming back at the beginning of the summer to pick up where they left off the previous year. Despite the physical rigours of the route I think the average age for anyone riding this trail must have been around 50.

When the team finally started to drift in around 10:30 there was much back-slapping and shaking of hands and I realised how much I'd enjoyed their company over the first month. Although I'd discussed the option of rejoining the tour with the Adventure Cycling office in Missoula, nobody in the group knew anything of my plans since we'd parted at Bannock back in Montana. Consequently they were more than a little surprised to run into me in the middle of Colorado nearly six hundred miles later. We caught up on the highlights of the intervening weeks over more coffee and cakes and I realised how lean and fit they'd become after so much time on the road and I started to feel slow and flabby by comparison. Most of them wanted to know if this meant I was back on the trail now, but I had to admit I didn't really know if I was up to it or not. I'd stick with them for the next couple of days, but after that it'd be a case of taking things one day at a time and see how things progressed. I was especially pleased to see Mark, Jack, Chris, Pierre and Sue again. I think Pierre was just glad of the opportunity to slip back into speaking French again, even if I did follow only around half of what he was saying. Wyoming had been quite an adventure, with gale force winds threatening to blow the tents away and stunning views of the Grand Teton Mountains. I was very sorry to have missed it, and watching videos in Stacey's house in Salt Lake City made a rather poor comparison in the life-enhancing-experience stakes. Still, I was back, for the time being at least, Colorado promised some of the best scenery yet, and from the little I'd already seen I doubted anyone would be disappointed with the riding yet to come.

Riding back from Clark to the KOA at Steamboat on an unloaded bike I was pushed to keep up with the others pulling fully loaded trailers, and I knew I would have to work hard to get fit again as quickly as possible if I was going to be able to keep up with them over the next few days. Which was why, of course, I spent the next two days eating too much, drinking and partying till late. We had a Margarita fest in one of the Mexican restaurants, went to see an appalling movie (since it was the only one on show – the X-men of all things) and took the opportunity of going to see the Rodeo while it was in town. Although it was interesting in a 'well now I've seen a Rodeo' fashion, I think small town rodeos probably have all the panache of the local amateur dramatic production of Puss in Boots. Rodeo is also an ideal TV sport with around 20 seconds of action followed by 20 minutes of bluster. Without the benefit of professionally produced commercials though, we were treated to what seemed like a particularly long and pointless lifetime of rodeo clowns performing 'magic tricks' that Tommy Cooper would have been ashamed of and telling jokes that Bob Monkhouse might've rejected (although you never know...). For those of you who may not be familiar with old-time British comedians, trust me, my sides were not aching with laughter. Still, picking up a full-grown calf and throwing it on its side is pretty impressive all the same. Personally I might have used a forklift, but call me a philistine. There were actually commercials during the show, but these were more of the nature of the announcer saying things like; "By the way, Folks, buy your hats at FM Light & Sons. They're really very good." Well, I was sold. One thing which they were very good at was involving the whole family in the show, and there were lots of events and activities specifically for children. If you were an animal rights activist (and you'd be in a very small minority in Colorado if you were) you might not enjoy the spectacle of 40-odd small children chasing a piglet around a dusty stadium, but you had to be there to appreciate its finer moments, trust me. It reminded me of a particularly mad chase scene from a Scooby-Do cartoon, everybody changing directions and running with their arms outstretched in front of them in that way that only small children and cartoon characters know how. Every now and again the piglet would double back and charge into the following pack, and one small toddler would somersault into the air above the heads of their friends as the pig rammed into their shins and flipped them back over his shoulder with surprising agility. Maybe the NSPCC would have been more upset than the RSPCA – whatever, that piglet was the star of the show for me. It made more sense to see the lassoing and horse riding events out here at least. In a small town Rodeo like this it seemed likely that at least some of the young men performing out there in the arena would be going back to day jobs on Monday where they might well end up using the same skills for real out on the range. Although I had to respect their courage and skill, we were almost close enough to hear the crunch of bones as they hit the ground and I could feel the bruises and the stiffness as they limped out of the stadium. Only the winners took anything other than bruises away from a show like this one, and even then it would be a very few dollars and a thin slice of glory for what seemed like a lot of risk and pain.

Although we set off together on the road to Lynx pass again, I had to stop on the steeper section and let the others go ahead. When I got to the campsite the others rather enjoyed telling me how the camp host had entertained them with the story of a British cyclist who had been there two days before chasing the chipmunks around his tent. With Mark to help pump this time I treated myself to a very invigorating wash under the old hand pump. If anything the water felt even colder than before. It might well have been snowmelt from the higher peaks, but it was more snow than melt by the time it reached this point.

The next day, en route to Kremmling, we would have to cross the Colorado River and it would be one of the biggest climbing days of the tour.

Colorado highs and lows

Mark and I were first out of camp again, getting back into the old routine, and on the road by 7am. The first descent was cold, really cold, and I was not looking forward to the first river crossing, since I already had a good idea just how fresh the water would be. We followed the river through another alpine meadow for a while and the water looked reassuringly low until just below the ford where an obliging Beaver had decided to erect his dam creating a good two extra feet of river. I looked at the dam, and looked at Mark and I KNEW he was wondering just how much it would take to give Mr Beaver a little construction project for the summer and let some of that water run off to where it really wanted to be – i.e. further down the hill (I certainly was). Before embarking on any wildlife relocation exercises though, we decided to scout out the river a little upstream and before long found a place that we thought looked easily walkable. We tossed a few big rocks in to improve things a bit, which had the net effect of damming the flow and creating more depth. You live and learn, even at our age. I don't know what Beavers sound like when they snigger, but I am sure there was one sniggering somewhere. Anyway, we got across without too much drama and without getting too wet.

While we were sorting our stuff out on the other side Richard arrived, took one look at the river and cycled straight through it. When I say 'through' however, I mean through as in 'through the water', but not I am afraid as in 'through to the other side'. He got about three quarters of the way across before his front wheel hit a big rock and he slammed to a halt, put both feet down, threw his head back and screamed as both boots filled instantly with icy water. In Richard's case this sort of scream was always the one that precedes hysterical laughter, so we weren't too worried about him, but we gave him a hand pulling his bike out and held it while he wrung out his socks all the same. Shortly afterwards Jack and Chris arrived and asked from the other bank if it was rideable. We told them almost truthfully that Richard had ridden it (he had his boots back on by this point), but either we were too careful with our semantics or they'd been around too long to fall for that sort of thing and they carefully picked their way through where Mark and I had thrown the rocks in.

As entertaining as this sort of thing was, we had a few miles to cover and a lot of hills between us and our destination so we moved off fairly quickly rather than wait and see how anyone else fared.

The next few miles were a roller coaster ride of half mile to mile long hills and valleys. The fact that I had to go slowly uphill in order to conserve my knees had no effect whatsoever on my downhill speed, to the extent that I became a little overenthusiastic at one point. While I was in Salt Lake I'd switched to semi-slick tyres which had very little tread on them by comparison with normal mountain bike tyres. This had one very big plus in that it significantly reduce rolling resistance and meant I didn't have to push as hard as the others to go at the same speed on the flat. It also had an occasional very big minus in that it gave very little grip in loose conditions and especially through fast corners. If I hit any loose sand or gravel I might as well have been riding on marbles. Although Mark was a very strong rider he tended to be more cautious going downhill. On the other hand, Richard liked to go hell-for-leather and had nice big knobbly tyres to help him stick to it. Thus it was that I left Mark near the top of one particularly steep incline and, following Richard at full blast I came round a sharp bend at something like 30mph to find hard packed dirt had turned to loose pebbles and gravel. The bike fishtailed instantly one way, I counter steered, the bike fishtailed the other way,

240

I put both feet down and prayed and the bike finally came to a halt about two feet from the edge. I thought I might reconsider using my brakes on the downhills every now and again.

Cresting the rise overlooking the Colorado River valley was an unforgettable experience. Deep below the narrow river twisted and turned, followed by the railroad along its length. The valley meandered into the distance in either direction and on the far side the red and sable hills rose steeply in a mirror image of those on which we were standing. The descent was fast and slippery and most of my good resolutions went out of the window fairly quickly.

We had been hoping for a store or a café near the bridge at the bottom, but were roundly disappointed, so Mark and I settled down on the riverbank to eat our sandwiches instead.

The downside of having a fast, free-rolling descent into something like the Colorado River valley is that unless you happen to have brought along your handy pocket inflatable whitewater raft there is only one way out again and that is to climb back up the other side. As we chewed our sandwiches we looked across the river at the hillside we had just come down, then craned our necks around to look at the mountain behind us and couldn't even see the top. The altimeter in my watch showed we'd just dropped something over two and a half thousand feet in the last three quarters of an hour. It was going to take a lot longer than that to get it all back again.

We followed the river for a couple of miles then turned right at 90 degrees to it and immediately began climbing. There would be a couple of climbs which were longer than this one during the rest of the ride, and at least one which was considerably tougher, but few would be more memorable than the next 20 miles. Even now I feel like I can remember every pedal stroke as we switchbacked up and across the side of the valley. Mark pulled away fairly quickly, then I was overtaken by Jack and Chris, then Richard, Sue and finally Pierre. I hung onto Pierre's tail for a while, since he was riding a little slower than the others, but inevitably lost him when I paused for a breather since the only thing Pierre ever stopped for was to take photographs. I came around one corner and looked up to see the others waving to me from a viewing point ahead and high above the river, but by the time I got there only Pierre was left and he was just about to move on. I stopped to enjoy the view anyway. Apart from the stunning perspective along the valley below I was just happy to be there. Given my condition at the time, this must have been one of the biggest challenges of my cycling career. I felt embarrassed and awkward to be going so slowly, but I was still moving and I was still climbing and I had every intention of reaching the top and carrying on when I got to the other side. After a long time, a very long time the incline started to level off a little, but the road still kept climbing, albeit more gently for another couple of miles. Finally I felt the pressure easing on my legs a little and I started to pick up a little speed as the road almost imperceptibly began to slope forward a little. Two minutes later I turned a corner and was slapped in the face by a strong headwind and had to pedal most of the way downhill to keep up any momentum at all.

Mark, Sue, Pierre and Richard had stopped under a tree just before the road joined the main highway into Kremmling and we cycled into town together and elated by the day's awesome ride.

The campground at Kremmling was probably the smallest, noisiest and buggiest we had encountered. A small, fenced-in piece of dirt behind the public toilets and just off the main square, about the only thing it had to recommend it was a steel barbecue which I decided to make the most of by cooking barbecued chicken for supper with corn on the cob for the vegetarians. The tents were wedged in like Lego bricks in a box and for some reason the place was swarming with mosquitoes. At least three people took one look at the accommodation and made straight for the nearest motel – probably the smartest move of the trip. Richard and I went shopping for supper while most of the others made a beeline for the town's one coffee shop and ice cream parlour and proceeded to denude its shelves and freezers of just about every edible item they possessed. This was probably a stroke of luck for me, since barbecuing enough chicken for eleven hungry people on one small grill was proving just a little ambitious. By eating in shifts we managed to fill most people with something hot and I quickly lay out all of the breakfast things ready for a quick getaway in the morning before diving into my tent to get away from the mossies and try to get some rest.

If I'd had a gun that night I would be writing this on death row now instead of a comfortable house in north London. At first there was a seemingly endless procession of cars and pickups who drove right up to the fence, lights full on, banged their car doors loudly, banged the doors to the public toilets loudly, then came back and banged their car doors again in the only way they knew how, which was, unsurprisingly, loudly. Did none of these people have toilets in their own homes? Not even the gents toilets on Clapham Common could compete on this place for midnight traffic. Once that had died down somebody decided the early hours of the morning were the best time to take their dirt-track racer out and see if they could improve on their lap-times around the main square. I sincerely hope they did improve their times because they were certainly practising hard enough. Probably the absence of any recognised exhaust system helped gain that extra half-second, I sure do hope so. If there is ever a 3am Town Square race near you I suggest you put your money on the man with the big 'K' on his back for 'Kremmling' because dedication like that is going to be hard to beat. Even he had to get some rest at some point though, or maybe who just ran out of petrol – who cared so long as it stopped. Before I could even roll over in my sleeping bag I heard someone moving around the campsite, banging pots and rattling plates. It sounded an awful lot like somebody was putting away all the stuff I'd laid out for the following morning. This was carrying tidiness too far, and I spent what remained of the night sharpening mental implements to deal with the culprit at daybreak. I was helped in keeping awake for this by the start of the early morning pee shift who were either taking over where their night shift brothers had left off, or were the same people coming back due to low-volume bladder capacity or high-volume all night drinking. Either way they practiced the same manly technique with door closure. I probably got more sleep going up that long hill the day before than I did overnight in Kremmling, and I was more than happy to be saying goodbye to it in the morning. In my keenness to get away I was up while it was still barely light to find that all the breakfast things had, indeed, been neatly put away, and started unpacking them all again and putting them back out on the table. In fairness I probably did this more noisily than I needed to, but if anyone else was asleep at that point it was going to take more than a little pot-rattling to rouse them. At some point Richard crawled out of his tent and started helping me to put everything out. I was just about to launch into a rather colourful panegyric on the arsehole who had got up in the middle of the night to tidy up when Richard got in first:

"Hey man, did you hear the goddamn skunk we had in camp last night?"

Hear him? A skunk? Not if he'd been tap dancing on a kettledrum with his Dutch mate's clogs on.

"Yeah, I kinda shoo-ed him away, but then I had to get up and put all the food away in case he came back."

Jesus Christ, the man 'shoo-ed away' a skunk? We had all been a great deal luckier in the night than any of us knew. I hate to think what it would have been like if our little black and white friend had gone off with all our tents together in such a confined space but from everything I've ever heard about skunks and from the very powerful experience of coming across even a dead one by the side of the road, I knew it wouldn't have been a happy event.

Still I thanked my lucky stars I'd kept my mouth shut long enough for Richard to get his explanation in first and I thanked Richard more openly for his selflessness in getting up to look after our food.

Those people who had had the good sense to book into a motel for the night turned up for breakfast looking bright, refreshed, unbitten and smug. I contented myself with the thought that if the skunk had really taken a dislike to Richard's shooing then nobody would have been looking very smug that morning – nauseous maybe, smug no.

After the epic ride of the previous day, the road out of Kremmling was pretty easy. We followed the river for six or seven miles then climbed quickly up out of the valley and cross a high plateau. The plain was dry and gorse covered, interspersed with occasional green valleys.

Although the Adventure Cycling maps were generally quite good, they focus closely on the designated route and don't give a vast amount of topographical information such as contour lines etc. Our most important navigational tool without a shadow of a doubt, was an accurate milometer. Each section of the route was accompanied by a narrative and notes which indicated key points along the way, junctions, passes, river crossings etc with detailed measurements of the distance between each. In fact each point had the distance from the beginning of that map section so whenever we located a landmark which was indicated on the map we would have to mentally zero our milometers and work out how far we had to go to the next marker. Thus, for example, the notes for the section through the Colorado River valley went something like this (notes in square brackets are mine):

1. Rougher surfaced road that will be quite muddy if wet.
2. Cross cattle guard and continue straight/left
3. Ford stream. Warning: if either this creek or the next one a mile up the road is too deep to safely cross, which they may be in May or June, backtrack to the highway and turn East. [This was where the beaver dam had raised the level of the water, but we got through anyway].Pass the rustic old Rock Creek Stage Station, an 1800s Wells Fargo mail station.
4. Ford Rock Creek
5. Turn right onto gravel FR212 toward Radium and the Colorado River. It's a major elevation loss to the river. You can ride the shorter highway route to Kremmling but you'll miss out on some incredible country. [This was an understatement].
6. Bear right downhill at saddle, as FR214 goes left. Start the long dive, keeping your speed in check as you descend through pinion and juniper covered hillsides. There are some dangerous sharp corners ahead. [I may have neglected to read this bit, or I might just have chosen to ignore it].

7.   168.1 High-point, with breath-taking canyon views. [Never a truer word put to paper]

As you can see, distances were given to the nearest tenth of a mile. Sometimes turns would be even closer than this or there could be as much as six or seven miles between landmarks. Generally the system worked pretty well and we would leapfrog successfully from one point to the next, but you had to trust the mileages on the map implicitly – enough to know that if you had gone a mile or so too far and still not found your turn the chances were you had probably gone wrong somewhere and would have to backtrack. Maybe because I was paranoid that every mile might be one step closer to a busted knee, or maybe just because I was lazy, but I got into the habit of never taking a turn without consulting the map first. Occasionally, though, we still got lost. Either an old dirt road had been recently paved, or a river dried up or, as on this occasion, I just misread the directions. At least this time Mark and I got so comprehensively lost that we managed to rejoin the main route before we even knew that we'd left it, and the only reason we knew we had gone wrong was that the mileages started coming up in the wrong places – that and the fact that Pierre and Sue suddenly appeared ahead of us without having passed us on the way.

At Horseshoe campground we pitched our tents among pine trees on the banks of a beautiful white rushing river and spent the remainder of the afternoon playing cards and drinking beer which Richard had very magnanimously dragged up the mountain from Kremmling. It was really no surprise that he was one of the most popular members of the group. Facilities at the Forestry Service campsites were usually fairly basic, consisting of a cleared area for camp fires, maybe a metal ring set into the earth, sometimes a water pump, but more often just a stream, and two pit toilets. Throughout Colorado and New Mexico though, these pit toilets shared one extraordinary feature in common. Every one had massive solid mahogany doors on them that looked like they had just been lifted from a medieval fortified town. This might have made more sense if the rest of the building were as strongly constructed. Most, though, had walls which looked as though they were built of papier-mâché and spit and in this particular case that huge door was held closed (just) by a small loop of rotting string hooked around a bent and rusty doornail inside.

That night we lit a huge campfire and talked a lot, but, thank god, not one person gave the faintest sign of any inclination to burst into song.

After the first really sound night's sleep in ages, I left camp early, ahead of Mark for a change, since we had a fairly long climb ahead of us to Ute pass (9,524ft), and I wanted to try to get to the top around the same time as he did. Part of the area we passed through was very badly scarred from an enormous strip mining operation. I've no doubt there would be plenty of people who were very upset about that, but it was most likely an important, if not the only source of income for the people living around there, there was still a lot of Rockies left for people like me to see, and maybe the locals here would go to Manhattan and complain about how the beautiful scenery had been ruined by all those blasted skyscrapers.

Mark and Pierre overtook me just before I got to the top, but waited for me and we took a few photos. On the way down I managed to cover five miles at an average of nearly forty miles per hour. Even so my lack of weight and the un-aerodynamic nature of my panniers counted against me. Mark and Pierre with their heavy (and more aerodynamic) trailers gradually started pulling away. As they got to the bottom and the junction with highway 9, I watched in disbelief as, without even touching the brakes, Pierre turned right and started pounding off down the road. Mark followed swiftly on his heels. I didn't, primarily because this was the route straight back to Kremmling and we were supposed to turn left towards Silverthorne. I shouted, screamed and waved but they had their heads down and were already a quarter of a mile up the road. At the rate they were going there was no way I would catch them so I settled down to wait to see if they would spot their mistake and turn back. After ten minutes there was still no sign and by the time Jack and Chris arrived it was clear that the others would not be turning around soon, so the three of us set off southwards, confident they would catch up at some point. Highway 9 was one of the busiest road sections of the entire route. After the peace and quiet of all those mountain trails, it was very unpleasant indeed to be back eating the dust from big artics and four-wheel drives blasting past your elbow at 50 or 60mph. Whatever the trials and tribulations of off-roading, it would always be far more pleasant than any road trip under conditions like those.

It was quite a relief to pull off the road in Silverthorne and stop for coffee and some lunch. Silverthorne is right in the middle of Summit County, the nesting ground for the rich and famous in Colorado and it shows, with lots of exotic delicatessens, fashionable coffee houses and designer outlets. I indulged myself with a new pair of knee-warmers which I am sure gave a considerable boost to the local economy and took my very un-designer dust, dirt and dishevelment out of town, across the top of a large concrete dam and up to a beautifully constructed cycle path which followed the shore of the Dillon Reservoir to the next town, Frisco. By this time Mark and Pierre had caught us up again, having completed a 30-mile detour and thereby neatly doubling the day's planned mileage. By way of compensation we treated ourselves to a huge iced coffee at Starbucks. The fact that we had nothing to compensate ourselves for was neither here nor there – it was a question of mutual solidarity.

I may not be much for designer wear, but I have a profound weakness for classy engineering. In one of the stores in Frisco I was compelled to part with a hideous amount of cash to buy a beautifully constructed Titanium cup and pan. By throwing out my old cup and bowl I probably saved the equivalent of a small packet of peanuts in weight, and the others had already started to cotton onto my obsessiveness about lightening my load and gave me an enormous amount of grief over it. Evan pointed out that the biggest weight saving was actually through all the cash I'd handed over in the shop. I didn't care, I looked on my little tin cup and pot in the way that other people looked on jewellery. They were things of great beauty and to this day it gives me great pleasure every time I take them out and use them. Besides, I was celebrating. Frisco represented a turning point for me in more ways than one. On the one hand it marked another crossover onto a new Map, Section 4 from Silverthorne, Colorado to Platoro, Colorado, and with only two more maps to go, psychologically at least marked a nominal halfway point on the trail. More importantly for me, since rejoining the trail back at Steamboat Springs I had covered nearly 350 miles over some of the toughest terrain we were likely to encounter from here on and climbed a total of nearly 14,000 feet, the equivalent of almost halfway up Everest. I was going pretty slowly most of the time, and almost everybody had overtaken me at some point. I was taking painkillers more or less continually and had shared practically every one of those 350 miles with a dull, aching throb in my leg. But I was still there, and that was what counted for me. Up to that point I'd been telling everybody I would just try it for a few days to see how things went. Once we reached Frisco I had become absolutely committed to completing this ride and getting to the Mexican border one way or another. Odd though it may seem, pouring a chunk of money into two silly little pieces of camping equipment that would be of no use to me for years if I bailed out of the trip at this point was a way of making that commitment tangible to myself.

…No, sorry, that's complete bullshit. I just made that up as one of many reasons for buying the damn things after the fact.

Breckenridge must be the plushest and certainly the wealthiest town on the entire route. There were supposed to be any number of film stars with properties there, which wouldn't have surprised me too much since they were probably the only ones who could afford it. In one real estate agent's I saw a small wooden shed (only slightly bigger than the one my father has in his garden) advertised for the price of a military jet. At first I thought they'd just forgotten to put the dot before the last two zeros, but it looked like it was considered vulgar here to suggest that denominations as insignificant as cents even existed. Nobody even bothered with that '999.99' business. No, Breckenridge was a town with a hankering for zeroes, and you'd better be packing a lot of them if you intended to stay for long.

Fortunately we didn't and were just treating it as an extended lunch stop, a chance to savour the delights of civilisation again before returning to the wilderness. Mark headed straight for the post office and was absolutely delighted to be sending home a total of 4 pounds and five ounces of extraneous kit. I'd already packed off my mini campstove and water filter, since from now on I was going to be relying on group equipment again. We found a launderette and between us practically filled the place with smelly socks, sweaty cycling kit and dirty T-shirts. While we were waiting for the machines to complete their cycle we decided to go in search of a coffee and found a Polish delicatessen just around the corner. Unfortunately, it appeared to specialise in Polish Customer Service more than Polish Food, to the point where I entertained myself going through the menus crossing out the word 'Service', as in ' A service charge of 10% ' and replacing it with the word 'Surliness' just in case anybody bothered to read it. After a little persuasion we managed to get some coffee, but lunch defeated our best efforts at international diplomacy. I also managed to get some 15 minutes of Internet time at the local library which was just long enough to send one rather cryptic message with lots of abbreviations in it.

From Breckenridge the road climbs up above the town for a few miles, and then switches to a disused railroad track for the climb up to Boreas Pass. Besides making for a gentle grade, the views from the trail on the way up were absolutely breathtaking. The side of the track was strewn with livid purple and pink wildflowers and there was still snow on the peaks of the mountains opposite. At 11,450ft Boreas Pass broke my previous altitude record for cycling by almost a thousand feet.

Our campsite that night was a very basic one, and the only water available had to be filtered from whatever puddles we could find in a boggy, mosquito-infested swamp a couple of hundred yards away in the valley below. Water filtering was one of the issues that caused what little friction there was within the group. Nobody liked to do it very much since it was boring, quite hard work and time consuming, but everybody needed water, and lots of it after a long hard day in the saddle. It was made worse at places like Boreas Pass since you were effectively meat on a plate for all the local insect life all the time you hung around any waterholes. Jack and Chris were our ace water gatherers since they were frequently among the first in camp and carried one of the better filters in their gear. Nine times out of ten, before they even got around to setting up their own tents they would fill one of the large plastic carriers we had with around a gallon of fresh water and set it up in the middle of camp ready for the cooking team whenever they arrived. Once the first load looked like it was getting low, Mark, Pierre or I would usually have a go at replenishing it. By the time the late arrivers got into camp though, it was often too dark or they were too tired to do much more than replenish their own water bottles and sit down to supper. As with any gathering of two or more people, these sort of differences occasionally caused resentment. Personally I wasn't too bothered. This might have been helped by the fact that I'd had a break from the trail which the others hadn't, and so I could put the whole thing into perspective a little easier. From my point of view too, I knew that when we early-risers left camp in the morning there was stuff that the others ended up doing to clear up the campsite after us that balanced out our evening activities. It struck me that it was, on the whole, a synergistic relationship that allowed everyone to work according to their own preferences but on balance benefited everybody in the group. As the first one up almost every morning I was quite happy to get the hot water on for whoever was making breakfast on the basis that I could leave it to someone else to clear up after me when I wanted to make an early start. There were still tensions around this and other aspects of group living, and most of these inevitably fell onto the natural schism between the 'early' and 'late' contingents in the group, but for most of the time these were pretty minor, and even when things came to something of a head later in New Mexico, they all got resolved fairly amicably in the end.

Richard and Bryan were normally part of the late shift anyway, but on this occasion were later than usual into camp. On the way through

Breckenridge they'd taken a detour to ride some interesting looking single-track, then stopped again at the top of Boreas Pass to hike up to the very peak of the mountain. On the way up the weather suddenly turned and they were caught out in the open, high on the mountainside in a massive thunderstorm with no shelter around and feeling very exposed indeed. As Richard put it:

"First we went past the tree line, then we passed the sensible line and left it way behind".

On the way down Richard found a Gore-Tex dog bowl of the sort hikers carry to be able to feed their dogs on the trail. He was wearing it as a hat as he arrived in camp and demonstrated its fashionability by doing a Cossack dance for us all next to the fire. It takes a special person to appreciate the fashion potential of a dog bowl, and Richard is a very special person Unfortunately, he would have to leave us at Salida to take up a new teaching job and we were universal in our sense of how much we would miss him.

Having left Breckenridge behind, the landscape and the lay of the land changed incredibly quickly. From a picture-book alpine village we moved back down the mountains to an area of vast and bleak plateaux.

The initial descent was steep and very rocky and followed a small creek through a narrow, steep-sided valley. Though less than 30 miles from one of the wealthiest parts of the state the houses here were so bleak, and isolated and impoverished you had to wonder what attitudes brought people to live out here and what activities kept them here once they'd arrived. Later the terrain opened up until there was more sky than ground and we swept along a broad rolling dirt road through gently rolling hills that looked as though they'd been shaved to the bone. Here and there were a few very stringy looking cattle and one tiny brilliant blue house stood out on the horizon.

If you were looking for a town which represented the antithesis of the chic, style and money of Breckenridge, you'd be pushed to find a better example than Hartsel. The place looked miserable from around five miles away when we first caught sight of it and it didn't get any more welcoming as we got closer.

We set up camp behind the old school, which was now a 'Community Centre' and pitched our tents between the concrete blocks, rubble and empty fading beer cans which were rolling around the back yard. The door to the one pit toilet on the site had been nailed shut which might have given us some indication of Hartsel's attitude to visitors. The waitress at the only restaurant in town had a face like a badly rutted dirt road in the rain and kindly informed us that they closed promptly at four, so we would have to order dinner by 3:40 if we expected to eat there. We went back outside and kicked around the dusty rubbish-strewn yard at the back of the restaurant to try to decide what to do. At least half of the others were unlikely to arrive before four and we were faced with the prospect of either ordering something for them and hoping we could stall until they arrived (stalling didn't seem like an activity our waitress friend would wear well) or trying to knock up a meal from cigarettes, milk and chewing gum bought at the gas station.

Things were starting to look pretty grim until we discovered Dorothy.

Dorothy was a diminutive silver haired lady who owned the back end of an articulated lorry parked at the back of the restaurant. In true American entrepreneurial spirit she had spotted a niche in the market (- like offering any food after 4pm) and was in the process of setting up her own business. She had painted the lorry trailer pink, cut a hole in the side for a door and an ordering window and spent half of her life savings to build a massive wooden ramp up to the window to enable disabled access as the law required.

This was "Dorothy's Tamales".

When we come across her she was still hand painting signs to go out in the road advertising her own homemade Mexican food. Unfortunately for us, she was not yet officially open as she was still waiting for yet another government inspector to approve her electrical hook-up. Dorothy, however, was not easily deterred. She offered to cook us a feast of tamales at her home and drive them over and deliver to us.

253

Could we get a drink as well?

No problem.

Dorothy scuttled off and five minutes later came back to tell us she has cut a deal with the local bar so we could take our food in there to eat.

Hands were shaken, money exchanged, supper sorted and problem resolved. With a powerful electron microscope you might even have detected a fractional upturn of the mouth on the sour waitress when we went back to tell her we wouldn't be troubling her for dinner that evening...or not.

The sudden reversal of Hartsel's bad auspices was reinforced when we discovered it even had a library. A small shed run by a couple of local ladies with no official funding, it might not have represented a great career move for a professional librarian, but they did have internet access. They were friendly and helpful and we all piled in one after another to check our email (again, for my younger readers: hard as it may be to believe, there was life *before* smartphones, mobile internet *or* social media). Between us we probably put enough cash in the donation box to keep them going for another 6 months. As Chris remarked:

"Sometimes even a shithole can grow on you".

In the evening the storm clouds which we'd watched brewing on the horizon for some time broke and it rained heavily for several hours. Fortunately, most of those were spent in the bar playing cards and drinking beer. The jukebox was kept spinning all evening, though in a place like this, to mis-quote the Blues Brothers - there were only two kinds of music- Country or Western. Dorothy's Tamales duly arrived, a delicious mixture of meat, chilli sauce and maize dough steamed in a little parcel of corn husks, and disappeared as fast as she could serve them.

Walking back to the gas station for a late night ice cream we spotted a very bedraggled figure huddling under the awning. 'Hero' was an exchange student from Japan, cycling across the country west to east. He had already had one flat today and was wet through. For what it was worth we offered him a share of our campground and he was so desperate he accepted right away.

Sitting inside my tent it would have been pleasant listening to the rain beating on the outside if only it had all been beating on the outside. Unfortunately a significant amount was finding its way through the two vents to drip slowly but persistently onto the middle of my sleeping bag. Too tired or lazy to do anything else I threw my rain jacket over the top of my bag and lay back listening to the sounds of the others gradually rolling back from the bar in varying degrees of sobriety. Chris's voice was especially easy to recognise. Having pitched his tent on a small patch of concrete to keep it out of the mud, he came back to find his little patch was the lowest point on the site and his tent and all his kit was floating in a pool of two inches of rainwater. Oh how he laughed.

By morning the rain had stopped but it was cool and damp. As usual I started off with half a dozen layers of clothing and gradually stripped down during the day.

For thirty miles or so Mark and I wound our way through the same open rolling countryside as the day before. Every few miles there was a tiny cabin set back from the road half a mile or a mile. These places were isolated in the summer; god alone knew what would possess people to live here in the winter. Their social calendar had to be somewhat restricted. Still the country had a raw beauty to it, which was attractive without being accommodating.

For the most part the day was a very long and quite empty one, and I was grateful for Mark's company as we swapped views on matters historical, philosophical, religious and political to while away the distance.

The final four miles to the main pass of the day climbed steeply and were very sandy making for difficult riding. Every now and then we had to shoo cattle off the road in case they got spooked by the bikes and accidentally ran into us (not a pleasant thought).

At the top of the pass we met a lone biker, Gregg, who had come up from Salida for a little training run. He very helpfully offered to guide us in and show us the bike shop, the restaurants and the campsites etc. and we gratefully accepted.

As we followed Gregg down from the high ridge, we took a sharp left and suddenly the whole valley opened out in front of us. The mountains in the background were high triangular peaks with a pinkish tint to them and were part of the Sawatch range, some of Colorado's highest mountains, many of them over 14,000ft, including Mount Elbert the second highest in the continental U.S.

Elbert seemed like such a domestic name for such a massive geological feature you might almost feel embarrassed for it, were it not such a magnificent sight.

While Gregg disappeared down the mountain with the contempt bred by familiarity with his surroundings, every one of us, to a man, slammed on our brakes and stood speechless at the edge of the road staring at the panorama before us. If God had any taste at all this would be his (or her) own country.

I almost got the chance to ask him (or her) on the way down, as enthusiasm once more got the better of common sense and loose gravel reiterated its disaffection for semi-slick tyres. Fortunately the road was a wide one and hubris was off my case for once, so I managed to pull the bike back round with an almost convincing "I-meant-to-do-that" kind of panache – convincing to anyone apart from me, that is.

We finally caught up with Greg and he was good as his word and following his cyclists instinct led us straight to the epicentre of our desires – a fantastic bakery and coffee house (where he happened to work) which was right next door to a bike shop (where he also happened to work). Serendipity in action.

Salida was so different to Hartsel it was difficult to believe they were in the same country, let alone the same state. Hartsel wasn't only a backwater, it had a bitterness of unfulfilled wants and a morbid envy which seemed to pervade so many of the people who lived there. Salida, by contrast, was a happy, healthy little town with a buzz and an optimism about it which was contagious.

We spent a very relaxed layover day collecting post, drinking coffee, eating cakes, and in the evening had a big celebration meal to bid farewell to Richard.

We would need all the relaxation we could get, there was still a long way to go, and ahead of us lay the biggest mountains we had yet faced.

Washboard and Wilderness

Want to know what it's like to ride the great divide?

Okay, you can ride a bike, yes? Let's start with riding your bike along a flat piece of road. The average person should be able to manage 12 or 15 mph without too much difficulty. Someone reasonably fit will do over 20mph but might be breathing harder. Let's start by raising the incline, not too much, so you are pedalling up, let's say a disabled access ramp. Okay, all of a sudden your speed drops off a bit and you start breathing harder. Now let's add a little weight, say a medium sized bag of potatoes, one at each corner. Now it's becoming quite hard work. Now the smooth ramp is replaced with an oversized piece of corrugated iron, with bumps 3 inches high and six inches apart. Everything goes 'wuh-wuh-wuh-wuh-wuh and to liven things up there are six inch rocks every now and again which smack you in the groin in no uncertain manner. Unfortunately we aren't finished yet. Someone has just tipped an inch of sand all over the ramp. This is just like riding with the brakes on. Finally, of course, they take away half your oxygen as you're doing all this at over 10,000 feet. You have to do this from seven in the morning until say one in the afternoon with two or three five to ten minute breaks. Of course, you get some downhill too, unfortunately, that seems to be the time when the wind appears and you find yourself having to pedal almost as hard if you want to make any headway.

This was more or less what happened on the long wind up to

Marshall Pass (10,842ft) from Salida. This may sound like hard work, but you should know there was an alternative route available which the map described as follows:

Very tough, but shadier and delightfully remote no-traffic alternative: at 'T' turn left onto FR203 and proceed up Poncha Creek. You'll gain nearly 3,000 feet in seven miles , much of it over a very rocky road surface, before rejoining the main route at Marshall Pass.

You may be surprised to hear that, to a man, we forbore the 'delightfully remote' alternative. From leaving the highway at Mears Junction to rejoining it at Sargents 30 miles later the only traffic we saw were two pickup trucks parked by the creek which looked like they belonged to a couple of fishermen, so we didn't feel overly bothered by the heavy traffic either. In fact, although it was a tough climb, and not helped much by the washboard, it was a very pretty route, and as we zig-zagged our way up into the Sawatch mountains we were treated to some terrific views back over the road we had climbed and down to the rivers and lakes below.

The fact that remoteness has come (by some at least) to be considered 'delightful', is very much a twentieth (or twenty-first) century phenomenon. Like most things its value has been increased by its rarity. In the 1800s, though, 'remote' was just about all you got if you lived out in this part of the world, and 'delightful' was not a word which suffered much from over-use ("Howdy, Ned. My, what delightful spurs you have there!", "Bartender, this whiskey is just delightful, but if you don't shut that god-damn piano player up I'm gonna blow his god-damn head off"). Many tributes have been paid to the men (and sometimes the women) who first came out to this wild area and made it their own (or took it away from the native Americans, depending on your perspective). In Boulder, for example, there is an Alfred E Packer Grill. Before eating there, though, you might like to do a little research into Mr Packer's history and exactly how he came to be commemorated.

Alfred E set out for the remote parts of the Saugauche range of mountains sometime in the winter of 1873/4, looking for gold with half a dozen other prospector chums. Sometime in the Spring he was to be seen back in town in the saloon spending lots of money on his own. It was also noticed that he appeared to keep his money in several different wallets. Even the sheriff thought this was a little unusual. When he was asked about the whereabouts of his friends he explained that they'd all killed each other in a big fight. When he was further questioned as to how he'd managed to survive the winter up in the mountains on his own, he indicated that he might have dined out, occasionally, on his friends' misfortune, so to speak. When the five bodies were eventually discovered they were all rather less than complete in the areas of the legs and chest. Parker was eventually convicted of manslaughter on his claim of 'Self-Defence' and pardoned by the governor after serving only five years in jail.

When we reached the top of the pass, we found it not nearly so remote as we might have expected on the road up. There were literally dozens of mountain bikers, swarming all over it, all on the very latest high-tech kit with matching sunshades, helmets and body-armour. After five minutes I gave up altogether saying hello to any of these ignorant gits. Our bikes looked well-worn, our clothes even more so and worst of all we had racks, bags and trailers attached – we were tourists! The fact that we had at least cycled all the way up the damn mountain rather than carrying our bikes up there in the back of a pickup to enjoy the free ride down counted more for us than it did, apparently for them. I wished them plenty of value from their helmets and body-armour on the ride down, and carried on.

From the top of the pass the wind started to pick up and my sail-like panniers meant that once more I started to lose ground to the more aerodynamic trailers on the way down. I could see the General Store at Sargents from a long way up the valley, but it took something like a century and a half to get there. Fortunately there was a warm welcome waiting in the form of "No Cycles" signs in the window, the car park, along the fence and on the toilet door. The latter was the one which disappointed me most since I had by now completely mastered the art of Peeing without actually getting off my bike to the point where it was almost second nature. On this occasion I would just have to manage without. I dropped my bike on the middle of the forecourt (the only place where I couldn't see a sign forbidding its existence) and went inside to buy myself an ice-cream. The anti-cycling paranoia was apparently occasioned by someone on a previous trip leaning their heavily-laden bike a little clumsily against the plate-glass window with an unfortunate and rather dramatic result. Still, I didn't quite see how the porcelain bowl in the toilet was likely to suffer the same fate.

Like a plague of locusts we cleaned out every piece of pie and all the ice-cream they had, filled up every one of our water containers from their tap and left to try to find a place to camp by the side of the road a little further down the valley.

From this point we were entering an area known as the "La Garita Wilderness".

The term 'Wilderness' has a very specific derivation in the US. Technically it is a federally protected area. Apart from a few designated trails, the only way you are allowed to travel through a wilderness area is on foot or horseback. No motorized or wheeled transport of any kind (including bicycles) is permitted. There were those in the cycling community who argued strongly against this, pointing out that the restriction should be against motorized vehicles only, but personally I couldn't get too worked up about it. There are few enough areas like this left in the world, and there were enough designated routes for us to work our way through without any problem. At the time we were there, there was an interesting debate taking place in congress (OK, I use the word 'interesting' loosely, maybe 'relevant' would be better) between the logging companies who wanted legislation to enable them to open up more roads in the wilderness areas and promote local industry and the environmentalists (most of whom earned their livings elsewhere, it has to be said) who wanted to keep things as they were.

Just before Cochetopa pass we surprised two mountain goats in the middle of the trail. These bear about as much resemblance to domestic goats as Mike Tyson does to Shirley Temple. For one thing they're nearer the size and weight of a small cow than the dandy little things we see in farmyards. For another they move more like cats

261

than animals with hooves. When they finally saw us they shot up a near vertical cliff face with a speed and agility that would have impressed Spider-Man. Competition in the Wild certainly seems to keep these creatures in shape. Personally I think they should have been tested for steroids all the same.

That night we camped at Luder's Creek, just below the pass on the edge of a high meadow, and drank cold, clear water as it came straight out of the ground from a mountain spring. The following day was to be a long, and very varied one. In many ways it was like a microcosm of the whole trip, packed into one 9 hour ride. What's more, it was my birthday.

Rather than try to do it justice in retrospect, I shall once more quote directly from my journal, written that evening in Del Norte:

What a magnificent birthday! The day starts with a long winding descent from Luders Creek campground. Through aspen and pine trees along a winding narrow valley. There is a short section of paved road before the long climb up to the top of Carneros pass. The climb is not too bad except for the last two miles, which are very rocky and rapidly start to take their toll on my knees again. Once over the top though there is another superb descent and we blap along at nearly 20mph for almost 20 miles. The road winds through Hoodoo country. Hoodoos (I am told) are the oddly shaped sandstone rocks and bluffs, which stand out from the rest of the terrain. Unfortunately, my cultural understanding of this phenomenon is such that all I can think of is a seventies rock song entitled "Who do you love?" Half way down we find ourselves promoted to impromptu cowboys as several small herds of cattle jump up onto the road as we arrive then, trapped between a steep drop on one side and a high bank on the other run in front of us for two or three miles. Those cows definitely lost some weight today, I can tell you. The terrain changes incredibly quickly from lush forest and meadow to open desert and sagebrush. Only 15 miles or so from Del Norte, after an already long day we are treated to a simply hideous road, sand and massive washboard across its entire width, and which soon begins to climb to add insult to injury. Looking at the map there would appear to be a perfectly decent alternative road which drops directly into the town and it's far from clear why the route would take such a meandering course. Finally though, we turn off the hellroad and all is suddenly made clear. Forget route 66, it's Saguache County route 665 to get your kicks on if you're a mountain biker. Less a road than a double jeep track through the desert, the tracks swoop, turn, flip like a mad roller coaster. For twenty minutes or so it feels like the wildest ride on earth. Truth be told the bike is actually under my control less than 10% of the time, for the rest I just let it go and try to hold on. If ever there was a sight I shall remember for the rest of my birthdays it was a bunch of 40, 50, and 60 year olds leaping mountain bikes with fully loaded trailers 2,3 and 4 feet through the air whooping like adolescents.

Mark, Jack, Chris and I checked into a motel to clean ourselves up a little. Pierre cooked crepe for my birthday which Evan tried to flambé and in the process lost all of the hair and half of the skin from his forearm. I was given a giant fluorescent plastic fly (which I strapped to my front mudguard) and a "Give me Coffee and Nobody Gets Hurt" sticker, which I put on my panniers. Were it not for the fact that I was still missing one birthday card that I really would have liked to have seen from back home, it was very nearly the perfect end to the perfect day.

Ahead of us lay the highest summit and the longest single climb of the entire trip, Indiana Pass.

From Del Norte the road rose straight up for 24 miles, gaining over 4,000 vertical feet without respite to the col at 11,960 feet above sea level. Before we left in the morning Lou asked me if I would keep an eye on Pierre during the climb, he'd had very little sleep during the night and was suffering from sickness and diarrhoea. I promised to try, but it wasn't going to be that easy. For one thing I wasn't convinced I could keep pace with Pierre if he'd had one leg amputated and was dragging a ball and chain on the other. For another he was not somebody who took to being 'looked after', and at 69 I rather suspected he knew his own mind on this subject. Instead I was reduced to leapfrogging him all the way up the mountain, pedalling like crazy to get past him then stopping further up the road to let him catch up (and try to get some of my breath back), so as not to look like I was shadowing him all the way. I knew he must have been quite sick or I would never have managed to keep up with him like this.

The day began fairly gently, with a paved road climbing steadily up the Pinos Creek valley. Twelve miles later we entered the Rio Grande National Forest, the road turned to dirt and the climb began in earnest. To my left I could make out Poison Mountain and Blowout Pass – these were not encouraging names. We climbed. The sun came out and I realised I wasn't carrying anything like enough water with me. Pierre gave me some of his. Who was supposed to be looking after whom here? I tried to keep to the shady parts of the road. We kept climbing. The road got worse. We still kept climbing. The road got still worse, with loose gravel and large rocks bumping and slipping beneath our wheels. There was still no other way to go but up. After six-and-a-half to seven hours of solid grind, I came round a corner to see Pierre's bicycle leaning against a sign – "Indiana Pass – Summit. Elev. 11,910' ". Parked right next to it was a Jeep. Inside the Jeep was a young couple, eating sandwiches and admiring the view. I only knew that their view from that summit was a very different one from mine.

After the pass the road continued to rise and fall without ever losing much altitude overall. We passed the euphemistically named "Summitville Mine Superfund Site". As I understood it, a company would come into the area, rip whatever it wanted out of the ground, sell it, and chuck away whatever it didn't want into the nearest river or water source. The Superfund was a way for the government to pay the same company to go back and try to clear up the mess afterwards. On the other hand this seemed like such a silly idea I must have got completely the wrong end of the stick. I was very glad of the extra water Pierre had given me as all the creeks running through this area were still heavily contaminated and not the sort of place to drink from unless you really were convinced that two heads were better than one. In fact the only water any of us got that day was a gallon and a half that Jack and Chris managed to blag from a passing RV and which we had to ration out for cooking supper and breakfast the next morning.

Park Creek campground was perched on the edge of a steep valley some ten miles after the pass but only 400 feet below the height of the summit. From where we pitched our tents there was a steep drop to a flat-bottomed valley with a dry creek bed, locked in by high jagged mountain tops on all sides. Towards evening a lone shepherd and his dog moved a vast flock of sheep into the valley looking for water. Later on we saw a train of riders with pack horses following the creek bed. At night the stars were bright enough to see by, even without the moon. There were more, and they were brighter than any I've ever seen in the northern hemisphere. I lay back inside my tent and listened to the wind moving through the valley and the tops of the pine trees. There could not have been many people in the world who were looking forward to waking up to a view such as would greet me in the morning.

As we left camp a young girl on horseback rode up to the road just ahead of us. She was one of the group of riders we had seen in the valley the previous night. She told us her father had fallen from his horse the day before and gashed his head, and she was looking for someone with a vehicle to run him down to the nearest town. Short of strapping him to one of our crossbars she was out of luck as far as our group was concerned, but we offered to look out for a car on our way down while she headed off in the opposite direction towards Summitville. She seemed very pleasant, if a little distraught, and I considered briefly asking her if she would like to go out for dinner instead, but decided that this was perhaps not the most propitious time.

The descent to Platoro was one of the roughest and rockiest roads we had come across this far. Because I was travelling much lighter than most of the others I was able to enjoy it more, but still the bike took one hell of a pounding. I had one aluminium bottle cage strapped to each leg of the front forks, holding a total of a litre of fuel for the group stoves. Within five miles both were broken and I had to strap them together with bungees and bits of tape. By contrast, both wheels, the main frame and the Italian made forks themselves seemed to be holding out incredibly well. This ride had to be one of the toughest tests of cycling equipment around, and the punishment they soaked up defied belief. If they lasted the next seven hundred miles they would have done well indeed. Still the bumps and shocks from the road took it out on my joints much more than the long climb the previous day, so I was very pleased to pull into the equestrian centre at Platoro where we all made straight for the restaurant and ordered the largest plates of burgers and fries on the menu. While we were waiting for our food I became aware of a constant, faint jingling sound in the background. Fortunately it wasn't the result of having shaken something loose in my inner ear, but rather down to the fact that almost everyone else walking into and out of the restaurant was wearing spurs. It was actually rather pleasant and I thought maybe everybody should have either little bells or rattles attached to their shoes. Maybe that was why they had all those gun battles face-to-face with each other in the middle of the street – it would have been practically impossible to sneak up on anybody with those things tinkling away on your feet. If I'd had to become a gunslinger I'm afraid I would have been the sort to wear Nike trainers and carry a Winchester rifle with a telescopic sight.

As I looked around our table, despite the fact that it had been a relatively short day, it became clear that the rigours of the journey were starting to take their toll on the human elements as much as the mechanical ones. Everyone was starting to look tired, even at the beginning of the day. Although Pierre seemed to have got over the worst of his illness he was still off-peak. Chris looked decidedly rough and was either coming down with the same bug as Pierre had or was suffering from a combination of dehydration and altitude sickness. Sue had a pinched nerve in her shoulder which was making riding sheer agony.

The next day we were due to cross over into New Mexico, our

fifth and final state (though only my third, having missed out Wyoming and a short section of Idaho), and when we set out from the Conejos river campground we knew that there would be a very hard day ahead. By the time we crossed our first pass at La Manga, Chris Sue and I had decided to take an alternative road route and meet up with the group again at El Rito, two days to the south. Both of the others were looking very rough, though for different reasons, and although I felt relatively healthy by comparison I doubted I would hold out well under another major rocky road assault, and I felt it would do no harm to have one more person accompany the sick crew on the tarmac. Just before the second pass we parted company with the others as they turned off onto a narrow dirt road going back into the forest and we wished them luck. Instead we headed down to the nearest town, Chama, to see if we could find a motel to rest up for the night, then make a long, but relatively straightforward road trip to El Rito the following day.

On the way down we spotted a plume of smoke up ahead. At first we thought it might be one of the many forest fires which had been raging across the west that summer. This far we had been very lucky, but by all reports the fires were getting closer and closer to us and in many places were simply burning out of control as all the available fire crews were wither occupied or exhausted. Instead it turned out to be a steam train, a real 'Casey Jones Special', and one of the last remaining operational ones anywhere in the states. When you saw how much smoke came out of the stack it was easy to see why it was one of the last, and in fact it was shut down two days later as representing too much of a fire hazard in the current very dry conditions. A little further down we were overtaken by a group of half a dozen road cyclists who shot past us, then pulled up a little further on where we stopped to talk to them. When we told them where we'd come from they told us how much they envied us our trip. We told them how much we envied their lightweight bikes, their skinny tyres and above all their lovely shiny white Sag Wagon – a great big van carrying all their extra gear and equipment which they took in turns to drive behind the group.

By the time we reached Chama both Chris and Sue looked completely whacked. We tried to find a hotel but soon found out of all the days in the year we had picked the worst possible one to arrive in this particular part of New Mexico. "Chama Days" are about the wildest, most drunken and riotous festival of the year in these parts – which would not necessarily be a bad thing were the three of us in slightly better shape and if there were any empty motel rooms for a radius of about ten miles around. We stopped at a small store and bought three ice creams while we contemplated our dilemma. We asked the woman at the store if she could think of anything to help. She said she thought her son might be able to drive us south to Abiqui in his pickup, there we might have a chance to find a room for the night and a short ride to El Rito in the morning. After three quarters of an hour trying to locate him though we decided we had probably better try our luck hitching while she continued to look. At this stage Chris was going downhill rapidly and it was clear the only way we were getting out of Chama together would be in some form of motorised transport. Fortunately, just about everybody around here drove a pickup truck, so carrying the bikes would not be so much of a problem as you might imagine. Getting a ride, however, in the run up to Chama Days, was another matter.

We parked the bikes outside the gas station and took it in turns to spot likely candidates and wander over to see if they were prepared to carry us south for a reasonable donation to their petrol fund.

After an hour or two of polite, and less polite refusals, we were beginning to wonder if we would ever get out of the place, when Chris stepped round the corner and quite literally walked into an old friend he hadn't seen for nearly eight years. It's difficult to know which of the two is more surprised to see the other, but frankly we don't really care. Charlie is like a gift from the heavens sent straight to us.

Charlie and Chris used to work in the Fire Service in California, but lost touch when Charlie moved out to New Mexico. He now lived in a large house in a small rural development around 8 miles south of Chama where he helped train the local volunteer fire department. He very rarely came into town but just happened to call into the gas station to get some cigarettes while his wife did some last minute shopping. Chris explained our situation and within minutes Charlie got into action over the phone. He quickly dismissed the idea of getting us a lift and insisted that we come back to his place first to get some rest (and clean up a bit too, though he was far too polite to suggest it). His car was too small to take the bikes so he called a neighbour with a pickup and trailer and got them to drive all the way into town to take us and the bikes back to his home. Meantime his wife, Sandra, had arranged for Chris and I to sleep at their friends, John and Mary, while Sue would stay in their spare room.

From Desolation Boulevard to being clean, shaved and in fresh clothes, with a cold gin and tonic in one hand and a forkful of hot food in the other took a little over an hour and a half. If anything the transformation was even more dramatic for Chris and Sue and they both perked up a little for the first time in two days.

We ate well, drank well and above all luxuriated in the comfort of knowing we were amongst new friends.

In the morning we had a luxurious lay-in until nearly 6:30 then wandered over to join John and Mary on their deck for coffee. At this time of the day their backyard was like the animal equivalent of Piccadilly Circus. Humming birds, thrumming around the feeders they had put out dive bombed me because of my fluorescent jacket and took a hopeful look in my ears for Nectar (no chance there!). Squirrels and chipmunks competed with stellar Jays for peanuts, which they had laid out along the handrail. The Jays, a beautiful blue with a Woody Woodpecker style crest are so canny they will walk along picking up each peanut in turn and weighing it so as to take the heaviest one first. Two or three full-grown deer wandered into the back yard looking for an easy breakfast. John pointed out what looked like a small war in the air, taking place over one of the bird feeders. Among the hummingbirds, apparently, is a small red-breasted one called a Rufus. This aggressive little dictator of the bird world will take up ownership of particular feeder, make a unilateral declaration of ownership and even when it has eaten or drunk its fill will hang around and fight furiously to keep the others away.

Frank, a friend of John's kindly offered the loan of his pickup so around noon we loaded up and headed off for El Rito. The contrast in the landscape since crossing over from Colorado was astonishing. Once we dropped down from the canyon where Charlie's house was, we were driving through classic western desert. The dirt was a deep ochre red and we were surrounded by high sandstone bluffs, stratified with many different shades of rock. We passed a vast natural stone amphitheatre and yet more Hoodoos (though they could have been Howdoos or even Whydoos).

Apart from the changing physical landscape there were other differences from Colorado which were equally marked. New Mexico is a predominantly Hispanic state, and there was clearly a lot of poverty here. El Rito could almost be in Old Mexico, with an adobe catholic church, a pair of dark and very battered general stores and the requisite pack of mangy, continually barking dogs.

Mark, Evan and Pierre turned up just as we are lifting the bikes out of the pickup and it was immediately obvious that we made the right choice in taking to the alternative tarmac route. The three of them looked like they had been run over by a truck, tipped through a dirt-o-matic and finished off with a bar brawl. By all accounts the road they took yesterday was the worst so far, a combination of steep hills, huge rocks and deep mud. It took Mark ten hours to make the campsite and the river there was dry when they arrived. As a result the whole group took to the paved road today and circumnavigated the second part of the main route. We tried very hard not to look smug, then realised that they were too tired to care and helped them unload their bikes and set up camp.

We said our goodbyes to Charlie and Sandra and promised postcards if and when we ever made it to the Mexican border, then pitched our tents on a scrubby little piece of grass behind the church. Two or three very iffy-looking dogs watched us curiously from underneath a car in the yard.

Sue and Pierre were the big animal lovers among the group and

Sue decided to befriend one of these local mutts by tempting it out from under the car and offering it some beef jerky. Having tried this stuff myself I would suggest that feeding it to a dog is a) tantamount to risking the wrath of the RSPCA and b) infinitely better than trying to east it yourself. Still, patience paid off and the dog certainly seemed to appreciate these gifts from his new friend. In fact, she was so successful that, having circulated the campground to sniff out her tent, he showed his appreciation by marking it as his own. I make a mental note that when not chasing cyclists a dog's favourite pastime appears to be peeing on them.

While we were sorting out supper and waiting for the others to arrive I noticed for the second or third time in as many days that one of my fingers had started to go numb, I presumed from the constant shaking through the handlebars. I decided to work on trying to transfer this technology to my arse as soon as possible. Personally, I wouldn't have cared if I never felt another thing though my cheeks for the rest of my natural. There should be an operation for this sort of thing.

By this stage just about everybody was starting to show some effects of the physical wear and tear of the ride. Chris was especially anxious to see his buddy Jack, and when he finally did get into El Rito, Chris's anxiety was shown to be well founded. Jack looked frighteningly pale, with great bags under his eyes and for the first time since I'd met him the boyish grin had disappeared from his face. Whatever was wrong looked very similar to whatever had struck Chris down, and we began to suspect something more than just dehydration and the cumulative effect of altitude sickness. What was amazing was the fact that without being able to eat anything and struggling even to keep reasonably hydrated he had managed to fight his way through the physical challenge of the last two days at all. To top it all it would be his 60th birthday in two days time. Those of us who could still face food hobbled, limped and shuffled along the road to a small Mexican restaurant where we began to discover some of the merits of being in New Mexico in the excellent spicy cooking. The others settled for drinking copious amounts of water and getting

271

in an early night. Fortunately for everybody we had already decided to take an extra rest day at this point and planned to make a side trip to the regional capital of Santa Fe for some rest and relaxation.

Having hired a couple of people-carriers we all bundled into them the following morning and headed off for the city to spend a day and a half enjoying the delights of the town before the final long push to the Mexican border. Being a very popular tourist spot Santa Fe's hotels were a lot more expensive than we were used to, so we carried our tents with us and set up base at a campground just outside the suburbs. Unfortunately half the group was still so sick that having had lunch in town they couldn't wait to get back to the campsite and just lie down for the rest of the day. Being part of the walking wounded list, Mark and I decided to use the afternoon to check out the Georgia O'Keefe museum. Ms O'Keefe was a much lauded local artist and had undoubtedly had a strong influence in the development of the town as an artistic and cultural centre for this part of New Mexico. The museum blurb described her as "A distinguished modern artist famous for pastel renderings of detailed flora and desert scenes". After twenty minutes of culture we made a unilateral choice and headed off to find the nearest Starbucks for coffee and ice cream. I took the time to buy two more water bottles and a 2 litre Camelbak (a cross between a water carrier and a rucksack). This gave me a total capacity of around 8 and a half litres or nearly two gallons of water, which would weigh nearly as much as all of the rest of my gear put together. At these altitudes though, that would be barely enough for two days personal drinking water – without allowing for cooking or cleaning. Despite the fact that we would still be above 8,000 feet for most of the time, shade temperatures were creeping up well into the low hundreds Fahrenheit (low 40s Celsius) during the day and we would be working as hard as ever with big climbs and long days still ahead of us. What was worse, it was rapidly becoming clear that the drought which had caused so many forest fires in the West had hit New Mexico particularly badly, as evidenced by the problems finding reliable water sources en route. Water was going to be THE issue for the remaining part of the ride and we needed to take it very seriously indeed.

After culture, coffee and shopping we sat down to relax in the main Plaza and were entertained by the spectacle of a wedding taking place on the bandstand in the centre. For some reason this was being officiated by a super-ecumenical threesome which consisted of a female Bishop, a Rabbi and a Methodist Minister. It struck me that this was hedging your bets in no uncertain terms. Maybe there was a city ordnance which required the representation of all minorities in any activity which took place on public ground – I checked to see if there was a disabled Buddhist or a Rastafarian Druid with dreadlocks just in case. Once the ceremony was complete (and it took a while to get through all three forms) it became clear that the Reception was going to be a very public affair too as the bride and groom cleared the stage for a very loud, frilly and glitzy mariachi band and everybody started dancing on the grass and the flower beds. Although not exactly my type of music they were clearly very popular and probably very good in a sort of irritating-bastards-with-a-guitar-and-trumpet-at-your-table-in-a-Mexican-restaurant kind of way. We left and made our way back to the campsite to discuss plans for our onward journey.

Deserts and Thunderstorms – the wettest drought in history

The next three days of the route were undeniably going to be challenging. Back roads and desert trails in New Mexico were generally extremely poor, and being very sandy had a tendency to turn instantly into thick, clogging mud within seconds of the onset of the (now daily) thunderstorms. More serious still, given the record drought conditions, the chances of finding water anywhere between El Rito and Cuba (the next town on our itinerary) looked extremely slim. The storms were too few and too late to replenish the now dry watercourses. Thus, ironically we got the worst of both conditions - too much and too little water; too much on the road, too little in the rivers. The walking wounded among us once again opted for the alternative road route to Cuba. The remaining five were prepared to carry enough water to try the main route, and if necessary turn around and come back if the rivers were completely dry. Although Chris was looking a lot better for his few days off, Jack was still not well and didn't want to push his luck. Neither Sue nor I had the heart to risk the rigours of what promised to be a very rocky road only to have to turn around for lack of water. Pierre seemed to feel he'd seen enough mud to last him for the rest of the trip.

We left El Rito the following morning uncomfortable about splitting the group, but each of us confident that we were making the right decision for ourselves and very much focused now on the single objective of just making it to the end of the ride. By the time we got to gas station at Abiquiu, though, and the turnoff for the main route, it was clear that Jack wasn't going anywhere. He had been weak from sickness and diarrhoea for several days now and his symptoms just continued to get worse until he could barely keep his bike upright. We parked our bikes and took him into the store to find a seat for a while and get him something to drink. It's a poor way to spend your birthday, but despite the brave face he put up we all agreed he could not continue and had to find a doctor, and if necessary get checked into hospital before he got any worse.

At this point the owner of the gas station-cum-store, Dennis, intervened. He was kindness itself. There was a clinic next door, but if necessary he offered to arrange a ride for both Jack and Chris into Espanola to the hospital within the hour. We had seen more of such kindness on this trip than the reverse, but each time I was surprised at how far people were prepared to go to help out.

After much dithering it became clear there was little else that the rest of us could do – Dennis would look after Jack and Chris and they agreed to meet up with the rest of us in Cuba in two days time or leave a message with the Adventure-Cycling office if they couldn't make it. Mark took a small dirt track back up into the hills, following the main route, while Pierre, Sue and I took to the alternative road south. Leaving Abiqui it wound through impressive red bluffs covered (sporadically) with scrub pine and sweet-smelling sagebrush. Despite the storms and the mud the others had encountered so recently, the land here looked so dry it was almost painful and the temperatures were high enough that each of us was carrying well over a gallon of water to last us through the morning. We climbed up and around the edge of what looked like a giant dry basin, until I realised it was supposed to be a reservoir from the white dusty concrete dam left beached and white in the sun at one end. All the rivers we crossed and which were supposed to drain into this area from the hills up to our left held nothing more than a few muddy pools of standing water left from overnight storms. Those hills were exactly where Mark and the others were headed and I began to have bad feelings about their likelihood of finding anything to drink once they got up in there. Once more Pierre thundered up the road like an unstoppable force but Sue was clearly suffering. Several times I caught the look of pain on her face and knew exactly how much each mile was costing her. At one point she simply dropped her bike and sat at the side of the road with tears coursing down her cheeks, seemingly unable to bear any more. After a few minutes rest she picked her bike up again, got back on and carried on down the road. Although we hadn't really spoken that much during the trip I started to develop an enormous admiration for this woman's dogged courage and absolutely fiery determination.

By the time we reached the road station at Coyote Crossing we were hot, tired and very hungry. This was too bad since the only restaurant in town was closed while the owner was out at the doctors – and in this part of the world we knew that was more likely to be a day trip than a matter of hours. Fortunately for us, Dave, the well-rounded and very friendly owner of the general store, offered the use of his microwave to cook some frozen pizzas (it never ceases to amaze me not so much what you will eat, as what you will actually enjoy eating if you are hungry enough) as well as allowing us to pitch our tents on his lawn. Actually, he went further and invited us to stay in his spare room, but I think we were all so habituated to our tents by now that we decided we would stick outside until we really felt the need for another motel visit. There were toilets in the launderette (which Dave also owned) and he offered to leave the door unlocked overnight so we could make use of the facilities there if we needed to. At first I assumed he lived out there on his own, but when we were talking later he told us his wife lived and worked in town and he stayed out at the store during the week with his Dalmatian dog, 'Buddy', to keep an eye on things. In the evening he set up a couple of trestle tables in the launderette and a young Mexican girl came in to help him make up dozens and dozens of sandwiches - "for the fire-fighters", he explained. Yet another huge forest fire was burning, more or less out of control, not more than 15 miles to the west and he was preparing packed lunches to be taken over for the volunteers called in to help fight it from all over the county. I thought of our modest struggle to get to Coyote Crossing and this man's daily grind to sweat out a living somehow between groceries, fuel, laundry and sandwiches, whatever it took to get by, and all with the risk of the whole damn thing going up in flames if the wind direction just happened to change on the wrong day or if lightning struck once more in the wrong place. As it started to get dark we watched another storm move in from the east and provide dramatic strobe backlighting to the dark hills, and we hoped our friends were not still out on the road somewhere over there.

We were just about to call it a night when two cars pulled into the car park, their doors opened and Chris and Jack stepped into the light from their headlights. We ran out to find out what had happened to them. After an hour's wait at the Hospital in Albuquerque the Doctor had diagnosed Jack as suffering from a bout of Giardia, a nasty little water-born parasite which announces its presence with violent diarrhoea, vomiting and nausea. These are not good cycling companions, and it seemed very likely that Chris and probably two or three of the others had been suffering from the same thing, picked up from a contaminated water source somewhere along the trail. Not everyone was very adept or particularly disciplined when using the water filters to pump fresh water from the streams and springs along the way. As water became more scarce we had been forced to use more and more dubious sources and the chances of the filters getting clogged with mud and inlet and outlet pipes getting mixed up became quite high.

Both Chris and Jack had been given a course of medication to kill off their unwanted internal tenants and recommended that anyone else who showed the faintest symptoms should obtain the same prescription and start taking it without delay just in case. Meantime Dennis had driven all the way back into Albuquerque to pick them up again and then arranged for two of the young people who worked in his store to leave early and drive them both down to Cuba where they could rest while waiting for the others to catch up. They'd seen the sign for the store at Coyote Crossing and assumed this would be where we would have stopped for the night, and just wanted to stop off and let us know they were OK. Though the news about Giardia was not so good, we were pleased and relieved that it was nothing more serious and glad that both the boys would be set to finish the ride with us soon.

We set out from Coyote Crossing fairly early in the hope of getting to Gallina fairly quickly and getting a cooked breakfast and some fresh coffee at a Café Dave had recommended. Instead it took us nearly two hours to cover a mere fourteen miles and we climbed over 1500ft in the process. By the time we reached Alma's café and had ordered most of the menu (Pierre was just a little disappointed there was no ice cream available) Sue was just about done in. While we waited for our food and coffee to arrive we decided to ask around to see if there was any chance of her getting a lift in for the remaining stretch to Cuba – which would have been fine if there had been anybody else around to ask. Alma herself was very concerned and tried to be helpful, but she clearly wasn't used to being run off her feet by the incessant flow of customers through her place and didn't seem to feel that the probability of Sue jumping into a pickup truck and zooming off down the road was so imminent as to require any rush making the breakfasts. An hour and a half later and I think Sue became more worried at the prospect of ending her days as an ageing wallflower in Gallina than she was of spending another 30 miles or so in agony from her right shoulder. We decided to head off together, take it slowly and try to shepherd her into Cuba on our own. Luckily, we seemed to have passed the highest point on the road, the going became much easier and we all got into Cuba sometime in the late afternoon.

Eventually we tracked down Jack and Chris and all checked into the same cheap motel. Pierre had been suffering from ice cream withdrawal for some days at this point, so while Sue bedded down with a bottle of painkillers to try and forget about her shoulder the rest of us took off for the nearest ice-cream parlour to try to satisfy Pierre's craving. From the way Jack demolished a huge bowl of double toffee fudge 'D'light the medication for Giardia appeared to be working well too.

We weren't expecting the others for at least another day and were sat outside on the patio speculating what sort of ride they'd had and whether they'd found enough water to drink or too much to ride through when Mark cycled straight past us, so we knew straight away that something must have gone wrong. We shouted, one person grabbed his bike, another found a chair, a third went to order more ice-cream and the fourth began the interrogation more or less immediately.

From the point where we'd parted back in Abiqui, Mark had started to climb a rock-strewn trail up into the hills. Although it was at least dry at that stage progress was difficult and slow. It took him at least two hours to get near the top and all he'd seen on the way up were dry watercourses, probably the beginnings of the same ones we'd seen down by the reservoir. After another hour and a half he reached the river crossing where they were supposed to camp that night to find a few stagnant pools and not much else. Things were not looking good. He waited another hour to see if anyone else turned up, then realised if he waited any longer they would be forced to stop the night there with whatever water they were carrying, so reluctantly turned around and headed back down the trail. He was nearly back to the highway turnoff before he met the next rider coming, such had been the attractions of Dennis's store in Abiqui, tempered probably by a natural reluctance to launch up that hill in the mere hope of finding water at the top. After a quick conference everyone voted to stay in Abiqui overnight, then follow our route via road the next day, but to set out early and try to cover the haul to Cuba in just one day. This was a long haul, especially having covered twice the ground the day before, and once more my opinion of Mark's endurance as a rider went up another notch. Only Paul had stayed behind, having succumbed to the mystery illness, and we explained to Mark about Jack's diagnosis with Giardia. He took the news with mixed relief, much as I had, since he and I were the only ones who had so far shown no symptoms and we were both wondering how we'd managed to avoid the same water source as all the others must have drunk from.

As a result of the shortcut by road and in order to allow everyone the opportunity to visit the clinic and get their anti-Giardia tablets, we took the next day off in Cuba.

Some habits are hard to break though, and the early risers began the day as usual with a 6am breakfast at the Cuba café opposite our motel. Unfortunately this left us with at least 16 hours to explore the delights of Cuba – by the look of things about 15 hours more than we would need. Somehow we managed to fill the day: laundry, ice-cream, nap, coffee, shopping for batteries, haircut, ice-cream, coffee, reading, journal, nap…and it was almost time for dinner.

My barber, Fred, operated a one seat hairdressers from a small wooden shed on the main drag, and clearly had either a past or future life mapped out as a London cabbie. In the space of a mere half inch of hair he gave me a full 35 year biography, a family tree stretching back to the conquistadors and a detailed economic analysis of OPEC's current production strategy. If there had been any donkeys in this town they would all have been dragging themselves around with their rear ends supported on little trolleys by this point.

Late in the afternoon we were back in the Cuba café and watched as the sky turned black as the ace of spades, thunder and lightning crashed almost continuously and what looked like four or five inches of rain fell in a couple of hours. This, at last, was the start of Monsoon, and no bloody good to us whatsoever. The rain would be nowhere near enough to refill the rivers or raise the water table back to the point where springs would start flowing again, but it would be plenty to turn dirt roads into impassable bogs.

A lightning strike started a new brush fire just half a mile or so away in the desert and in full view from the window of the café. We watched the town fire engines start up and drive off in the opposite direction. The wind seemed to be blowing it away from town and with any luck the rain would be heavy enough to put it out before too much damage was done, so maybe they had higher priorities elsewhere.

American Pie

After much discussion, as a group we decided to continue on the alternative road route as far as Grants, two days ride from Cuba. Although it was possible to carry enough water for two days, it might take longer than that if the roads were as bad as we suspected now that the monsoon had broken, and we still had enough people who were either sick, or just recovering from sickness to warrant being cautious.

Our caution was rewarded with a very pleasant ride out of Cuba, along a wide valley then up and out onto a broad desert plain. After around 15 miles we turned west and a stonking tailwind had us hurtling down the road at an average 20-25 miles per hour.

The land we were travelling through was almost all Navajo reservation. Although I was told repeatedly that the Navajo got exactly what they wanted, if that were true I would have to admire their lack of ambition if not their perception of real estate values – you really had to like sand and rocks to appreciate this place.

Having said that, and although it was clearly a very poor area, the drivers were among the most courteous we had encountered, and always waved to us. Everywhere we stopped people were friendly and interested in our trip. A hint of more serious social problems, though, was provided when we stopped at one of the few general stores on the reservation and found the checkout fenced in behind a large steel security cage.

At Pueblo Pintado we stopped at the final store to stock up on water before turning off the road for a couple of miles to make for a site known as the Chaco ruins.

According to local historians the Chaco culture dated back over a thousand years and was closely linked to some of the Aztec remains also found in this area.

At the top of a small hill in the middle of the desert we found the remains of what used to be an enormous three storey building. The ruins themselves had been dated at between 950 and 1000 AD and were in surprisingly good condition. A large fort, almost a city, filled with people once looked out from this hill – over what? It was difficult to believe it had been as arid and barren then as it was now.

We poked around for an hour or two, sifting through the detritus of lives which were so far distant from ours, it was difficult to know how to even begin to connect with them. The ruins were impressive and thought-provoking, but then as I pointed out to the others, there were houses in my street at home only a few hundred years younger, and they had the benefit of a roof and central heating now.

During the evening and most of the night lightning storms ranged all around us, but somehow we managed to escape with just a light sprinkling of rain.

Mark and I were both up before light, much to the annoyance of our fellow campers, but since we knew the day was going to be a long one we were anxious to cover as much ground as possible before the heat of the day set in, and try to arrive before the now regular evening thunderstorm threatened to blast us off the face of the planet. An added bonus of being up so early was that we got to watch the sun come up behind the ruins and contemplate the fact that it had done so at least 360,000 times since anyone had last lived there to watch it.

First stop was five miles back the way we came where we could get a decent coffee at the store, dump all our garbage and most importantly perform our morning rituals in the comfort and privacy of a real bathroom (there are no trees in the desert).

Despite our fears the day started mercifully cloudy and, if anything, a little cool – much like an overcast English summer day,

282

and just perfect for cycling.

For the first thirty miles or so the road twisted and turned through some beautiful canyon country. There was hardly any traffic but some significant, steady climbs and for some reason or other my legs simply didn't want to play today. Maybe they'd got wind of the long distance ahead of them, or maybe they were planning an insurrection. Either way it was only by sheer willpower that I could keep the pedals going round. Unsurprisingly the knee decided to join in with the muscle rebellion and was being particularly cranky. We had at least fifty miles to go before the first store, gas station or café, and I was counting off every one of them. Once over our last crest we crossed a long straight flat plain and at Ambrosia Lake passed the old Uranium mine. I wondered whether it was called Ambrosia lake before or after the mine was established - nice sense of humour if it was after. The mine was closed now (demand for Uranium having probably tailed off a bit with the end of the cold war). Probably someone will re-open it as a health spa soon ("For that all over glow").

The others sighted a herd of Elk just off the road to our left, though I missed them. At first we thought they were domesticated but later learned that they were wild animals, come down from the mountains in search of water. This did not bode well for us. If even the Elk had the sense to come down, should we have been planning to head up there for a week at a time?

As we rolled into Milan, only Pierre was brave enough to eat at the Uranium Cafe (complete with luminous green sign). Jack, Chris and I opted instead for the Dairy Queen fast food option next door where the nearest we were likely to get to radiation poisoning was a microwaved fruit pie.

A little further down the road at Grants itself we took one look at the campsite, another look at the building clouds and unanimously decided to check into a motel. Yet another Stirling silver decision as it turned out.

Sue and I cycled out to the local Wal Mart to get some films developed when the most almighty thunderstorm broke. Within

283

seconds the car park was inches deep in water and getting deeper rapidly. As we stood in the doorway and watched the rain dropping like Niagara on a wet day, we looked at each other and realised after so much desert, it might actually be fun to be out in so much water (especially since we had a warm dry room to go back to). We bought a couple of emergency plastic ponchos (read bin-liners with armholes punched in them) for 50c each, put our helmets on over the top and headed off into the storm. It was difficult to tell who was laughing the most, us or all the people in the restaurants and cars we passed watching us dice with the elements. The ponchos made very little difference to our weather-worthiness but were money well spent in terms of entertainment value.

Grants really is a classic strip development, the whole town is stretched out along either side of the highway in one long chain. This is not too surprising when you realise its principal claim to fame is that it lies on the old (now broken up and renumbered) Route 66, one of the earliest and most important trans-continental highways in the US. Not only did we follow the Continental Divide, we also got to cycle along part of the most famous road in the States. Unfortunately, though it was in its time one of the busiest routes in the country, the old road had since been bypassed and the town, which tied its fortunes to the highway, was in similar decline. There were dozens of old motels, many of which had now closed down and many of the old restaurants had gone too.

It was around this time too that Mark got some bad news. His mother-in-law had been taken seriously ill and he was finding it very hard being so far from his home and family at such a critical time. It was now his turn to agonise over whether or not to continue with the ride and he was torn between carrying on for just eight more days or going home now. He spent hours on the phone trying to organise flights, talking to his wife and daughters and working out what options were open to him. In the end he gave up. It would have taken days and an enormous amount of money to organise a flight out of New Mexico at such short notice, no one could tell him how bad his wife's mother really was, and it wasn't so clear how much he could do if he were there anyway. He decided to carry on and take his scheduled flight back in ten days time. Those of us who had already come close to quitting (and by now that was almost half the group) knew just how hard a call it was.

By now, too, the mental fatigue of the ride was starting to tell. The fact that that finish line was nearly in sight, didn't in any way defuse the stresses and strains brought on by homesickness, rough roads, illness and concerns about water supplies and friction began to build over our proposed route south from Grants.

We would all have liked to follow the off-road route as far as possible, but we also all wanted to finish. One thing we had learned through carrying ourselves and our equipment across so much of the West was a much greater respect for the land and an awareness that even in the 21st century, the wilderness was not so lightly to be conquered.

Most of us agreed a compromise whereby we planned to follow the trail through the desert for two days, then skirt around the main wilderness area and take an alternative loop for the remaining three days ride to Silver City, our final layover point.

The road out from Grants climbed steadily up into the high desert. For nearly thirty miles it followed the edge of a massive, 2000 year old lava flow, black crumbly rock rising about 6 to eight feet up from the desert floor and spread across the valley for four or five miles to the other side. We skirted between the lava and high sandstone cliffs on our left, through an area known as The Narrows. There was also giant natural stone arch etched into the side of the cliffs here. After something like thirty miles we turned off onto a narrow little dirt road and continued a roller coaster climb through more open scrub desert.

Looking for a water source to camp by was a waste of time - there was no water anywhere, other than what we carried, so we simply picked the best-looking campsite we could find once we had ridden into public lands. It was pleasant enough, very sandy and peppered with rocks the size of cars and (more of a problem) nasty little cactus plants, just like the ones people keep in their kitchens at home, with inch long thorns. By way of extra incentive to watch where you were

285

putting your feet, there was a large anthill in the middle of the only open space. I was particularly wary of these little fellows. Earlier in the day I stepped off the road a little way to lighten my load and walking back to the bike felt a really sharp stinging around my ankle. At first I thought it was a thorn, but the stinging got worse and continued for at least half an hour. This was my introduction to Fire Ants, nasty little buggers who had wandered up here from South America. They were as pugnacious as a Saturday night drunk looking for a fight and carried a very nasty venom to add some real punch to their bite.

In the evening we were treated to the most magnificent natural firework show I had ever seen. I was told New Mexico lightning would be special, but couldn't have anticipated anything like this. Enormous forks of lightning started almost right over our heads and blasted the ground on the horizon. The force with which they struck was such that there was an orange afterglow, which flared up immediately after the white light faded. Once the storm had passed the clouds cleared quickly and I sat out under the desert sky, on top of a huge sandstone boulder watching more stars appear than I will probably ever see again. The best view in New Mexico is looking away from Earth into space.

Despite the glory of the desert, though, I was finding those last few days hard going. In my journal I wrote:

I am tired now. Tired of dirt road, tired of rocks, which jounce and crunch my knee, tired of washboard, which shakes my teeth loose, tired of endless hills and headwinds. Yesterday was a hard day, and today was just as hard. I am pushing myself forward each day now on willpower alone and looking forward to the Mexican border and a return to civilised life. It's not that I'm sorry to be here, or that I would ever regret coming. I've just had enough and feel the need for a change.

Not surprising, then, that I was looking forward to some good food and fresh coffee at one of the very few watering holes we were to cross in our journey through the desert. With a name like "Pie Town", in fact, we had all been looking forward to it for days.

When we arrived, around 11 o'clock in the morning, we discovered that Pie Town, in fact, lacks only two things for the tired cyclist – pie, and town. A collection of dusty shacks and a rundown RV park was all we managed to find. At the RV park we were told there was such a thing as the "Pie-O-Neer" café, just down the road (Hurrah!) but it only opened on Thursdays (guess what?) and there was nowhere else to eat in town. We used their tap to fill up all our water containers which took around twenty minutes given how much water we were carrying at this point, then, for another five minutes stood around wistfully looking at each other, looking for a reason to stay longer or hoping to materialise a café by wishfulness alone. When nothing appeared we turned around and headed back out on the trail. It was long, washboarded, sandy and went up and down a lot – what more can I say?

After a while we climbed a little higher, leaving the desert mesa behind and gradually saw more and more trees – at first just the odd tall rangy juniper next to an abandoned windmill or a derelict ranch house, then pinons, small pines and finally we entered the Apache National Forest.

Just inside the forest we found the first running water we had seen for days, a small creek no more than six inches wide in places and only a couple of inches deep. It was enough for us and we set up camp just before the first of the afternoon storms rumbled in. In between showers I dashed in and out of my tent to stir the supper, which was cooking in the shelter of a large tree. I was nervous of it blowing over so hung around for a while to keep an eye on things. It was while I was doing this that I spotted three more cyclists, not part of our group, on the road up above me. I shouted and waved and ran up to see who they were. Two young girls and a boy of around 23 or 24 they were clearly pretty fit and seasoned Divide Riders. They'd set out a little later than us but had been riding longer days and planned to finish a day or so ahead of us, in time to get back to college. From the look of them I had no doubt they'd do it, but asked them where they were headed for that night, since the weather was already starting to close in. They told me they wanted to try and make a spring which was marked on the maps at Valle Tio Vences, another five miles up the trail. I wished them luck and went back to my haute cuisine. An hour and a half later two out of the three of them were back with more mud attached to them than a Mississippi mud wrestler. They were literally dragging their bikes behind them where the thick gooey dirt had built up around the wheels and locked them solid, packed between the tyres and the frame. They'd only made it around three quarters of a mile up the road before they'd ground to a halt as effectively as if someone had simply locked both brakes on. One had stayed to set up camp by the side of the road where they stopped, and to look after their gear, while the others dragged their bikes back down the hill to try to wash some of the mud clear in the tiny creek where we were camped. Any smugness we may have harboured was well tempered by the thought of negotiating the same road tomorrow morning after what promised to be more rain during the night. We helped them as much as we could with the bikes and offered them a share of our supper to save them using up any more of their own water for cooking when they got back. The pleasure of our own supper was somewhat alloyed by the discovery that most of the others had been a little more persistent than we had back at Pie Town and had not only located the eponymous Pie-O-Neer café, but had banged loudly enough and repeatedly enough on the door to persuade them to open up, Thursday or no. The descriptions of mammoth portions of cherry, apple and rhubarb pie with crisp pastry and thick fresh cream did nothing to enhance the gastronomic experience of stodgy rice and tuna a la Grecq (someone found an old tin of olives in their bag). This time when the Coyotes sang their way along the valley at night I could have joined in, mourning with them, having missed out on the fabulous Pie Town Pies.

We left camp late (8 am!) to try to give the road a chance to dry out. There was a short climb up to the continental divide (the 21st crossing on the route and the last above 8,000ft), and although the road was still muddy, it was rideable. This type of mud was sneaky. Instead of your normal gloopy, common-or-garden slop, this stuff looked ok, until, as you worked your way through it, you realised it was gradually accumulating thicker and thicker on your tyres. If it got really bad it would eventually just clog everything up and leave you with a bicycle which might as well be fitted with square wheels for all the chance you had of actually riding it anywhere. This time though, we managed to make our way through it (just). For once I was helped by having slicker tyres than anyone else. Although they provided less grip, there was practically nothing on the road to grip anyway, and the absence of any tread to speak of just meant there was that much less for the mud to stick to. For the first time in ages I started to pull ahead of the others going uphill and started to feel some of the strength coming back into my legs at last. Once over the divide the road dried a little and as the descent steepened and swooped along the speed gradually threw all of the mud that as left from the tyres (and onto whatever else was available – generally the face of anyone foolish enough to follow too close behind).

Once we turned onto the highway the road down to the small town of Reserve was an absolute gem. Dropping very gently most of the way, it wound its way through a long and beautiful valley, the first real greenery we had seen in weeks and livestock whose ribs were discretely covered in polite quantities of flesh. A clear indicator that it was a much richer area than any part of New Mexico we'd seen outside of Santa Fe, was the fact that it registered a mere 2.4 on the beer-can scale. The simplest measure of any (populated) part of New Mexico was to count the number of empty beer cans by the side of the road. In some places this got as high as sixty or more per mile before we got bored counting. The roads here, by contrast, were almost can-free. There were even two or three small country stores strategically placed along the route for breakfast, coffee and lunch. At one tiny place we had to rouse the octogenarian owner from her mid-morning nap to serve us. She claimed to have owned and operated the store continuously for the last sixty years. I refrained from pointing out that some of the stock looked as though it had become very familiar with the shelves over that time. Bizarrely, though not much inside had changed since the forties, she had just had built, outside a pair of the most massive and luxurious log-cabin outhouses I had ever seen. The interiors would have raised no eyebrows if they had been installed at the Ritz, though the exteriors looked more like a set for Santa's Grotto or Hansel and Gretel's house in the woods. One by one we trooped through them just in order to savour the experience.

Gradually the country opened up more and became drier again and the pinons gave way to scrub grass and small thorn bushes.

At night we thought we heard wolves, quite a different and more haunting sound than the baying of Coyotes we had become used to, and in the morning Jack and Chris thought they spotted one slinking along a dry riverbed next to the road.

The Silver-Grey Wolf had recently been reintroduced into the wild in this area by conservationist groups. Not surprisingly this had not gone down too well with the local population, who were mostly ranchers and whose ancestors had spent a lot of time and effort going out of their way to *ex-troduce* the wolf from the countryside in order to protect their livestock. The argument as it raged among the general populace, though, seemed to have more to do with the principle of the Wild West Vs Washington & Federal Government than with the real economics of ranching, especially given the numbers of wolves they were talking about. Most places we went there were posters up in the Post Offices making it clear that anyone found guilty of killing a wolf faced a fine of up to $25,000 dollars or 3 years in jail, whatever the circumstances. It interested me, by contrast, to find a separate poster advertising the forthcoming county fair, and listing as one of its attractions the 'Coyote Weigh-In'; first prize $100 for the most coyotes (dead, I assumed), second prize $60 for the heaviest, third prize $40 for the lightest ("No Bill, don't shoot that one, get the little feller over there, he's tiny!")

It struck me that if this continued the Coyotes were going to get REALLY pissed off at the wolves for lowering the tone of the neighbourhood. Maybe the wolves were the ones who are wily after all.

In Buckhorn the walls of the cafe were decorated with photos of Heidi X, of the 'Didn't Miss' Taxidermy, and her trophies. Heidi apparently specialised in stuffing bear and mountain lion. I wondered whether she could lend me a couple of hundred stuffed coyotes in time for the county fair ("Well they're DEAD, aren't they?"). Maybe we could spend the prize money on Acme gift vouchers for the remaining coyotes to buy rocket-propelled roller skates, dynamite and birdman outfits to escape the wily hunters.

By now we were back down to just over 6,000 feet and in real desert country for the remainder of the ride. There were flowering cacti by the side of the road and huge fields of giant Yucca. If it grew here it was going to be a) Tough and b) Spiky. Unsurprisingly our toll of punctures, hitherto fairly rare, began to mount rapidly.

I picked up another sign for my growing collection.

High up on one board, in bold red capitals it read:

"WORMS!"

The below, in smaller type on another board:

"Need Help? Try God".

I suppose if you are a worm that's about the only place you're likely to get any help. Evidently coyotes either can't read or don't deserve any help since there was no mention of any assistance programmes for them anywhere along the way. There was one creature which we came across more and more often (though we never actually saw them) and which definitely did need help, or at least counselling - cicadas. Huge numbers of the neurotic little buggers hid from sight in the trees or the grass all around us, and you would have no idea they were there. Then one of them would start chirruping, another one joined in and suddenly a chain reaction started which set the whole lot off. Wave after wave of sound would ebb and swirl all around you. The noise was like an incredibly loud garden sprinkler, the type with a little paddle that splashes in and out of the water jet, spraying it everywhere. Slowly it would die down and fade away, then go quiet for another five minutes until one of the little herberts would set the whole damn show off again.

Snake, rattle and roll

By the time we reached Silver City we had only two days riding left and were pretty much in party mood. We celebrated with an extra large breakfast, a trip to the cinema, and a farewell meal for everyone in the evening. Most of the tensions of the previous few weeks had dissolved, though there was still a slight nervous anticipation in the air. After three months on the road we had all become fairly settled in a new way of life. Our tents were our homes, this strange mix of people had become our immediate family and our bicycles were our work. When we had first met in Whitefish all those months back it had been difficult to imagine getting to this point – it was still twelve weeks and nearly three thousand miles away, and we really had only a very vague idea of what it would take to get there (assuming we made it), what we would see and feel on the way and how it might change us in the process. I think we were all looking forward to going home, but we had all changed at such an accelerated rate over the summer, we would never quite fit straight back into the hole we'd left in our previous lives.

Still, we had a little more time to contemplate that, and the next two days held a few more surprises for us yet.

Between Silver City and our final destination Antelope Wells on the Mexican border was a whole load of nothing much according to the map. About the only point which offered any intermediate respite from the desert was at Hachita, some 82miles south of us.

Since we knew it was going to be a long day we were once again up well before light and failed to endear ourselves to the motel staff by banging on the door of the restaurant at 5:30 am demanding to be fed. The sky was black with rain and lightning rattled around the horizon. I decided the safest response to this was to order an additional short stack of pancakes and a fried egg to supplement my complimentary 'continental' breakfast of coffee and cereal – you don't cycle 80 miles on an empty tank.

By the time we were ready to roll, light was just starting to pick out the edges of the clouds and the rain appeared to be holding off for the moment.

On the way out of Silver City we passed the gigantic Tyrone mine. I hadn't realised that was where all the Tyrones came from, but why anyone would want to dig them out of the ground and how so many of them ended up In Liverpool was anybody's guess. The highway south was a very busy one, and having had my elbows shaved a few times (usually by huge articulated lorries or 'semis', or almost equally large RVs) I was more than happy to turn off after around 18 miles to follow a narrow dirt trail into the desert. The track meandered between giant Yucca plants and little fat cacti and alternated in a very disconcerting and unpredictable fashion between hard packed dirt and soft sand. Unsurprisingly, most of the sand was to be found at the bottom of the hills, and, depending on the depth, you could either experience the delight of going from 35mph to zero in a tenth of a second (optionally accompanied with an introduction to free fall flight if caught unawares) or the equally entertaining sensation of having the handlebars disconnected completely from the front wheel.

Eventually we climbed once more up to the level of the Continental Divide and were rewarded for our efforts by an astonishing view. Every time I thought I had exhausted the potential for this ride to surprise me it threw up something new. For nearly 15 miles the ride followed the line of the divide itself as we rode along the very top of a high sandstone ridge. The desert stretched away on either side, spotted with giant Yucca and in the distance the mountains rose, jagged and misty, up into low clouds. As a finale to our dirt riding experience it was quite simply, magnificent. Even after so long on the road, with so many miles still to go, with aches and pains in most of my joints and half of my muscles I loved it and felt privileged to be there.

As we dropped off the ridge I finally spotted my first Roadrunner, making a dash off into the desert. I shouted "Meep-Meep" to him as loud as I could, but he didn't seem too interested in conversation. Once again I felt myself coming out in sympathy for the Coyotes. Damn, those little birds were fast, and scrawny with it! If that was all there was on the breakfast menu out here it wouldn't take much to persuade me a career change was in order, from scavenger to rustler.

Around four in the afternoon we finally rolled up outside the Hachita Gas Stop and Café. Over the duration of this trip I had come to use the word 'Town' to describe just about anywhere I could buy food or drink, and that just about summed up Hachita. What it lacked in size, though, it made up for in quality.

Alma, the owner/waitress/manager of the Hachita café was a pure gem.

She had a permanent smile fixed to her face, could not do enough to help us and was a great cook. The other, semi-permanent residents of the café were Patricia, a retired nurse from California, and Jim, a large bearded gentleman with an artificial leg and a scar running from his chin to his waistband.

Patricia could have competed with Fred the barber in the talking stakes, but had a wealth of information on the history and the current gossip of the area, most of which got mixed up together as though Pearl Harbour happened yesterday and who was marrying Marie-Helen from the Circle-G ranch was a matter of world import.

Jim informed us in a very matter-of-fact way that he had come here to die. He didn't elaborate as to how or why, and we didn't ask - but from the look of him he had already made a good start to the process.

In the evening we were treated to yet another spectacular display of natural pyrotechnics, with forked lightning filling the sky every two to three seconds. In places it was still so warm that although we could see the rain dropping from below huge black clouds, it seemed to evaporate again before it even hit the ground.

For our final day on the road we had a long flat ride straight to the border. For a mile or so we found ourselves being shadowed by a curious coyote (presumably thought we looked slower and a lot fatter than those pesky little roadrunners – and with good reason I might add).

Around midday, Mark, Sue and I were riding three abreast along the quiet, straight road when we spotted a dead snake on the tarmac ahead of us. As we got to within less than a couple of feet of it though, there were two problems with it which we hadn't anticipated. One: it was a rattlesnake, and Two: it wasn't yet dead. It suddenly reared to strike, rattling its tail viciously and three bicyclists changed direction like someone had let off a hand grenade in the middle of them. When we pulled ourselves back together again and made sure nobody had been bitten we looked back down the road, but were so far away we couldn't make out if it was still there or not. Nobody volunteered to go back to check. It must have been hit by a car later, because Dean told us it was dead by the time he arrived, so he cut off the rattle for a souvenir – sooner him than me all the same.

A few miles further on we encountered a much friendlier roadblock – a tortoise, a real, wild tortoise. I know it might not have been everyone's idea of a wildlife safari, but personally I was delighted. It was the first, and probably the last time I was ever likely to see a tortoise in the wild and became one of the abiding images of the trip for me.

As we got closer to the border we were all counting down the miles. At first 20, then 9, then 5, then suddenly Mark seemed to turn on the turbo boost and we were all hammering through the last three miles as though our lives depended on it.

Then...we were there, Antelope Wells, border crossing with Mexico, the target of months of work and years of planning, the end of one road, and the beginning of another.

We had a couple of hours for tired muscles to unwind while we waited for our shuttle bus to Tucson, and after all the shouting and celebrating was over, all our minds started to turn to getting back into our day-to-day lives again.

It had been a great summer, and a magnificent journey – two thousand miles and over a hundred thousand feet of climbing. For myself, I was just happy to have got there. I hadn't cycled all the way, I hadn't even stuck to the suggested route. I'd taken two weeks out and missed Wyoming altogether. I'd ridden buses, cycled the highway and carried less gear than anybody else. It certainly hadn't worked out the way I'd planned, or even the way I would have liked, but in the end, one way or the other and with a little persistence, I'd managed to get to my destination eventually – and isn't that the way it works out for most of us?

Discovering Japan
A Very Volcanic Summer
Sept. to Nov. 2003

2003 was a very Volcanic Summer, one way or another. First Iceland, then I spent two months cycling around Japan.

I began my trip there by spending a couple of days with a friend in Tokyo, then caught the overnight sleeper to Sapporo in Hokkaido, Japan's northernmost island.

Having cycled across the middle of Hokkaido I flew down to Kyushu in the far south of Japan where I spent another month completing a figure-of-eight tour of the island.

Finally, I rounded off the trip with a manic one week train tour of Honshu, the mainland.

Commuters, Cauldrons and Samurai Cows

Arriving at Narita airport just outside Tokyo you can't help but feel the contrast with the experience of the poor travellers who come to the UK for the first time and turn up at Heathrow full of expectations of Olde Englande looking for charm, courtesy and that fabled English politeness....to be faced with a dirty, smelly run down dump manned by glowering monosyllabic grumps. Passage through Narita by contrast, was clean, swift and clichedly efficient.

At immigration I was asked politely "Why two months in Japan?"

"For a bicycle tour."

The slightest of raised eyebrows. "OK, but please be sure, you no work. This is tourist visa. No working, understand?"

Well, all right then, if you put it like that. How nice to be encouraged to be a layabout.

At baggage claim there was even an airport official waiting for me with my bicycle UPRIGHT - a significant change from the tangled wreckage that usually trundles past on a conveyor belt at Heathrow. I became slightly more suspicious of this level of service, though, as I made my way through the airport complex towards the railway station. At the head, and the foot of each escalator a white-gloved senior citizen bowed and ushered us onto, then off the steps. Now I may be being a little cynical here, but even if you've just arrived from the depths of the Borneo jungle, a moving stairway might be a little surprising, but it's not that complicated to operate, and since there were solid walls on three sides at the bottom, it was equally unlikely that any of us were going to get lost when we did manage to dismount.

There is an interesting approach to unemployment in Japan which fosters a suspiciously low official statistic for the not-so-great unwashed (something like 1.2%). This is not quite so surprising when you take into account the seemingly endless array of people you encounter whose sole function is to bow, smile and wave you in the right direction. They all sport obligatory white cotton gloves and a degree of seriousness I would find very difficult to reconcile with that sort of task. It is just this seriousness that throws me. It would all smack very much of digging trenches and filling them in again were it not for the fact that these guys are trying really hard to help. It adds a whole new perspective to the concept of 'the dignity of work'. Whatever they are doing may be of no use to man nor beast. But it's clearly important to them to do it as well as they can. What the hell, I'd rather pay them to do that than soak up daytime TV and clog up the post office every Tuesday morning.

For the first few days I was staying with a friend in a neat, if small apartment in a tidy low-rise block on the outskirts of Tokyo. 'Outskirts' is not quite the right word, since it's impossible to say where the city ends. I assume there is a logical division, some form of prefecture, but the buildings just keep going on and on. At least there were a few trees out here and more houses and low-rise buildings than big blocks. The sense of space was exacerbated by the large baseball ground next door. By now it was lashing down with rain and I was grateful to be indoors looking out. As I was standing on the balcony the chainlink fence surrounding the baseball ground suddenly began to rattle. Then it rattled rather a lot. Then the balcony started wiggling around. My first earthquake, and a reasonable size one at that, 5.5 on the Richter scale. Actually, not quite my first, as there was a very minor one in Montana that wobbled the laundromat I was in ever so slightly. This one left me with the uneasy feeling that the ground was continuing to move for at least a couple of hours afterwards.

After lunch we took the train two stops further up the line to Tachikawa. First up was a visit to one of Tokyo's many huge department stores. The predominant sensation here could be summed up in a single word - cacophony. Radios blaring, people trying out electronic keyboards, shop assistants shouting (sometimes into megaphones) and above everything a series of maddening, endlessly looping, plinky-plink jingles coming over the store tannoy. The concept of noise pollution has some ground to gain here.

Later, a fine supper was had at a revolving sushi bar. The food itself was not that different from Sushi to be found in London, but the quality of the fish in this particular restaurant was clearly very high, and there was a much larger proportion of slimy, tentacly or generally just unrecognisable dishes on display. At first we were a little put out when the staff insisted we sit just inside the door, rather than further in where there was clearly more room, but all was explained when, five minutes later the chef came out. The first thing he did was to cause a pile up...of Sushi that is. Putting his hand across the conveyor he backed up all the remaining dishes into one long, joggling line. The, having let them go again, he deftly whipped out a couple of extra sections of conveyor, flipped a barrier across and with a grin that would have sat well on the fat controller himself redirected all the traffic onto a new, shorter circuit so that all of the remaining dishes now looped quickly in front of the few remaining customers. Very neat.

On the way home my friend translated a small poster at the station, it politely requested that gentlemen abjure from groping the schoolgirls - an unpleasant, but apparently very common problem on Japan's very crowded trains.

The following day I wandered into downtown Tokyo to find the Tourist information centre. En route I passed through the new International forum, an impressive glass exhibition centre guarded (honestly) at the entrance by a plastic samurai cow. Cool.

The TIC were very helpful and gave me a map of Tokyo (my third) and some rather skimpy notes on camping and cycling in Japan, so I headed back to Tokyo station to pick up a tour bus as being the quickest way to get an overview of the city

The theme of the tour seemed to be "There's not much to see in Tokyo so let's not kid ourselves and get this over with as quickly as possible."

Our guide was a nifty septuagenarian, Nakagawa San who insisted we call him by his Americanised name, Ned. As if to emphasise the nature of the tour as being about not very much he would punctuate his description of the sights with such gems as "oh, and on our left we can see a blind man. With stick. Aaaahhh. Must be very difficult to be blind man in Tokyo, no?"

First stop was Tokyo tower that was, well a tower, with aerials on it. The most striking thing about the view from the top was that whichever way you looked, all you could see was Tokyo. Buildings, as far as the horizon, with the one exception, far off and topped by clouds, the base of mount Fuji.

Ten minutes then back onto the bus for our next stop, which wasn't - we drove past the Parliament building, at least I think we did, we went past so quickly I couldn't guarantee which one was the parliament building, though there was a tower which had recently been struck by lightning. Then, the imperial palace, though again you couldn't actually SEE it. We wandered through the grounds up to one of the entrances from where we could just pick out bits of a green roof through the trees, then, back to the bus. Next stop Buddhist temple and shopping centre. With what appeared to be a 'if you can't beat em, join em' attitude the priests who had set up this temple had actively encouraged traders to set up nearby in a 'fair and honest' trading zone. Outside the temple was a large iron cauldron filled with sand studded with sticks of incense. People crowded round and wafted the smoke over themselves 'for good health'; so apparently passive smoking IS good for you. Inside for 100 Yen (about 60p) you could see your fortune. To do this you would pick up a small octagonal aluminium drum and shake it. From a small hole at one end would drop one of about 50 or so bamboo sticks, each with a number on it. From the relevant drawer you could then pull out a piece of paper describing your fortune. Out of curiosity I snuck a look at half a dozen different sheets and amazingly they were all remarkably similar!

New York may be the city that never sleeps, Tokyo is the city that never stops commuting. The rush hour seems to run from around six in the morning until 11 at night. In the evening I headed for Shibuya, Tokyo's equivalent of Soho. Even at 8 or 9pm the railway stations were packed to capacity. When I got to Shibuya itself I couldn't believe the sheer volume of people there were just milling around.

This is the area where all the bright young things hang out. Some of them were very young. On just about every street corner were packs of young girls in school uniform, and while most of these were certainly quite innocently watching the world go by, there are also, apparently, significant numbers trawling for randy salarymen to pick them up and 'show them a good time'. This practice is apparently widespread enough for it to have generated its own euphemism: "Compensated Dating".

Even if I had been so inclined, my chances of finding a date that evening would have been pretty slim since I was booked into a capsule hotel and I somehow think that might not have been seen as much of a compensation.

Most of the capsule hotels are all male affairs and they largely owe their existence not so much to the intense pressure on living space in central Tokyo as to the extreme work ethic that pervades so much of Japanese industry. Capsule Hotels are explicitly designed for the tired Salaryman who has just finished an 18 hour day, has been obliged to top it off with a few beers with the boss and is too tired/drunk/late to get the last train home and still get back in time for work in the morning.

At the reception desk you are handed a pair of slippers, a Yakuta (a thin cotton dressing gown) and a locker key. In the locker room everyone strips down to their underpants, dumps their clothes in the locker and slips into their Yakuta. In a bizarre way, its a great leveller. Once checked in, everyone looks the same and its a little like being in some obscure gentleman's club. There is a smoking room, a massage parlour, a huge communal shower room and hot bath, a restaurant/bar and TV room. When you finally decide to retire for the night you make your way to the dormitory corridors where your capsule awaits you. These are generally stacked two or three high, made out of cream coloured fibreglass and something like an oversized coffin. Once you have scrambled in there is just enough space to sit cross legged. There is a TV, a radio and alarm clock as well as air conditioning and of course a thin mattress and duvet. Generally there's just about everything you would need in a hotel room except the space. However you would need to be fairly drunk to get any real sleep since it's an overwhelmingly noisy experience and the fibreglass serves to catch and magnify every noise from the corridor which is only ever closed off from you by a thin curtain. In the morning disposable toothbrushes, toothpaste and razors are all provided free of charge and in the foyer shirts, ties and even suits are on sale for those who may have arrived a little smudged the night before.

It was a unique experience, and a great introduction to some of the finer points of Japanese accommodation etiquette before I slipped away from Tokyo and caught the sleeper train for the 800km ride north to the island of Hokkaido.

Sapporo and the central highlands

"**I**ce-e-creamu, ice-e-creamu..." ...at 6 in the morning for god's sake? At some point during the night we had passed through the long tunnel joining Hokkaido to Honshu and I woke up to a grey, drizzly morning on Japan's northernmost island. In the corridor the trolley lady was still doing her best to get rid of her Cornettos but I didn't see anyone getting crushed in the rush to get the last one. Outside through my convex tiny window I could see low clouds pushing down on thickly wooded hillsides. Although Hokkaido is traded as Japan's 'Big Country' with wide-open spaces, at this stage at least it was clear that Montana it ain't. Yes, I could see fields for the first time since I arrived here, but alongside the railway track was still pretty much one continuous conurbation. The main difference so far was that the houses are ever so slightly bigger, many have a parking space and the roads between them are wide enough for two cars to pass without folding in their wing mirrors.

After 16 hours on the train I felt like I'd grown sea legs - everything kept rocking around me. At least I'd be ready if there was another earthquake.

After a quick cup of coffee in the station I set about putting my bike back together as quickly as possible. I tried to fit myself into a small corner as out of the way as possible, but before I was halfway through I saw a station official making a beeline for me so I braced myself for a lecture on passageways, fire hazards or some other sort of nonsense. By the time he reached me I could see he was a tall, slightly gaunt grey haired man, probably in his late fifties.

"Where are you from, please?"

"London"

"Ah so, desu ka?" (Oh really?). "Bicycle here in Hokkaido?"

"Yes, touring".

"Ahhhh....I wish you very happy journey" and he turned and left.

It took me ages to work out what had felt so strange about that encounter. The best I could come up with was the fact that he simply didn't behave as though he was wearing a uniform. His questions and his wishes were not only friendly, they were purely personal. In a small way I was lifted and strolled out of the concourse with a smile on my face. Even the cleaning lady bowed. smiled and held the door open for me as I wheeled my dirty bicycle across her freshly polished floor. Oops.

Outside it was raining steadily, in a way that suggested that it could go on for as long as it felt like, so I made a swift decision to spend the day in Sapporo. The lonely Planet guide suggested two Ryokan or traditional Japanese style inns only a block or two away from the station, so I decided to take the plunge and see how much of a fool I could make of myself in taking the full brunt of Japanese traditional etiquette. The guidebook itself gave very good descriptions of both places omitting only the final detail of exactly how to find them. Although there was a map too, this indicated a small dot in the middle of a large square so it was not immediately obvious which side of the block the ryokan faced onto the street. To make absolutely sure of confusion none of the streets were named or numbered either. Still, after about 15 minutes of riding around I finally tracked down one of the two.

I was greeted by a charming elderly couple. Without a great deal of English they managed to make clear to me that there was a room free, that it would be 4000 Yen for one night. but they were a little bit concerned- I did understand that this was Japanese-style inn, shared bathroom?

Using my best bluff- of course I've done this lots of times before,

I'm not silly you know- voice I explained that would be fine and hoped to god they didn't find me shaving in the washing up bowl or showering in the ladies only toilet or something.

My room itself was a small square, covered with tatami matting and not much else in it apart from a floor cushion, a low table and a lacquer ware bowl containing a green tea kit.

After I had settled in the elderly lady came back and made tea for me, explaining how to use the various bits and pieces and asked if I would like my futon rolled out now or later. I settled for later and headed off to explore downtown Sapporo. By this point it was fairly lashing down with rain, but somehow when you know you've got somewhere dry to stay and you're idly wandering in and out of warm shops it doesn't seem to bother you so much as when you're cycling up a mountain to a cold, dark campsite. Sapporo was a pleasant, clean and thoroughly modern city. Still not quite as many recognisably western branded shops as say, Singapore or Penang, which was nice. Out of idle curiosity I headed for Susukino, "the largest entertainment district outside Tokyo" to find it was essentially one long string of girlie bars. Since the male gene which wants to pay £50 for a beer while some hapless girl sits next to you talking rubbish and pretending to like you is missing from my particular chromosomes, I turned around and went back to the shops which were much more interesting.

The next morning I was shaken awake at around 5am. The only trouble was, when I sat up and looked around I couldn't see who it was that had been doing the shaking. What was more the shaking itself was continuing quite vigorously. I got onto my knees (that seemed far enough at the time) and looked out the window to see the ten storey building opposite doing a shimmy that would not have looked out of place on an 80's dancefloor. Nearer to me I watched a tall streetlamp trace a 45 degree arc through the night air. For a few seconds I was awake enough to debate the correct protocol under these circumstances - should I run naked screaming into the street, should I stand by the window? by the door? In the corner of the room? In the middle of the room? By the time I'd gone through all the options the rumbling and shaking had started to die down so I did the most sensible thing and went back to sleep. About an hour and a half later the whole thing repeated itself. Fortunately the epicentre of the earthquake was somewhere out to sea, but talking to a number of locals later that morning it was still the largest shake in living memory in that part of Japan.

I finally emerged around half eight and after a quick Japanese-style shower and shave I packed the bike and headed off to Starbucks for breakfast. Suitably fortified and caffeinated I set out for route 3 south. This was fortunate indeed as there was a strong north wind blowing and thanks to the gods I found myself bowling along with a stonking tailwind nearly all day. Although there was a fair amount of traffic heading out of Sapporo, it was fairly slow moving and the streets wide with a good wide shoulder, making for fairly pleasant cycling. After an almost uncountable number of traffic lights I finally broke free of the city and for 35km rolled across a broad, largely flat plain. Eventually I branched off and spent a very pleasant afternoon climbing steadily into the hills. Yunburi was a nice little town. When I got to the campsite, although there was a small army of people sweeping and tidying it I was slightly disconcerted to find I was the only resident. As a result I pitched my tent directly under the shelter of one of the cooking areas - wisely as it turned out since it rained quite hard during the night.

From Yunburi I rolled downhill with the wind behind me for almost 19km before leaving the main road and turning back north again. For a long time the road wound gently from side to side, following the broad river down below and gradually climbing up towards the mountains ahead. The trees were just starting to turn and providing a good sample of some of the glorious colours yet to come. In outward appearance the area was very much like parts of France or Germany, the Alsace say, but the mountains here were peakier and every now and again there was a glimpse of an out of place clump of bamboo of some other exotic flora to remind you that you were on the other side of the planet.

The infrastructure in Japan, roads and rail, must surely be the best in the world. The roads are wide, superbly surfaced, well maintained and, with the aid of a lot of tunnels, cut a gentle gradient through some seriously lumpy mountains.

Most of the road signs were in Kanji (Japanese script), so I found myself inventing my own shorthand for map reading- "Ok, crow on a picnic table next to a backwards 3, a pregnant woman and a TV set, where was that again?" A few, though were translated into English, with some charming variations. "Caution- this area infested by bear".

By 1:30 I'd already reached my destination. I pitched up initially at a broad, well laid out picnic site next to the lake. Only problem was the campsite (official) was 500m further back dark, damp, gloomy and particularly unprepossessing. I decided to wait till dusk and take my chance on pitching at the picnic ground, on the basis that I'd be up and away before anybody turned up the next day and hopefully no-one would mind too much.

The following morning I awoke to a very wet tent and a distinct chill in the air, having again rained hard during the night. I got up fairly early to pack the tent away though. Amazingly, even at 8am on a wet Sunday morning there were still one or two tourists wandering around taking photos. Having fortified myself with a heavy cup of coffee I made the fatal mistake of wandering off to the loos leaving all my stuff spread out on a nearby picnic table. Now, strangely enough in Japan, generally you can do this sort of thing and get away with it. The level of petty crime is remarkably low and people are generally very honest. However, nobody told this to the crows. who are thieving bastards wherever you go. I got back to find most of my food scattered all over the campsite, but worst of all one bugger had ripped open my sacrosanct supply of Starbucks coffee, coffee which I was going to have to ration over the next two weeks. I was not impressed. The trip to Furano was relatively uneventful apart from one short stretch - this was my longest tunnel so far at 2.5km. Up to this point I'd always been able to see the exit. This one made me a little more nervous. I covered myself with as much reflective material as I could, lots of flashing red LEDs, put my head down and pedalled like Billy-oh. Mostly the traffic was fine, but the thought that if anybody did get it wrong there would be nowhere for me to go acted as an excellent incentive to set a speed record and I popped out of the other end like a champagne cork.

Furano was a pleasant enough town, but definitely on the backwater side of populous. Still I found an excellent sushi-to-go restaurant that had the added advantage that they didn't seem to mind when I didn't actually go, but proceeded to eat mine on the premises. so much so that they even brought me a cup of tea. As the weather was still lousy I checked myself into a nice Ryokan by the station and spread my tent, sleeping bag and assorted clothes around the room to dry out-, which was just as well since next morning, amazingly, it was raining again.

On the map the journey from Furano to Biei looked like a relatively easy day, which just goes to prove you can't always believe a map. I had enormous trouble getting out of Furano. For some reason I just could not make the combination of town and road maps and compass bearings match what I could see on the ground. Eventually I worked out it was because I had assumed I was on the other side of the railway station and, having checked with a local taxi driver pedalled off north on the main road at last. To begin with at least I had a tailwind, unfortunately it brought with it some fairly foul weather and by the time I started climbing up into the hills it had turned seriously sour. What began as a gentle climb, too, soon turned into a serious slog. For about two hours I sweated up a steep gradient, switching backwards and forwards, in lowest gear into the teeth of a lashing headwind and pouring rain. At times I was reduced to stopping every half km just to get my breath back, swear a bit, then pedal some more. It reminded me of a long climb I'd had over the Andes many years back in similar weather, and I used the same mantra to get me through it as then: "So long as the pedals keep going round, you'll get there eventually. All you have to do is keep them going round". Still it was a graft, when I finally reached the top I rewarded myself with some lunch, then added a few more layers of clothing for the long descent into Biei. I was hoping the views might have made it all worthwhile, and they might have done. had I been able to see them. Instead all I got for the first 20km was thick fog, then more rain to follow By the time I got into Biei I was not in the best frame of mind, I struggled to find the tourist information office, struggled to smile when a little Japanese lady quite deliberately butted in front of me, then struggled to find the minshuku (guesthouse) only two blocks away with the map and directions they had given me. I think that Japan, like the US in some way, has suffered from its isolationism in some odd ways that we in Europe have not. Both countries rely very heavily on written signs and tend to use symbols much less than multi-cultural Europe. As a result, unless you can read Kanji it's very hard to tell a bicycle shop from a hotel. In this case, to complicate matters further, it turned out the bicycle shop WAS the hotel. Still the lady was very nice about me dripping all over her floor, despite her lack of English and my lack of Japanese we managed to negotiate a room, although I failed abysmally to conjure any supper. I used the word for 'dinner' and she showed me to what was clearly a dining room, then left me to it. I have no idea if I was supposed to find and cook it myself or what, but after an hour and a bit, I gave up and went back to my room for a beer and bananas.

The next day dawned reasonably bright, and dry at least, but cold and there were low clouds on the horizon. On balance I decided against another trek up into the mountains on the assumption that however nice it was. once up there I would be unlikely to be able to see much of it anyway. Instead I opted for a very leisurely roll into Asahikawa, the 2nd biggest city of Hokkaido. The fog eventually lifted, though the clouds still sat gloomily over the hills. Although the traffic was fairly heavy it never felt uncomfortable and I sailed through a landscape of small farms and rice paddies. by 10:30 I was in Asahikawa and heading for the station to pick up a town map. I made a mental note to try to set off early the following morning as it was likely to be a longer ride. For the first time on this trip the lonely planet guide had come up with what turned out to be a useful suggestion. The Teikyo Ryokan was very close to the centre of town, not too expensive. friendly and helpful. I'm beginning to like the Ryokan, preferring the simplicity of the rooms, futons and tatami mats to conventional western style rooms with beds. The strange smell, a combination of green tea and tatami is even growing on me too. Having arrived early I spent the rest of the day feeding myself up (I think I've been losing weight too quickly) and just chilling out in the sunshine. I say sunshine, but although the day stayed mostly fine the ominous black clouds were never far away and I remained unsure as to what tomorrow would bring weather wise. One momentary picture stuck in my mind as I was cycling into town - a grey haired grandmother, complete with pinny being dragged along by her tiny grandson, him full of energy, enthusiasm and bounce, she laughing and clutching in her other hand a wilting yellow dandelion flower obviously freshly plucked for her. It struck me as a universally happy picture and made me smile.

The evening meal at Teikyo Ryokan was awesome. I was initially ushered to my cushion at a very low table in the dining room. The first problem was that since I'm physically incapable of sitting cross-legged I had to kneel - which was fine for about 5 minutes, then increasingly painful. Spread out on a tray in front of me was an alarming array of beautifully presented dishes, one or two of which were vaguely recognisable. To this were quickly added a bowl of rice, some green tea and a large fondue-type device with a sizzling slice of beef, onion and green chilli inside. The only problem I had was (literally) knowing where to start. I got around this on my own way by trying a little of everything in turn.

Breakfast was remarkably similar to supper, if anything marginally less recognisable, my only regret that I didn't think to take a photo before I destroyed its artistic layout.

Cycling out of Asahikawa was painless enough, much as when leaving Sapporo, just an hour or so of endless traffic lights. The afternoon more than made up for it though, climbing steadily through a long, narrow and very steep gorge to Sounkyo. Either side were sheer cliffs, their side riddled with curling flaws and lines like scrolls. at the very top and right up to, and often just over the edges, a fringe

311

of trees in every autumn colour available. The sun even tried its best to hold out, giving up finally at the point when I was just reaching for my camera, naturally. Still, the day was thankfully dry, and in many ways a beautiful autumn day, though it had been getting progressively colder. Sounkyo itself was fairly unprepossessing, a nest of large concrete hotels crammed into a pretty location to the point where they almost smother it.

My good mood up to that point was sorely tested by the tribulations of trying to find anything in Sounkyo. There were, to begin with at least 3 different variations on where to find the tourist information office- including a map RIGHT OUTSIDE THE OFFICE directing me to the other side of town!?! Eventually I passed the first trial. The next was to find a hotel. This wasn't helped by the fact that everyone except me seemed to know that the one recommended by the guide book had now changed name, so I was on a loser from the start tying to find Pension Milky Way, even with directions, when it was now calling itself Hotel Gran Lusso or some other such nonsense. Finally, given that the whole reason for the existence of this place is supposed to be the presence of the hot springs or spa, you might have assumed that they would have been easier to locate. after half an hour's detailed searching I found THE spa, down a back alley, through the entrance to a restaurant then on the 3rd floor of a large concrete block. 3rd floor? Natural spa? Must be some water pressure underneath that thing. I walked away in disgust.

Fortunately my hotel had a perfectly respectable hot bath that I soaked in for about an hour to ease my aching back and soothe my bad temper.

I had almost forgotten how many highs and lows you could fit into one day's cycling, Physical, mental, moral, altitudinal and attitudinal. To wake up to torrential rain and stormy winds, then after breakfast set out against the wind, but dry at least, Within an hour the sun comes out and you are just beginning to appreciate life and feel what a good day this could be. Then it dumps rain on you like the sky overflowed and the temperature plummets a good 10 degrees. You keep pedalling and keep climbing against the wind. Gradually the rain eases a little, then stops. You keep all your rain gear on in the hope that all the heat you are now generating will somehow dry you out from the inside. The road rises then falls again and you resent each drop because you know up ahead is a high pass and you hate to lose height before then. Finally, and almost always when you're not expecting it, you reach the top and pause for breath and maybe a banana or cheese and bread. There's just the hope of some sunshine on the way down, but the view is a full panorama of golds, blues and greys and you have no idea which you will hit next, so you keep your waterproofs on against the cold of the descent. On the way down there are flashes of sunshine and glimpses of stunning views through the trees, then for no reason you hit a sudden patch of melancholy and the day seems to be dying on you, then another short climb, a little sun and you're flying again. I reckon if you can stand the pace you could get at least 3 lives out of one like this, but you'd probably be grey early and mad as a biscuit as far as anyone else was concerned.

Still, on balance I would have to say it was good day. At Nukabira I'd hoped to try out the youth hostel, or even the campsite, guilt at my luxurious lifestyle so far finally getting to me, but the youth hostel was closed and the campsite had turned invisible again so I opted for another dollop of guilt and checked into a very pleasant looking onsen and reached for my wallet.

The bath this time truly was fed by a hot spring, and was seriously hot. Before long I began to worry that I'd end up on the evening menu if I sat there for more than a minute or two more, and climbed out while I was still only partially cooked.

In the early evening I took myself off for a stroll along the old road that ran around the lake. There were any number of signs and barriers that I took to indicate this was off limits and circumnavigated anyway on the basis that as a Gaijin (foreigner) I had the perfect excuse for being dumb. On the way back I surprised a small family of deer. What surprised me about them was the way they called out in alarm, exactly like the shriek of a small child.

Dinner was absolutely outstanding - local mushrooms, fresh local fish, about the size of sardines, cooked whole in batter in a sort of sweet and sour sauce, hot chilli soup with green vegetables and the usual array of pickles, rice and unidentifiable object. it was all, without exception delicious.

The final treat of the day was the discovery of the ultra high tech loo. Not only did this have a pre-warmed seat, when you sat down it automatically triggered the extractor fan. On a sort of armrest to the right were a bewildering number of symbols and buttons that I'm afraid I just didn't have the courage to press (certainly not while sitting down anyway), but looked fascinating nonetheless.

The following day was very much in two halves, the sublime and the dismal. An excellent breakfast at the pension in Nukabira and a glorious blue sky made for a great start. Still, as the staff at the pension turned out in force to wave me on my way I had spent long enough on the island to know that the clear weather would only last so long.

I spent a very pleasant couple of hours dropping swiftly down to the lowlands again, the sun bright, even if it was still a little cool. Heading down a narrow avenue of birch trees on a small backroad I came across a young man cycling the other way. He rang his bell furiously and hurtled towards me, clearly not wanting me to miss his desire for me to stop. Although our linguistic abilities were poor even in combination, his enthusiasm made up for much. We 'chatted' for a while, shook hands and waved goodbye, neither of us much the wiser, but both happier for the encounter.

Every 5 or 10 km I came across yet another set of road works of some sort or other, each one had a full contingent of flag waving, whistle blowing warning men (and women), often outnumbering the actual workers. Whilst this hardly makes economic sense, it certainly paid off for me at one point where, due to the works taking place inside a tunnel I was given my own personal escort, mounted on a folding bike and pedalling like fury in front of me, blowing his whistle and waving a red light stick to clear our path. We were almost a convoy. I passed through the town of Ashoro barely noticing it, then turned onto route 241 for a long climb.

314

Although the sun was still out I could see the clouds building and around noon (and 50km mark) I passed my last accommodation option for a while, a lonely 'rider house' catering specifically for motorcyclists. I decided noon was too early to stop and hoped I could make the next campsite before the rain broke. I didn't. What's more I had badly misread the map and judged the summit of my climb to be around 15 km earlier than it really was. So it was that by 1pm the rain was already lashing down and I was still climbing. Rather than bother even looking for the campsite I decided to push on regardless for the next town, Akan Spa. It was a long, cold and very wet haul. Under such conditions even reaching the top of a climb is not much satisfaction, since you can look forward to absolutely freezing your butt off on the way down. Which I did (freeze, that is, rather than look forward to it, which I didn't). By the time I got to Akan I was in no mood to mess about. I eyed the glitzy modern hotels on the shore before deciding they probably wouldn't even let me drip on their reception carpets, so opted instead for what turned out to be the fawlty towers of Japanese Ryokans. The owner was a grey haired shuffling git, who simultaneously fawned on his few salarymen clients while grumpily tossing me a key to an upstairs room, muttering something which required no dictionary to translate as the equivalent of "...and don't drip on the carpets you grubby little oik". So I did. Lots. With great satisfaction. The dining room could just as well have been from the same school of hotel management. I felt a little more sympathy for the poor maid, who looked tiny and very brow beaten. For some unknown reason too she seemed to have lots of silver in her mouth, but mostly between the teeth, rather than as fillings in them. I couldn't work out whether it was some sort of complicated brace or just very drunken dentistry. When she tried to explain to me what the menu was, and I apologised for not speaking Japanese she kindly went away and wrote it down for me in Kanji, which, of course made everything quite clear. When I still failed to understand she shook her head sadly and put me down as a lost cause.

The bathroom in the basement had the unattractive combination of freezing cold water coming out of the showers (under which you are meant to wash yourself) and an absolutely scalding bath, fed directly from the hot springs (in which you are meant to soak). I compromised by dipping a bowl in the bath, topping it up from the shower and dowsing myself with it.

In the evening I phoned my friend from Tokyo, Julian, to check on arrangements for meeting him the following Friday. While we were on the line he checked the weather forecast for Hokkaido on the Internet.

"Hmmm...it says here sunshine with 20% chance of rain."

"Does that mean it will definitely rain on 20% of Hokkaido? That there is a one-in-five chance it will rain somewhere? Or that they're 80% sure it'll be sunny?"

"Hmmm....doesn't say"

Funny that.

Finally I did the most sensible thing I could do under the circumstances which was drink two beers quickly and go to bed.

Lake Kusharo to the Sea of Okhotsk

I knew before I woke up that it would be blue skies and sunny. In the same way you can see by the quality of light through the curtains when it's snowed overnight, I think you can hear and smell rain, or the absence of it. Whatever. it was dry, which was what counted, so I raced through breakfast a) because it was worth rushing and b) to get on the road as soon as possible. I was damn sure that 20% would hit me with all its statistical punch by mid afternoon and I wanted to be wherever I was going to get by then.

From Akan-Ko another uneventful climb, another high pass then a whirling, brake scrubbing, chicaning drop down to Teshikaga which, frankly, as a town was a complete non-event. There were signs for a campsite, but these were 2km out, and as I knew now from experience by the time I got anywhere near it would have evaporated from the face of the earth, and so it proved. Since the rain had held off so far I decided to push on a further 20km to the shores of lake Kusharo where I was confident, campsite or no, I could find somewhere to pitch my tent. and so there was. By 2:30 I was camped on a small promontory poking out into a beautiful blue lake. All along the sandy shore were little wisps of steam where natural hot springs bubbled up and out into the lake. So much so that you had to be careful when you went paddling not to end up with cooked feet. Officially, of course, the campsite was closed, but other than removing all the taps (why?) that made precious little difference to me. If anything it just meant it was quieter, for the time being anyway......

I decided there and then this was too good a spot to miss, I was well ahead of schedule and this looked like the best spot so far to spend a rest day, do some laundry, drink some beer, and chill.

The next day I decided was my rest day. Still, it didn't feel right to do absolutely no cycling, and I needed to stock up on beer and other essentials...well, actually on beer and a few fripperies such as fruit, cheese and bread. So I cycled along the lake a little to the next town, Kuwaya to find the nearest convenience store.

Convenience stores form such a core part of modern Japan, it's difficult to overestimate their importance, they're not a convenience, they're a necessity. Unlike at home where they are scattered mostly around city areas there are six or seven key chains here and they are almost literally everywhere. Also, unlike home where you might just use one to top up on the stuff you forgot at the supermarket or grab an extra bottle of wine after hours, they seem to be one of the key places people go for their essential supplies. I have seen relatively few supermarkets so far, particularly outside the cities (and there they are really Hypermarkets).In fact the only ones I have seen have been the co-ops.

On my way back from my shopping excursion I stopped off to dip my feet in the town hot-spa-paddling-pool. Although this was clearly a very popular event of a Sunday morning, everyone kindly shuffled up enough to squeeze my skinny western butt in on one of the benches. An old lady flashed her gold teeth at me from under her bonnet and a young couple tried to keep their small son under control (unsuccessfully). It was all very communal. The bonnets, by the way, are almost obligatory wear for any old lady over the age of 60 ish, especially out in the country. I saw one old dear working on a construction site with bonnet firmly tied under chin and bright yellow hardhat perched at a jaunty angle on top.

Back at the campsite a bunch of young lads had taken up station right next to my tent and decided to dig their own hot spa. Having been at it all morning and half the afternoon the beach looked like a simulation of the Normandy landings, but they had managed to create at least one hot pool to a depth of a foot or so. Around 4 they cheerily packed up and cycled off home leaving their earthworks behind them. It had one advantage which was that I was able to preheat some water for my coffee by sinking my metal water bottle into the beach!

I awoke to a grey overcast morning but the skies gradually cleared and had warm sunshine for my ascent of the Bihoro Toge Pass. By this stage I think I'd finally begun to get my cycling legs back, and although I wouldn't have set any speed records I cranked my way up the mountain quite happily and when I got to the top I could just as happily have turned around and done it all again. The view was, as advertised, 'panoramic' but to be honest had been at least as good at any one of a dozen spots on the way up and a lot less crowded, so I didn't hang around for too long.

I was very foolishly already congratulating myself on having a good day when, with only 10km or half an hour to go to my destination I cycled straight into a mini typhoon. I couldn't actually have got wetter if I'd been cycling under water (which I very nearly was). At Bihoro itself I made my way as usual to the station, ready to call a halt despite the fact it was barely past noon. Through a series of small kindnesses I was passed from one lady to another and eventually wound up dripping all over the floor of a small minshuku. Maybe it was because I was tired and wet, maybe just because they were as unsure of me as I was of them, but despite the best intentions we tripped through a whole series of misunderstandings. First they took off my jacket and over-trousers, I thought simply to hang somewhere to dry but instead they laundered them (in fact I had a whole kit load of underwear that would have been better in the washing machine). Then I wandered out of the loo still wearing the toilet slippers. Then I wore the ordinary slippers on the carpet when I should have been in my socks. Oh god, the complexities of etiquette in these places and the different boundary lines for differing types of footwear brought me near to despair I must admit. Still, despite these faux pas they remained friendly enough, to my face at least, though god help the next gaijin who turns up dripping on their doorstep!.

319

I arrived at dinner forearmed with my not-so-trusty phrasebook and did my best to suggest I would a) eat anything and b) would like to go with their recommendations. Unsurprisingly given my total lack of familiarity with slipper etiquette the young lady who was my waitress looked at me rather sceptically but after questioning me repeatedly on the topics of 'rice?ok?' 'Pork?ok?' and 'Vegetables?Ok?' Seemed to feel that if I didn't like it then I would only be getting what I deserved anyway. Still, she looked back over her shoulder at me two or three times on her way back to the kitchen just in case I should suddenly shout out, "No, no, I was only joking - just give me a beef burger and ice cream please!"

Still, I did indeed get Pork, Rice and Vegetables, as well as fish, tofu (which I still can't see the point of) and soup. And it was indeed, good (except for the Tofu).

Top item on the news that night was the fact that Asahidake, one of the central mountains, was already covered in snow. Why did this not surprise me?

Whilst the TV was on I glanced up at it occasionally. After the weather the main event of the evening was a game show. Fortunately where TV of this sort is concerned nothing could be more superfluous than language, since you would be hard pushed to find anything worthy of the term 'meaning' in it. In this case the latest boy band hashed their way through an over-engineered cloying pop-rock single, then put themselves through a number of demeaning (but only just the right amount of demeaning) 'games' which doubled up as demonstrating that hey, they were just cool kids too. In fact it was no different from pop TV anywhere.

From Bohiro I cycled first to Memanbetsu airport to scout it out prior to meeting Julian there the following Friday. Then a quick drop into Memanbetsu town, likewise to check out the accommodation options. On the road in from the airport was the Nakahori Coffee and Inn. Only trouble was, nobody was (Inn) and 'Inn' could mean anything from Hotel to cafe. Still, I decided it was worth a try later on if only for its proximity value. In the town itself I managed to locate the campsite on the lakeshore, which was pleasant enough but a bit dark and damp. I also found the public library, and hoping to pick up some email went in to see if they had Internet access.

"Internet, Yes. Pubric, No" was my answer. I'm sorry, but this sort of thing really pisses me off. You spend a small fortune of taxpayer's money to build a lovely new library. You pay a lot each year to keep it staffed. You even pay to have broadband installed. And why? So that only the staff can use it? Borrocks.

So I left Memanbetsu and headed for Abishiri and my first look at the Sea of Okhotsk, the wintry stretch of water that separates Japan from Russia. Abishri town will probably always distinguish itself in my memory for having the worst cacophonic medley of street muzak anywhere in Japan. At one point there were at least four different rock/pop idols screaming for my attention disharmonically.

One of Abishiri's key attractions though, is its geographical position at the eastern end of a masterpiece of cyclo-engineering: The Okhotsk Cycle Road. this is the equivalent of the M4 built solely for cyclists: Two lanes, smooth tarmac surface, with its own bridges, cycle parks, rest stops and underpasses it runs for 26 magnificent kilometres between Abishiri and Tokoro, skirting first the large inland Lake Abishiri, then following the coastline of the sea of Okhotsk. The sun shone, for once, the leaves were golden and I spun the full length of it without meeting another human being and without a care in the world.

From Tokoro I followed the coast road for another 30km or so until I finally pitched up at a completely deserted campsite on a bleak peninsular, looking out across the sea towards Russia. Just offshore was a horseshoe shaped sandbar with a line of Herons spaced evenly along it, each with their own licensed fishing territory. The only problem with having an empty campsite is having too much choice. I must have wandered up and down for three quarters of an hour before realising that wherever I put my tent it was still going to be bloody cold, so I settled in the end for a room with a view over the shore and my neighbours, the Herons.

321

I had just dragged together a small pile of driftwood and was settling down for a rousing evening of solo Campfire Karaoke (NOT) when the place was suddenly flooded with people- well, two actually. she was a young girl by the name of Makiko, touring Hokkaido by car and she spoke a little English. He was a stocky, silver cropped hair Japanese in his late fifties by the name of Mr Ichikawa (or Ichikawa San) and he didn't.

Makiko had come out to see the sunset. Mr Ichikawa had come out to see if there were any bikers out here. Makiko translated:" He says he would like to buy us both dinner. He says he is Millionaire". Now this latter point might have been slightly more credible, but a great deal less intriguing had Mr Ichikawa arrived by helicopter, say, or driven up in a large Mercedes. Instead, he stood beaming next to a 50cc Suzuki moped, swathed in what looked like 14 layers of clothing, rubber waders and had what looked like a piece of asbestos covered in silver foil poking out of the back of his jacket. Intrigued, I weighed my options and decided campfire karaoke could wait for another evening. Ichikawa-San climbed back onto his trusty steed and I bundled into Makiko's little Mazda and we followed his little red tail light into the night. Over supper of raw clams (a local delicacy as testified by the small mountains of clam shells I had cycled past during the day) and a large beer, Ichikawa San narrated, through the long suffering Makiko, how he was an expert ski-er, skilled in Judo and Karate, keen cyclist, owned several properties, was in the process of building his own house locally and re-iterated his claim to millionairedom. As much as I was warming to Ichikawa San during the course of the evening, it had occurred to me that his first name might well be Walter, when he started to produce his photos from somewhere within the many layers of clothing. Ichikawa San on racing bicycle. Ichikawa San with daughter dressed as Geisha. Ichikawa San doing backflip on short skis. Whether he really was or wasn't an eccentric millionaire I don't know, but I found him an immensely likeable person, I related to his openness and his sense of hospitality and community with anyone who happened to be travelling on two wheels, and I found it impossible to persuade him to let me pay for my supper. Makiko offered to drive me back to the campsite and I waved goodbye to him thinking I'd really given him very poor value for money, and wishing I'd had more than a few words of Japanese to delve deeper into his intriguing story.

On the way back to the campsite I was wishing even more that I had a greater fluency in Japanese as Makiko demonstrated an alarming incapacity to be able to drive at night. We ricocheted from side to side along a dark country lane. Ahead of us I could se quite clearly a T-junction, lit up like Blackpool illuminations with two giant opposing flashing red arrows. Only when it was already too late did I notice that Makiko was fixated by these two arrows like a rabbit mesmerised by car headlights. Without showing any sign of slowing down she drove straight at them. Fortunately for us both she snapped out of it at the last moment, jammed on the brakes and came to rest with the front wheels on the edge of a ditch and the bonnet resting neatly centralised between the two red arrows that were lighting up each of our startled faces in synchrony. To be fair, this might have been a momentary lapse of concentration, were it not for the fact that at the very next junction she was clearly unsure of they right way and resolved this dilemma, again by driving straight at the mid point of the junction and then jamming on the brakes. Eventually I was delivered back to the campsite in one piece and waved goodbye, hoping for her sake that there weren't too many road junctions between there and where she was staying in Abashiri.

After a bitterly cold night I woke to a fine and sunny morning, and having watched the Herons breakfasting over coffee (my coffee, not theirs) I packed up and headed back to Abashiri with the intention of just chilling for a day or so at the campsite by the lake there, ready to go meet Julian on Friday.

I had a very pleasant ride back along the Okhotsk cycling road, dropped into Abisihri to pick up some food, set up camp on the lake shore, did some laundry and was just about to call it a day when I was very nearly Shanghai'd. Ok, so a naval expression based on a Chinese city may not be entirely appropriate for a Japanese port, but the principal remains the same. Just as I was wandering back to my tent from the bathrooms, two guys cycling by spotted me, jumped on their brakes and ran over to hug me and start taking photos of us together. I like to consider myself an amenable sort of chap but did feel this was just a little bit forward of them. During the course of a very stilted conversation I managed to work out they were Vladimir and Wolla, Captain and Bosun respectively of a small Japanese crabbing vessel in the port, but based out of Sakhalin, Russia. The fact that we could manage around 3 common words each in Russian, Japanese and English proved no deterrent whatsoever to their determination to socialise. The Bosun was rapidly dispatched in search of more beer while the Captain I attempted to exchange pleasantries. After the usual formalities of age, marital status, geographical origins and work experience we sailed into the conversational doldrums for a while. Undeterred the captain again picked up the mantle and launched into a comparison of the relative merits of Russian and English culture. Here at least I felt I could make some contribution, however trite. Ah yes, I beamed, "Tolstoy, Dostoyevsky, Tchaikovsky, Rachmaninov".

"Da, da," he beamed back , (though I failed to point out that Dada was in fact, Spanish), "Charles Dickens, Rudyard Kiplink, Dick Francis, Iron Maiden, Ace of Bass".Hmmm, well clearly this was not going to be a conversation out of the South bank Show. Sure enough, it was only a matter of minutes before the Beatles surfaced, to be followed swiftly by a truly heart rending rendition of 'Yellow Submarine'. He had, of course, been on submarine duty in the Russian Navy. I pasted a fixed grin on my face and prayed for the hasty return of the beer-bearing bosun. Not that the conversation could be said to have flourished when he did return. Instead we moved on to the topical subject of the price of prostitutes in various harbours of the Pacific Rim (Not, I am happy to say, a subject I would normally play my joker on). For those of you interested, Korea, I understand, offers the best combination of exotica and value for money at around $50 for a Korean girl or $100 for a Russian if you're feeling flush or homesick. Once again the poor bosun was dismissed, this time for Whiskey and Food ("Chup, chup"). At this point I tried vainly to indicate that a) I had had enough and b) if they insisted I could at least pay my share. The Captain, though was having none of it and insisted that we were 'All seamen together'. This worried me slightly since by no stretch of the imagination could I be construed as anything other than a dyed in the wool landlubber. He also asked very nicely to see my visa and compared it carefully with his own (work) visa.

The conversation continued very much in the same vein as before," Ah, Elton John, beautiful....Lady Dee, beautiful.." yeah, yeah. Unfortunately the conversation had now reached the point where it became almost obligatory to exchange addresses, which we duly did, and I apologise here and now if anyone actually lives at 35 Arbuthnot Grove, Hampton Hill, London and are receiving a string of dirty postcards in Cyrillic script of brothels around the world.

Finally I persuaded the two of them it was time for me to climb in my tent and there really wasn't room for more than one in there. Before they left, though, the captain insisted again that I come to visit them on their ship at noon tomorrow for lunch before they sailed.

Now it may well be that I was being very unfair, but it had occurred to me that there was just a possibility the captain had somehow found himself one crew member short and the list of candidates was not too extensive. Either way, it's always difficult to make a judgement call in these circumstances. Most people you meet really are genuine in my experience, and you can't always make the cautious choice or you will miss out on some of the real experiences of travelling alone. You can either go with your instinct or try to make the best judgement you can. Personally, I have found the Homer Simpson "Doh!" methodology quite useful. Rather than try to work out what were the odds of something going wrong if I should take up the captain's offer, I preferred to think how stupid would I feel after the event if something had gone wrong. *Soooo...You wandered onto a strange boat, in a foreign port, with two Russians who bought you a drink the night before, ...and you woke up in the middle of the Sea of Okhotsk with someone shouting at you to come and pull up the lobster pots...*DOH!

I thanked the Captain very much, promised him faithfully I would see him at noon on the morrow and bade him and the bosun goodnight.

Unfortunately noon found me eating a banana and sipping apple juice on a small hill on the far side of the lake and enjoying it rather a lot. Oh well, 20 years ago I might actually have considered sampling the life of an Okhotsk crab fisherman for a month or two. Now I'm comfortable enough to let the opportunity slip me by.

After a long and leisurely loop of the lake I fetched up again in Abashiri. Although quite a fan of sushi something somewhere in my western digestive system had decided it had had enough of fish and was driving me towards some red meat from a creature that had once been warm-blooded. I had an unnerving craving for a steak, and there was only one place in Abashiri that was likely to offer me succour, and that was Victoria's Steak Soup and Salad bar. My head told me it would probably not be very good. My stomach told my head to shut up, mind its own business and get us in there and order fast. Whether it was a case of absence making the heart grow fonder, or whether it really was a good steak I don't know, but it certainly tasted like it was, and sated, mind and body at one again I pedalled back to the campsite.

I pottered back into Abashiri to take the alternative, hilly route back to Memanbetsu. At Memanbetsu I decided to stop again at the Nakahori Coffee and Inn on the road to the airport and took an instant liking to the charming silver-toothed old lady who ran the joint, She proved a perfect example of how a reasonable intelligence, openness and willingness to make a fool of yourself can be more than adequate tools for surprisingly complex communication. In the face of almost total ignorance of each other's language and armed with only a very sketchy phrasebook we conversed more than I had done for the past two weeks combined. Having determined (apparently) that it was, indeed an Inn or at least that she had a room where Julian and I could stay (more of which later), I decided to cement our nascent friendship by handing her an enormous pile of sweaty and very smelly laundry and asking if I could use her shower even though it was only mid day. In the interests of avoiding any potential confusion, however, I decided it was simplest to tell her that Julian was my brother, as man of my age sharing a room with another is open to all sorts of construction which would be well beyond our impromptu linguistic abilities to explain. Truth to tell, Julian looks about as much like me as my real brother does, which is not very much, but I was banking on a degree of all-foreigners-look-alike, and besides it would be most un-Japanese to put such a question directly, even if it was noticed.

This only left me with the question of what to do with the rest of the day, so I wandered down to the lake, swatted some flies, ate some lunch and generally goofed off.

Memanbetsu airport had a lifecycle reminiscent of a Mayfly. There were long periods of inactivity interspersed with brief, but intense bursts of hustle, bustle and for all I knew mating dances too. There were so few planes going in and out the locals had taken to waiting somewhere near the town end of the runway till they saw their plane actually come in to land before they could be bothered to drive the 3km out to the airport terminal to meet their loved ones. Being brought up on Heathrow madness I cycled out an hour early and sat alone in the arrivals lounge for 55 minutes. Given how little petty crime there is in Japan, and people's lax attitude towards security of their own possessions there was one strange process in place that I have not seen at any other airport (probably because of the volume of traffic). A young lady at the gate was scrupulously checking each piece of luggage passengers had picked up off the carousel against the baggage claim stickers on their plane tickets. Even with this the Japanese fear of confrontation or dealing with exceptions kicked in instantly, and when she saw Julian, a big nosed Gaijin dragging a large bicycle and medley of plastic bags towards her, she bowed and waved him straight through.

Back at the Nakahori Coffee House Mrs Nakahori was delighted to be able to converse properly with my 'Brother' and filled in a few of the gaps in my understanding while satisfying some of her own unanswered curiosity over supper. Top of her list of curiosities (having sorted out all my laundry that afternoon) was quizzing Julian over the nature and purpose of my padded cycling shorts. Julian duly assured her (at least he told me that he had) that they were quite normal bike wear and all serious cyclists wore them and no they weren't incontinence pads or a cod piece to impress the ladies..."Ah, sooooooooo,,,,,desu ka?" (Ahhhhhhhh, really?) She also explained that she didn't really like working much any more (she was in her late sixties), so mostly when people turned up she told them she was full and sent them away. We were lucky that I had asked only for a coffee first, then got engaged in our conversation before alluding to accommodation in only a sideways manner ("Do you know if there is a guest house near here?") More by luck than design I must say, but then this is very much the Japanese way to approach things and maybe I had begun to pick a little of that up by osmosis.

Over the course of our meal (which was huge and very good) the conversation ranged far and wide and I understood how we had managed to communicate so much with so little while at the same time feeling frustrated that I couldn't join in more. On one topic she was adamant. In the recent elections she had gone to the polling station because it was her duty, but had immediately and deliberately spoiled her vote because she couldn't stand and wouldn't trust a single one of the politicians standing. I knew there would have been many reasons why I liked her.

Mrs N again provided us with an enormous breakfast to send us on our way, but in deference to our western tastes had anglicised it considerably. Thus in addition to rice and fish we also had eggs sunny side up, frankfurters and toast. The toast caught me off guard when I went to pick up a piece to discover it was all one slice at least 2" thick. Julian explained that a thin slice would look like meanness, so the thicker the better. I wasn't complaining.

As we wound up breakfast Julian and I then had a very Japanese debate about whether we should ask if we could stay there on our return the following Tuesday. If we asked directly, it would be tantamount to insisting on it, as she would not be able to refuse without losing face. We already knew that she didn't particularly want guests and she had clearly gone to considerable trouble to fed us. In the end we decided that since we had to come back to Memanbetsu anyway it would be much worse if we stayed somewhere else and then bumped into her on the street, so Julian asked as indirectly as he could if we might be able to make a reservation and after only a fractional hesitation she said yes.

Finally we wobbled off down the road, our bellies nearly as swollen as our bags, Mr and Mrs Nakahori turned out to bow and wave us down the road.

As we worked our way east we wove backwards and forwards across the main coast road following smaller local roads wherever we could. One reason I knew Julian would be excited to be in Hokkaido at this time of year was for the Salmon run. Although we were at the very end of the season, every river we came across was teeming with mighty black salmon, either nosing forward on their way to spawning grounds, drifting gently backwards having spawned and waiting to die, or dead and littering the bottom of the river. It really was an amazing sight. Sadly the spawning grounds now are almost all restricted to a very short estuary area as there isn't a river in Japan that hasn't been clogged with kilometre after kilometre of concrete cofferdams designed to 'reduce erosion'. It struck me as highly unlikely that these monstrous eyesores would actually do any good to anyone and much more probable that they were completely screwing up the rivers ecology.

Julian had brought a small rod and lure with him just in case and was unable to resist the temptation offered by the sight of so much fish flesh, so we stopped every now and then by one of the smaller rivers and I would pull out some bread and cheese and munch quietly on the bank while he did his man the hunter bit.

After a while though it became clear that food was the last thing on these fish's minds. It was Sex or Death and nothing else mattered much. Julian and I agreed that more direct methods were required. Taking his shoes and socks off he waded into mid stream armed with a large branch and launched himself furiously at the first fish to come within clubbing distance. Clearly they were thinking about sex or death but not contemplating suicide as none of them were quite stupid

329

enough to be caught by these sort of antics. Still it whiled away an entertaining half-hour and amused a couple of passing farm workers no end. I took a short video to email to our friend Simon back home. Simon is a fly fishing aficionado, a true English sportsman and I thought he might appreciate our impromptu angling technique.

At Utoro, on the Shiretoku peninsular, we stopped at the local information centre to check out campsites. There were apparently 3 in town, but only one still open at this time of year. Fortunately this was the one with the Rotemburo, an outdoor hot water spa. Decisions don't come much easier than that, so we headed out of town and climbed the short but steep hill up to the site. There we quickly pitched the tent on a small plateau, sank a swift beer and went to soak in the glorious hot pool, looking up at the stars and staring out to sea to watch the fishing boats coming back to port.

As we packed up our gear in the morning I was entertained with the thought of how many different approaches to camping there were. Within minutes we had practically everything loaded into two small bags on the back of my bike while our nearest neighbour was struggling with a large trolley he had brought specifically for the purpose of transporting his gear backwards and forwards from tent to car. It took him several trips. It would be fair to say he had a lot of gear.

From Utoro we had a straight, steady climb for the next 14km up to the top of the Shretokotoge pass. As we wound our way up gradually we stripped down to T shirts and shorts, then started layering up again as we got nearer the top and began to climb into cloud and fog

At the very top Julian chatted briefly with a young lad who had just cycled up the other side. His bike was probably carrying as much baggage as both of ours put together and to top things off he had a medium sized rucksack strapped to his back as well. He spoke in a very squeaky voice, almost Disney like and even without following the conversation I could see something was strange. Julian told me that he hadn't been able to make head nor tail of his replies and we concluded he was either in the process of escaping form some sort of secure treatment facility or delirious from carrying all that kit up a mountain.

The drop down the other side was fast and hairy with strong winds threatening to throw us off course and get us down the mountain even faster. Julian particularly was struggling with the steering on his bike that was shaking its head like a bad tempered horse at every corner. Still we rolled into Rausu safely enough some twenty minutes later having done pretty nearly a steady 40mph all the way down.

From Rausu we turned north and pedalled into a strong headwind to make our way out to the far end of the peninsular. At every river mouth we saw more Salmon, dead or dying or having sex. After a while it became just a bit morbid. At the end of the road we stopped to watch a few fishermen listlessly trying to haul some of them in. A couple of old guys wandered past, oblivious to the others, carrying their fishing gear out towards the head. Julian chatted with them briefly and found out they were heading away from the river to try to catch some younger fish at sea. The old man shook his head. These ones are no good, he said. They have used up all their fat in the push to come and spawn, and the flesh is lean and tasteless. It made us feels somehow better in our abject failure as hunter-killer-foragers. The rotemburo at the end of the peninsular was closed and had been boarded up, so we turned around and headed back to Rausu for the night.

Back in town we rolled along the main street and pulled up outside a very unprepossessing building with the symbol for an onsen on boards outside. Inside it was pitch black and showed no signs of life, but we slid back the doors and poked our heads in just in case. We were just about to turn around and leave when I spotted a TV flickering in a corner of a room off to one side and we rapped on the window.

The owner was a grey haired man with a short ponytail, probably in his early sixties. His best friend was his Old English sheepdog, 'Busu' or 'Ugly'. He welcomed us with open arms. Our Onsen turned out to be the oldest in Rausu, built at the turn of the 19h century and was delightfully run down and comfortable. We were given the best room in the house, and not only was the basic rate very reasonable but he absolutely insisted on giving us a Y1000 rebate. The onsen was clearly from a genuine hot spring and had a strong smell of sulphur to it. The water coming out of the feed pipe was scalding hot but the bath itself very soothing after a long ride. The owner explained that originally our room had had a wonderful sea view, as the onsen was on the edge of the main road through Rausu, but with a suspicious level of cynicism the government had built a new road on the seaward side, on reclaimed land and funded it by selling off retail plots which had subsequently turned his road into a backwater. Still he was fairly laid back about it. He explained that he owned another onsen in town, run by his son, and within a week or two he would shut this one down for the season and go and hibernate in the other.

In the evening we took a brief stroll through the town (brief because there wasn't much town to stroll through). On the way past the local police station, not for the first time in Japan, I noticed a small police car parked outside. keys in the ignition and the engine left running. It was still there and still running when we walked back 15 minutes later. further up the road a lady walked out the front of her house and deposited a large salmon in her freezer. Her freezer was sat outside the house right next to the road. I tried to imagine how long either police car or freezer would stay in situ if this were Liverpool, but couldn't remember the word for a small enough segment of time.

On the climb back up to the pass I had to let Julian go ahead as there was no way I was going to be able to keep pace with him. I hadn't anticipated I would be a slug shaming 45 minutes behind by the time I finally reached the top, and he, poor devil, was very nearly turned into a human lollipop. The 20km descent however made the climb look like a summer party. We dropped through fog, howling wind and lashing sleet until cheeks, hands and feet had all passed through the pain barrier and simply become too cold to feel any more. Around 4km from Otaru we pulled off the road into the local visitor centre. I was so cold I had trouble unhooking my fingers from the handlebar and found my lips wouldn't move properly to speak. I must have sounded like a badly synchronised foreign movie. We

332

stumbled into the visitor centre dripping water, shed all our outer clothes, even took off our boots and socks and spread everything out over the nearest radiator while we sat down waiting for the shivering to stop. Had we been in Austria. Germany or Switzerland, a supercilious official would have arrived within minutes and turfed us ignominiously back out onto the road. In Japan we were either politely ignored or actively sympathised with, and we were able to relax and bask in the warmth and dry. So much so, in fact that we spent almost the whole afternoon there, waiting out the rain and gently roasting socks, hats and gloves until they were moderately dry again.

Finally the rain eased and we rolled the last 4k into town. The lady at the information desk explained we were lucky because only the previous night Utoro had been full, but this evening everyone had headed home and we would have no trouble finding accommodation. As nice as this was to hear I think we both suspected that her conception of 'full' might be a little different from ours. Perhaps she'd had a rush of four people asking for hotels, or maybe there had briefly been a traffic jam in the centre of town, something like that.

The following day saw dark lowering skies, stormy seas and rain. The morning had not promised much and we hung around in our hotel room until 8am hoping for some improvement. Eventually it eased a little and we prepared to sally forth. Among other things this included putting on most of the clothing we had as well as taping plastic carrier bags over our feet in a vain attempt to stay dry for as long as possible. We looked like the contents of a rubbish bin mixed with a jumble sale - elegant we were not, but hopefully at least dry.

Eventually we made our way back to Memanbetsu and boarded the plane, Julian to head back to Tokyo while I was heading for the far south and (hopefully) much warmer clime of Kyushu.

Fukuoka Everything

Loading bikes and luggage at check-in in Memanbetsu Julian and I had been just a little apprehensive. Although both on the same flight, and both with bikes, he was getting off at Tokyo, while I had about an hour to change planes for Fukuoka. The potential for one or both bikes going astray seemed enormous. This was, however, Japan. Everything was carefully labelled by the girl at the desk, a handwritten note was copied and attached and when I finally picked up my bike in Fukuoka airport, where I had casually taped some bubble wrap around the chain, the Memanbetsu luggage handlers had carefully and skilfully wrapped it up neatly in tough brown paper. It put even my best efforts at Christmas present wrapping to shame. I half expected to find a ribbon on there somewhere.

Fukuoka is a great city to arrive in. I walked straight out of baggage claim onto one of the main roads into town and within 15 minutes of busy but pleasant cycling I was whizzing past the central train station. Unfortunately I spent another 45 minutes circling the same block cursing the Lonely Planet editors as I was looking for a Ryokan which they had spent two paragraphs lavishing praise on, but had failed to give either the Kanji characters for, a phone number or directions. The 'map' (read blob and squares drawn at random)was also hopelessly inaccurate. Eventually, with some help from Julian and Japanese directory enquiries I managed to track it down about a block away from where it should have been, and it has to be said it was worth the looking for, a very pleasant place to spend a few days.

Having dumped bags and bits I cycled off to a) get some more coffee and b) have a quick evening inspection of the town. My first, and very Japanese discovery was a shop in the station concourse named, in a very open and frank manner 'Colon Booth' that as far as I could see, stocked a wide range of health products for the digestively challenged.

My second was that the pedestrian crossings, when turning green, played a Rolf Harris Stylophone version of 'When a body meets a body comin' thro' the rye....' At least the north/south ones did. The East/West ones played a sort of mobile phone fu-manchu jingle. Surreal.

Fukuoka, though, grabbed me immediately. A pleasant, broad streeted city, it straddles a small river and makes much of the river frontage with cafes and food stalls strung along the banks. Lots of flashing neon and bustle

I had already decided to stay an extra day in Fukuoka, and the delight of being somewhere warm and sunny at last made me doubly sure I would enjoy my stay. The first shock, though, was having to pay for bicycle parking! Having located the Starbucks in the station concourse I discovered that parking a bicycle anywhere near a station was subject to a Y100 (60p) charge. There were even 'parking attendants' on hand to enforce it. Whilst normally I would balk at such nonsense I decided to give it a try this time if only to find out how it worked. The attendant smiled at me happily and waved me into a small slot facing a row of coin boxes with chains attached. He unhooked one of the chains and threaded it through my front wheel. When I Proffered the money he waved me away, but motioned that I should add a lock of my own if I wanted to find my bike still there when I returned. So the Y100 goes into the slot when you want to release your bike...clearly not exactly a massive deterrent to any potential thief. The idea that you should put a lock on your own bike that anyone can undo with a small coin solely so that you should be sure to pay for your own parking is so Japanese it stunned me for a moment. I couldn't see this working anywhere else in the world, but here it was the norm.

One item that was also the norm in Fukuoka as in other main cities was the crossing countdown mechanism. In rush, rush, hurry, hurry Japan there is always a tension between the ever present need to hurry and the cultural inhibition at jumping a red light, even a pedestrian one. Presumably as a way of containing the pressure, most pedestrian crossings have countdown lights. These are a tall triangle of lights next to the normal red and green men. When the light first turns red they all light up red, then gradually go out from the top down as the time ticks away until when the last line goes out the green man goes on. The same then happens in reverse with green lights all the way down to tell you if you can make it to the crossing before it changes or if you have to run.

At the bank, while changing some traveller's cheques I found another example of simply indeterminate Japanglish. A small sign on the desk gave the rates for dollar exchange.

At the top was '*Cash*'. Underneath '*Buy* - 106.65', '*Sell* - 112.65' .

Then '*Travellers Cheques*'. again, underneath '*Buy* 108.65', '*Sell* - 110.65'.

Then, bizarrely, '*And So On* - 108.46'?????

Walking over one of the bridges I thought I'd spotted the most imaginative solution yet to the parking crisis when I saw a motorbike dangling from a large hoist over the middle of the river. Turned out it was simply advertising a bike shop....for any passing motorcyclists.....on the river?

In town the cycle parking went to extremes with first of all multi storey cycle parks, then what could only be described as bunk bike parking where cycles were actually hoisted up into the air on a steel frame to squeeze more in below. Jeez, there were a LOT of bikes here.

That evening as I was strolling back along the riverbank I came across yet another mystery. alongside all the food stalls (and an outdoor pet shop) was one stall with a number of white plastic crates on the pavement. The crates were full of water and in the water were live eels. Not so strange so far. Until I stood and watched for a while.

An old man came up, handed over some money and in return was given a small stick, slightly longer than a chopstick, with about a foot of line attached to it and a large hook on the end. He the proceeded to try and catch himself an eel. I couldn't workout whether it was some sort of arcade game, a fortune telling gimmick or simply a way of adding spice to choosing your evening meal, "Look what I caught on the way home from work dear!" Man the hunter.

Fashion at the moment for any young lady in Fukuoka dictates boots. It may be 20 degrees, you may be hot and sweaty, but you will wear boots, at least calf length and the spikier and longer the heels the better. Fashion also generally dictated you should have brown hair rather than black. At the extreme end there were also a few women, but enough to notice, wearing eye patches on the streets. The chances were relatively high that these were not from careless accidents with wild chopsticks or misused chainsaws but actually the result of eyelid surgery, one of the most popular cosmetic operations, heavily advertised here and designed to give a more 'western' look.

Almost everyone here cycled on the pavements, and while I was conscious of a degree of impatience from drivers when I ventured out onto the road, to be honest I found it much less terrifying than dealing with the pell-mell of old ladies students and office workers hurtling at and across each other on bicycles or on foot on the packed city pavements. Fortunately most seemed to have developed a sixth sense and I never actually saw a single crash, but there must have been thousands on a daily basis.

Fukuoka province is, it has to be said, a smutty-minded Englishman's dream. Being one myself, I watched with glee as the airport staff attached any number of official looking tags to my luggage and bicycle, all of which had 'FUK' in bold letters across them. Today I was nearly blasted off the road by a large truck that had emblazoned across the back 'FUKKA EXPRESS', which was spooky as that was almost exactly what I was thinking at the time. Later, wandering around Karatsu, I came across 'MENS SHOP FUKA-SAKE', presumably for those ultra impatient guys who just hate shopping, "For Fuka-Sake, just give me that one and let's get out of here."

I took my usual breakfast at Starbucks and was pleased to see how very much quieter the centre of Fukuoka was of a Saturday. Eventually I broke free from my caffeine fix and headed west to follow the coast road. The sky was a glorious azure blue and before long it was warm enough to strip down to T-shirt and shorts, a welcome change from Hokkaido's thermals. The roads too, even the minor ones, were much busier and generally much narrower with a distinct absence of that lovely wide shoulder I had become used to. Still, before long I was singing as I was bowling along a wonderful coast road, narrow golden sandy beaches to my right and green mountains close to my left. Kyushu matched my preconceived images of Japan much more than Hokkaido.

There were many more traditional style houses with thin walls and heavy, ornate roofs with intricate glazed tiles. The towns and villages were squashed up against each other in whatever flat land there was with the odd pocket-handkerchief rice paddy here and there.

After a while I noticed I was being tailed by an older guy wearing wraparound shades on a lightweight mountain bike. We played tag for a while, enjoying the company without needing to talk, then I lost him in a maze of small streets in one of the villages. Shortly after I pulled up at a luxurious 'Cyclists Rest Spot' specially built on the coast, as too good an opportunity to miss to grab some lunch. I was just clearing up the remains of my Ham, fresh pineapple and raisin bread snack-a-rama when he re-appeared and rolled up next to the table. Again, frustrated at having so little Japanese I would have liked to talk more, but we managed the basics, compared bikes for a bit and I think his name was 'Wirram', or something close to that, but since I can't remember English names for more than a fraction of a second, it could have been anything to be honest, but it didn't seem to matter. After a while we headed off together, him leading. At first I was a bit unsure, as I like to know where I am and consult the map fairly frequently, but after a while I decided it was too nice a day to fret and just went with the flow, confident that wherever we ended up would be ok one way or another. As it turned out, Wirram was an excellent, if taciturn, guide. First stop was a Sumo school. Unfortunately we missed the competition, but rolled up just in time to see the prize giving. The boys were all around 6 or 7 years old, and didn't look like five of them together could make a decent Sumo's lunch, but they made up for size in their earnestness. At the cape we stopped by a line of roadside stalls run by three old crones, all vying for Wirrams business. In the end he bought a small bag of what looked (and tasted) like deep-fried and salted sweet potato chips. They were certainly tasty but probably had enough salt, fat, sugar and starch in them to kill you in a week. Finally we pulled into a small courtyard next to a large traditional style house and barged straight through the front door. Inside it was more like a barn with a high ceiling, small cast iron stove and chimney pipe. There were two wonderful tables made from a bizarre combination of two 3 foot wide slices of whole tree trunks laid on top of a line of cheap plastic crates. On top of the tables was a range of crude, but well formed pottery, mostly sake cups and vases. After a degree of bellowing Wirram rousted the proprietor, an elderly lady who appeared from a back room and proceeded to make us tea. They talked pleasantly for while, I picked out the odd word - 'Jitensha' (bicycle) 'Rondon' (London) but not much more. Eventually we left without Wirram proffering much in either the way of thanks or payment - so much so that I wondered if it was his Mum's place? Finally we came to the parting of the ways, shook hands and he sped off back towards Fukuoka while I carried on west to Karatsu. I just love the idea of dipping into the warp and weft of other people's lives like this. Especially when travelling you seem to switch from a strong diet of close and meaningful relationships, friends, family and lovers, to a Meze of brief encounters with strangers, or like a Japanese meal, a kaleidoscope of small dishes, each unique, enough to sample the taste without really becoming familiar with it.

I had planned to camp in Karatsu, it being such nice weather, but the campsite wasn't simply closed for the season, it was out for the duration, and probably just as well as it appeared nothing more than a

339

mosquito infested bunker anyway. Karatsu itself was a pleasant enough town but surprisingly short on Minshuku or ryokan. I stopped at a cycle shop to ask directions. Fortunately the owner spoke very passable English and recommended that I try one of the business hotels near the station. When I got there even that was full, but in traditional Japanese service manner the young girl on reception would not let me go till she phoned around half the hotels in town and found me an alternative room. After so long in Japanese style Inns, I realised how dull and impractical western style hotels are. So I checked in, washed my undies and went out for some food.

How can you get the Sunday blues when you don't even know which day of the week it is? Some days you just have lead in your boots and some days you just have sludge in your head. The next day was a dull, uneventful ride to a dull, uneventful town. In Imari I faced one of those classic moments of indecision. It was clouding up heavily and looked set for a real storm at some stage. I had a headache. But it was only just after noon and only around 60k on the clock. I debated my options. I could stay put. I could continue along the coast. I could turn inland and head towards Nagasaki. Looking at the sky I decided the safest thing was to call it a day so I checked into the unimposing Imari Hotel. The man behind the counter smiled nicely, accepted my money then told me check in time was 4pm! Bugger. I now had the worst of both worlds, stuck in dullsville and not even able to have a bath and chill. It didn't take me long to figure out there was not much to keep me entertained in Imari, so I cycled another 5k out along the coast road, got fed up with the traffic, came back and sat on a concrete wharf overlooking the river for an hour or two reading my book.

Peace and Turmoil

Working over again the amount of time I had available and the things I wanted to do, I decided another change of plan and headed directly for Nagasaki. Although the weather in Kyushu had been wonderful, far better than Hokkaido, the roads were nowhere near as nice, much narrower and very busy. Apart from short stretches even the coast road was likely to be fairly busy so I decided I might as well get my head down and give myself more time in the cities and around the volcanoes in the national parks.

The ride to Nagasaki was not especially pleasant. Even busier road and if anything, even narrower, but by driving through I managed to get to Nagasaki just after noon. Dropping down towards the harbour and the centre of town I pulled up at the Peace Park, around 5km from the centre. At the end of a small green space stands a plain black stone obelisk, maybe twenty feet high, which marks the hypocentre of the bomb blast. A little way away, and just up the hill is the Atomic Bomb Museum. Once inside I descended the long spiral walkway that reminded me a little of the Guggenheim museum in New York, But there the similarity ended. Most of the museum is quite simply laid out, and dedicated to the task of trying to convey the factual as well as the humanitarian impact of an explosion the size of which stretches the limits of human comprehension, and it does so very effectively. I don't consider myself an especially sentimental man, nor do I sit comfortably with those who condemn the bombing as a simple atrocity. I don't feel such over simplification does justice either to those who died or to those who instigated the bombing. It seems to me unlikely that there are ever any 'good' deeds in war just less bad ones, and whether god or bad, once begun, the events which led to the dropping of the bombs were as inexorable as the chain reaction within the Uranium or Plutonium which released such devastation. Still, within twenty minutes I had seen enough, and, choked up, had to leave. As I came up and out into the light I struggled to reconcile the darkness of what I had seen below with the brightness of a normal sunny day outside, and failed. How much greater can the contrast have been for those who survived between their normal, straightforward lives before 11:02, August 9th 1945 and what faced them in the days weeks and months after.

In sombre mood I left the park and cycled the rest of the way into town where I checked into the Nishiko-Si Ryokan on a small hill overlooking the city centre. The Ryokan itself was clean, cheap and run by a small round lady who looked as though she would sell her own grandmother for a reasonable profit (and probably already had). Having weighed me up when I first arrived, evidently I had not hesitated for long enough when she quoted the room prices to me, Half way up the stairs she changed her mind, and direction and told me the room she had given me was over there, but this one was soo much nicer and only Y500 more. What the hell, I thought, it WAS a nice room and for £3 extra was I really going to argue? I dumped my bags gratefully and fell straight into a shower, to wash off the sweat of the ride as well as the itching I had on my skin ever since I left the Bomb museum.

In the afternoon and early evening I took a swift walk around the main shopping district, Hamano-Machi at the foot of the hill, and retired to bed early with an ominous ache from my right knee.

Unsurprisingly, I hadn't slept well, so was up early, brewing a fresh coffee to watch the sky turn brilliant blue while reading my book from a seat in the window. After a substantial breakfast (delivered to my room) I wandered to the main station.

At Kinko's I spent an hour (and a small fortune) on the Internet typing up an update email to all and sundry only to lose the entire thing when I tried to send it. Apoplectic or what?

From the station I caught a tram to the Glover Gardens area of town. Glover was one of the chief European (actually British) traders based in Nagasaki, founder of Kirin beer and builder of the first railroad in Japan. The houses of the early traders spaced out up the hill in Glover Gardens, though not fantastically large, were elegant, delightfully cool inside and really very attractive.

After another long debate with myself, I decided to stay another day in Nagasaki, largely since yesterday had proved rather unsatisfactory in purely practical terms, but also because there were still a few sights I wanted to check out. Once again a swift trek to the station where the information desk staff proved unfailingly helpful. My quest for more reading matter was swiftly satisfied as there was a bookshop in the building next to the station with a reasonable range. I even found a Lonely Planet guide to Hiking in Japan, but decided that one set of useless disinformation was more than enough.

Back at Kinko's, this time making multiple backups of my email as I typed. After an hour I decided not to push my luck any further and hit the send button. This time it seemed to go ok....I think....

From there I crossed the road and climbed the hill to the Fukusai-Ji temple - an 'interesting' piece of architecture in the shape of a giant silver turtle carrying an 18m high statue of the goddess Kannon on its back.

Next-door was the more conventional Shofuku-Ji temple, with a wonderful enormous bronze bell outside. I was so tempted to swing the large log suspended in front of it to ring it I had to leave quickly.

One more temple, confusingly called Sofuku-Ji and one of the oldest in Nagasaki, built by a founder of Zen Buddhism and I was about templed out. More interesting was the amazing collection of white, golden and brown carp gathered in the murky river under one of the bridges where they were being fed by a young man, his wife and their toddler. I had no idea how these fish came to be in the river, what was more surprising was how they came to stay in the river given how valuable each one of them must have been.

I started the next day wondering really whether I was bored of cycling by now. The road rose and fell as I headed out along the coast to the Shimabara peninsular, and although it wasn't particularly physically challenging I struggled to find the motivation to push myself along.

Somewhere along the way I was overtaken by a small moped, piloted by a scarecrow of a man who could easily have been Ichikawa San's son. He too was wrapped up in an indeterminate number of layers, including several different hats all crammed on underneath a construction worker's hardhat that was his concession to wearing crash helmet. As he passed, he wobbled violently, cut in front of me, then helpfully slammed on his brakes while he stared in the mirror. After a while he pulled away, but a few km down the road he had pulled up and was waiting for me.

"You spik ingrish, yes?"

I was duty bound to stop really, so I pulled up just in front of him.

"Yes, English"

"Ah, sooo, desu ka? Tour Japan, yes?"

"yes"

"How many kids?"

"Sorry?"

"Kids, how many kids?"

"Two"

"Ahhh.Good. Where are you going now?"

"Unzen"

"ooh....coold, very cold. I am going Unzen too"

Hence all the layers presumably

"I wish you very good journey"

"Yes, thank you. You too."

And with that he pulled one of many layers up from his chin to his nose and was gone.

After around 40 (fairly tedious) km I turned off onto a small side road as a shortcut up and over the mountains to the volcanic spa of Unzen. The road soon narrowed to a single track and began switching back and forth again and again as it wound its way steadily up the mountainside. Finally, once again, I found myself enjoying the ride and the climb One thing which helped was that unlike in England where the hairpin bends are the steepest part of the road, here in Japan, they had done it properly and actually flattened the gradient at each of the bends, which made it much easier to turn and line yourself up for the next short climb. Ace.

Unzen itself is a bubbling. steaming, boiling sort of a town. Everywhere you go is the smell of hydrogen sulphide and every wall, garden or pavement seems to have steam coming out of it somewhere. The Jingoku ("Hells") were even more impressive, bubbling, whistling, grunting mud baths and geysers

I checked into the Keysu Ryokan, a lovely wooden structure with a wonderful, hot, smelly ofuro. The little old lady who checked me in was about 300 years old and two foot tall, but couldn't have been any friendlier and couldn't do enough to make sure me and my bicycle were comfortably settled. So much so she changed her mind at least three times about where the best place to put it would be, settling in the end for the foyer.

I decided to stay in Unzen an extra day in order to climb mount Fugen Dake. Fugen Dake is a rather ill tempered volcano that last lost its temper in 1994 when it blew its top completely and buried one the nearest towns in ash and lava. It hasn't entirely regained its cool yet and still smokes ominously from the top while slowly pushing another lava cone up from inside.

One of the ladies from the Ryokan very kindly gave me a lift up to the base of the climb, and well loaded with food, clothing and drink I started up.

By the time I had reached the top (or as near as you could get given that Fugen was still considered active) I was feeling pretty chuffed with myself. As I sat and ate my lunch with glorious views over half of Kyushu I was just pondering the loneliness of the great athlete when I was swamped by a party of around sixty 6 year olds who had just hiked up all the way from the town and were fresh enough to still be jumping around and playing tag at the top. To make things worse they were followed shortly after by the Derby and Joan club of Japan whose average age had to be at least 75. At least they weren't playing tag and had the grace to look knackered.

On the way back down it was at least quieter and I stopped for half an hour at a tiny Buddhist shrine just for the sake of sitting and enjoying the stillness.

I poured the Buddha a small dram of whiskey from my hip flask as an offering of thanks for such a nice day, but I think he may have misinterpreted my wishes as two minutes later I bumped into a short bespectacled Scot from Edinburgh hiking up the same path. He very kindly offered me a banana ("one less to carry up, eh?") before carrying on his way.

Back in Unzen and one final sightseeing trip to complete the set. This was the 1300-year-old Buddhist temple. The building itself didn't quite look that old, but the giant Buddha inside was very striking. Gilt sparkling in the sun he was probably 20 feet high, but most intriguing of all had, for some reason, bright blue hair. The Blue Rinse Buddha? Who knows? All around the temple gardens were dozens and dozens of small statues, each around 2 foot high and on a small plinth. As was the custom here, too, each wore a small cloth bib tied around their necks. For some reason though, it looked as though the local WI had had a hand in the bib making and got a little carried away. A large number of them were made from 1960's flower power patterned cloth with lacy trimming around the neck. The net effect was to make them look as though they were all sporting 60's style ladies knickers -very disconcerting.

Supper was once again exquisitely presented. The Tatami- matted dining room was neatly divided up with small wooden hurdles separating the guests, each sat on a single cushion on legless wooden chairs at the low tables. My appetite was marred slightly by the seemingly endless array of slurping, sucking, chomping, belching, farting and other digestive noises being produced by the old man opposite me. Now, though I am normally fairly tolerant of differing etiquettes, and I know that in Japan it's considered quite proper to slurp your noodles, this chap was working on turning it into an art form. He combined it with that pointed (and deliberate) obliviousness to the existence of anyone else, that only the truly ignorant old git can attain. Once everyone else had gone I could bear it no longer, and decided the only way to live with it was to see if I could actually out do him in the art of digestive oratory. For a few minutes we conducted a symphony of slurp, chomp and belch (even I couldn't bring myself to join in the farting), but in the end I had to concede defeat, I was up against one of the grand masters and that was that. I retired to bed, bested, but satisfied that I had put up my best performance, and one that I truly hoped I would never be required to repeat.

Castles and Calderas

From Unzen I had a short climb, followed by a lovely, long swinging descent down into Shimabara and to the port where I planned to catch the super fast catamaran ferry across the inland sea to Kumamoto. At the ticket office in the ferry terminal the young lady behind the counter was remarkably uninterested in selling me a ticket and much more concerned to get me to take my bicycle out of the building and into the parking lot. Eventually we settled on a compromise whereby I agreed to go AFTER she had given me a bloody ticket for god's sake. She thanked me kindly for my reasonableness over the affair (at least so I chose to interpret her comments) and I wheeled my bike out...taking the long way through the terminal by mistake.

Kumamoto castle, destroyed in the nineteenth century but rebuilt in the 1960s was impressive if only in terms of scale. Built in the centre of the city with a perimeter wall of some 9km the grounds were vast. Like most Japanese castles, though, it seemed to consist mostly of walls within walls, all some 30-50' high, of giant blocks of stone, neatly fitted together, curving upwards increasingly steeply from the base. At the centre was the comparably small keep, again as with all Japanese castle, incongruously built of wood and therefore perpetually susceptible to fire. This probably has as much to do with why there are so few original structures like this remaining as it does with Japan's feudal warring history. What the Japanese didn't burn, the Americans did.

In the evening I had an unexpected bonus in the form of the Kumamoto Street Art Plex. Normally I would be as attracted by the idea of organised street art as I would by a cactus toilet seat, but I was very pleasantly surprised. All over the town different musicians and bands were performing in the shopping malls and the parks. My favourites were a troupe of drummers, a young man with a squeaky voice and a Samisen (a traditional 3 stringed banjo) and a completely mad jumble of a band that included a couple of percussionists, more samisen players, a tuba and a superb saxophonist. They played a mixture of Japanese folk songs and western jazz/pop but all in their own style. Most effective of all though was their sheer infectious enthusiasm for their music, and when they left the stage to begin dancing in the street a huge crowd joined them waving their hands in the air and chanting along. It was just how music should be, energetic, participatory and above all huge fun.

The usual series of traffic lights working my way out of Kumamoto, then turned off onto a narrow 'B' road which turned out to be a real gem, winding its up along the valley floor, following alternately the river and the railway line, through paddy fields and small villages for around 20km.

The payback was having to go back onto the awful and busy route 57 for the last 20km climb to Aso.

At Aso station I sat for a while to eat a banana and ponder my options. While I was chomping, an Australian couple came out and in the course of conversation recommended the youth hostel up the hill. Karma, I thought so pedalled my way up.

The Hostel was run by an octogenarian woman and her nonagenarian husband, but they were friendly and helpful. I dumped my bags and started cycling up the mountain towards Naka dake, one of the most active volcanoes in Japan.

Aso itself sits in the largest caldera in the world, a huge bowl, blown out of the face of the planet some two million years ago, but these days the key action takes place in the mountains that form the rim of the caldera, and Naka Dake in particular. So much so in fact, that the local authorities recently took the precaution of constructing concrete bomb shelters all around the rim should Naka decided to start misbehaving unexpectedly (as it did last time in 1989 killing an unfortunate young woman who had gone there for her honeymoon).

I got about two thirds of the way up, and although the views were spectacular the wind was getting stronger and stronger against me. With a big day of climbing ahead of me the day after and knees still dodgy from the day before I opted for the easy way again and rolled back down the hill to the Youth Hostel to get the bus back to the top.

By bus or by bike the trip was certainly worth it. Staring down into the crater of an active volcano is an experience I can highly recommend. Way below at the centre of the crater steam and smoke swirled and boiled. The sides of the crater were deeply scarred with ravines and multi coloured from yellow, green to russet brown.

In the youth hostel I shared pleasantries over supper with three other guests. Miyazaki San was a retied salary man from Tokyo. Having worked for Hitachi all his life he was now trying to scrape by on a 'very, very small pension'- not that he was bitter at all. Still he was a very pleasant chap. Kendo San said a lot less but smiled a lot more. Probably in his mid thirties he was the opposite of a salaryman and was 18months through a tour throughout Japan on a 50cc moped. In many ways this was probably the ideal means of transport for that type of tour, but I thought the hugely overloaded plastic crate strapped to the back of the seat was perhaps lees than an ideal way to handle his luggage. Finally there was Margot in her late twenties from Paris. She was expansively Parisian with strong opinions that she wasn't afraid to use. The most striking thing about her though was her hat. Round and woollen it came up to an extraordinary point in the centre, making her look like nothing so much as a recently sharpened pencil.

I didn't get very far the next day. 2km out of town the bike was making an unusual noise and didn't quite feel right. I stopped at a 7-11 to investigate and discovered a broken chain, one half of a link hanging off. Bugger. I had, of course, left the chain tool at home as I'd

350

never needed it before and decided it was just excess baggage. I walked the bike back to Aso, dumped my kit in left luggage locker and got the next train in to Kumamoto. Not much help there either. Chances of finding an 8 speed chain- nil. I couldn't even find a chain tool to buy. Fortunately a guy in the bike shop took pity on me and gave me his spare. I hopped the next train straight back to Aso and managed to get a temporary fix in place at least, but didn't really know how strong it was or how long it would last.

When I arrived back at the youth Hostel to check in again it could have been a scene straight out of Groundhog Day. The old boy (the nonagenarian, remember?) smiled politely, took my name and then went through exactly the same spiel as he had done the day before about rules and regs, where the shower was, what were the local interest points etc. I felt like Bill Murray, reliving exactly the same day again, but being the only one who remembered doing it all before, Bizarre.

The second time I tried to set off from Aso It was a great deal colder than before and I was nursing my patched chain very gingerly. After a few kilometres along the busy rote 57 I turned off onto a minor road 265 that was an absolute gem. A long climb up to the edge of the calderas, but a beauty every inch of the way. from there the road continued to rise and fall, but it gradually got warmer, the traffic was fairly light and the views marvellous.

I made Takachiho by just after noon. By 12:15 I was once again apoplectic with the Lonely planet guide. The maps had been drawn with all the cartographic skill and regard for accuracy of an autistic 3 year old. Not one item on the map appeared anywhere near where it was supposed to be and this tosser had the front to call the local tourist office inept. Spending paragraphs praising a wonderful restaurant to then say "Look for cartoons of cavemen" really doesn't help very much. One hostel was on completely the opposite side of the road. Another hotel had been closed for years.

Off my own bat (and out of sheer fury) I found a perfectly acceptable ryokan not mentioned anywhere in the book.

Having dumped my bags I rode down the hill, and down again to the very bottom of an enormous gorge which is THE local tourist attraction. Like almost every Japanese tourist attraction it shared a number of features;

1. The path along the bottom of the gorge was massively over engineered, paved to extinction and fenced off with natural wood effect concrete posts

2. The designated coach party gorge walk (i.e. the bit which could be reached by a bus at either end and wasn't too steep or slippery for elderly feet) was choc a bloc with people

3. The remaining 1km of path was completely run down, overgrown and had nobody, NOBODY, else on it at all.

Guess where I went.

There were plenty of restaurants in Takachiho, but as with the rest of Japan I could never find a way of working out what type of restaurant any of them was. I tried learning the Kanji for Sushi, Ramen and Yakitori, but the problem was a) Restaurants always favoured a dramatic style of calligraphy for their signs which may have been very artistic but was like trying to decipher a doctor's handwriting on a Chinese prescription, and b) That I suspected the only thing they put outside was the name anyway. Sometimes there would be a glass case with wax models of speciality dishes outside, which helped, Otherwise I would just have to go in, be seated look at the menu blandly (and blindly) and consult my phrase book for 'What do you recommend?'

In this case I think they were used to Gaijin or took pity on me and just brought me a mixed plate of sushi and a beer. Either way it was delicious and great value at about £8

The following day I lost my way coming out of town and frustratingly ended upon the busy main highroad to the coast rather than the smaller road I was looking for. After a few kilometres I stopped at some road works to ask for directions and check whether the road they were working on dropped down into the valley to join the one I wanted. After five minutes there was no one left doing any work on the road and they were all crowded round my map, pointing and arguing as though they'd never seen a map before. I found this a little disconcerting and couldn't help wondering whether this meant there were itinerant troops of road crew wandering the country just looking for bits of road that looked like they needed some work done. They certainly weren't able to identify where they were on a small-scale road map (in japanese!). After a while I thanked them for their time, smiled politely and headed off anyway. They were still arguing as I left.

When I did get to it the smaller route along the valley floor was a beauty. Narrow, often only single-track and with very little traffic it wound its way along the steep sided valley, weaving and intertwining with the river and the railroad track as though they were playing with each other.

Sake in the Street

At Hyuga I found a bicycle shop that actually had some spares and not only that, had the right size chain. The owner kindly fitted it for me too (though in truth I don't think he was too busy that morning). I felt much happier with a new chain. Apart from the risk of having to walk a long way if my dodgy repair gave out, odds were that when it did go, it would be while I was standing on the pedals heaving up some huge gradient at which point two things would happen: The pedals would suddenly swing free and as I dropped to the ground my balls would be knocked up somewhere near my Larynx. This was not an experience I was too keen to embark on.

I nearly made up for it though when I came down to join the coast road. At a crossroads with a single red traffic light flashing (meaning go if you're quick?) I came up to the junction with two cars in front and a car and truck pushing hard from behind. The two in front went so I decided to follow and pulled straight out into the path of oncoming traffic from both directions. Fortunately both were going slowly enough to stop, and etiquette in Japan forbids the screaming of 'What the f*&$ d'you think you're doing you %$£@!' out of the window. Both drivers wiped the sweat off their brows, smiled politely at me (thinking, of course, 'What the f*&$ d'you think you're doing you %$£@!') and waved me through. Close. Nearly a waste of a new chain, I thought.

In Hyuga I checked into a small run down business hotel near the

354

station. The three ladies at the check in desk covered their initial panic by giggling a lot, with their hands politely covering their mouths of course as all Japanese ladies are taught to do. Then they dragged out a dusty hand written crib sheet from somewhere with key phrases in both Japanese and English. Fortunately most of these were the same phrases I had managed to learn in the process of checking into and out of similar establishments over the last month, since their pronunciation was a little erudite shall we say.

In the room itself was the usual small panel above the bed with controls for the radio, alarm etc. The labels were in both Japanese and 'English', but it took me a while to work out that 'Room Right' was simply the phonetic rendition of the nearest the Japanese tongue could get to saying Room Light.

In the morning I opted for the 'American Style' breakfast just for a change. While it was nice enough, I hope to god they never serve it to a real American. There was omelette with a dash of tomato ketchup and a half of a cocktail size frankfurter, which was fair enough. What someone from Idaho would have made of the cup of chicken and sweet corn soup, spicy noodles and usual square block of unidentifiable gelatinous mass I'm not sure.

While waiting I watched the construction workers at the site opposite line up then begin their early morning warm up exercises together. Ok it's conceivable that somewhere else in the world construction workers MIGHT do some warm up exercise in the morning, but lined up? In sync? Only in Japan.

The ride to Miyazaki was not the nicest I've had so far, weaving on then off the busy route 10, taking parallel side roads wherever possible, but the sun shone all day, and for the last 7km I found the Miyazaki cycle road which was a pleasant well surfaced path snaking through the forest next to the ocean.

In Miyazaki itself, after riding around for three quarters of an hour, I eventually fell into the amazingly cheap Myazaki Family Business Hotel where a room with bath cost about the same as a bed in a shared dorm at the YMCA. At first I thought the lady at reception had misunderstood when I asked for two nights and was only charging for one, but she smiled sweetly and thrust my notes back at me saying, no, that was the correct rate, and was I sure my bicycle would be ok where it was? Cool.

In the evening I decided to try a local Thai restaurant, but immediately fell into the old slipper zone trap again when I took off my shoes to sit at the bar. The waiter was flummoxed and tried to point out that I only needed to do that if I was going to sit at one of the tables on raised tatami platforms. I equally tried to point out that by that stage my shoes were off, my feet were hot anyway and I was buggered if I could be bothered to put them back on again. He settled for one of those 'Gaijin, who knows eh?' shrugs and left me to it.

As much as I liked Myazaki, it's a fatal flaw in any city to find there are no coffee shops open before 9am. After I'd been pacing the streets for half an hour in sheer frustration it did occur to me that caffeine might actually be addictive, but then since I couldn't see any relevance to that either way I carried on pacing. Eventually the nearest branch of Tully's opened up. Tully's is only one of many unashamedly close copies the Japanese have made of Starbucks. I don't comment particularly on the morals of this, but I admire the gusto with which they plagiarise at least.

In the afternoon I took a busman's holiday and cycled down the coast to the tiny island of Aoshima. Although quite pretty in itself its key claim to fame is in the unusual washboard effect that the surrounding rocks have eroded into. If you came across it unknowingly it would be quite striking, but as with most tourist attractions here it has been so over hyped that when you get there it's difficult not to think 'oh yeah, washboard rocks...ok.'

In the evening a full-blown street festival was taking place in town. There were Kodo drummers, lion dancers, and shamisen players, samurai dancers the works. One lion, being operated I suspect by two young boys, couldn't resist the temptation to break ranks and chase a small pack of young girls snapping and screaming down the street.

The samurai dancers wore a strange sort of straw hat, which was like a large circle folded in half and then plonked over their heads. The net effect was almost of a mask as it was impossible to see their faces. Strangest of all though were the flute players who wore what could only be described as see through straw waste paper baskets over their heads. Maybe they were just really, really ugly, who knows?

The food stalls were pretty impressive too, you could buy just about anything to eat provided it could be threaded onto a stick. There was chicken, pork and beef of course, then rice balls, squid, cuttlefish and octopus, not forgetting toffee apples, toffee plums and toffee grapes (on a stick) - actually they were rather good.

In the middle of the street was a heath Robinson affair that consisted of a series of bamboo tubes running over a charcoal brazier, which turned out to be a form of hot sake fountain. Best of all the sake was free at the other end. Free hot sake at a street party? It could only end in tears at home, but here everyone was very well behaved. There was so little for the 'security' staff to do they had to content themselves with trying to make people walk in opposite directions on different sides of the street - unsuccessfully I must say.

The next day started in an ugly mood and soon took me with it. It was overcast and muggy. The road out from Myazaki was busy and I was soon forced to spend much of my time on the pavement. By lunchtime the road and the traffic had improved slightly but by then it was raining steadily. Myakono Jo did nothing to lift my mood.. What was probably a dull backwater town at the best of times was even less impressive in the steady rain. I did feel slightly sorry for them as they were doing their best to carry on with the town festival (turned out this was a long festival weekend across the country) but somehow the damp efforts at jollity only turned out more depressing.

From Myakono Jo it would have been a reasonably pleasant ride up to the Kirishima National park were it not for the low brooding black clouds again. By the time I had climbed up to Kirishima town itself it was raining again and I decided invisible mountains were the worst of both worlds. They were still bloody hilly and you didn't even get any views for your pains. So I turned and dropped back down to the coast along the very pleasant route 60. Unfortunately the pleasantness passed all too quickly as I was soon back on the very busy coastal route 10, very wet and in a very foul temper.

In Kagoshima it was again festival time, but by this point the crowds, the rain and the screaming p.a. were a shade more than my frayed nerves could take and I barged my way through in a very ill tempered hunt for some accommodation. I was saved by the kindness of the owner of one of the (full) ryokans who took it upon himself to phone around town, and keep phoning until he found me a reasonably priced room not too far away.

Kagoshima was a nice enough town, but still somehow slightly disappointing. So far, outside Tokyo, only Sapporo, Fukuoka and Kumamoto have felt anything other than parochial.

Highlight for me though was the wonderful Kagoshima Aquarium. It was housed in a spacious, sweeping new building by the harbour. From the entrance a narrow escalator took you up a deep blue tunnel to emerge in a spectacular darkened viewing room with one enormous glass wall facing the main aquarium.. Prize among the exhibits here was a huge whale shark, just cruising around the tank, his vast mouth gaping.

Among others there were turtles, tuna, sturgeon, giant crabs, seahorses shaped like seaweed, jellyfish, eels. Among my favourites though, the tuna stood out more than most. With dinosaur like serrated backs and glistening bodies they looked almost mechanical. But the speed with which they suddenly accelerated was the most striking thing about them. I don't think I have ever seen any creature move so fast.

After I had wandered around the tanks for an hour or so I finished up in the arena where two young girls were rather lamely trying to train a dolphin to retrieve a ball for them. The Dolphin definitely had the air of the one with the upper hand.

In the evening I fell foul yet again of the complexity of Japanese food etiquette. I thought I would try another type of restaurant. I think it's called an Isikaya. Anyway there were lots of kebab like sticks arranged under glass along a long counter with stools. I went in and sat at a stool hoping I could just point. Instead I was presented with a menu. I tried choosing an item with a picture that looked like chicken, but the implication from mine host was that this would not be enough for a growing lad so he suggested another dish too which looked like pieces from one of the kebabs so I agreed. First thing to arrive was some pickled fish, which was ok. Next came a bowl of raw cabbage with vinegar, which again was ok. Next came the suggested dish, which was slices of raw red meat and chicken, and now I was trapped. I had no idea whether I was supposed to eat it raw, season it and pass it to the chef, cook it myself or what. I waited. My cooked chicken arrived and I ate it. Everyone else was getting heaped plates of steaming smoking cooked kebabs. Nobody else had raw meat. I was hopelessly lost. In the end I timidly nibbled a bit of each, decided it wasn't such a great taste it was worth risking salmonella for and left it, presumably much to the amusement of the waiters.

It might seem like a small example but as I walked back to my hotel this struck me as one of the problems with Japan. It is not so much that there are too many traps for the unwary, as a traveller that's your lookout really. No, it's more that it feels like a society at risk of becoming hidebound by its own immense culture and tradition. Sometimes it appears that there is a Japanese way of doing almost everything, and sometimes just for the sake of it.

Just across the bay from Kagoshima sits the ill-tempered Volcano Sakurajima and I decided to catch the ferry across and cycle around it to see if I could get a better view.

In between gaps in the clouds you could catch glimpses of smoke still coming out of the top of he volcano. The road around the island was quite pleasant, if hilly, and traffic was light. By the time I'd reached the opposite side of the island though it was already spotting with rain and the clouds were even lower. I decided there was no point in climbing back up into the mountains again and carried on around the north shore rather than going back up via the mainland. There was a steep, but satisfying climb up to the viewpoint on the volcano, even if there wasn't that much to view, and then I dropped back down to the visitor centre in Sakurajima itself. There were some interesting pictures and video of some of the previous eruptions. I was still surprised by the violence of some of the explosions.

Later I caught the ferry back to Kagoshima and checked into the Nakozono Ryokan, a very friendly and comfortable inn.

That evening there was a terrific downpour, which eventually developed into a full-blown tropical storm.

Samurai Gardens and Kamikaze Kids

I t was still raining the following morning so I decided a non-cycling day was in order.

From Kagoshima I first caught the bus to Chiran. Chiran is actually a very pretty little town, straddling the banks of a small river up in the hills of the very southernmost peninsula of Kyushu. There is a narrow stream, no more than a gutter really which follows the main street down a gentle slope, but is full of the most beautiful (and large) carp.

Chiran has two claims to fame. The first is its samurai gardens. Running parallel to what is now the main street and just one block back from it are the remains of its origin as a fortified feudal medieval town. A narrow lane leads up between two low stone walls each of which is topped with a short hedge. Set back from the lane on either side are the 'Samurai Houses' where the feudal lords would have lived. The houses have all been rebuilt many times over by now, but the gardens are supposed to have been maintained very much as they were. there are 7 in all open to the public, each very similar, none of them as big as half a tennis court, yet every one clearly laid out to a plan of the most intricate detail. Rocks, trees, plants, "borrowed features" - i.e. hills which can be seen in the background, even the rake of the gravel all set to a purpose. I could see their beauty of a type, yet they were both too Spartan and way too precious for my taste. Give me a ramshackle rambling sweeping lawn with a few balls, bats and a swing any day.

Chiran's second attraction is also on a martial theme but rather more sinister. During WWII (or the part of it that the Japanese refer to as "The Greater East Asia War" Chiran was the main airbase for the Tokko, the special attack forces - to you and me the Kamikaze.

These boys(between 1000 and 5000 of them, depending on who is counting) were often taken straight out of school or university, in theory as volunteers to be trained specifically to kill themselves for the Emperor.

As the Americans prepared to invade Okinawa, the first of the Japanese homelands to be attacked, the theory was that if Japan could just strike one crushing blow, in particular against the American fleet, it would crack the American spirit and enable Japan to negotiate an 'honourable' peace.

With neither the technology nor the aviation fuel to compete, it was decided the only way to do this would be by filling small planes with high explosive and charging their pilots to crash them directly into the enemy ships. "A Battleship for every plane" was the motto. In fact planes were not the only form taken by the Tokko. There were other suicide bomb vehicles from manned rocket bombs, to high powered speedboats and the Kaiten, or manned torpedoes.

Walking around the Kamikaze Peace Museum on the old airbase I was at first sad, but soon just very angry. Wall to wall there were photos of young, silly, goofy boys. The Museum tried to dance a very thin line between respect for the 'courage' and 'valour' of these men and talk of a 'tragedy that must never be repeated'. What bollocks.

The war was already over and Japan had lost by early 1942. Hardly anyone would now dispute that, but what is more it should have been crystal clear to Japan's leaders even then (and was in some cases). Instead a mad, anachronistic Emperor and a bunch of militaristic throwbacks clung desperately to the hope of retaining their own power, whatever the cost to anyone else.

These boys didn't die defending their homeland. They were last-ditch chips tossed on the gambling table by a drunken loser.

From Chiran I got the bus back to the coast and then south a little more to Ibusuki to be buried. In fact being buried is all the rage in Ibusuki.

In a small modern building near the beach, for a small fee you are given a towel and a cotton Yakata. Once you've changed you walk through then out onto a covered area of the beach where a small army of labourers wait with shovels to heap hot sand all over you. The beach sits on top of a natural hot spring and for 10 to 15 minutes you gently cook under a mini mountain before rising mummy like from it to go and shower the sand off.

It is, to say the least a strange experience, though not unpleasant. I suspect that the lightness felt afterwards is a direct result of dehydration. For some obscure reason, though, whilst lying under the sand the strongest feeling I had was being able to sense my own pulse, in my feet of all places.

Still, Lazarus-like I rose again and got the train back to Kagoshima.

Walking back along the beach the moon was shining through thin clouds onto a calm sea. The photos of all those young boys flashed across my mind again. "What a stupid, evil waste," I thought.

Still the sun came up next day, the sky was blue and it turned into a wonderful day for cycling. A nice, steady climb up and out of Kagoshima, not too much traffic, then a lovely ride through the mountains on a narrow side road which skirted high above the shore of a huge manmade lake, and finishing by crossing above the Seigo falls, at least as big as anything I'd seen in Iceland, but quite unexpected.

Apart from the ride, which was well worth coming for, the only other event worth noting was when I stopped to ask one of the construction workers on the dam for directions. Once again, either he had no concept of how to read a map or he genuinely had no idea where he was. Either way he was about as much use as a chocolate teapot, but in a very friendly smiling sort of way.

In Okuchi I doubted whether they saw one western face from one Christmas to the next. The owner of the hotel was so pleased he invited me for coffee, but I don't think it was long before he regretted his generosity as my very limited Japanese conversation skills, combined with a general social truculence and being tired and sweaty meant we lapsed into a rather painful silence while I tried to drink my scalding coffee as quickly as possible to get into a hot shower.

The climb out of Okuchi was one of the finest so far. 14km rising to 700m on a newly surfaced, quiet twisting mountain road with some superb views. Almost from the beginning of the descent the other side, though, the traffic began building. Following a long river valley down I was able for part of the time to switch sides of the river to a much quieter country road on the opposite bank, but where I was forced back onto the main road the traffic was heavy and ill tempered. Finally for the last 40km or so into Kumamoto I was on the extremely busy route 3 and back into the old pattern of dodging back and forth between bumpy, unpredictable pavement or being swept into the gutter by passing trucks and buses. At least the pressure added wings to my heels and the last 30k went reasonably quickly, only my shoulders beginning to feel the strain. By a little after 4pm I was back in Kumamoto and my cycling expedition to all intents and purposes over.

Bullets, Ambition, Bombs and Blade Runner

From Kumamoto I picked up the ordinary limited express train to Fukuoka, having stopped off first to return the chain tool I was given by the nice man at the nearby bicycle shop. Since he wasn't actually there I have a strong suspicion that the woman who took the tool from me was convinced this was some mad kind of Gaijin festival where we go around handing out tools to worthy shopkeepers. Still she smiled and nodded as people so often do here.

The most ordinary thing about the limited express train was that it left on time and arrived on time.

The Shinkansen (or Bullet Train) is an awesome piece of equipment. Much wider than our trains, with a long shovel shaped snout it really looks like it enjoys going fast. What can I say? It's smooth, quiet, clean, comfortable fast, punctual and keeps you informed in both Japanese and English by announcements and display boards all the way. Just like home really.

The Shinkansen was once a source of huge national pride for Japan. Now it seems to have slipped down the scale a little, possibly a victim of its own, blandly continuing success. Personally I'm all in favour of dullness in its right place. Dull trains that run on time every time are OK by me. Dull cars that start every morning. Dull people who just get on with their lives without ever feeling the need to conquer the business world or start any wars. There's a lot to be said for them. The Company, which builds and runs the Shinkansen, however, obviously thinks differently. The new Nozomi super express train is called "Ambitious Japan". Advertisements for it show a line of young aggressive businessmen jumping forwards, as though at the start of a race, eyebrows low, hands almost, but not quite clenched into a fist, mouth snarling. The caption could almost be "Banzai" and the parallels are obvious. These are supposed to be the peacetime warriors.

At Osaka we were joined by a small group of German trainspotters who stood out like a pork pie at a Bar Mitzvah. The combination of leather coats, moustaches and rat's tail mullets made it difficult to pick them out from the locals at first, but then they gave the game away with their over polite deference to a pregnant lady, a small boy and an old woman when getting on the train (not).

Coming back from Tokyo central to Julian's I was forcibly reminded there really is no time when it's NOT rush hour on Tokyo's trains. Fortunately everyone found it terribly funny to be squeezed onto a packed commuter train at the end of a hard days work and then trip over a dirty bicycle loosely wrapped in bin liners or be boffed in the face by a very lumpy rucksack. Still I found that by just wedging the bike in between a pack of commuters I didn't need to bother holding it up at all, and once I'd let go of it and we'd been through a few stations, by scowling heavily at my next door neighbour I managed to plant at least the seed of a doubt in some people's minds that the big awkward parcel might actually belong to him, rather than the Gaijin tourist with the rucksack. In London, of course I'd have been thrown off the train, possibly with a kick up the arse for good luck.

Carrying awkward parcels aside, there are only four things to do on the trains in Tokyo, and I list them here in descending order of preference:

1. Sleep. It really would be a good idea to provide some sort of neck strap or headrest device. At least 50% of the people you see on commuter trains, whatever the time of day, will be sound-oh.

2. Text. Given the complexity of the Japanese character set this can't be easy. I seriously doubt it is possible to come up with any form

of truncated Kanji that would compare with "C U L8ER". Most people seemed to dedicate at least half an hour to a single message. Around 30% of the occupants will be so occupied

3. Read. More books than newspapers, the Tokyoites appear to be avid readers. Apparently the publishing industry was one of the first to recover post war. A further 15% will have a book in hand

4. Finally, the remaining 5% will be fully, wholly and concentratedly dedicated to moving large lumps of phlegm backwards, forwards, up down and around inside their heads with full accompaniment of sound effects. In winter this percentage might be higher, I don't know.

Heading south again from Tokyo my first stop was the old capital city of Kyoto.

Temples. Kyoto is big on temples, and the temples in Kyoto are BIG. There are also quite a few tourists and for the first time western faces are fairly common. Despite that it's a relatively pleasant town, more laid back than Tokyo. Kyoto is very neatly parcelled up into different areas. By the station is a rather bland business area, just north of there the shopping sector, across the river and up the slopes of the surrounding area the older town, temples, restaurants and souvenir shops set amid narrow cobbled streets and wooden houses.

In one of the temples there was a Buddhist ceremony taking place. There was much chanting, ringing of bells and clacking of wooden clappers, but at least there didn't seem to be any preaching, and the overall effect when combined with the heady scent of incense was actually quite peaceful.

One of the reasons given for Japan's very late adoption of wheeled transportation was that the country was just too hilly and there were too many rivers (though wheeled transport was also prohibited by imperial decree for some time - except for the Emperor of course). Almost all the rivers though are very shallow, especially at this time of year, and the ducks in the river running through Kyoto couldn't decide whether to try and sit on the water, or just stand in it.

Having already visited Nagasaki I was interested to see how Japan's other atomic city, Hiroshima had coped with its trauma in the post war years and this was my next stop.

It was a beautiful sunny autumn day, blue skies, and a wisp of high cloud, a few last leaves hanging on to the trees next to the river. I stood in the Peace Park, quietly composing my thoughts having just emerged from the Atomic Bomb museum. Three round, bright red school caps bobbed into my vision, about navel height. Simultaneously the three caps tipped back and three round faces appeared staring up at me with a mixture of awe, glee and fear.

"Excuse..scuse me please. Can we ask you some questions ..tions" they chorused, very nearly simultaneously (the one on the end, with spectacles, was just a little slower than his pals).

"Yes, of course you can"

"My name is Tiger..uo..ira. Please to meet you...you"

"Nice to meet you too. My name is Patrick" Now this was just plain cruel. I have never yet met a Japanese who can cope with the full version of my name and sure enough this was greeted with a degree of blankness, like an actor on stage whose colleague has suddenly decided to improvise. There were a few sideways glances and a degree of conferring, then one started to write and the other two settled for copying whatever he put down.

"What Japanese food do you like...ike?"

Ask me a hard one, "Sushi"

(relief) "Ahh sushi" (scribbling)

"Where do you come from...om"

"London"

(more relief)

"Do you make rice in your country....in your ....country?" Specs was falling further behind at this stage. I decided after the name business it would be unfair to try to differentiate between growing or cooking with rice, so I went for the simple

"Yes"

"Thank you very much. Have a nice day...ice...er" Specs was again caught out as his pals were already scurrying off, but I called them

368

back for a photo before they disappeared. If you're under thirty five or so it is obligatory in Japan to pose with two fingers held in a V sign for any photographic opportunity. The V can be forwards (as in victory), backwards (as in up yours) or sideways (as in Benny Hill saluting) or it can be double. But it has to be there or it isn't a real photo, so they duly obliged. Specs even removed his glasses for the occasion.

The flame in the park is not supposed to be eternal. In theory it will be extinguished when the last nuclear weapon has been disassembled and reworked into a refrigerator. or something like that. I hoped they had a good supply of gas laid on and a big stack of coins for the meter since it was likely to be burning for some time.

As at Nagasaki I had very ambivalent feelings about the museum here. There were all the usual platitudes about the tragedy of the bomb, about nuclear proliferation and campaigns for World Peace. But platitudes are frankly piss poor payment for the monstrosity of all the suffering that the people of this city paid, and they paid it for an immensely complex historical event that was the result of the even more complex combination of forces of greed, money, aggression, stupidity. What's more, and here's the rub, mixed in with those were a whole bunch of other things like honour and humanity and courage and concern.

The item that finally broke me in the museum was a rusty, mangled and tyre-less child's tricycle. Its two year old owner had loved it so much he had ridden it every day...every day including August 7th 1945. When the bomb went off he wasn't killed outright, but he was badly burned. He died the next day. Rather than bury him some way off where they thought he would be lonely, his father dug a small grave in the garden where their house had stood and put him there, together with his favourite tricycle and his toy steel helmet. Many years later he was disinterred to be moved to the family mausoleum and the tricycle was donated to the museum.

Somewhere around 100,000 people were killed at Hiroshima. I couldn't grieve for 100,000 people if I tried, but I could oh so easily shed tears for that boy on his tricycle.

369

At a straightforward level the museum works very well in putting a human face on the experience of being the victims of an atomic explosion. At a deeper level it stops well short of provoking any serious enquiry into the mechanics of cause and effect, any really open discussion of what led up to that event. There was not even a straightforward recognition that of all of those who could actually have prevented it, the Emperor Hirohito and Japan's wartime leaders, held the greatest capacity and therefore must have shouldered the greatest responsibility.

To specs and his pals though, all that was pretty well irrelevant and hopefully they will all outlast their own tricycles by many, many years.

All else aside, I liked Hiroshima. Like Fukuoka, there was something about its wide leafy streets and the way it embraced and made the most of its river frontages that spoke a very open, positive and upbeat approach to city life

By way of contrast, my next stop was Japan's 2nd city, and some would say its commercial hub, Osaka. The only reason Dante stopped at the 7th level of hell was because he'd never seen Osaka on a Saturday night. Streets as packed as a Tokyo subway train, young women tottering on ridiculously high heeled boots, dudes in sharp suits cut wide with no lapels or collars, wannabe rappers with crotches to their knees and baseball caps at a jaunty 45 degree angle (oddly reminiscent of Norman Wisdom of all things), raucous music screeching from every open door or window, no to mention the sound coming out of the Pachinko parlours which is as near to white noise as you can probably get. It was an experience. I have now experienced it. That will do thank you. At night it also bore a rather spooky resemblance to the futuristic cityscape in the science fiction film Blade Runner.

On a side note, one part of Osaka I did enjoy was Dotemburi Street. Just off this busy shopping street was a narrow, but long arcade entirely dedicated to catering supplies. This being the country of 'anything on a stick' and 'ooh, what we can we do with THIS weird sea creature' though, the variety of tools, implements and artefacts here beat all others. A Favourite was the enormous display of wax food items to be used as a kind of 3d menu in glass cases outside the front doors of restaurants. Not that seeing the things would necessarily make you any the wiser as to what went into their making of course...

From Irashimassia to Antimacassar

I thought it might be interesting just to list some of the commonplaces of Japan, the things which every Japanese sees so often they don't even recognise, but which might strike western eyes as different or unusual, so here goes:

Bicycles: There are bicycles everywhere. In most major towns and cities they seem to outnumber the people two to one. Everyone rides them on the pavement, no matter how crowded. Parking around the train stations is at such a premium that you have to pay to leave your cycle anywhere near and there are even specific (often multi storey) cycle parks built nearby.

Muzak: If you like the sound of silence you won't take to Japan too well. It often seems that the native inhabitants must be terrified of any lack of noise. As a result you will find the most dreadful tinny Muzak piped everywhere (there were even loudspeakers buried in the shrubbery alongside one of the otherwise peaceful riverbank walks). More often than not you will also find two, three, four or more sources of music competing fiercely with each other in the street at the same time. If you want a real definition of cacophony though you would just have to step inside any Pachinko parlour...

Motorbikes: While there are quite a few of these about, there is some sort of reverse psychology going on that says the toughest guys carry the biggest loads on the tiniest motorbikes. Generally you will see a 50cc moped so laden with boxes and bags that its rider is almost

372

invisible from behind. At the other end of the scale, in the cities you might spot a Japanese 'Hells Angel' cruising the streets on a large Harley or a Harley lookalike, dressed in leather, chains and chrome helmet. The effect is spoilt slightly when he bows politely to the little old lady pushing her bicycle across the street.

Petrol stations; Nothing much different about these, until, that is, you watch the entire staff run out of the office to bow out a customer who has been good enough to fill up there.

Irashimassia: The most common word you are likely to hear in Japan, and you may well hear it a hundred times a day. Something like 'Welcome', but every single shop assistant, stallholder, barman or waiter is morally obliged to bellow it out to every single customer, potential customer or approximate passer-by within sight.

Taxi drivers: Every one of them wears white cotton gloves and a white plastic covered Captains hat with a broad black peak. They will also take any spare moment to jump out of their car and start polishing it (as indeed do the bus drivers!)

Lacey antimacassars on car seats: No Toyota/Nissan/Honda saloon car would be complete without a full set of gleaming white lacey covers on the seats and headrests.

Picnic areas and public loos: Beautifully maintained, spotlessly clean and found just about everywhere. The only downside is that it is not uncommon for the gents at least to have a wide, low window opening onto the street so that passing traffic can have a good look at you in mid whizz.

Packaging: The Japanese are the kings of packaging and sometimes carry it to extremes. It is almost impossible for example to buy a packet of biscuits such as you would find in the uk. Oh no. After opening the outside wrapper you will find a neat moulded plastic interior. In individual slots within this you may find shiny silver foil sachets. Within each of these will be a colourful cellophane package and if you haven't got bored by then you may be lucky enough to find a single biscuit inside each of those. You are unlikely to squeeze more than ten into a pack this way, often as few as five, but without the patience of Methuselah you'd probably never get around to opening them all anyway.

Baths and onsens: The Japanese love baths. The catch for a westerner, though, is that under no circumstances are these to be used for washing in. Baths are for SOAKING. It is absolute etiquette to shower thoroughly and rinse BEFORE you get in the bath, which will often be a shared affair. The best baths are fed from natural hot springs and have often been made into small hotels called Onsens. From my point of view, the very best, too, are out of doors, giving you the chance to soak underneath the stars.

Vending machines: You would be hard pushed to find a part of Japan remote enough that couldn't provide a drink and a snack (and often a hot drink at that) from some sort of vending machine. Usually these are stuffed full of either energy drinks or readymade coffee in ring-pull cans. It's not uncommon though to find beer vending machines on the streets and hotels often offer toothpaste, socks or even shirts 24 hours a day.

White gloves: I've already mentioned taxi drivers wear them. You've seen images of the guards pushing people on trains at rush hour wearing them, but the market for white cotton gloves must be absolutely enormous. Just about everybody seems to have a pair handy somewhere to pull on when they're driving/smoking/gardening/loading in fact doing just about anything with their hands. It did strike me that black might be a more practical colour, but white is de rigeur.

Bowing: I defy anybody to spend more than a week in Japan and not start bowing like one of those funny model birds that keeps sipping from a drinking glass. It's endemic, but after a while actually quite pleasant.

Roadworks: There must be a law in Japan that even the most insignificant of roadworks requires at least one guard on duty to warn the general public of the dire peril they stand in if they come anywhere near. The guard (and often guards) are equipped with a flag and a whistle and aren't afraid to use them. In one tunnel I went through they even had a fold-up bicycle which was duly unfurled and used to provide me with a private, flag waving escort of my own all the way through.

Car names: Often silly, occasionally downright bizarre. My favourites included the Nissan Gloria and the Cedric, the Daihatsu Naked and the Daewoo Willy.

Smoking: You'd have thought nobody had ever heard of the health campaigns we have had running in the west for the last 40 years. Nearly everybody smokes like a chimney. The latest fashion accessory is to carry your own portable ashtray so you can light up anywhere without creating a mess.

High Tech Toilets: Heated seats, a control panel that would not look out of place on the deck of the enterprise and all sorts of spraying functionality that few but the brave would care to try out - I predict someone will start marketing these in the west very soon. At least the heated seats are very cosy.

Meandering in my own backyard
The slow route from Land's End to John O'Groats

N ot really an ultra-long endeavour, but in the Spring of 2000 I spent three weeks slowly pedalling through the British countryside to see what I had been missing in my own backyard. The journal below documents some of my more memorable experiences along the way.

Day O
23 miles, 1100 ft ascent
The day starts with a gentle cycle from Enfield to Paddington, courtesy of a light tailwind. Even the traffic seems more courteous than usual, though that might be simply because I left home later than usual, and though the traffic's heavier, it's going much slower.

At Paddington I'm reassured to find that privatisation has done nothing to infect the resilient British Rail culture with any traces of customer care. The ticket collector informs me that cycles are stored in the middle of the train, next to the buffet. This is possibly true if you can disguise a 35 pound mountain bike as a stale bread roll. After I've found the guards van at the front of the train, a Cro-Magnon man in uniform indicates with primitive grunts and gestures that I'm to be permitted to mount my bicycle in a small rack at the back of his cave, then heads off down the train - presumably to club himself a mate and drag her back by the hair.

Opposite me sits a very friendly elderly gentleman who tells me he is on his way from Harlow to Dawlish to visit an old friend. He has droopy eyelids and a wide, narrow mouth which is constantly hunting to find a comfortable position around his dentures. His daughter arranged his ticket through an organisation called Journey Care, to make sure he was helped with his bags. Neither of us is very surprised that the help has so far consisted of no-one at Harlow, no help on the underground and (yes) no-one at Paddington either. But he takes this with a fair degree of equanimity, as I suppose you do as you get older. Fortunately, one of the more highly evolved guards was able to help him with his bags along the platform at least. We chat quite happily for most of the trip, he perhaps because he is a little nervous and because people don't often have time to listen, me because he is an intelligent interesting man. I fetch him a drink and a sandwich from the buffet, and discover that he worked for NatWest (or the Westminster Bank, as it was then) most of his life, and that his niece is a famous TV personality. He tells me how he once cycled to Portsmouth and back over the weekend, which "nearly killed me", and which prompted him to buy a new bike with state-of-the-art Sturmey-Archer 4 speed hub. All in all it's a very British conversation and at Exeter we part in a very British way, with a firm handshake and a mutual "enjoy your trip".

I'm a tad wary when the Penzance train pulls into Exeter and turns out to be a 2 carriage shunter, with no sign of a guards van anywhere. Fortunately the staff are a bit more helpful this time and the bike is shoehorned into something which looks like a cross between a toilet and a broom cupboard. I think the brooms must have been left behind anyway, because the floor of the train is fairly well covered with crisp packets and sweet wrappers.

As soon as we leave Exeter the countryside changes and we cross any number of narrow, twisty valleys between short steep hills.

Plymouth is not a pretty town, and is matched by a grey depressed sky. As the train fills up I find myself looking forward to the solitude and independence of the road. Inevitably, further into the ride, I will find myself looking forward to the speed and comfort of the train.

At Redruth four women get off the train. They are all, shall we say, in their "middle years", of substantial girth, clutching clear plastic cups of beer and, to a woman, pissed as farts. The last one, the tail end charlie, intriguingly has a large plastic "L" plate pinned to her ample bosom and another one, which has turned over and is no longer legible, pinned to her back. They sway very happily, if a bit unsteadily towards the ticket barrier, the Learner looking just a little lost bringing up the rear.

The ride from Penzance to Sennen is a fairly easy gentle roller coaster road, though I will later come to dislike just this sort of up-and-down climbing without really getting any higher. Along the side of the road are old stone walls, completely covered now in grass, gorse and wildflowers - a whole marching band of bluebells streams along the top of them, just below eye level. The bluebells, in fact, will be a uniting theme following me all the way up the country.

Nearing Land's End everything becomes the "First and Last". The "First and Last Stores", the "First and Last" filling station, post office, inn, the First and Last Fertility Clinic and Funeral Home - well OK I made that one up, but there could be an opening there for the imaginatively minded.

At the Old Manor Hotel Shirley and Jen are charming, friendly and very welcoming. Dinner is followed by a swift walk down the road to check out the start point for tomorrow.

A miniature theme park now graces the point at Land's End. As these things go it's relatively well done, but it still seems like a blot on the landscape. At least at this time of night it's quiet enough to enjoy watching the sun set on the British Isles in peace.

Day 1 - Par

62 miles, 4000 ft ascent

During the morning an overcast sky is complemented by a b%$ £*&% headwind, bringing progress down to a grinding 5 to 7 mph, bottom gear all the way, even on the flat and often having to pedal to go downhill as well. If this is fun, I'm a sick bunny.

By Truro the wind has abated a little and the sun has come out, but it still looks like being a tough day.

I stop for lunch at the Tea Cosy Cafe, Probus. Why does a Cornish village have a Latin name? The food is excellent but God my backside is sore. I think I can cope with that provided the knees hold out. A technique I've used before is to use as low a gear as possible, so although my little legs are spinning like a Hamster on Benzedrine I'm putting the minimum amount of pressure on the joints - such I guess is the wisdom of age which makes us calculating but dull.

At Par I eventually manage to locate the campsite, despite the total absence of signage and the fact that it is all of 300 metres from the village but no-one has ever heard of it. At this stage of the day you get paranoid about the thought of cycling any distance unnecessarily, especially if it might be uphill.

Still, it's a very pleasant site. Arriving at Reception, a very pleasant lady tries to book me in. She tuts and moves to another terminal. Another lady joins her there. They move back to the first terminal. A third joins them. They look at a third terminal, hunker around a fourth briefly, then return to the second. After further five minutes when the other three ladies have gradually drifted off or found other more rewarding tasks calling their attention, my first point of contact scribbles my name on a piece of paper and takes £3 from me.

There are lots of ducks (why DO ducks so love campsites?) and a nice beach despite the large and very prominent chemical factory at one end of it. Bizarrely there are four swans swimming in the sea close to shore, something I've never seen before. I sit on the dunes above the beach and there is a skylark high above the shore, a dog barking down in the surf and a persistent whine from the chemical factory. Still, it feels very peaceful, but a strong northerly breeze bodes ill for tomorrow.

Day 2 - Moretonhampstead
57 miles, 6500ft ascent

The day starts with another of those bizarre encounters that brook no explanation. Climbing up and out of Par along a tiny sheltered lane I am about three miles outside the village at around 8 am when I come across two young girls making their way along the road. One is standing a little further up the road than the other, hands on hips looking back at her friend with a 'come on for God's sake' look on her face. Her friend, trailing behind, is kicking a large brown plastic suitcase along the road. This does not appear to be the most efficient method of transporting luggage, and certainly the suitcase does not appear to be benefiting much from it, but she is young, pissed off and persistent.

"Scuse me, how far's the beach?"

"About two miles down the road"

Kick. Kick.

How they got out there at that time of the morning, how long they'd been walking or where they came from I have no idea. What was clear was the likely fate of the brown suitcase, which was going to be worn to a sliver by the time they reached Par.

Outside Tavistock I am lured away from a perfectly good road onto a signposted 'cycle path'. This meanders alongside the road for a while, then starts to drop gently, then more steeply into a culvert, ending in a large set of steel barriers and a small side road going underneath my original route. A helpful sign points across the road at a steep flight of steps as the continuation of the 'cycleway' back up to re-join the main road. What genius builds these blasted things?

Dartmoor is simply a nightmare, not so much the climb (though difficult enough) as the gale force wind blowing across the top. I'm down to 3 mph at times and even reduced to counting off the hundredths of a mile on my little computer to try to convince myself I am making progress. I am reduced to swearing at God for creating his blasted north-east wind. If he does exist he no doubt finds such antics very entertaining. I wish I could say the same.

At Two Bridges in the middle of Dartmoor I pause, hunkered down in a small hollow against the wind. I don't even like the WORD moor any more. I will never be able to think of Othello in the same light again.

By the time I reach Moretonhampstead it's fair to say I am shattered. Bugger the thought of camping tonight, I check into the first B&B I find. God my arse is sore. On closer examination (calling for some major contortions using a bathroom mirror which would probably have me branded as a major pervert if anyone else could see them) I discover a hole the size of a 20p piece where nature did not intend there to be a hole. This is not good.

I decide some anaesthetic is called for and waddle to the nearest pub for comfort.

One thing about the relative remoteness of this part of the country is that the term 'Home Cooked Food' still appears to mean food actually prepared on the premises. This need not necessarily always be a good thing of course, but in this case it makes for a pleasant surprise. I opt for a second dose of anaesthetic to be on the safe side then head off to see how well I can sleep face down.

Day 3 - Taunton
47 miles, 3300ft ascent
This morning the anaesthetic has worn off and my backside feels like it lost a fight with a power sander. At least the rest of me is only stiff. The bad news is that the wind is even stronger and topped off with the occasional thundery shower. Lovely. I set out with no idea how far I'll get today, I'll just have to try and see. Thank God I'm not crossing Dartmoor in this at least.

My thanks may be a little premature as the climb up and out of Moretonhampstead is a pig. Moreover it's swiftly followed by a bottle-testing drop and, yahoo! - another climb. Oh what fun these West Country hills are.

For the first and last time during the trip I'm forced to push the bike for twenty yards when, halfway up a 20% incline I have to stop for a tractor coming the other way. Every time I try to start again the front wheel just lifts in the air as the bike rotates around the pedals rather than vice versa.

By the time I reach Taunton my knees are creaking like rusty hinges and I decide I'd rather not bother with any forensic examination of my rear end this evening on the basis that a) I will certainly not like what I will find, and b) there is nothing I can do about it anyway. I don't know whether it's the headwind, the shorts or the saddle, but my body is definitely rejecting this bike implant in a big way. Apart from anything else the bike feels way too heavy. Either I should go back to using a trailer or lose some gear soon.

At Taunton I check into a clean, if rather fussy B&B and look for the nearest source of more liquid anaesthetic.

Dinner - how many people sit at home to a nice curry and think "I know what this needs to set it off - I'll just get a bit of soggy lettuce, two quarters of tasteless tomato and, oh yes, some grated carrot would be perfect"? There must be thousands of them since this 'side salad' comes as standard with every pub meal I've ever eaten. And while I'm on the subject, whoever fries one mushroom for breakfast alongside their stringy bacon, half piece of fried bread (always cut diagonally) and tablespoon of baked beans? Bizarre.

Day 4 - Bath
48 miles, 2200ft ascent

I have a cunning plan. It requires a large Elastoplast, two pairs of shorts on top of one another and a fistful of Neurofen. These are my weapons in the battle to get me as far as Bath.

At least the wind has dropped a little and for the first time my speed on the flat breaks into double figures (actually, not quite for the first time - yesterday as an experiment I turned around and went with the wind for a few hundred yards to see what it was like. Result: 8mph into the wind, 21mph with it. Heartbreaking).

Then, cutting across the Somerset levels to Glastonbury, for almost the first time on this trip, I find myself actually enjoying the feeling of cycling.

At Wells I decide to stop for lunch and to savour my newfound pleasure before taking on the Mendips. In a small Deli I asked for a cheese sandwich.

"I'm sorry we can't do sandwiches"

"Could I have one of those bread rolls then?"

"Certainly"

"And a small piece of that cheese"

"Of course"

"And would you mind cutting the roll in half and putting the piece of cheese in the middle?"

"Okay, okay"

Splendid.

Sitting in the churchyard eating my un-sandwich I'm joined by two old fellas eyeing the bike and all the bags. The first is a charming old boy, born and bred locally who practically shared his life history with me. Born just outside Wells in 1915 he was baptised in Camberwell. His father had been called up in the first world war and his mother, convinced she would never see him again took her new born son up to London to say goodbye. Fortunately his father survived and the child grew up to be first a bicycle Telegraph boy, then a delivery boy for a greengrocer. He was delighted that someone would still use a bicycle for travelling such a long distance. Later his turn had come to be called up for a war of his own. He too had survived, but was wounded at Normandy - "Lost a kidney, part of a lung, and one of me other bits..." indicating, I assumed, a testicle, though it could have been anything from a testicle to a toe given the direction he was pointing in, and I didn't like to ask. He reminded me somehow of one of Shakespeare's yeomen. Not witty, not gifted but solid, honest and decent. By the end of our conversation he shuffles off as though he were afraid he might have exhausted my patience. Yet I feel as though it has been a privilege to meet him.

The other chap is a youngster by comparison, a sprightly 60 and a lifetime cyclist. He tells me how he did the end-to-end two years ago in only 13 days. Next month he is doing the round Ireland tour which is even longer. At this point I start looking for my yeoman friend and his stories of telegraph delivery, being more in the vein of things I want to hear. Still, it does at least give me enough of a kick up the (painful) backside to shake off some of my early depression and get on with the job. It also confirms that I'm well overladen for this job and will need to shed a fair amount of equipment once I get to Bath to give myself the best chance of completing on time.

Much to my surprise I practically sail up and over the Mendips, with some lovely terrain across the top and drop down into the narrow, twisty valley which eventually leads to a friend's house just outside Bath.

In Bath I settle for a weekend off to repair my battered body, post about four kilos of stuff home and generally have a good time.

Day 5 - Tewkesbury
63 miles, 3000ft ascent

The day starts with a satisfying climb up and out of Bath past the racecourse then a very pleasant morning working my way through the Cotswolds. The one exception is the arse in a red escort who decided too late he didn't have enough room to get past, so pulled in anyway and pushed me off into the verge. He is already fat, and bald and ugly, but I decide these are not really sufficient punishment so have to hope that he will die soon to gratify my sense of vengeance. Firm, but fair I feel.

It is hot, hot, hot, but (whisper it for fear the gods will grow jealous) for once a light tailwind is helping me on my way.

Cheltenham is pleasant, but the lack of shade and my inability to find a convenient coffee shop push me on through the town.

At Tewkesbury I step into a small greasy spoon for a cup of tea before trying to locate the campsite. The young girl behind the counter takes one look at me and disappears around the back. Since this is by no means an uncommon occurrence for me I remain unfazed and wait her out next to the counter. When eventually she does poke her head round the door (to see if I'd gone presumably) I lasso her verbally with a quick (and I hope incontrovertible) order for

384

a large cup of tea and a scone.

Although the countryside is changing, by far the most noticeable aspect of the distance travelled each day is the changing accent of the people I meet. I'm now thick in Brumspeak and have already been caught off guard a couple of times not understanding what the hell someone is saying to me.

Once I have set up my tent the couple with the tent next to me reappear having been walking their dogs along the river. One (of the dogs) is almost completely blind and navigates his way solely by following the scent of his mistress. While she is chatting to me he winds his way across the field to us, following where she was running along the tramlines of her past. Unfortunately, since she came over I've moved my bike and the poor old fellow, nose glued to the ground walks smack into it. If a dog can look surprised I swear he does.

Day 6 - Telford
57 miles, 3500ft ascent
Once again the wind is being kind and there are some nice views across the Shropshire countryside. I stop briefly to admire the original iron bridge at the imaginatively named town of Ironbridge. It is truly impressive, though the town itself looks too much like the set for a BBC period drama to feel real.

Three guys around my age are sat on a bench with their bicycles parked next to them. I stop for a quick chat, though they are clearly the strong silent types. The one subject which does bring forth comment is my British made front pannier bags. These are the subject of much praise and patriotism until, rather unwisely, I suggest that the German-made ones on the back might actually be better. This prompts a flurry of comments about durability, repairs etc. By this time I think we have extended the debate beyond its capacity to interest either party, so we wish each other luck and I go on my way better informed if not necessarily wiser.

As the weather is starting to close in I cycle up the hill into the outskirts of Telford and stop at the first B&B I find. Telford is not a place I would normally recommend for a stopover. The B&B is friendly enough, I think they were a bit surprised that anyone should want to stop there. Unfortunately I have to walk a mile and a half to find anywhere offering any food. In fact, most of the pubs seem to keep their front doors locked and aren't that keen to open up the back. Must be a Telford thing.

In the one pub which does serve food there is a Glaswegian at the bar. I know he is Glaswegian because he says so....very loudly.....every four minutes. I try to tune out his conversation, which is more of a monologue, but one phrase keeps coming through concerns his holiday arrangements. It is not where he is going that he is so keen to broadcast so much as the fact, repeated ad infinitum, that it is 'booked and paid for, booked and paid for'.

Outside it is such an extraordinarily clear evening that it's like looking at everything in 4D - stunning! An almost full moon, stark white cumulus clouds and a ridge of pine trees overlooking the valley. Life has its moments.

Day 7 - Warrington
58 miles, 2200 ft ascent.
A zooming day. Mixed tail and side winds, sunshine and showers and nice, gently rolling country.

Whitchurch is a little disappointing. I don't know what it is that determines the fate of these little old market towns. Some of them seem to gentrify and thrive, living off tourist cash while others slowly decay like bad teeth, with shopfronts boarded up to left and right and £1 discount shops plugging the gaps. Still the town's only cafe appears to be thriving with an odd mixture of pensioners and young wives in over-tight trousers.

In Warrington I stay with friends Dave and Kate who have just launched out setting up their own software consultancy. In the morning I'm looking out the window at the thick grey sky and heavy persistent rain. I think of them staying behind in the house, trying to drum up new customers and realise, a bit blandly but with no less truth in it for that, that we each of us set out on our own little adventures every day. Each of them takes a little bit of courage to take on the uncertainty. It occurs to me that it's the uncertainty which keeps us alive.

Day 8 - Settle
62 miles, 2900ft ascent
It's throwing down with rain and blowing a strong north-westerly. There is no way I'll make my target of Kirkby Lonsdale today so I will do my best to enjoy the day as much as I can. My first tea stop is at Golborne after only 8 miles. I expected the countryside around Warrington to be a mess of industrialised suburbs, but so far it's been a delightful mix of little country lanes and attractive villages, marred only by the odd electricity pylon.

Despite the weather I laugh out loud when I cross the M6 and see a massive tailback in both directions.

Just outside Wigan I come past a shop which proudly advertises itself as "Dishcloths and Pet Food". Obviously the dog lovers of Wigan have well fed, if slightly messy pets. I entertain myself for a few miles imagining a scene inside the shop........

.......Ding....aling.........aling (goes the little bell on a coiled spring over the door)

"Morning Mrs Wainthrop"

"Morning Mrs Udderscale. What can I get you?"

"Let me see... 2 tins of Pedigree Chum, beef & chutney flavour, 2 of Felix dolphin delight, oh and a pound of birdseed please."

"Anything else?"

"Yes, there was something....now what was it?"

"A dishcloth maybe?"

"Now hold on, it'll come to me..."

"How about a dishcloth?"

"D'you know I must be going daft..."

"Perhaps you need a new dishcloth?"

"I know. I've got it! Can I have a new dishcloth please?"

"I'm sorry, I'm afraid we don't stock them any more. Demand dried up, you see........"

Further up the road in Blackburn Mr Roe Lee is evidently doing much better for himself. First I pass the Roe Lee clinic, then Lee's restaurant and takeaway and finally Roe Lee's Garden Shop and Hardware.

By Clitheroe the wind is so fierce and the clouds so low I decide I would be pushing my luck to try and cut across the moors, so take the long way round through the vale of Ribblesdale - a lovely road, but spoiled by the very heavy traffic and huge number of motorway construction trucks thundering past my elbow at 60. At least the weather makes the moors look pretty spectacular.

Eventually I fetch up in Settle and decide to call it a day before I get too tired and ratty.

Day 9 - Appleby-in-Westmoreland
62 miles, 3200ft ascent

In the quaint (and cheap) Whitefriars guesthouse this morning the landlady obviously mis-hears my request for two boiled eggs and brings me a full cooked breakfast. We spend about three minutes doing a very English two-step apologising in turn to each other for the misunderstanding and trying to decide whether to swap breakfasts or not, before she finally whips the plate away. Later, with a superb intuitive grasp of my desire to get under way she launches into a full length recitation of the history of the building, built apparently as a "Dowager House" -

"What's that?" I ask, on cue. Apparently a house provided by the Lord of the Manor for his new Mother-in-law to ensure that she is not to be found a place in any corner of his own home. Expensive, but given the options, probably good value.

Coming up and over the moors I find myself roped in as unofficial assistant sheepherder. A farmer is moving his flock along the road using a four wheel bike, but he and his dog are having a fun time trying to stop any animals sneaking past them. Since I am not going to get past them easily and since they aren't going a lot faster than me anyway I cycle happily alongside him, hustling the flock on their way. Not being an experienced shepherd and for want of anything better to say I settle for shouting "Hey sheep, MOVE!" at the top of my voice. As we pass a car coming the other way, the woman passenger gives me a filthy look, presumably for frightening the poor little sheep. In return I very maturely stick my tongue out at her and herd on.

The views across the Forest of Bowland are spectacular, but I pay for the skyscape with a couple of good drenchings.

By the time I reach Appleby my shoulders are killing me and the saddle would be in the bin, were it not for the fact that it is all that is separating me from an even more uncomfortable piece of metal.

Outside the White Hart Hotel the (printed) menu proudly advertises;

VEGITARIAN options, but several of the main courses are also served with VEGIATABLES, which is nice. After a particularly windy day I was especially tempted by the TORNADOS ROSSINI, but since my arse was so sore I went to the Crown & Cushion instead where I was served a superb lamb sausage with redcurrant sauce.

Day 10 - Annan
59 miles, 1800ft ascent
A glorious morning, blue skies, no wind and marvellous cycling along the lanes of Cumbria. There are too many startled rabbits to count and lots of quite happy young lambs, viciously head-butting their poor mothers in the belly and tails rotating like propellers as they feed.

In Annan I dine out at the Cafe Royale (Fish & Chips shop). Although undoubtedly cheap, there are a few minor irregularities in the presentation of the food. For one thing my pot of tea has everything in it except a teabag - I have to go and request one specially. My bread and butter consists of just that, a single slice of bread and a piece of butter. A further slice costs 30p. Evidently I am in Scotland now.

Wandering back along the street I am shadowed in the gutter by a large, black and very dishevelled looking crow. To be fair I probably don't look that clever myself and he may well be considering the odds of dining out on one of my eyeballs before the evening is out. Today at least he is to be disappointed. The crow seems almost to be the national bird of Scotland and as I make my way north I come across larger and larger numbers of them. I know many people dislike them but I have a sneaking admiration for their glossy coats and air of cunning survivability. I certainly find them far less distasteful than the keepers trophies I passed today, strung out along the top line of a barbed wire fence a dozen or so tiny black moles hanging from their snouts, arms and legs stuck out cruciform and blowing in the wind. I will accept none of your country lore on this subject, and no I'm not a particular fan of moles, but the person who has both the time and inclination to perform this sort of ritual is not a well individual in my books.

Day 11 - Cumnock
69 miles, 3000ft ascent
Just outside Annan in the morning I bump into Neil from Powfoot (great name for a village) out for a Sunday ride. He escorts me all the way into Dumfries, chatting about bikes, work and weather on the way. In Dumfries we meet his 3 pals gathered for the weekly outing and I take the opportunity for a quick break and a chat. A nicer bunch of four old duffers you couldn't hope to meet.

If I were to compile a list of my Top 'n' places to visit, 'n' would have to be one of those mathematically impossibly large numbers to get Cumnock on the list. If anyone reading this comes from Cumnock, I'm sorry - not for slagging off your town, just for the fact that you have to live there.

When I arrive the 'Municipal' campsite (why does that word 'municipal' bode so ill?) is locked up, smashed up and generally screwed up. The lone B&B, when I finally persuade someone to answer the door, presents a broken-down old lady who says simply she has decided to give up, has put the house on the market and is not taking guests anymore (though it's evidently not worth the trouble taking down the signs). I am left with the Dumfries Hotel, which, though friendly enough, is freezing inside and obviously has no plans to turn its heating back on before next November.

The town appears to have some sort of connection with Keir Hardie and the Hotel is obsessed with him. There is an election photograph of the man, dour, bearded and in a deerstalker with his catchy campaign motto underneath: " Vote for: Home Rule, Democratic Government, Justice to Labour, No Monopoly, No Landlordism, Temperance Reform, Healthy Homes, Fair Rents, Eight Hour Day, Work for the Unemployed". Which all sounds remarkably familiar. About the only thing which might not go down so well now is the Temperance Reform, not a big vote winner these days and likely to meet some opposition from the brewing industry (maybe that's what "No Landlordism" means?). As for No Monopoly, I'm all in favour of that provided we ban Trivial Pursuit and Scrabble too.

On the way out of town one sign says it all:
"WEST SCOTLAND WATER"
"CUMNOCK SLUDGE TREATMENT PLANT"
"ESTIMATED VALUE £60 MILLION"
Yeah, right.......

Day 12 - Tarbet
88 miles, 2700ft ascent
The route today weaves a fairly tortuous path in order to try and work a way around the industrial heartlands of Glasow, and by about midday I'm crossing the Erskine Bridge and getting closer to the highlands. Just before the bridge I pick up and follow a young couple who are part of an organised tour doing Land's End to John O'Groats. Although all their luggage is carried for them, they're putting in some long days and high mileages, and certainly today they don't seem to be enjoying themselves very much

If I have picked up one golden rule of cycle touring during this trip, it has to be: "Never, EVER follow designated cycle routes, paths or trails if you want to get anywhere. These are, almost without exception badly conceived, badly surfaced, badly signed and badly maintained. They are a favourite place for local Yoof to strew broken bottles (ha, ha). Even if you can find your way and aren't shaken to bits and don't get a puncture and don't wind up in some desolate industrial wasteland or a sink council estate, you will ALWAYS find yourself, every 5 minutes or so, having to wrestle your bike through or around some huge wrought iron barriers specifically designed to stop cycles. WHY? These things are designed and built by town planners who presumably never use a bike, designed for weekend leisure cyclists who do no more than 2 or 3 miles with nowhere in particular to go - which is fine if you want to potter along safely with a couple of kids in tow, but no damn good at all if you want to get anywhere. The Glasgow to Loch Lomond cycleway is no exception to this, though even I have to admit the section from the Erskine Bridge to Dumbarton is pleasant, currently well surfaced and gets you off a fairly murderous dual carriageway. Never say never again?

Everything south of Glasgow seems to be connected with killing: Kilmarnock, Killmaurs, Kilwinning, even Killmalcolm (which seems a bit harsh). To top it off there are even the Killpatrick hills (which didn't, as I didn't cycle over them).

Just north of Kilmarnock graffitti on a bridge reads "Fuck the Pope". Nice to see religious toleration still thrives in these parts.

Later on another memorable sign on a garden gate reads:

"Vicious Dog. No responsibility taken"

Well I guess that's vicious dogs all over, they're like that, they just don't care.

The final stretch, although it looks nice on the map, along the shores of Loch Lomond, turns out to be a very busy road and by the time I roll into Tarbet I'm ready to call it a day.

Tarbet, unfortunately, is another town with very few eateries, so I take a pleasant evening stroll to the next village, Arrochnar to find a restaurant.

The only other people in the room are a very young couple who are so intimidated by the place (or by me) that they conduct their entire conversation in church-like whispers. This in turn makes me yearn for something like a packet of very noisy crisps to break up the air of sanctity which is being created.

Despite the winds and despite feeling completely knackered, I feel like today I finally found my legs (they were inside my trousers after all).

Day 13 - Spean Bridge
78 miles, 3300ft ascent

A magnificent day in strange ways. Weather conditions are just appalling. The rain is coming down steadily, and occasionally heavily and strong winds ensure that just about everything gets a thorough soaking. The wind shifts from one minute to the next, head, tail, side, head. Still, the long climb up to Rannoch Moor and Glencoe is worth it. Even when half covered in cloud and lashing rain the scenery is just stunning.

On the other side of Glencoe I stop at a teashop and stand, dripping all over their carpet. Still, they are very nice about it.

At Fort William I finally buy a new saddle, which I will try for the rest of the trip at least. I also throw away my fabulous "SEALSKINZ" gloves (as used and recommended by Navy Seals) which proved to have all the insulation, breathability and comfort of a pair of rubber washing up gloves without actually being in any way shape or form waterproof. Marvellous.

Also at Fort William I take up the entire staff of the small railway station for a good 40 minutes trying to organise my train journey home. This does not make me a lot of friends among the other paying customers, but at least I got my ticket in the end.

My sturdy British front panniers are also leaking (which comes as no great surprise) and the only dry stuff is in the Ortliebs on the back.

I also manage to break my speedo cable, so it is a testing day in many ways for man and equipment.

As I leave Fort William for the short stretch to Spean Bridge the rain picks up again.

Day 14 - Dingwall
65 miles, 3000ft ascent

At breakfast this morning I am joined by an American couple at the next table.

"God does it always rain here?"

"Gaahhhd! Look, its raining again!"

"I don't care where we go, as long as it's not raining"

They have been here for all of two days and have at least had the privilege of observing the weather from the inside of a warm car.

Cycling along the unimaginatively named Loch Lochy.....

"Duncan"

"Jamie?"

"What d'ye think we should call this Loch?"

"Ah cannae say"

"Well a name should be descriptive. How would you describe this loch?"

"Ah cannae say"

"Well, what's it LIKE?"

"Like? Well it's like a loch of course"

"Right then. Loch Lochy it is...."

Another day of mixed showers and sun, but the wind keeps mostly behind me as, coming out of Drumnadrochit, a tough, steep climb is followed by a marvellous swooshing run across the moor at the top and a sight of my first wild (I think) deer.

Day 15 - Helmsdale
66 miles, 3100ft ascent

The day begins sunny, but again degenerates into ever more frequent bouts of rain (are you sensing a theme here yet?). I am beginning to sympathise more with the Americans at this point. A couple of fair climbs are followed by a frustrating roller coaster of a road, continually climbing and dropping, with heavy, impatient traffic.

The B&B at Helmsdale is a real gem, a lovely house set up on the hill, a stunning view out to sea with a smokey blue sky and at its back a livid yellow hill covered in gorse in full flower.

In the village I have "Fish Tea" at "La Mirage". The fish was fresh and chips were crisp, but La Mirage is decked out like a tart's boudoir. The owner/proprietor, though not visible in person, dominates every wall and has made this place her own private grotto, dedicated to images of herself and notions of celebrity. Wide and white haired, very much in the Barbara Cartland mould, there is even a picture of her alongside the old Dame herself, they could almost be twins - definitely from the same Rigor Mortis school of makeup artistry. I have no idea of her history, but somehow she must have found herself in this far flung corner of the island and decided to carve into it her own little vision of 'the greater world'.

As I watch the fishing boats sail out against a cold evening breeze the world of the aptly named La Mirage seems so out of kilter to the harshness, toughness and realness of life in this place, I wonder what sort of dementia could have spawned it - such a powerful need to turn in on itself (the place was also full of mirrors).

Day 16 - John O'Groats
53 miles, 3500ft ascent
In the morning I catch up with a large and well laden Dutch cyclist.

"Morning!"

"Morning"

"Going far?"

"Yes"

"Nice day"

"Ye-es"

OK, time to be on my way. Sometimes the Dutch can make even the Finns seem garrulous.

Once I am through Wick, though, with only another 17 miles to go, for some reason my energy levels are dropping and dropping. Even with a tailwind it is a real struggle to climb the final hill and drop down at last to the John O'Groats Hotel by the harbour. Once I'm there, though, I think I know why I was struggling. This place was never my destination in the first instance. It was just a target. Once hit, there's really not much to keep you here, and after the obligatory photo I'm more than happy to turn around and head for home.

In Wick I find a small B&B on the way out of town. My landlady has a bizarre accent which takes me a few minutes to place as half Scots, half Italian. In the morning she tells me her life history in the time it takes to butter and eat four pieces of toast.

Born in Tuscany, she married a Scottish soldier at the age of 17 and went back with him to his hometown of Wick. I try to imagine the shock a 17 year old Tuscan girl might have experienced, at a time when there was no TV and precious little else to prepare her for life outside her own little part of Italy. The cold, the strange light, the language, the people. At first it was hard, she says. The streets were so wide, and yet so empty of people. She struggled with the language, she said, but liked the people. She found them very sincere, and liked the strong sense of tradition. She stayed.

And then, a few years ago, she thought about retiring back to Italy. She wanted to be sure, though, to make sure she was making the right decision, so she visited. She stayed for nearly two years before finally deciding ("What about the husband?", I thought). So she came back to Wick one last time to put her house on the market... and then she met and married her current husband (-"So that accounts for the first one, but a fast worker anyway").

And so, here she is after all, 72 and still living in Wick.

Like I said, everyone has their own adventure...

APPENDIX
Gear and General Advice

As you have gathered by now, this is a very personal memory of a wide range of bicycling adventures. What follows is a very personal list of suggestions and ideas based on my own accumulated experience. Take whatever feels relevant to you from it, or leave it as irrelevant nonsense, but please don't hold me responsible for any of it when something goes wrong!

In terms of bikes I tend to favour reliability and maintainability over lightness and efficiency. A single breakdown can cost you days or weeks or even jeopardise your tour. There are other ways to save weight (see below).

BIKES
I've used all sorts of different bikes for my trips (including the three-wheeled recumbent Windcheetah, a 1950s BSA with 3 speed Sturmey Archer and a wicker basket on the front and a replica Dursley-Pedersen with hammock seat). Sometimes the bike itself is part of the adventure. If you want to minimise some of the unexpected adventures for your trip though you could consider some of the points below:

FRAME
Steel is best. Really. It rides best, with a good combination of spring and damping. It's strongest, whether bouncing along an unmade track or fending off the attentions of hammer-wielding baggage handlers. If you bend it you can make a good fist of straightening in out yourself without worrying it will suddenly snap.

Worst case scenario just about any third world garage or blacksmith can weld it if it should break.

For a fast European tour I've used a titanium frame before, but thin walled tubes are especially vulnerable to careless handling on planes, trains or ferries.

I don't like aluminium. It's fragile and when you are riding all day it feels harsh to me, transmitting every bump and ripple in the road.

Carbon fibre - wonderful material, irreparable once broken. One mis-step and your tour is pretty much over.

WHEELS

Use a cheap frame by all means but spend money on a decent set of strong wheels. Most modern bikes come with cheap wheels which are not intended to last because they rarely cover more than 50 miles in their lifetime. 80% of all problems I've seen on the road are linked to wheels. With a heavy load and over rough ground they take a hell of a pounding. Good quality rims, 36 (plain) stainless spokes, decent but not the most expensive hubs. I've never had so much as a spoke break but only because this was where I spent the most money.

TYRES

Again worth spending on. There are great puncture resistant options available these days from the likes of Schwalbe. It's the nature of the beast that you'll go miles without a single puncture then get 3 on one day - either there is a nasty variety of spiked plant nearby or local yoof have been scattering broken glass all over the municipal bike path you decided would make a nice shortcut. Anything that minimises the number of times you have to stop, *unload all your gear* and fix a puncture makes a big difference.

For off-road touring don't be tempted to go too radical. Big knobbly tyres are slow, noisy and hard work when its dry. When it's wet they suck up mud like nobody's business. I went for a relatively wide tyre with a hard central section and short tread pattern towards the edges - they rolled well in the dry and although I lacked grip in the wet I didn't have to get off every ten minutes to unclog my rear wheel and subframe. Of course I did nearly slide off the side of a mountain at one point as I scrabbled for grip on a particularly tight downhill corner - but I (and you) should go slower downhill, you miss all the scenery otherwise.

GEARS, HUBS, BEARINGS AND BRAKES

Buy good, but not the most expensive ones you can find. Why? Because the expensive ones are usually fancy-schmancy racing kit, made to be lightweight and replaced reasonably frequently. The next grade or two down is usually heavier but more durable.

My favourite for some time has been a Rohloff 14 speed hub gear. A bit like the old Sturmey-Archer 3 speed but with a huge range of 14 gears all packed into a slightly oversized hub. Hardly any heavier than a full set of gears plus derailleurs but incredibly robust and low maintenance. Combine one of these with a Hebie Chainglider plastic enclosed chaincase and apart from a little oil every now and again you can almost forget those messy maintenance stops. More recently I've discovered the delights of belt drive. No oil, no mess and nearly silent. Squeaks a bit when it gets dusty but just pour a little water over from your water bottle and its sorted.

Brakes: Good quality rim brakes work in all weathers and are easy to maintain. Magura hydraulic rim brakes are lovely but difficult to fix if they should get cut. These days discs are the norm and I have yet to have a problem with them.

RACKS and BAGS

Along with wheels, racks are the most common breakages. However robust they may look in the shop, put 40 kilos on them and bang them repeatedly for 8 hours a day and they will soon show their mettle (or metal). Steel beats aluminium nearly every time again (even though it is heavy). Tubus seem to be a good brand.

When I first went to South America I met a couple of Dutch guys on bikes. It had been raining continuously for 7 days. Their gear was still dry. Mine wasn't. They had Ortlieb panniers. At that time only Ortlieb made truly waterproof bags - simple roll-top designs made from the same stuff the make flexible lorry sides from. There are a lot more, cheaper versions of the same design now and all pretty good. I still stick to Ortlieb though, not least because they once (literally) saved my life. Crossing an ice cold glacial river I was carrying two Ortlieb panniers over my shoulder when I slipped and fell into the water. The current was fast and I was immediately carried away. Fortunately the bags are SO waterproof they acted like floats and I was eventually able to use them to kick my way to the shore. So thank you Mr Ortlieb.

TENTS and CAMPING GEAR

More of a personal choice here. Some people are happy with a Bivvy bag. personally I prefer a lightweight tent with at least enough room to sit up in at the end of a long day or to sit out one of those inevitable days when it's just too wet/windy/horrible to be bothered to ride in. A vestibule of some sort is handy for keeping wet bags and things away from dry sleeping bags.

When choosing sleeping bags and mats remember it's hard to cycle all day long if you haven't been able to sleep because you were too cold in the night.

STOVES and PANS

I love the feeling of independence of having everything you need on one bike, and wild camping beats noisy campsites hands down. For me it offsets the extra weight and pfaff of carrying your own cooking gear and food any day.

These days gas canisters are much easier to find. You can get tiny folding gas stoves that sit on top of these cheaply and easily and they're quick, clean and efficient. If you're heading to less developed areas or into the wilds you may prefer a petrol burning stove, but these are heavier, dirty and smelly and more pfaff to set up and light. In Europe it's getting harder to find somewhere that will actually sell you half a litre of petrol but in more remote areas you can almost always scrounge some from someone - take a clear plastic tube for siphoning.

Pans, bowls, cups and spoons - titanium all the way. Just don't go overboard. One pan, cup, bowl, fork and spoon is usually enough to serve any home cooked meal.

CLOTHING

All depends on the climate where you are going. I always take stuff which is lightweight and dries quickly. You can layer up to stay warm and with luck wash and dry stuff overnight so you don't have to carry too many spare clothes. A friend of mine cycled from the UK across Europe, Asia and China and ended up in Japan. He took a toothbrush with half the handle cut off to save weight and just three socks* which he rotated daily: left, right, washed. He is, of course, mad as a biscuit.

*He did have other clothes too - but cycling in just socks would make a great adventure. Do let me know if anyone out there decides to try it.

OTHER

Take at least one luxury with you. Doesn't matter what it is, something that makes you feel good. It's always different for me. In the early days I took a Sony Walkman Professional so I could record some of the sounds of my trip - I have a great cassette full of the howling wind in Patagonia. Other times it was a small feather pillow. More recently it's been a very lightweight folding chair - I never liked sitting on the ground and these days if I do I can't get back up again.

General rule - less is always more. Even now I still end up taking too much stuff and I've never gone more than a couple of weeks without posting some stuff back home. Be careful in your choice of luggage because whatever you take you will fill it and more. On the Great Divide trip I tried all sorts of configurations - including a trailer. These were surprisingly nimble - watching a 60 year old jump one over a six foot berm was truly impressive. Their main problem is they are *too* capacious - take one and you will fill it for sure and half of the stuff you put in it will never see the light of day on your trip. In the end I settled on two large rear panniers with tent and a mid sized dry bag strapped across the top of these, sleeping mat strapped under my handlebars (because it's light) and numerous platypus waterbottles strapped to any spare surface depending on how far you may have to go between water sources. Water is by far the heaviest and most important thing you may need to carry, so be sure you leave enough spare capacity for whatever you might need.

Phones, Satnavs and other gadgets are great, of course, but remember the fancier they are the more attention you risk drawing on yourself. One of the best bits about travelling by bike is the ability to slip under the radar a lot of the time. Local ne'er-do-wells will generally prefer rich flashy tourists in travel hotspots to grubby cyclists off the beaten track. When I'm walking around I usually carry my valuables in a plastic supermarket bag. Bumbags almost always have something of value in them but who wants to nick groceries?

TOOLS

Go minimal. A puncture repair kit and pump are essential. You shouldn't need them often but when you do you'll realise just how glad you are you have them.

Allen keys and/or some sort of multitool come in handy for minor adjustments and maintenance. Anything else and you're probably better off winging it, otherwise it's just excess baggage. I've only ever broken a chain once and that was my own fault. At the time I didn't have a chain tool but I was able to improvise enough to get me to the next town where I could borrow one. Try to avoid having anything on your bike that requires really specialist tools.

HYDRATION and FOOD

It took me years to learn to stop and drink a little and eat a little every hour on the hour. It's very tempting to just crack on, whether the going is good or bad. Of course by the time you notice you're thirsty it's too late and we all hit the 'bonk' at some point - suddenly you feel drained of energy and every pedal stroke seems a monumental effort - usually down to low blood sugar. I keep dried figs and dark chocolate in my handlebar bag but I am a BAD

PERSON - you will no doubt find much healthier options. The good news is if you are cycling 8 hours a day you can eat pretty much whatever the hell you like. In the states I have been known to wolf down three pop tarts for breakfast. If you have never come across these delights they are the most sugary, disgusting concoction of pastry-like bread (or bread-like pastry) filled with sickly jam. They have about 3m calories each, but by 11 am I'd burnt them all off and was hungry again.

Drink lots, eat lots and enjoy it.

DANGERS

Forget about spiders, snakes and wild animals (except, in certain specific cases, bears) - *people* represent the biggest danger you are likely to face. The thing is, though, there is no such thing as a risk free adventure, and if you are too guarded all the time you risk missing out on a huge part of the experience. The sad reality is large parts of the world are still much, much more dangerous if you are female, but there are still risks at home too.

The good news is, as a cyclist, and especially a lone cyclist, you pose very little threat to anybody. You will regularly be approached by people who want to know who you are and what you're doing. They may just want to practice their English. They might offer to help, show you around, or even off accommodation. I try to keep a low profile, I try to stay observant, I try to start off at least polite but I have also come to trust my instincts and if something feels vaguely wrong I will risk offending an innocent stranger rather than be taken in by a con artist. It's a big world and there are plenty more people to meet. Anyone genuine you accidentally offend will either understand or have forgotten about it by the next day.

Printed in Great Britain
by Amazon

41681452R00225